The Fa... ips,

Themes in Comparative History

General Editor: CLIVE EMSLEY

PUBLISHED TITLES

Clive Emsley
POLICING AND ITS CONTEXT, 1750–1870

R. F. Holland
EUROPEAN DECOLONIZATION, 1918–1980

Ian Inkster
SCIENCE AND TECHNOLOGY IN HISTORY

Dominic Lieven
THE ARISTOCRACY IN EUROPE, 1815–1914

Rosemary O'Day
THE FAMILY AND FAMILY RELATIONSHIPS, 1500–1900: England, France and the United States of America

Pamela Pilbeam
THE MIDDLE CLASSES IN EUROPE, 1789–1914

Jane Rendall
THE ORIGINS OF MODERN FEMINISM: Women in Britain, France and the United States, 1780–1860

Ken Ward
MASS COMMUNICATIONS AND THE MODERN WORLD

FORTHCOMING

David Englander and Tony Mason
WAR AND POLITICS: THE EXPERIENCE OF THE SERVICEMAN IN TWO WORLD WARS

Joe Lee
PEASANT EUROPE IN THE EIGHTEENTH AND NINETEENTH CENTURIES

Peter Rycraft
PEASANT REBELLIONS, 1400–1600

Series Standing Order

If you would like to receive future titles in this series as they are published, you can make use of our standing order facility. To place a standing order please contact your bookseller or, in case of difficulty, write to us at the address below with your name and address and the name of the series. Please state with which title you wish to begin your standing order. (If you live outside the UK we may not have the rights for your area, in which case we will forward your order to the publisher concerned.)

Standing Order Service, Macmillan Distribution Ltd,
Houndmills, Basingstoke, Hampshire RG21 2XS, England.

THE FAMILY AND FAMILY RELATIONSHIPS, 1500–1900

England, France and the United States of America

Rosemary O'Day

MACMILLAN

First published 1994 by
THE MACMILLAN PRESS LTD
Houndmills, Basingstoke, Hampshire RG21 2XS
and London
Companies and representatives
throughout the world

ISBN 0–333–37293–X hardcover
ISBN 0–333–37294–8 paperback

A catalogue record for this book is available
from the British Library

Printed in China.

I dedicate this book to my far from simple co-resident nuclear family – David, Daniel and Matthew Englander – and to my wider family

Contents

List of Family Trees

General Editor's Preface

Since the Second World War there has been a massive expansion in the study of economic and social history generating, and fuelled by, new journals, new academic series and societies. The expansion of research has given rise to new debates and ferocious controversies. This series proposes to take up some of the current issues in historical debate and explore them in a comparative framework.

Historians, of course, are principally concerned with unique events, and they can be inclined to wrap themselves in the isolating greatcoats of their 'country' and their 'period'. It is at least arguable, however, that a comparison of events, or a comparison of the way in which different societies coped with a similar problem – war, industrialisation, population growth and so forth – can reveal new perspectives and new questions. The authors of the volumes in this series have each taken an issue to explore in such a comparative framework. The books are not designed to be path-breaking monographs, though most will contain a degree of new research. The intention is, by exploring problems across national boundaries, to encourage students in tertiary education, in sixth-forms, and hopefully also the more general reader, to think critically about aspects of past developments. No author can maintain strict objectivity; nor can he or she provide definitive answers to all the questions which they explore. If the authors generate discussion and increase perception, then their task is well done.

CLIVE EMSLEY

Preface

I owe an enormous debt to a great many people for their help with this book. I have space to mention but a few. I thank the Arts Faculty Research Committee of the Open University for their generous support, financial and otherwise. Secondly, I thank the extremely helpful staff of the Open University Library, especially all those who processed numerous inter-library loans. Thirdly, I am grateful to the archivists of the Folger Shakespeare Library, Washington, D. C., the Bodleian Library, Oxford, the Guildhall Library, London, and the British Library. I was assisted considerably in my archival work by Dr Angela Raspin and Ms Sue Donnelly of the British Library of Political and Economic Science (LSE). I owe a debt which I shall never be able to repay to Jane Isaac of the Lichfield Joint Record Office. I learned this summer of her tragic accident. She and David Robinson, her predecessor, always made working at Lichfield a delight.

The writing of this book has been made pleasurable by my colleagues. My students Sally Gosling and Margaret Smith gave me the benefit of their stimulating conversation. The 'Women in the Humanities Research Group' at the Open University has always proved a source of psychological support. Professor Ruth Finnegan and Professor Michael Drake gave me the opportunity to develop my ideas about the families of the poor in the nineteenth century. Dr David Englander has lent me the benefit of his brilliant mind, and, even more important, his sympathetic ear!

I thank Mrs Wendy Clarke for assisting in the production of the typescript. Finally, thanks to Beverley Tarquini of Macmillan Press for seeing this book through the press.

ROSEMARY O'DAY

The Open University

Introduction

In the dim, dark distant past, when this book was first conceived, it seemed that it would be both desirable and possible to study the history of the Western family and place it in a comparative perspective. It seemed, if not a simple, then a reasonably straightforward enterprise. Of course, these proved naïve beliefs.

First, the more I read purported histories of the family, the more I realised that they often did not focus on the family as a unit or cell at all but rather upon the institutions which hedged it – marriage, divorce, inheritance – or the roles played by individuals within families: wives, husbands, mothers, fathers, children, siblings, or of attitudes to these same subjects. Some such histories were nigh on indistinguishable from histories of women. Having written this book, I am more than usually sympathetic with the authors of these studies but also more and more convinced that we now need to focus on the family rather than upon its constituent members.

I started by reflecting on what is meant by 'family' today and whether this can or should be seen as having any relevance for the world that we have lost. Today most of us live in families but we only occasionally attempt to define what the family is and what it means to us and in our society. The 'family' may seem an institution common to all in our society, with features which are, for example, class specific; yet I dare say that as much separates my family from all the rest in our immediate neighbourhood as unites us. If a family is often perceived as a microcosm of a 'state' then there are many more variants on family than there are on state.

'Family' is also one of those concepts which seems to unite our world with an earlier world but which, on closer inspection, proves not to do so in a straightforward fashion. Indeed, contemporaries find it almost impossible to agree on the nature of the family in today's world. The transferability of the modern concept to the past is fraught with dangers. Certainly the people of the sixteenth, seventeenth, eighteenth and nineteenth centuries used the term, but what they meant by it often seems very foreign to modern developed societies. The term 'family' was used to describe the household or domestic economy, the co-resident members of the biological family, and the wider group of non-resident kin. Also there is a separation, not always clear-cut, between theories of the family and attempts to shape the family, on the one hand, and the form and behaviour of actual families. I comforted myself with the knowledge that today, also, we use the same word to cover a variety of meanings and shades of meaning. Constraints of space permitting, I resolved to try to make it clear in which sense I am using the word 'family' at any particular time and, where possible, to use the word 'household' when I am referring, in an economic context, to co-resident members of a domestic group which included non-kin members.

Why a comparative perspective? Historians use comparison and contrast in the course of their work in a perfectly natural and unreflective way as a descriptive, explanatory and analytical tool. Such comparisons tend to be casual and unsystematic. Some assumptions, however, have an underlying comparative import and dimension which demands, but rarely receives, further attention. One of these of direct relevance here is the assumption that the 'family' is in some sense a reflection of or response to the 'economy' and/or the polity prevailing. If this is indeed true then it would seem to follow that similar economies and/or polities should display similar families. Is it true that, as the nations of the world pass through different phases of economic development, the form of the family and the nature of family life show very similar characteristics? That is, that all 'traditional' economies, 'market economies' or 'competitive capitalist' economies, whenever and wherever they occur, produce the same family forms. Conversely, can it be shown that families in the countries studied are never comparable on a purely chronological scale unless their economies or polities are comparable? For example, can it be demonstrated that the families of England, France and North America were not comparable in, say, 1820? Then again, does the family merely replicate the state? And, if so, are all the families in one state extremely similar? Historians have argued that the family in England, France and early America was, like the state, a monarchy. It was characterised, to a greater or lesser extent, by patriarchal relations. If this was indeed the case, then is it not strange that this period saw civil war and revolution in all three societies? The call to obedience was not uniformly answered.[1]

The emphasis of this book is upon the English family. It is possible, of course, to use a comparative approach within such a national framework. To some extent, this strategy is followed here. I compare the family of the seventeenth century with that of the nineteenth; that of the town with that of the country; that of the middling sort with that of the poor, that of the widow with that of the married couple. Such comparisons and contrasts come naturally and they help to show what is distinctive about the family experience for each type. Typology is important. International comparisons are similarly helpful. Whereas one might be tempted, if we concentrate exclusively on England, to see features of the family as wholly English, comparison can often prove the lie. Who knows England, who only England knows?

One of the criticisms of comparative history, systematically pursued, must be that it tends to underline those aspects which are comparable at the expense of those which are not. These other features might be equally important as tools of analysis. It may well be that the family, while responsive to economic, political, religious or social forces, is yet never a simple reflection, replication or response to any of them. The historian should attempt to generalise about the development of the family within the scheme of historical change. Where appropriate, bold comparison and contrast both between societies and between economies over time and space must be used. But the historian should also strive to show what makes the development of the family in each society and at each time distinctive.

Above all, reducing everything to the level of absurdity should be avoided. We all know, if we think about it, that the experiences of families in early modern Britain, France, and North America were very different one from another and, equally, that living in a family in industrialised America was different from living in a family in early industrial Britain – these differences can be simply ignored if we make statements such as 'all early modern families displayed similar membership and structures' or 'the family was a reflection of the factory system'. The history of the family must be, to some extent, a history of the economy in which the family exists. The family is a unit which is demonstrably responsive to economic forms and to economic change. But it must be something more than this.

Why Britain, France and America? It early became clear that to broaden the basis of the comparison would obscure rather than clarify the issues which I wished to tackle. The countries chosen allow for both comparison and contrast in all aspects of their history – they are neither so similar nor so different as to make the exercise futile. All began as largely agrarian economies. All have trodden the path towards becoming competitive capitalist economies with a large industrial base. All have had chequered political histories. There was some real interaction between the three at political, socio-economic, religious and cultural levels. Yet all three had distinctive cultural, political and socio-economic histories and traditions. It is true that more comparisons could have been drawn by including Spain, Portugal, Scandinavia, Russia, Germany, Austria and other parts of central Europe. This would have been at the price, I think, of 'hopping around' and removing a firm basis for coherent comparison. It is left for others to expand upon what I have said here in these other geographical, economic and political contexts.

Until quite recently scholars have been afraid to study the history of personal relationships. To chart the changing structure and composition of households was one thing, to attempt a history of family relationships another. The major contribution of women's history should be acknowledged here. Historians of women have made the history of personal relations not only respectable but essential for any understanding of the past. Those scholars, like Lawrence Stone, Edward Shorter and Philippe Aries, who have picked up the gauntlet in a more general context, have been attacked by others for producing overly schematised chronologies of change in human relationships. Yet our understanding of the world that we have lost has been much enriched by their endeavours. We should not be deterred by the difficulty of the enterprise from attempting to understand the interplay between the desire for harmonious and satisfying human relationships in the past and the accepted mechanisms and structures of everyday life. We do not diminish the importance of ideology by recognising that agencies and institutions such as church, state and local community did not have uninterrupted access to the domestic circle. And this was not merely because people were not necessarily exposed to this teaching through reading or oral communication. It is as important that we understand how the family protected itself and defined itself within the state or church as well as how it acted for the state or church.

Personal relations in this book, however, is not shorthand for power relations. It is unfortunate that the dirigist approach has been so largely employed. If we examine the family experience in the early modern period we see how important harmonious relations were to the individuals who made up the family and indeed to the family itself. There was undoubtedly a tension between the way in which external agencies wished to use the household, and especially the head of the household, and the manner in which members of the family wished to use their family. We need to recognise this tension for what it was and determine to what extent it was a productive tension for the family as an institution and for its members. After all, the family was not simply a passive recipient of society's ideas, and it was within the family that individuals defined themselves. If we rest content with a discussion of the 'oppression' of women and girls within marriage and the family we will not progress very far. Families developed their own distinctive ethos which surrounded and influenced the development of individual identity. The sources reveal that wives and female children were seen as component parts of a body. While the head was important, it could scarcely function as a body without its members. And each member had important roles to play – valued roles, which often had repercussions in the wider world. The 'caring' nature and roles of the adult woman, for example, or the religious and moral sensibilities of women, nurtured in the family experience, were developed by women themselves in their lives outside the family. We may regard this definition as restrictive, but perhaps the family definition of the capacities and roles of an adult male was also, in its own way, limiting.[2] How these family roles were played in particular families varied enormously even within one society at one time. The family was a powerful agent in society and as such should be viewed as an independent variable, alongside class, education, religion, and gender. It did not act alone and the historian must identify the areas of interaction.

The book which follows has an unashamedly unorthodox plan. The book is divided into five long chapters, each of which treats extremely important issues involved in arriving at a coherent history of the family, and provides provocative material for both seminar discussion and future research. Two of these are avowedly methodological. Is historical demography an adequate substitute for a history of the family? Can we discover what societies wished the family to be? Two others seek to describe and analyse the family forms of the period 1500–1800 in England, France and North America and to ascertain in what senses these forms were either distinctive or comparable. These chapters also attempt to illuminate the importance of 'family' for individuals, communities and groups within these societies, and implicitly to identify the conflict which existed variously between theory and practice and between the external and internal functions of the family. There is some consideration of the implications of this argument for the history of the 'middle-class' family in the modern period. The final chapter seeks to pinpoint the poor working-class family, both as a target for state and social reformers and as a feature which acted to bind together the working class. The brief conclusion draws together some of the main statements of the book and suggests where discussion and research should go from here.

The Open University   ROSEMARY O'DAY

1. The World that Slips through our Fingers: A Framework for the History of the Family

In his excellent introduction to *Historical Demography*, T. H. Hollingsworth described it as 'the study of the ebb and flow of the numbers of mankind in time and space by a combination of geography and history using statistics' and its main concern as that of achieving 'accurate estimates of human numbers'.[1] If this were all there was to historical demography then it is doubtful whether the historian of the family would need to concern him or herself with it. But, as Hollingsworth proceeded to explain, historical demographers are concerned to estimate the distribution of the population by age group and gender and may need to estimate the number of people residing in the average household in order to establish the total population.

It is because historical demographers have in the past half century exploited data about households in order to deduce statistics about population behaviour in past centuries that historians of the family must concern themselves with their work. Without the data provided by such specialists, historians of the family are in danger of inferring characteristic institutions, habits and experiences from the equivalent of literary evidence: stray historical examples. Peter Laslett once likened the manner in which historians and

1

others had taken the example of Juliet's early marriage as 'typical' of Elizabethan marriage age to a future historian inferring ordinary sexual habits in the twentieth century from a reading of *Lolita* or *Fear of Flying*. We require a statistical framework for the history of the family which will display the broad lines of development over time and highlight similarities and differences in both time and space. In other words, it will facilitate comparison. The close co-operation between historical demographers and historians (both use one another's skills and sources and it is sometimes difficult to decide whether a given individual is a demographer or a historian first and foremost) has obscured the fact that demography alone (applied to the past) cannot answer all the important questions about the household or, indeed, the population. Examining the experience of real people in real families and households will always be important and will always interact with the work of demographers in interpreting and in suggesting new questions which must be broached. But it *is* vital for the historian of the family to situate individual examples correctly within the statistical framework, to establish whether they are typical or atypical, to judge their relationship with other examples and so on.

In this chapter our concern is not primarily with the methodology employed by historical demographers nor with the fine detail of their work over the past decades. It is, rather, with surveying the picture of household formation, size and composition which has emerged through their endeavours in the light of this methodology. Nevertheless it is very important to say something about the initial inspiration for the demographers' work and its development because this in part explains the nature of the questions tackled and of the conclusions reached. In addition, it is necessary to discuss the terminology, definitions and concepts which have emerged in historical demographic approaches to the family of the past if we are to succeed in interpreting the framework they have presented to us and relating our own knowledge of the past to it.

Historical Demography

While historical demography was not born in 1964, with the foundation by T. P. R. Laslett and E. A. Wrigley of the Cambridge

Group for the History of Population and Social Structure, we could be forgiven for thinking so. With vigour, enthusiasm and conviction, researchers here applied techniques originated by French demographers to English sources. Initially the work on parish registers produced simple counts of baptisms and burials (indirect vital statistics), from which were derived counts of births and deaths to gain basic information about the growth and decline of populations. But the work has become increasingly sophisticated over the years, involving extensive family reconstitution, analysis of the time series and aggregative back-projection. E. A. Wrigley and R. S. Schofield's *The Population History of England from 1541 to 1871* was made possible only by computer manipulation of the data.

In the 1950s and 1960s a French demographer, Louis Henry, developed techniques of family reconstitution, involving record linkage between materials on baptisms, marriages and burials to produce 'genealogies', which permitted certain demographic calculations. Henry's own chief concern was to study the natural fertility of past populations, and to this end he reconstituted some forty French parishes, or about one in every thousand French parishes, down to 1830. These new techniques were enthusiastically adopted by historical demographers throughout Europe and North America.

Work of this kinds on the parish registers is, of course, important in constructing a framework for the history of the biological family, and allows us to say much that is useful about the role of church marriage in the formation of biological families, but it does not permit historians to comment on the composition of the units in which individuals lived. There is no necessary correlation between 'biological family membership' and co-residence. T. P. R. Laslett has contributed greatly to our knowledge of co-residential patterns and, therefore, the whole concept of family life by careful analysis of listings of households and their members. It is to these two strands of demographic research, the one treating the biological family, the other the co-residential unit, that historians of the family must turn if they wish to create a sturdy, supportive scaffolding for their studies.

Cambridge-breed historical demographers early saw their role as revisionist: by examining the quantitative data systematically it would be possible to re-evaluate assumptions about the population and social structure of past times. In 1965, for example, Hajnal demonstrated that low nuptiality, high numbers of life-long spinsters, and relatively late age at marriage characterised pre-industrial Western European populations.[2] This challenged the general acceptance of the idea that marriage was inevitable and child marriages extremely common. Peter Laslett's revelation that co-residential nuclear family units predominated in England and much of Europe from the sixteenth century onwards rocked the preconceptions of those who remained wedded to the idea that early moderns lived in extended households in which several generations of the same family dwelt together.[3] Others cast doubt upon the prevalence of high fertility and high illegitimacy rates in past times. Even high mortality did not escape the revisionists' axe.

If revisionism marked the later 1960s and 1970s, the 1980s and early 1990s have seen the revision of the revisionists! Increasing sophistication in data collection, manipulation and analysis, coupled with more determination to ask questions informed by historical understanding of the data have led historical demographers to refine both their approaches and their conclusions; to move from a broad-brush approach to a more detailed picture of the ways in which individuals lived in the past, how they responded to the socio-economic and religious milieu, and how this interaction affected or was affected by their demographic behaviour. As a result the apparent comparability of household structure and composition and, even, demographic behaviour to which the historical demography of the 1960s pointed has tended to disappear.

Sociologists and Frédéric Le Play

To the extent that there was an accepted picture of the fundamental unit of social organisation before the Cambridge researchers set to work, it was informed by the common supposition that, historically, domestic groups were universally larger and more complex than those in industrial societies. This assumption owed much to the work and theories of Frédéric Le Play (1806–82) and the way it was read by later historians and sociologists. As we note in Chapter 5 below, Le Play discerned three basic family forms: *the patriarchal* – stable and traditionalist, it kept all the sons in the household after marriage; *stem* – similar in many ways, but the parents selected only one of the sons as heir to retain in the household, married off and dowered the remainder, thus allowing them to found new households, or supported unmarried offspring within the original household; *la famille instable* – a household formed on marriage, which grew with the births of children, shrank when they married and left home, and came to an abrupt end with the division of any inheritance on the parents' death. Le Play approved the patriarchal and stem domestic organisations but saw in *la famille instable* one of the chief sources of social decay.

In part, the problem of the historical demographers seems to lie in their partial misreading of Le Play, or rather, their reliance on what sociologists have said of Le Play. Laslett, for example, states that Le Play assumed that the stem family, or *la famille souche*, was the predominant form in several named areas of France, including the South, for hundreds of years. Such a family would consist of a co-residential, downwards extended family of two married couples with their children. Unmarried siblings might also live in the household in addition to servants. The heir of the first-generation conjugal unit might be the youngest or the oldest son, or, in the absence of a direct male heir, a favoured son-in-law, nephew or cousin. The important point, however, is lost – that Le Play associated his preferred family form with inheritance practices characteristic of England, which he hoped to introduce throughout France. These were not those of primogeniture or ultimogeniture nor yet of equal partition, but of the freedom of testation.

In the early 1970s Laslett explained how Le Play's theories had informed sociological and historical work on the family.[4] The assumption had been that this French model fitted the rest of Europe, including England. It would have been more accurate to say that Le Play believed that the English model, which had pertained in parts of France before the Revolution introduced compulsory partition of estates, could be transferred to France. It is no less the case, however, that modern demographic research into the family has been in large part a reaction to what the demographers believed Le Play's theories to be. Laslett proceeded to examine the 'reality' of the co-residential domestic group in early modern England and to compare this with the historical model he thought had been sketched by Le Play. Yet he barely touches upon inheritance practices nor yet upon the love and affection within the family which dictated testation of property according to Le Play. It is not the size of the family/household that concerns Le Play but the way in which the family/household system operates.

Peter Laslett and the Household

The criteria for a household were, according to Laslett, co-residence, shared activity and, in some but not all cases, kinship. Common subjection to a 'head of the household' or acknowledged fount of domestic authority made servants, apprentices, journeymen, trade assistants and live-in agricultural labourers as much part of the householder's 'family' as his or her own offspring. Something like 12 per cent of English people in early modern times were servants. The distribution through the various age groups differed greatly, however. Many servants were agricultural rather than house-specific and as many were men as women down to the 1800s.[5] In 1851, 42 per cent of households had additional residents on census night, of whom a high proportion were servants. Children who have left home cannot be included as part of a household; neither can kin who live near by, share in the same work and even frequently eat with the 'family'. Retired members who co-reside are still part of the household.

For his work, Laslett invented a vocabulary to describe household forms of the past which has since been refined and augmented but never superseded. Precise classification of types was necessary for statistical manipulation and it has introduced a discipline into historical thought about family types for which we should all be grateful. As we shall need at many points to consider the significance of demographic findings it is as well to become familiar with these forms and how they are to be differentiated. The *simple family household*, for instance, is the term for a household based upon what is variously described as the 'nuclear', 'biological' or 'elementary' family. The conjugal relationship is the structural principle in such households, which may include a married couple, a married couple with their children or a widowed person with children. There must be at least two members.

Servants may also be present but are considered not to affect the 'family' structure. An *extended family household* consists of the conjugal unit plus other relatives, and once again may exist with or without servants. Where the resident relative is of an older generation than the conjugal couple, the extension is said to be upwards. It is downwards if the relative is a niece, nephew or grandchild. Presence of a brother, sister or cousin denotes a lateral or sideways extension. *Multiple family households* are those comprising more than one conjugal unit connected by kinship or marriage. Such complex household formations would include Le Play's stem family but also those in which the conjugal units of brothers and sisters co-reside. A widowed parent might be present. But where the siblings are connected only by a linkage to a no-longer present conjugal unit, the household is known as a 'frérèche'.

It is worthy of note that Laslett's categorisation of households confuses two phenomena. On the one hand, a household cannot exist where there is not subjection to a common authority, and servants of all kinds are counted as members of a household on this basis. (In the light of Laslett's own work on patriarchy, this emphasis is unsurprising.) On the other hand, it is assumed that marriage 'forms' a household. The conjugal unit is used as the point of reference for all Laslett's categories. Servants are discounted. In Laslett's 'dictionary of household types' there is no possibility of a 'household' where there is a single or widowed person plus servants. When the conjugal unit disappears so does the real household. It is kept alive quite artificially by him in the event of a widow living with the one or more offspring – she and the heir are 'counted' as a conjugal couple. But the family of the widowed aristocrat Anne Clifford, in her old age, for example, simply would not exist. She would be counted as a solitary. Her own children lived away with their families in the south of England. That which she spoke of as her 'family' on her estates in the north – a considerable menage by all counts – would be discounted by the historical demographer. Joyce Jefferies' spinster household would not be a household or a family either.[6] There is an unhappy conflation in Laslett's work of the 'biological' and the 'co-residential' family. This confusion in Laslett's categories does lead to problems for the historian of the family. We have to decide upon consistent criteria. Is the family experience that of the co-residential household or of biological/kinship links within a co-residential household? Or is, perhaps, the family experience wider than that of any domicile?

It is also unfortunate from the perspective of the historian that Laslett chooses to divorce the concept and the reality of the household from the ownership of property. Comprehensible though such a divorce is in demographic terms, in historical terms it is a nonsense. Not only was 'marriage' as an institution bound up with the transmission of property, but also 'families' were preoccupied by its existence. This was not only because individuals were its guardians, stewards, farmers, inheritors and purchasers but also because so many were dependent upon it. In Richard Gough's Myddle it was the physical house which defined the co-resident household (not kinship, conjugality or name) and its right to a church pew and an established place in the community.[7] Keeping a house in the family meant retaining a place in the community. This sense of identity was of course strongest in those socio-economic groups with the most secure title to property (which seem, perhaps coincidentally, to have also been the largest and most complex domestic units) and weakest in those with the least. Nevertheless, a recent study of will-making in Bedfordshire in the early sixteenth century shows how important it was, even for those with very little property, moveable and immoveable, to see that it was bestowed to the advantage of their families.[8] Perhaps the absence of land, as much as demographic factors, may have argued for the simplicity and early dissolution of labourer and pauper households. My work on Katharine Buildings in the 1880s seems to indicate that, for the nineteenth-century lower-working-class 'family', four walls did not a home make – their households were fluid even if their families remained strong and constant. Disenchantment with Le Play's general model of the multiple, stem family (as a household of two conjugal units, downwardly extended) need not lead historians to disregard his insistence that the stewardship of property was a fundamental concern of the stable family nor the inference that disregard for or lack of property was a concomitant of an unstable family. It should be apparent on reflection, also, that while the household and the property were closely connected, the property itself could have considerable significance for members of the family who did not co-reside in the house. Thus property acted as a cement to bind together disparate parts of a 'family', and not simply to divide one co-resident group from another.

The Early Modern Household Unit

Laslett's work in the late 1960s and 1970s revolutionised scholarly views of early modern social structure at the primary level. The commonest form of household unit was the simple family house-hold with or without servants and, within this category, the nuclear family of father, mother and children predominated. The size of such households was by no means formidable – the mean size being around 4.75 people. The idea that the multiple family household, the stem family of Le Play, or even Laslett's extended household, was the ordinary domestic institution of non-industrial England was confounded and with it the comforting picture of the social support network provided by the family.

> It is not true that the elderly and the widowed ordinarily had their married children living with them, or that uncles, aunt, nephews and nieces were often to be found as resident relatives. It is not even true that the casualties of earlier, harder times, the victims of age, sickness, bereavement or want, could usually rely on their kin for continuing maintenance even though they did not live with them.[9]

What is more, these conclusions tallied not only with sugges-tions from medievalists that households in England had for long been relatively small,[10] but also generally with data collected for Western Europe, North America and even Japan during the *ancien régime*. At one blow the orthodoxy that the modern simple nuclear household originated in the American colonies was demolished. Unfortunately, however, precise comparison was rendered impos-sible by the difficulty of collecting equivalent data for comparable dates. One had to assume, which of course one should not, that mean household size remained as constant elsewhere as it was demonstrated to have been in England between 1599 and 1881. One had also to assume, and it proved a dangerous assumption, that within Europe and America there was no regional or local variation. The figures also apparently laid to rest the assumption that the simple (nuclear) family household was a product of industrialisation. Though early modern (or *ancien-régime*) households were larger than today's,[11] the difference is accounted for by the presence of servants in earlier households and their absence in modern. Even the very large early modern households were very large chiefly because they were prosperous households with many servants. Philip Greven's analysis of the Federal Censuses of eleven American states in 1790 revealed that although the average family was larger in colonial America, it was still of the simple (nuclear) family type, and was considerably swollen in size by the presence of servants and slaves.[12]

Other work suggests that, on average, New England couples married two years earlier than in England. The average number of children born per marriage rose, as a result, to 8.2, as compared with 7 in England. What was much more remarkable was the survival rate of these children. In New England, 7 out or 8 lived to adulthood; in England, 4 or 5. The average number of children born to New England families dropped by the eighteenth century and the rate of survival much more closely approached the English. In much of Pennsylvania and New Jersey the situation was similar. Because most immigrants came as families, family life was the norm here from the start, unlike in the Chesapeake. Men married at about 26, women around 22. Yet here also there were some exceptions. Among the Quakers, for example, the average age of marriage for females was 25. In eighteenth-century Virginia, once the sex ratio became more equal, marriage became more common and the age of marriage of gentry children more closely approximated the English, and, with improved physical conditions, more children survived to adulthood. Only among the poorer sections of the population did men and women marry earlier.[13] Interpretation of this evidence is difficult but it does seem that purely demographic factors provide no satisfactory explanation for differing ages on marriage or for changing rates of infant mortality. Economic conditions (including inheritance customs), the pattern of immigration, the physical environment, and the conditioning of the young were of immense, if variable, significance. A recent study of Paris in the seventeenth and eighteenth centuries confirms the general impression of small nuclear families, varying in size by the unequal distribution of servants, throughout the population.[14]

The Household Life-cycle

Laslett's calculations smoothed out the development of households in terms of size and composition. Once servants were removed from the equation, the commonest forms of household seemed, since the thirteenth century at least, to have been small and nuclear. There was, in effect, no history or development of the household in terms of size and composition, servants apart, from the middle ages to the present. Lest we give up the history of the family in despair, it is necessary to remind ourselves though that family size and composition tells us relatively little about family experience, which is, as I shall argue elsewhere, as affected by the relationship between the household and the 'outside world' as it is by mere facts of demography. Laslett, having shown servants to be members of the household in one part of his work, proceeds to ignore the very prominent presence of different categories of servant in shaping the family household. The lower incidence of servant-keeping in France, for example, might point to a very different practice of family life from that in England. Admittedly, Laslett discounted servants in his classification exercise for sound demographic reasons – his task was not to examine family experience – but it would be a great mistake if historians of the family were to adopt his conclusions in this respect.

Closer examination of the statistics which Laslett provided of the spread of different household forms also tells a rather different story from that conveyed by his overall figures for mean household size. When he examined 100 English settlements between 1754 and 1821, he indicated the spread of household sizes of between 1 and 11 or more. Although the commonest household size was 3.0 (16.5 per cent of households), nearly a half (47 per cent) were between 3 and 5 people in size; and significant percentages were larger. Eleven per cent of households, for instance, had six occupants, and over a third of households had between 6 and 11 or more occupants.[15] Does this mean that Laslett's presentation of a mean household size is indeed a meaningless mean? No doubt it serves its demographic purpose but the distribution around the mean is of immense significance for the historian of the household/family.

The American historian, Tamara Hareven, has stressed that 'families and households evolve different types of structures

organizations and relationships, which are generally obscured in
the snapshot approach' based upon census analysis.[16] Martine
Segalen took up this idea in her study of Saint-Jean-Trolimon, a
village in Finistère, from 1836 to 1875.[17] In this village of scattered occupation, the household, she states, is the unit of production and consumption in which members co-reside for a
number of 'economic, patrimonial, technical and affective reasons'. She attempts to chart the evolution and changing composition of the domestic group over time, using Laslett's classificatory
system for households. In so doing she considerably undermines
Laslett's bold assumption that small and simple family forms
were characteristic of Europe. In this village the mean size of
household was high, at least until the First World War, and there
were a large number of complex households, either of the multiple family variety (Le Play's stem family) or the upwardly
extended type. Solitaries were few in the nineteenth century.
Interestingly, it was the relatively prosperous 'farming' households which were largest (because they contained servants) and
which tended to be complex. The households of labourers, on
the other hand, tended to be small and of the simple family
model. The study pioneered the attempt to relate these observations, which were still based on the snapshot approach, to the life
cycle. Thus two thirds of households were 'simple' in their first
phase (i.e. on marriage), and a third 'extended'; more became
simple in their second phase. There was a high fecundity rate in
the village and with each generation 'the succession problem is
again posed, which has a direct bearing on the household structure'. Families with property could give their children money and
tools but could not give them land until the death of one of the
original conjugal unit. Thus one often found two conjugal units
living together along with unmarried siblings acting as servants.
In this village it was most often the youngest child who remained
in the household because older siblings had obtained land of
their own to cultivate. When the older generation died, the
youngest child and his or her spouse inherited the farm. Labourers, on the other hand, had nothing to bestow and would not
support their children. These children went into service and
when they had saved enough founded households of their own
away from their parents. Le Play would certainly have been well
content with these conclusions!

Laslett himself was aware that households were not static but developing entities. This was in part because of the unit upon which they were based, a marriage between two individuals, was itself changing and developing from the wedding to the funeral. For this reason there may have been a tendency in traditional societies for households to develop into extended-family or even multiple-family households, even though at any one time relatively few such existed. This might have been a factor of mortality rates as much as anything: early death prevented two generations co-existing and co-residing into maturity and old age. A study of the households of Saint-André-les-Alpes, in eighteenth-century Haute-Provence, revealed that in three-quarters of the marriages where there was appropriate information the bridegrooms had already lost their patents and could not therefore ever have formed an extended household (78 per cent of 686 marriages, 1628–1792). During the same period, at least 568 out of 1,254 marriage contracts envisaged the married couple living in the same house as the parent/s of one of them. These two sets of figures combined suggest that a tendency towards extended, multiple households was present, and that it was often modified by mortality.[18] In addition, complexity was perhaps introduced into many households on a strictly temporary basis: the visit, more or less extended, of a grandparent, grandchild, brother, sister or more distant kin. For the historical demographer it may be sufficient to note the presence of the household cycle and to declare that, whatever their preference may have been and whatever the small fluctuations in size of domestic unit, early modern people lived in small households which were essentially nuclear in composition. For the historian of the family it is much more difficult to establish the significance of a small mean size if in fact small households might stand a high chance of becoming larger and more complex at some point in the cycle before shrinking and perhaps dissolving. In this case, the 'family experiences' of members of developing households were also not static. Other features of demographic behaviour (for example, age at marriage, mortality rates and patterns, length of widow or widowerhood) may have determined the longevity of such family experience as much as preference. It is also evident, although not often noted, that while the number of simple family *households* in a given community may have been the largest single category, *more of the population* actually lived in larger, complex households. Nevertheless, one cannot deduce from statistics the extent to which early modern people saw their early knowledge of a small nuclear unit as the abiding and shaping experience of their lives. In the twentieth century it seems that each generation associates itself with the decade of the mid-to-late teen years – 60s people are those who achieved a certain amount of freedom and independence during the 1960s. Their tastes, philosophy of life, and memories are to a great extent dictated by this single decade. If this were true of the seventeenth century, for example, it might be that the predominant household experiences of many a man and woman were within the home of a master rather than of the natural father. The historian of the family, therefore, must move from a demographer's perception of generation to the generations of experience.

In the event, as has already been intimated, Laslett's suggestion that a relatively low mean household size, and by implication a simple 'nuclear' family household, was common throughout *ancien-régime* Europe and America, proved precipitate. As Martine Segalen shows, the type of household was socio-economically specific, but there seem also to have been other reasons for difference, perhaps deriving from local conditions. When Philip Greven examined the evidence for household size in eleven American states in 1790, he discovered that the mean free white household size, although nuclear, was very large (about 6 persons) in comparison with the English and French means, but also that there were considerable regional variations. Free white households in the coastal areas of South Carolina, especially around Charleston, were relatively small – about 4.49 persons. In part, he claimed, this could be explained in terms of the unhealthy character of the region. But it could also be explained by the relative lack of need for white labour – the plantations were worked by black slaves, who swelled the size of households therein; these slaves were generally absent from urban families in Charleston itself. Although the average size of families was still higher than in England or France, there were marked variations between states and sometimes within states. The mean size of free white family ranged from 5.42 in South Carolina to 6.04 in Maryland. Both within and between states there is a suggestion that newly settled areas were characterised by smaller family and household sizes than the longer established settlements.[19] Greven also indicated that change in family/household size might occur over quite a short period of time: in a number of towns in Massachusetts where figures are available for both 1764 and 1790 the trend was towards smaller 'housefuls'. He surmised that this was a continuation of a much longer trend.[20] E. T. Pryor Jr, who, unlike Greven, had information regarding household composition as well as size, posited that, while both extended and multi-generational households were relatively few in 1875, they were much more common among the rural community than the urban.[21] S. Ruggles has argued that the prevalence of the simple family household in the early modern period in both England and America was due to a combination of poverty and demographic factors such as the short life expectancy; once people lived longer and were more prosperous larger and more extended family patterns asserted themselves.[22] He discovered a resurgence of the extended family household between 1750 and 1900. All the detailed work on family and household in North America indicates that the co-resident family experience therein totally defies generalisation. To draw comparisons based simply upon the size or even upon the composition of households is, in the end, of little meaning. Race, ethnicity, religion, class and geography acted separately and in varying combinations to determine the family experience.

In France there appear still to have been wide regional variations in the seventeenth, eighteenth and even nineteenth centuries. The nuclear family, or simple family, was prevalent by the seventeenth century in northern France, whereas elsewhere, particularly among the more prosperous peasantry, a more varied picture emerges and the preponderance of the simple family household, even where present, is not as marked.[23] In areas such as the southern Alps, Gascony and Limousin, double households in which lived two married couples with their offspring and, occasionally, an unmarried brother or sister who worked for their keep were common. In such cases the family was closely identified with property and a house (taken together, the Estate), which was regarded as inalienable and indivisible. Joint households of this type, therefore, tended to belong to the peasantry of at least average wealth. The head of the household selected an heir (normally from among his children and usually, but not inevitably, the eldest son), who lived in the household, brought his wife there, raised his family there and worked there until such time as he came into the inheritance. Common though such households were, one would expect the simple family household to predominate among those poor peasants who had nothing to hand on to their descendants. Perhaps more surprising is the fact that large, complex family groups appear to have been common, especially in livestock-rearing areas, in the centre of France. In the mid-eighteenth century more than two-thirds of the parishioners of La Courtine, in the present département of la Creuse, had lived and still dwelt in households which always contained at least two conjugal units, surviving unmarried offspring and a number of young children. Here the dowry paid to the head of the household with the bride of the heir was used to buy out the unmarried sons. The newly married couple lived in the communal household. Many instances of similar arrangements have been found in the west of France: in Poitou the large, forty-hectare sharecropping farms demanded male labour, and complex families of the joint type seem to have provided it.[24] Variations on this theme were probably common enough in northern France also, but seem to have died out largely by the seventeenth century. Even more complex family communities, including frérèches, appear to have occurred in the Nivernais province, the Bourbonnais and parts of Limousin and Berry. Households of between twelve and thirty individuals, all related, shared a large farm, amply stocked, and household. Everything was communally held. The men elected one of their number as 'household head' and he alone acted to sign leases and marriage contracts. Such marriage contracts were normally arranged between members of two such communities. If anyone wished to leave the community they did so, but could take with them only their personal belongings and a few coins. The experiences of co-resident family life of the *ancien-régime* French were probably more varied than those of the English during the same period.

The historian Jean-Louis Flandrin, in *Families in Former Times*,[25] provides an excellent corrective to the demographic historians' reluctance to link household structure and composition with inheritance patterns and the nature of property. Le Play, of course, had already drawn attention to this linkage. Flandrin observes that Le Play was incorrect in assuming that egalitarian partition of estates was an innovatory imposition of the Revolution. It had been traditional in northern France. In southern France before the Revolution, however, the patrimony had been passed in its entirety to one heir according to Roman Law or (as in the central and western Pyrenees) to customary law. In some areas (until 1555 in Béarn, and until the Revolution in Aure, Lavedan, the Barèges Valley and the Basque provinces) the sole heir was the eldest child, male or female. The younger children received only a legitimate portion of disposable goods and chattels. This custom was so strong that the people of the Pyrenees found ways of evading the insistence of the Revolution's civil code, that estates must be partitioned equally between heirs, and thus ensured the continued existence of the complex multi-family household in that region. Elsewhere, as in Limousin, such customs continued well into the nineteenth century but resistance was less effective. In Périgord, as Jean-Noël Biraben has demonstrated, the impact of the civil code upon household structure is apparent. Whereas in 1644 36.5 per cent of households were complex, the percentage had declined to 14.6 per cent by 1836.[26] The unequal impact of the civil code upon the practice of testation makes it dangerous to assume that inheritance customs no longer have any relevance for a study of differences in household structure after the Revolution. On the other hand, there were existing traditions of egalitarian partition in southern France, as in Bazadais, which seem to have produced simple family households. In the most egalitarian areas, such as Normandy, occurred the lowest proportion of complex households. Insufficient research has been done into the household structures of those areas in which the rule of primogeniture prevailed (that is, from the mouth of the Seine to the Pas de Calais) to indicate what implications this had. Moreover, there were so many different inheritance customs in the north that any generalisations about household-structure patterns deriving from such customs must be undertaken with extreme care. Whereas it may be possible, as Flandrin does, to distinguish between the lineal spirit (ties of blood or person) which bound the Norman family together and the house spirit (property) which bound those of, say, the Pyrenees, there can be no broad generalisation concerning where this applied. Each locality must be studied. The household spirit, which he suggests is characteristic of the French peasantry as a whole, identified the family with the household in the present – on its dissolution, property would be divided only among those who had been living in the house, not children who had already left. Further research is needed to see whether this also was

region-specific. This does not seem true of England.[27] One cannot
but echo Flandrin's cry from the heart: 'British historians have
made no efforts to discover any connection between the history of
the rules of succession and that of family structures ...' comparable to that of the French. It remains to bring together all the valuable work accomplished by students of inheritance and the studies
of the historical demographers.

The nature of agriculture may also have been important in
determining household structure. Guy Conquille, in the sixteenth
century, suggested that 'in so far as the labour of the rustic household is not only tilling the soil, but also feeding the animals; and
this requires a great number of people'. Flandrin suggests that the
habit of forming *communauté taisible* arose from the need to find
sufficient labour to make the poor soil productive during times of
low population growth and high wages. Thus they appeared in the
period 1400 to 1550, when such conditions prevailed. Fertile land,
on the other hand, when combined with high fecundity and low
wage rates, would foster the use of wage labour on independent
farms. He admits, however, that this is not a sufficient explanation
because in some areas, fitting the latter description, wage labour
was little used. And, even where prosperous farmers could maintain independent farms, the middling and poor might still engage
in *communauté* contracts. For community enterprise to be feasible,
the area had to be one in which peasant proprietorship predominated. In Sologne in the eighteenth century, *communautés taisibles*
were not characteristic, despite the infertile land, the low population growth and the high wage rates, simply because all the land
had been bought up by the nobility. Similarly, in so many infertile
areas of England landlords had taken up the land for pasture
farming and excluded the possibility of such common enterprise.
The example of North America indicates that in some circumstances the demands of agriculture were met by employing large
numbers of slaves rather than by expanding the number of the
farmer's or plantation owners's children.[28] While land use and
economic conditions might dictate household structure in the
above ways, there is a good deal of evidence to show the linkage
between complex family/household structures and prosperity. Figures for Valenciennes suggest that extended families were most
common among the bourgeoisie and skilled master craftsmen,
and least amongst the journeymen or day-labourers. Bardet has

noted that in Valenciennes extended households were relatively rare among the nobility, indicating perhaps that other factors than wealth were important – Flandrin has suggested that this means either that the nobility were outstripped in wealth by the bourgeoisie or that they were less deeply rooted in the town, having arrived there without their wider families.[29]

Defining Generations of Experience

To do those concerned justice, many historical demographers have taken the point and sought to approach their serial statistics with greater sophistication. Demographers can on occasions help us to define generations of experience. This can be done in several ways. For instance, in their tables demographers have demonstrated that there were considerable differences in the household experience of the various socio-economic groups. In France, as we have indicated above, complex households seem to have been much more common among the reasonably prosperous than among the poor peasantry. Over the period 1574 to 1821, in England, the households of gentlemen and clergymen were much more likely to contain relatives other than children than even the nearest groups, the yeomen and husbandmen. Labourers and paupers were the least likely to do so by far. Gentry and clergy households were also more likely to have servants, and the mean size of child group was larger than in most groups (husbandmen had the largest mean size of child group). By the mid-nineteenth century this situation seems to have been changing. The poor and very poor were the most likely to have live-in relatives. The determinants of such trends may have been demographic or they may not have been. Demography might, however, provide a clue. Before the twentieth century, levels of infant and child mortality affected the numbers of children growing up to become members of an older generation quite dramatically. This did not only reduce the possible number of surviving children in a household at any one time (for which see below); it reduced the number of single aunts and uncles and cousins requiring 'hosting' in their relatives' households. Mortality, moreover, discriminated between socio-economic groups: the presence of more kin in middling and upper-class households might have been a direct product of this.

Perhaps, though, more purely economic factors were at work. One suggestion has been that, whereas the gentry and professional classes had housing standards that were relatively expensive to satisfy, it was astoundingly cheap to establish a cottage household and relatively easy to obtain the necessary permission from the Justice of the Peace. The fact that the more prosperous households were tied not only to marriage but to property more often than were those of landless labourers and paupers, may also have encouraged more relatives to 'hang around'. Ideology also may have played a part. The more prosperous classes may have been more conscious of an allegiance to a wider kin group and of a social and moral obligation towards its members. The demographers cannot help us to identify which, if any, of these factors were significant. It is not possible with certainty to deduce ideology from statistics.

The experience of the child, adolescent and young adult can also be charted to some extent in demographic terms. In 1983 Laslett described the experience of a poor inhabitant of an English village in this respect:

> a boy, or a girl, born in a cottage, would leave home for service at any time after the age of ten. A servant-in-husbandry, as he might be called if he were a boy, [sic] would usually stay in the position of servant, though very rarely in the same household, until he or she got married. Marriage, when and if it came, would quite often take place with another servant. All this while, and it might be twelve, fifteen or even twenty years, the servant would be kept by the succession of employers in whose houses he dwelt. He was in no danger of poverty or hunger.[30]

If we can assume that this experience belonged to a full 90 per cent of the population of rural seventeenth-century England, then this has enormous implications for the associalisation and acculturisation of English men and women. Their biological family background was relatively unimportant because so short-lived. Some historians have suggested a far earlier age for departure from the parental home. We are informed that in the poor cottages of southern France six was the age when children left the family of their birth. Laslett implies that the young servants, while thenceforward committed to a life of service until marriage, did not remain in a single household. It is unclear from where he derives this information. If it is reliable, this would suggest that the poor had a highly volatile experience of domestic life even when they left the biological family. He also indicates that the children of the poor became the servants of the better-off – husbandmen, yeomen, gentry, clergy and so forth. If this is the case then the impoverished child put squalor early behind him and the servant-housing families could be regarded as fulfilling the function of charitable-nannies to the potentially starving, even though their motivation was clearly economic. At almost every level of society it was common for children and adolescents to live, for some time at least, in other households than their 'own'. When one takes into account the large numbers of apprentices and journeymen, the importance of this common experience is emphasised. The suggestion is, however, that such young people were in some sense exchanged by families of the middling sort rather than placed in superior environments. Their movement was dictated by the economic necessities of individual families – be it to offload a youngster at a given age or to import labour.[31]

This picture of the youthful household experience of 'average' early moderns demands refinement. For England, Richard Wall has gone some way towards refining it by asking important questions arising from a knowledge of the way household economies functioned in a rural and pre-industrial environment, which in some ways show the weakness of Laslett's sweeping generalisations. Wall posits a gradual decline in the number of servants in the household in the late seventeenth and eighteenth centuries, followed by an acceleration in this development down to 1851 and a marked falling off between 1851 and 1947. The high-point from which servant-keeping is deemed to have fallen is itself doubtful. Whereas 'between the ages of 15 and 24 as many as 3 out of every 4 inhabitants could be servants', there were enormous local variations. This over-view masks, however, more than it reveals about the experience of servant-keeping and servant-providing. A study of Colyton in the nineteenth century indicated that servant-keeping was indeed common, although the suggestion that about one in five households had resident servants and or relatives must make us cautious about Laslett's view that about one third of all families were participating in a sort of service-exchange in pre-industrial England, even if one accepts that resident servants were

by now less common than they had been. Wall's analysis demonstrates, however, the immense variety in the practice of providing
servants. There were differences, for example, in the ages at which
girls and boys left the parental home. In labourers' homes it was
more common for boys than girls to leave in the 10+ age group;
even craftsmen sent more boys away at this early age than girls.
This exodus was yet more marked as the boys grew older. It was
only the tradesmen and farmers who demonstrated a marked
tendency to retain boys rather than girls in the household. There
may be several explanations of a socio-economic nature for this
phenomenon. Perhaps there were more opportunities for outside
employment for poor boys and more opportunities for indoor
employment for poor girls. Thus many sons of labourers were
found working for farmers who had kept their own sons at home.
This would tend to suggest, as Wall argues, less a labour-exchange
mechanism at work than a labour redistribution. Perhaps farmers
and traders had greater need for male labour; perhaps they
displayed a greater interest in finding suitable marriage partners
for their daughters by extending their social circle, or perhaps
there was a limit to how usefully young girls could be employed
around a farm.[32]

Many intriguing questions emerge from Wall's studies. If
Colyton can be considered representative, it may be the case that
poor girls were retained in the parental home far longer than were
poor boys. As women were regarded as the chief home influence it
might be argued that the result of this would be to perpetuate the
values and organisation of labourer homes into future generations. It would indicate also that the 'shared activity of the household' might only involve certain members of it and habitually
make redundant one sex or the other. One might expect a labourer's household to be girl-heavy, because girls had a function as
child minders, house workers and perhaps income-earners within
the household. A farmer's household, however, would be predict-
ably boy-heavy, affording only sufficient year-round work for males
(more than the farmer and his wife could produce of their
bodies), the farmer's wife and one or two daughters. The childhood experience was not defined by how long the individual
remained in the co-resident family of birth. Labourers' daughters,
frequently retained in the household through adolescence,
attended school, in general, only to the age of seven; craftsmen's

daughters might attend until they were eleven. These girls made an earlier appearance in the labour force than did boys of the same groups even though they more commonly worked at home than did the boys.[33]

Historical demographers have helped show just how inadequate is our conception of the pre-industrial family as a tightly-knit, stable and supportive unit. For example, Michael Anderson has produced statistics which indicate that while it is true that, when compared with the later nineteenth and earlier twentieth centuries, late-twentieth-century families were much more commonly disrupted by marital breakdown, death had always disrupted the expected shared experience of many families. More startlingly, his figures demonstrate that before the twentieth century marital breakdown rates (whether by death or other cause) closely paralleled those of the later twentieth century and, moreover, that, because death struck parents and the childless indiscriminately, pre-twentieth-century disruptions of family life affected children more frequently than did modern marriage breakdowns (which apparently occur most often among the childless).[34] Anderson's findings for Britain echo some of those for North America. Whereas the inhabitants of New England appear to have imported English marriage and family patterns, those of seventeenth-century Chesapeake did so much less successfully. Here immigrants married late and died young. Half of the marriages solemnised in the second half of the century were disrupted by the death of one or both spouses within seven years. Their families were small by comparison with those in New England but, this notwithstanding, the orphaned young presented a problem for this society. The incidence of households with step-children was, therefore, high. As were the number of households containing the children of kin. The exaggerated comparison with the society of New England, where marriages took place earlier, families were more numerous, and marriages longer in duration, was considerably reduced even by 1700 as new social and economic factors came into play. From the situation where the family was not the norm but the exception, the demographic characteristics and domestic organisation of the population by the eighteenth century much more closely resembled that of New England. The sex ratio was less skewed. Marriages lasted longer. The family had arrived.[35] The element of comparison which Lorena Walsh introduces into this work, however, underlines the point that average figures mask a multitude of variations on the general theme, which demography alone cannot reveal.

By all accounts this high possibility of nuclear-family breakdown was not compensated for by deeply-rooted and easily maintained links with community and kin. The idea that entire families put down and maintained roots in a single community, in which they dwelt, worked and died and in which their descendants also lived out their days, has suffered many nasty knocks. Early modern people were mobile, albeit over what we, in an age of rapid transit, would view as relatively short distances. Gough's *History of Myddle* is interesting here because it is less a history of the individual families (which as often withered completely on the vine as put down deep and sprawling roots) than a history of houses, which passed from family to family, often with but tenuous links with the community of Myddle. This mobility (and its effects upon 'family') was if anything increased by industrialisation. A sample from the 1851 Census indicates that well under half of the population were living in their birthplace; that two-fifths had moved from their native place by the time they were fifteen and that around one sixth had moved by the time they were two years old. This was as true of urban as of rural populations. Clearly, in an age without telephone or motor car, it was at the least difficult to maintain close ties with relatives over quite modest distances.

Michael Anderson has provided us with a glimpse of what the important demographic developments of the nineteenth and twentieth centuries have meant for the life experience of the average married couple and their offspring. Children were now more likely to live beyond infancy and to the age of 25. Mothers were having their first child at a much younger age than previously and these children were themselves marrying and having their first children at younger ages. The children of a marriage now tended to be clustered in the earlier years of marriage and there were fewer of them, although as a proportion more survived. This meant that the married couple had a longer period together in a childless house. It also meant that more saw and knew their grandchildren. The 1861 cohort was the first where a majority would know all their grandchildren. Subsequently, men and women could expect to live long enough to see all their grandchildren marry. As Anderson points out, this development had considerable implications – grandparents could care for grandchildren while mothers worked; children could care for their parents in old age. But this did not allow for the idiosyncrasies of the market place or individual preference. Women preferred to work rather than to look after grandchildren or to support their aged parents. The reciprocal pattern of behaviour apparent in the period 1861 to 1940 was a short-lived phenomenon. Clearly demographic factors alone do not shape behaviour.

Probably more important for a comparative framework for the history of the family is the argument that family life in the later twentieth century has attained 'new' characteristics of age-gradedness and predictability. This is not necessarily a demographically-induced situation. A uniform education system, a uniform retirement plan, laws regulating human behaviour indicate the age at which infancy ends, childhood begins, adulthood begins, working life ends. People in Western societies feel relatively confident of living out their life-span. These people feel in control. They feel able to 'plan' their family life. Insecurity characterised the family of earlier times. A feature of this insecurity was enormous diversity in the patterns of family life in a practical demographic sense as well as in economic and ideological ways.

Conclusion : Confusing the Family with the Household

Valuable though these demographic studies are, they display grave deficiencies from the perspective of the history of the family. One of these is that they are almost entirely census-derived descriptions of the people, with all the source-association limitations. Censuses were produced for many reasons. The national census was designed to record, above all, the occupancy and occupants of 'houses' on a single date. The census, therefore, defines a household. There must, first of all, be serious reservations about the census definition concerning a distinct household.[36] Leaving these aside for the moment, historical demographers tend to confuse the household of the census with the family of experience. This identification is not self-evident. Historians must not allow themselves to assume that it is. The census does not permit us to determine whether there was in fact a wider family, or to study the relationship between this family within the household and other parts of the family. Martine Segalen boldly states 'We shall deal here with a particular type of family, a household co-residing as a domestic group. We consider such a group to be the pertinent unit of observation.'[37] Her use of the census as the basis of her study indeed locks her into such an assumption. Historians have begun to accept that household equals family. Thus Flandrin writes that family can be defined, in the words of the *Dictionnaire de l'Académie* (1694), as 'Toutes les personnes qui vivent dans une même maison, sous un même chef', although he avoids this exclusive definition himself. In part, the assumption that household and family are the same arises from the emphasis on the household to be found in contemporary writing.[38] In part, it arises from the deductive reasoning of the demographers.

While no-one sensible would deny the importance of co-residence as a family experience, it may be that other types of family experience are equally important to family members. It may also be the case that its importance varies from country to country, group to group and time to time in the same way as its size and composition appear to. It is just conceivable that the demographers may arrive at a formula for a population multiplier, but it is surely clear that they are not capable of arriving at an experience multiplier. They have not claimed such skill and historians of the family must not conclude that they have. For example, Laslett assumes that, because there is no census evidence to suggest that kin supported their aged or disabled relatives in the household, therefore it is proved that no important support was offered. Whether it was or not is really of no importance to the demographer in search of accurate population statistics, but it is crucial for the historian's understanding of the family. We must look to other sources for evidence to confirm or contradict the demographer's proposition.

Within the discipline of historical demography there is a tendency to think of variations to the pattern of 'family' structure in terms of life course. There have been a number of studies exploring this possibility. Some of them point to rather different conclusions from those their authors have elected to draw. For example, Segalen's study of Saint-Jean-Trolimon in fact indicates that household composition and structure were as dependent upon external factors such as availability of land, number of dependents, national economic and social change, warfare, and the laws of inheritance as upon life-cycle in any strict sense. Although she agrees with Jean Cuisenier that 'the phases of the cycle and the economic history of the domestic community are one and the same process', it does seem an agreement in contradiction of her own evidence. There are other factors which might have an impact upon household structure and yet which are rarely explicitly mentioned and almost never, if ever, emphasised by demographers. Ultimately, it must be said that demographers (and indeed all historians who rely on serial statistics for their evidence) are able to handle satisfactorily only those features which large numbers of households hold in common and declare. The historian, however, must wonder whether there are equally important and perhaps less predictable aspects of family experience. As a consequence, other types of source and other methodologies must be employed to study this possibility.

Historical demographers tend also to exaggerate the importance of the average in historical development. It is the average married couple, the average baby, the average child, the average household, the average town, the average village that are singled out for analysis. Not only does this ignore the relative importance of other structures and experiences, it can often do so even at the expense of the most numerous categories. Sometimes this results in strange anomalies: in pioneer Peter's Colony, Texas, between 1845 and 1850 the average household size was indeed low and the society was characterised by low fertility, but when one perceives the skewed demographic composition – a very high number of single males (795) and widows and widowers balancing 896 married couples (with 3.3 children on average) – the actual family pattern for the region seems much more comparable with the American norm, albeit that family cohabitation was not a possible option for much of the population.[39] At other extremes, even if there were fewer extended than simple households, more people may have lived in them than did not. For the historian it is often difficult to determine, from tabular presentations of data, what the basis of analysis is and what precise criteria have been used in making unit definitions.

So one of the dangers inherent in historical demography is that it may seem to offer a spurious exactness and certainty to our knowledge of demographic behaviour and performance in the past through its statistical tables, its precise definitions and its explanations and defences, which are nigh-on incomprehensible to lay person and scholar alike. Historical demography offers no miracle-cure in the face of inadequate data. While it might, on occasion, offer strategies for off-setting its absence by sophisticated manipulation of the evidence that does exist, it is essentially a descriptive science. The interpretation of its conclusions remains highly speculative and ultimately dependent upon a knowledge of the past derived from other sources. The questions which historical demographers seek to answer in statistical terms are historical questions to which, more often than not, there are no strictly demographic answers.

Historical demography offers the historian useful and usable tools to use in the quest for a convincing history of the family in a comparative framework, but the framework it itself offers is not intended to be, and should not be allowed to become, a substitute for a history of the family.

2. The Prescriptive Family, c.1450–1700

Throughout the modern period external agencies have sought to make the family 'work' for them. As a consequence much has been said and written, agitated for and legislated for about what the family ought to be like. And also, as a consequence, it has been only too easy for churchmen, educators, governments and civil servants, as well as historians and social scientists, to believe that the family *is* indeed what they would like it to be – to treat *prescriptive* sources as though they were *descriptive*. Such is perfectly understandable – the sources for the early modern period are so scant and incomplete and so biased towards coverage of the élite, and those for the modern period are so diverse and difficult to use, that there is a great temptation to accept the perspective adopted by agitators, campaigners and polemicists with little or no question.[1]

Understandable it is, but not desirable. As the previous chapter demonstrates, many of the preconceptions which commonly have been accepted about the nature of the family in the past are at the best questionable and in some cases definitely erroneous, yet these misconceptions inform both everyday debate and important central and local government decisions. Just one or two examples will suffice: in a television discussion programme on 26 November 1991 one participant – a young woman in her thirties, who spoke to defend the idea of mothers working and pre-school children attending childcare facilities – argued fiercely that 'children have *always* been brought up in an extended family with grandparents, aunts and cousins sharing in childcare'. In another context, one of the arguments for ceasing to provide places in old people's homes and mental hospitals in the 1980s and 1990s has been that such 'caring' has historically taken place in the family home and should be returned to it. On the breakfast programme on 28 November 1991 a psychologist, opposing the return of mothers to work before their children achieved three years, declared without hesitation or qualification that mothers in the past had given birth to many children and had stayed at home to rear them.[2]

Clearly historians and social scientists cannot afford to ignore the ideas which our predecessors expressed about the family's role in society, but we should seek to study these as 'ideas' or theories and not as descriptions of the family in the past. It will always be difficult to make a strict separation between the prescriptive and descriptive elements in the views put forward, for example, by Protestant preachers. Arguments are drawn from personal and vicarious experience; from misunderstanding or lack of understanding; from wishful thinking; from idiosyncratic perspectives and so on. But the attempt to make the separation is vital if we are to understand what the family was in the past as opposed to what contemporaries would have wished the family to be.

Why there was Interest in the Family

In the centuries under discussion, Church and State displayed tremendous interest in the family. Why? The family was potentially extremely useful as an organ of social control and economic stability: it could supervise closely its junior members; it might channel the energies of the economically productive and physically strong members of the biological family into providing for and caring for weak offspring and elderly kin. Biology provided the clue to the strength of the family unit: it was because people had a natural affection for their close relatives, that was strengthened by co-residence, that they were eager to perform these tasks, which the State, the community and the Church regarded as socially and spiritually valuable. At a time when in all the countries under discussion central control was weak, discipline from within the household and the local community was crucial. The Church was essentially interested in the individual soul. Only individuals could be saved, not families or villages or nations. The family was none the less important because within it the individual was nurtured, trained up, controlled. The Church was primarily interested in the natural biological unit and the strength and utility of the bonds it created. The State was not so much interested in the individual as in the strength of the nation. Sarah Hanley has suggested the existence of a Family–State Compact in France, which was 'designed to bring family formation under parental (that is patriarchal) control in the first instance and under the magisterial control of the Parlement of Paris in the second' and which 'regulated family matters (marriage regulations, reproductive customs, inheritance rules, and marital separation arrangements)' to this end.[3] There are strong similarities here to the position in England. The appeal of the State and theorists of the State was always to self-interest or, in some prominent cases, to the interest of the co-residential unit, the household. In many cases the State was not concerned necessarily with the biological family but rather with the actuality of the household, comprehending as it did the biological family, adoptive and step-members and residential servants. The household was a valuable agent of social control at village and town level. In theory it prevented young bachelors running riot; it prevented unwanted pregnancies among unmarried females; it provided succour for each individual in terms of food, clothing, warmth and shelter; it made it easy to count and account for the population; it made it simple to tax the population. Properly managed, it could ensure that the number of household never exceeded the capacity of the land to support the population. Jean Bodin wrote in 1576, 'Les familles étant bien gouvernées, la République ira bien.'

The family continued to be viewed as an important socioreligious institution throughout the seventeenth and eighteenth centuries. It is clear that this was, in part at least, because of its convenient location between the individual and the church's ministry. Richard Baxter in 1656 wrote by way of advice to pastors:

> The life of religion and the welfare and glory both of the Church and State depend much on family government and duty. If we suffer the neglect of this, we shall undo all. What are we like to do ourselves to the reforming of a congregation, if all the work be cast on us alone; and masters of families neglect that necessary duty of their own, by which they are bound to

help us? If any good be begun by the ministry in any soul, a care-
less, prayerless, worldly family is likely to stifle it.[4]

To avoid this situation he advised that ministers should 'get information how each family is ordered,' visit each family and inquire
about the practice of religion within the family for 'it might be well
to get a promise from them that they will make more conscience
of their duty for the future', teach them to pray as a family, provide
them with books and set readings, and show them how to spend
the sabbath as the Lord's Day.

    Neglect not, I beseech you, this important part of your work.
    Get masters of families to do their duty, and they will not only
    spare you a great deal of labour, but they will essentially pro-
    mote the success of your labours.

This work was still being reprinted in abridged form and
recommended as a principal work on the pastoral office in the
nineteenth century.
    But the family was a secret unit. Some of its features could
indeed be turned to advantage by the State and the Church but it
also threatened the aims of these outside agencies by its very existence. It set up a barrier around itself which was difficult to penetrate. Its intentions were not always friendly or sympathetic to the
goals of the wider society or the Church. Blood was certainly
thicker than water but it was also, on occasion, uncomfortably
stronger than allegiance to God or state. In 1552 Hugh Latimer
commented of the married man who declined an invitation to the
king's marriage feast that he 'saith "I cannot come"; because his
affections are more strong and more vehement than the other
men's were'.[5] Even in an age of little personal privacy and poor
house construction how could anyone, least of all a relatively
powerless State or Church, discover all that really went on in the
marital bed or round the proverbial hearth?[6]
    It was also in some senses a temporary and a fluid unit. A child
belonged to its parents' family until it became independent and
set up in a 'family' of its own. It seems also to have been assumed
that the child was associalised and acculturated within the parental
home and that the values and norms which a child acquired in the
family were a more powerful and lasting bond than that provided

by the authority of the parents over the child. Yet this is an assumption rather than a proven thesis. Moreover, as 'new' families are created every time a man and woman marry and set up a separate home together in which to raise their children, the individual adults concerned have to create, presumably from their pooled resources, the values and norms of their new family unit. Without labouring the point, the young wife has to find her feet in the extended family of her husband, and the husband in that of his wife. Yet different problems were raised when a new conjugal unit was added to an existing one to form a multinuclear household. The type of relationship that exists between husband and wife will determine whose values and norms dominate. The historical debate about the nature and extent of woman's oppression in the past takes on a new importance for the history of the family.

What, also, of that large number of children who during childhood lost one, even both parents and, as a direct consequence, lived in may be several 'families', albeit perhaps always in the same building? Can it really be safe to assume that the ways and values of each of these 'families' were identical and unchanging?

The ambivalent attitude to the family as an institution was apparent from the beginning. The family/household as we know it has a relatively short history. It owed as much to the traditions of the German tribes as to the practices of the Roman Empire, and it was from the middle of the eighth century AD that it emerged in a recognisable form. From this date both State and Church endeavoured to shape the family and to use it. But it was from the eleventh century onwards that this attempt was most successful, as the Church made a vigorous and, according to some historians, effective effort to reorder secular society. A systematic theology and canon law of marriage was in time developed. The Church was granted the right to judge marriage cases in the Courts Christian. The rules of affinity and consanguinity were applied.

The Scriptural Origins of the Church's Teaching on the Family

It was in fact the Church alone which developed a coherent teaching on the family, and, therefore, most of this chapter is dedicated to describing this teaching and, where appropriate, to pointing out where this teaching differed in a national context. The approach of the Church towards the family was, from the first, eclectic and ambivalent. This was perhaps inevitable because the main sources for its teaching on family relationships were themselves contradictory. The family was regarded as a God-given institution because it figured in the Bible narratives as a 'natural' state and, moreover, because the Bible contained major teaching on human relations within the biological family. Yet there the clarity ended. On the one hand, Adam declared 'Wherefore a man shall leave father and mother, and shall cleave to his wife, and they shall be two in one flesh.' On the other hand, in the Book of Deuteronomy no pronouncements were made extolling the marriage relationship, but only the parent–child relationship. 'Honour thy father and thy mother' ordered the fourth commandment. The wife was regarded as 'property' on a par with the neighbour's ox. The first text made true patriarchy an impossibility – when a son or a daughter married, obligation passed to the spouse. The second text made respect for the parent mandatory. What position should the Church take? The evidence suggests that churchmen related their understanding of such texts to other traditions of contemporary import rather than to the historical context in which the texts themselves were produced. For instance, we know that in Roman times two forms of marriage had been known: in cases of marriage *in manu* the authority over a girl held by her father was passed to the husband (either by a gift of bread in compensation, or by straight purchase, or by fulfilment of a given period of cohabitation) so that the wife stood in the place of a daughter to her husband; in cases of free marriage a daughter remained under her father's authority despite taking a spouse – while on first sight this might seem to suggest a worse condition, it in fact profited a woman's independence quite considerably. Free marriage became the norm after the second century AD. The opposing, Germanic, tradition to which the West was heir in the Middle Ages was one in which there was widespread sexual promiscuity and polygamy and extreme emphasis, as a result, upon relationships through the female line. It was indeed a wise child who knew his own father. Yet the forms of marriage echoed the marriage *in manu* and the free marriage of the Roman Empire. We are able to trace their persistence in the laws of marriage and inheritance. Thus the contradictory positions on the authority relations between husband and wife, and parents and children, were part of the fabric of Western culture; they were echoed in the teachings of the Church and they remained unresolved by the Church.[7]

The Church, however, regarded the natural family with a certain suspicion. At its best, human love, whether based on a biological bond or upon sexual attraction, was seen as competing with the absolute and overwhelming love of the individual for Christ. It could certainly stand in contradiction to the authority of the Church. Christina of Stomelm was tempted by the devil: the temptation took the form of a vision of a happy family group of husband, wife and baby. The wife was playing with the child and, looking up at Christina, said, 'There is no delight greater than this delight, like to this delight, which a mother has in her child'. In the eleventh and twelfth centuries there may have been a resurgence of the tendency to overplay the authority of the father in the family. Some historians believe that the teachings of Peter Lombard, bishop of Paris, on the consensual nature of marriage were a direct response to this theologically indefensible trend. Lombard taught that to achieve a valid marriage the bride and groom, who were otherwise free to marry without impediment, had simply to consent to the union in words of the present tense. Such a doctrine forbade any individual or institution from interfering. Father, master, lord, king, priest, bishop, Pope – none could control the marriage of a man or a woman. When Pope Alexander III (1159–89) endorsed these teachings in a series of decretals, the power of the Church was set behind the principle of consent as the basis of union. True patriarchy could not develop for as long as this principle held good. These twelfth-century decisions, the fruit of suspicion, had far-reaching consequences in terms of social organization in the West.[8]

At their worst, family relationships were in themselves far from satisfactory, permitting individuals to sin with impunity against the commandments of God – daughters did not have happy relationships with their mothers-in-law; husbands beat their wives and children, indulged in incestuous or adulterous relations; children were disrespectful towards their parents and neglected their care in old age; parents neglected their offspring. Was the confessional the only window into the family's soul? Or could inquisitors and court officers also penetrate the fortress that was the family?

Christians suspected the natural family but they were forced to accommodate it in their teaching and to spend their own lives within it. St Paul, who regarded virginity as the ideal state for the devotee of Christ, none the less sanctified the family. It is interesting that it is the relationship between husband and wife rather than between parent and child that first commands his attention. The husband has authority over the body of the wife and she over his. Either can demand the marital debt, even when the other partner is unwilling. Divorce among Christians is forbidden. The husband is placed in authority over the wife as Christ is placed in authority over the Church and can no more leave her than Christ can leave the Church. The husband, by analogy, has spiritual governorship over his wife – he is concerned for her salvation because, just as the Church is part of Christ, the wife is part of her husband. She is his rib. Only then does Paul consider parent–child relations. If children obey their parents 'in the Lord' (that is, when obedience is consistent with God's will) they will receive their contracted child's portion from God – prosperity and long life. And parents should not take advantage of their position and drive their children too far, rather they should bring them up according to God's commandments. There is no word in Paul of patriarchy. The analogy of God the Father is not employed. Mutuality in both spiritual and physical terms is emphasised. All relationships will be governed by God's commands that have been made in the interest of His people.

It may seem strange to use the words of St Paul to introduce a discussion of Church attitudes towards the family in the early modern and modern periods. After all, Paul was addressing a small group of Christians in first-century Ephesus not seventeenth or eighteenth- century Britain or France. This is to miss the point. Christians, be they Catholic or Protestant, used the Bible as their conduct book. These same words of Paul, along with other scriptural texts, were the basis of Christian teaching on the family in Britain, France and the United States down to the present. Now it will become evident that interpretations were not always in agreement. Committed Christians were subject to many different influences. Tradition, meditation, vision – all had their part to play in informing Christian teaching on the family.

It is important to note, however, that throughout our period theorists of domestic life concentrated upon the proper relations within a household based on a simple nuclear family. They offered no counsel on relations within complex households of any type or upon relations with the wider kin group after marriage. How should a wife regard her parents or a father his married son, daughter-in-law and grandchildren? This obsession with the simple nuclear household (which, we should observe, included servants as well as biological relatives) arose out of the teaching of the Bible and represented wishful thinking rather than a statement of actuality. It means that theory never addressed the problems experienced by extended or multinuclear families.

The Holy Family

The fourteenth and fifteenth centuries saw large-scale attempts by the Church to interpret these scriptural injunctions and to model the human family on that of the child Jesus. The family would become a holy institution. The child would love and obey his or her parents. The mother would nurture the child. Nursing at the breast would enlarge her love for the baby. The mother, like Mary, would be an intercessor, a means of facilitating the frequently difficult relations between one male generation and another. The father, like Joseph, would be patron and protector, accepting God's will (as did the mother) without demur. The bonds of love between individuals in the family would always be second to those owed the person of Christ and His Church – just as Jesus had put obedience to His Mother second to His obedience to God. The natural bonds, however, would be strong enough to encourage the parents to 'look after' their children's spiritual as well as their physical welfare. The family would assist rather than impede the individual's progress on the road to salvation.

Within this institution there were attempts to alter the balance of roles. In the fourteenth century there was a growing cult of St Joseph. Traditionally he had been a neglected figure, who only came into his own as a figure of comic stature in the stories of the nativity. Now Church leaders wished to regard him as the respected patron of the Holy Family. Jean Gerson, Chancellor of the University of Paris, argued that Joseph should be given his own major feast day. He was not the 'old, ugly, ineffectual' and incapable man of the mystery plays but a young, vigorous and capable head of household who steered the Holy Family through dangerous times in Egypt. Bernadino da Feltre was overwhelmed by a vision of Joseph's devotion to the child Jesus. His role was not only that of servant protector: because Mary and Jesus had both acknowledged Joseph as in authority over them, he was by rights the ruler of the world. Pierre d'Ailly, the French theologian, echoed the opinion of da Feltre that Joseph had been taken up with the Holy Family into heaven. In 1479 Joseph's saint's day was added to the Roman Calendar. But the campaign to overcome the popular cultural stereotype had only partial success: the name Joseph, in its Italian form of Giuseppe, came into fashion in Florence only in the sixteenth century; while St Teresa of Avila and St Francis de Sales popularised the cult in Spain and part of France, there is little evidence that it gained popularity in England.[9]

There were certain advantages in according Joseph importance in the Holy Family, model for Christian families. One was that he provided a 'human' role model for a father. The only other available Christian role model was God himself. For a Church none too keen to suggest the omnipotence of human father, analogies with the authority and power of God were not considered apposite. Joseph, like Mary, possessed authority, but it was demonstrably authority under God rather than as of God. Did his low profile in English Christian thought about the family tip the balance in favour of patriarchy?

Christian marriage was seen to dissolve one family and begin another. Childhood – that is dependence on the parents – ended on marriage and not before. On marriage a son became independent and a daughter replaced one authority – that of the father – with another – the spouse. Obligations to a former family were overridden by those to the present family. An old covenant is replaced by a new. Yet one could not defend an analogy in which it was even suggested that God the Father's authority could ever be cast aside. The presence of Joseph in the human Holy Family simplified matters considerably.

St Paul's somewhat grudging acceptance of marriage as a Christian institution also left a profound legacy in the medieval and early modern West. Until the early sixteenth century both France and England shared this legacy. The Catholic Church regarded vows of celibacy and the state of virginity as infinitely superior and preferable to vows of marriage and sexual intercourse within marriage. Marriage was necessary but not desirable:

it existed to protect the individual against sins of the flesh; it existed for the sake of the human race and for the family. These were views to which even the advanced thinker, Montaigne, subscribed. The legacy was difficult to shake off in later years. When Protestants rejected vows of virginity among the clergy, some still saw celibacy as evidence of 'superior moral endowment'. The Elizabethan apologist for the Church of England, Richard Hooker, spoke of single life as 'a thing more angellicall and divine' than married life and saw marriage as necessary for the continuation of the human race. 'The state of perfection is virginity, so much commended by our Saviour, so highly esteemed by St Paul', wrote John Cosin. George Herbert saw the married state as guarding the individual against fleshly lusts.[10]

The Spiritualised Household

At some point in the late fifteenth and early sixteenth centuries orthodox teaching about the family and relationships within it were subjected to considerable stress. The task before the historian is to determine why, when and how traditional church teachings were either rejected or modified in the face of this.

Not so long ago, historians were accustomed to argue that change was brought about by the Protestant Reformation and that it found its most sophisticated expression in the Elizabethan and Early Stuart puritan concept of the spiritualised household. Thus, Keith Thomas was able to write that, 'The Reformation, by reducing the authority of the priest in society, simultaneously elevated the authority of lay heads of households', adding that the idea that the head of household was responsible for the religious instruction and discipline of its members 'was part of the protestant inheritance'. So, in a sense, it was; but only, as Margaret Todd pointed out, because English Protestants shared in a common European heritage of Christian humanist thought and scholarship. Christian humanists had, in the late fifteenth and early sixteenth centuries, challenged contemporary orthodoxies. Of key importance were the writings of one who was neither a Church leader nor a Frenchman nor an Englishman: Desiderius Erasmus. His colloquies ('Courtship'; 'The Girl with No Interest in Marriage'; 'The Repentant Girl'; 'Marriage'; 'The Young Man and the Harlot';

'The New Mother'; 'A Marriage in Name Only'; and 'The Lower House') and *Encomium Matrimonii* (1518) and *The Institution of Christian Marriage* exposed the underpinnings of contemporary teaching on the family and invited open discussion. By the mid-sixteenth century his works were readily available in translation in France, Britain and the other major European languages. Not only theologians and preachers read his writings – generations of schoolboys raised in the humanist tradition were made privy to his thoughts. 'Courtship', for example, via an entertaining dramatic dialogue, offered the important and controversial argument that marriage was a desirable state preferable to virginity.[11]

> PAMPHILUS: A maiden is something charming, but what's more naturally unnatural than an old maid? Unless your mother had been deflowered, we wouldn't have this blossom here. But if, as I hope, our marriage will not be barren, we'll pay for one virgin with many.
>
> MARIA: But they say chastity is a thing most pleasing to God.
>
> PAMPHILUS: And therefore I want to marry a chaste girl, to live chastely with her. It will be more of a marriage of minds than of bodies. We'll reproduce for the state; we'll reproduce for Christ. By how little will this marriage fall short of virginity! And perhaps some day we'll live as Joseph and Mary did.

Unusual in this respect, Erasmus was more traditional in his acceptance of the nature of marriage and the remedies available to *The Discontented Wife*, Xanthippe. While husbands were supposed to 'cherish their wives as Christ has cherished his spouse the Church', the wife is not absolved of her duty to offer obedience to her husband because he has failed to observe his own duty of love. 'Whatever your husband's like, bear in mind that there's no exchanging him for another ... you must be husband and wife until the day you die.' The wife afflicted by a boorish, brutal husband must for her own sake make the best of a bad job. By using her feminine wiles she may win him over to better ways.[12]

Juan Luis Vives, who was tutor to Mary, elder daughter of Henry VIII, wrote very much from within the Erasmian tradition. In the *Instruction of a Christian Woman* (1523) he argued the superiority of the married state and the necessity for happy union. The emphasis upon companionate marriage was developed again by Vives in *The*

Office and Duties of an Husband as well as by Erasmus in *Prayse of Matrimony* and Thomas More in *Utopia*.

Erasmus's German contemporary, Martin Luther, also expressed considerable interest in marriage. To him, marriage was the only institution in which human sexuality could be expressed with God's blessing. It provided a 'hospital' for lust. Sexuality could not be denied but required proper direction. When a marriage ceased to offer this protection there were grounds for divorce: for example, if a wife denied her husband sexual gratification and tempted him to adultery, or if adultery took place. Marriage was there for pleasure as well as for procreation. Luther's emphasis was upon the chaste, respectable woman, whose natural role was within marriage as wife and mother. The woman's role in the family was enhanced in importance but restricted and domestic in its sphere. The spinster and the nun were equally regarded as 'abnormal'. Indeed, the 'normal' role for all Christians was within a family. Family discipline was binding for all Christians. The family was patriarchal and hierarchical in its ordering. The husband had authority over wife and children and servants.[13]

Erasmus was from the Low Countries, Vives from Spain, Luther from Germany. Why are their views important in our study of the family in England, France and the North American colonies? Simply because they were part of the cultural and intellectual curriculum of educated élites in early modern England and France. Elizabethan puritans in particular, it is claimed, developed a distinctively Protestant teaching of the spiritualised household and drew their ideas from Luther, from Calvin and, above all, from the writings of Heinrich Bullinger. Books and pamphlets of Christian counsel on domestic matters proliferated in the later sixteenth and seventeenth centuries. They claimed as their authorities, Scripture and the Continental reformers.

This claim does not bear close scrutiny. While it is true that the immediate source for such writings was often either the Bible or the works of Bullinger and other reformers, the views expressed in them can be traced back as much to Erasmus, always a Catholic, as to the reformers. Erasmus, like Luther, urged that marriage was advised by Scripture and practised in nature. For neither was virginity the ideal. Marriage was a superior estate. Erasmus described religious celibacy as 'a forme of lyvynge bothe barren and unnaturall'. The Elizabethan puritan Bartholomew Batty, in his turn, said something remarkably similar: 'marriage is the most excellent state and condition of life ... which all the godly both by preaching and example have commended unto us, and placed the same in the toppe of all good works'. Luther emphasised the importance of the woman's role in marriage as wife and mother. Erasmus stressed the need for companionship within marriage – it is 'an especiall swetnes to have one with whom ye may speake even as it were with your own selfe'. It was a sentiment which seems echoed by the puritan, Robert Cleaver, 'There can be no greater societie of companie, then there is between a man and his wife.' The concept of the household as seminary of church and commonwealth was common to both the humanist and the Protestant. Similarly, both saw the importance of the parents as educators. This was seen as a joint responsibility and considerable emphasis was placed upon the woman's role. It was Erasmus and Vives who first called for an end to the wet-nursing of infants: all children should 'have all one both for their mother, their nurse and their teacher' because then maternal affection would reinforce proper moral, Christian training. The home was a nursery for Christian education. Elizabethan writers such as William Gouge, William Perkins and Bartholomew Batty did little more than agree. Puritans regarded men and women as spiritually equal and taught that the woman should always obey God before her husband where their wills conflicted. But this Protestant teaching was far from novel. There was little here that Erasmus, Vives and Thomas More had not already said. It was Erasmus and other Christian humanists, then, who first laid emphasis upon the importance of the spiritual-ised household and the valuable role which the wife and mother played within it.

Identifying common strands in the domestic theories of humanists, Continental Protestants and Elizabethan writers does not, of course, prove that English Protestants derived their teaching from either humanists or Continental reformers. They could have reached their opinions independently through study of the Scriptures. Even if there was a debt to Erasmus and Vives, it might have been indirect. Many of the early sixteenth-century reformers, Luther included, themselves had been heavily influenced by Christian Humanism. Bullinger's *Christen State of Matrimony* was heavily reliant upon the Bible, the Ancients and the Christian Humanists. Thus it may have been that ideas about the family were passed down to Elizabethan Protestants. It was just as likely, given the educational curriculum of the period, that Scriptural and classical ideas would be mediated to Elizabethans by the writings of Christian Humanists themselves. In fact, the Elizabethan writers acknowledged their debt to Erasmus and Vives as well as to the study of the Scriptures and the Ancients. There was little distinctive about English Protestant domestic theory, and its proponents had no wish to claim its originality.

If there was an innovator in domestic theory it was Erasmain humanism and not English Protestantism. Moreover, English Protestant domestic theory should be seen as part of a continuing tradition in late medieval/early modern thought rather than as a simple consequence of the Reformation.

An examination of Tridentine attitudes to marriage and the family might appear to give the lie to this statement. The Council of Trent seems to have viewed the spiritualised household and the nuclear family with suspicion. Tridentine Canons and Decrees gave bishops the authority and responsibility for religious teaching, not parents. Unauthorised religious teaching was forbidden. The superiority of the celibate state was asserted: 'If anyone says that the married state excels the state of virginity or celibacy, and that it is better and happier to be united in matrimony than to remain in virginity or celibacy, let him be anathema.' Religious authority was returned to a celibate priesthood. The historian of the spiritualised household urges that the Tridentine decrees 'led to the demise of the family as a holy and religious institution in Catholic teaching'. Whereas the great Elizabeth puritan preacher, William Perkins, described marriage as 'a state itself far more excellent than the condition of a single life', the Catholic Cardinal Bellarmine held the sharply contrasting view that 'marriage is a thing humane, virginity is angelicall'. It may appear ironical that marriage remained a sacrament within the Catholic Church but not in the Protestant Churches.

It is possible to argue that, without the Reformation, Erasmian attitudes to family issues, to sexuality and to women's roles and abilities would have died. Protestantism can be seen as ensuring the continuance of the Christian Humanist tradition. It is also possible, however, to argue that without the perceived threat of Protestantism, Catholics would not have been forced on to the defensive at Trent and Christian Humanist ideas would have been preserved as one strand among many in the broad Catholic Communion. As it was, the Catholic Church was forced into a corner on domestic issues. Erasmus's views on marriage and the family became identified with Protestantism. The Catholic Church declared Erasmian views not only unpopular but totally unacceptable – anathema.

In sharp contrast, the spiritual household was carried by English settlers to the New World. A covenant was formed between the family and God. 'The Puritans', as E. S. Morgan says, 'thought of their church as an organization made up of families rather than individuals'. The family engaged in regular devotions, which included scripture reading as well as prayer. There was in New England, though, some debate about whether it was the family or the household who entered the religious covenant. John Cotton believed that 'the Covenant is made to the householders and their servants', using the example of Abraham as his support, but the equally influential John Davenport argued for the exclusion of servants.[14] We should not, however, exaggerate the importance of the family unit in the life of the colonies. In many churches families did not sit together for worship – instead the congregation was divided accordingly to sex and age, in marked contrast to the English arrangement.[15]

Conduct Books

Historians studying 'religious' positions on the family should constantly remind themselves that the men and women who, as it were, spoke for the Church were influenced by both secular and practical religious concerns as well as by the inspiration of Holy Writ. As a result, theory and practice were almost inextricably intertwined. If we study, for example, the English marriage conduct books of the Tudor and Stuart periods we can see how teachings on the proper conduct of conjugal family life were influenced by the belief amongst these authors that the ideal was not being fulfilled in contemporary society. These authors were addressing their writings to an educated group among the middling sort in English society.[16] In other words the families they addressed were not the impoverished and simple nuclear families of labourers and cottagers but households based upon an 'independent' nuclear family which included servants, apprentices and farmhands. These were not, then, the majority of biological families, although from the religious point of view they could be regarded as the most influential. It was the co-resident household rather than the biological family that could be used as the nursery of true religion. It is not insignificant that historians write not of the 'spiritualised family' but of the 'spiritualised household'. We should interpret William Gouge's oft-quoted statement in that light: 'Necessary it is that good order be first set in families: for as they were before polities, so they are somewhat the more necessary: and good members of the family are like to make good members of Church and Commonwealth.[17]

Generally speaking, of course, such households were based at some stage in their cycle upon the conjugal relationship of husband and wife, but it is a social and economic organisation of which Gouge, Stubbes and the rest write. And they found good and convenient scriptural support for their teaching. In that same Epistle where he pronounced upon the proper relationships between husband and wife and parents and children, the apostle Paul wrote,

Servants, be obedient unto them that according to the flesh are your masters, with fear and trembling, in singleness of your heart, as unto Christ; not in the way of eyeservice, as men-pleasers; but as servants of Christ, doing the will of God from the heart; with good will doing service, as unto the Lord, and not unto men; knowing that whatsoever good thing each one doeth, the same shall he receive again from the Lord, whether he be bond or free. And ye masters, do the same things unto them and forbear threatening: knowing that both their Master and Yours is in heaven, and there is no respect of persons with him.[18]

This and other New Testament texts – for instance the parable of the Prodigal Son – described relations between servants and masters and made it abundantly clear that, while these were not the same as those between children and parents in the biological family, they, like the relations between parents and children in the household, were to be governed by obligations. Members of a family/household were to behave towards one another as children

of light, bearing always in their minds and hearts the knowledge
that in Christ there were no social divisions and that His salvation
was for all those who believed in Him. Ignoring the differences
between the society of Ephesus in the first century AD and that of
England in the sixteenth and seventeenth centuries, it was tempting to transpose this very specific teaching of Paul to contemporary households which were also composed of nuclear families and
servants. Indeed, the values and norms of Christianity were
regarded as timeless, they were those of the 'eternal' family. While
it is true that the authors of many of the conduct books can be
described as belonging to the puritan wing of the Church of
England, there is little or no evidence that this teaching was distinctively puritan or that only 'puritan families' were at the receiving end.

Sermon Literature and the Application of Christian Values to Family Life

It was not only in conduct books, of course, that the relevance of
Christian values in human families was taught. Popular sermons
have been insufficiently studied in this context. Hugh Latimer, in
mid- sixteenth-century England, emphasised the importance of the
'family' of God to which all Christians belonged. The authority of
Father God was stressed. He insisted that Christians have all
acquired God's values which must permeate their lives in human
families. When a Christian man and woman set up house together
and have children there is no dispute about the values and norms
of their household for they already share the 'pattern' of the Christian family. These are values which are never cast away, never grown
out of, but which are passed on from generation to generation.

> That man and that woman that live together godly and quietly,
> doing the works of that vocation, and fear God, hear his word
> and keep it'; that same is a religious house, that is, that house
> pleaseth God.[19]

In the petition, 'Give us this day our daily bread', according to
Latimer, children pray for godly parents and tutors because without them they cannot be 'brought up in godliness', and man and

wife pray one for the other. 'For one is help unto the other, and so necessary the one to the other: therefore they pray one for the other, that God will spare them their lives, to live together quietly and godly, according to his ordinance and institution ...' Servants, in particular, should be well supervised in their adherence to God's values because they have no natural bond with the master and mistress to reinforce their acceptance of God's family rules: 'those that have servants must not only command them what they shall do, but they must see it be done: they must be present, or else it shall never be done'. Latimer uses the analogy of mundane tasks – for example, the servant left to care for his master's fields – but he is addressing rather the spiritual life of the Christian servant and its expression in social conduct.[20]

What were these Christian values and how would they be translated in family life? In another sermon, Latimer explained the 'armour of God' with which Christians must gird themselves against assaults of the Devil in terms of family life. Truth in the first weapon: 'For it is seen nowadays, that children learn prettily of their parents to lie; for the parents are not ashamed to lie in presence of their children.' 'Suffer not your children to lie, or tell false tales. When you hear one of your children to make a lie, take him up, and give him three or four good stripes ...' The second is justice. To be just is defined as 'to give every man that which we owe unto him.' 'So likewise between married folks there shall be justice; that is to say, they shall do their duties: the man shall love his wife, shall honour her, shall not be rigorous, but admonish her lovingly: again, the wife shall be obedient, loving and kind towards her husband, not provoking him to anger with ill and naughty words. Further the parents ought to do justice towards their children, to bring them up in godliness and virtue; to correct them when they do naught: likewise, children ought to be obedient unto their parents, and be willing to do according unto their commandment. Item, the master ought to do justice unto their servants, to let them have their meat and drink, and their wages: again, the servants ought to be diligent in their master's business ...' Christian children will love to hear the word of God, will have faith, and, therefore, salvation.[21]

Latimer used a miracle, the raising of Jairus' daughter, as the occasion for exploring the divine purpose behind the relationship between parents and children. 'The same fatherly affection and love of the parents towards their children' as Jairus had 'is the good gift of God' and it is implanted in human parents for two reasons. First, for the sake of the children: 'it is an irksome thing to bring up children' and, moreover, a cause of great expense – love is the compensation 'which taketh away all the irksomeness of all labour and pain'. (Surely such understanding on Latimer's part suggests he had a family!) 'For what is the child when he is left alone? What can it do? How is it able to live?' So love inspires parents to provide for their children. Second, from the human example 'we might learn ... what affections he beareth towards us' 'the chosen children of God' 'For the love of God towards us is more earnest and more vehement than is the fatherly love towards his natural child: which thing shall comfort us in all our distress.[22]

Preachers throughout the sixteenth and early seventeenth centuries showed how the fundamental Christian virtues provided a sampler for family life. What changed was not the basic Christian message but how it was made relevant to contemporary circumstances. To spring forward into the later sixteenth century, William Perkins, a don and a cleric, discussed the duties of parents towards their children in broadly similar terms to Latimer but with marked differences of detail and emphasis. (What he described as duties, Latimer would have seen as justice.)

> The duties of parents are especially two; one to bring up their children; the other to bestow them, when they have brought them up. Touching education or bringing up of children, the parents care must be, both that they may live, and also that they may live well. Eph. 6.4. Touching the preservation of the life of the child, there are as many duties required of the parents, specially foure. First the mother is herselfe to give the infant sucke, and to wrap it up in swadling clothes. Paul commends it for a note of a good wife, to nurse her owne children.   1 Tim. 5.10.

The parent will provide 'meat, drink and clothing', will lay by something for the future maintenance of the child, and will, having observed the inclination and the natural gifts of the child, 'bestow it in some honest calling and course of life'. And the parents' first 'care must be for the Church, that those of their children which have the most pregnant wit, and be indued[23] with the best gifts be consecrated unto God, and brought up in the studie of the scriptures, to serve afterward to the ministery of the church. Thus Anna dedicated Samuel her sonne unto God by vowe. I Sam, I,II' The parent will provide that the children may live well and lead a godly life by baptising and naming the child, ensuring that it is catechised, and seeing that their children's religious instruction is geared to their age, inclination and needs, 'that they may take it with delight'. Words for reproof and the rod of correction are a last resort. The Bible will provide a sufficient conduct book for parents' relations with their children (from the arrangement of marriages to the treatment of the errant child) and for children's relations with their parents (with regard to marriage, choice of calling, household chores and care for the aged).[24]

Perkins's teaching on the family and parent–child relations within it, then, was Bible-based and, in essence, very similar to Thomas Becon's much earlier Catechism, but it also reflected more contemporary views on educational matters and child management and the lively debate about the future of the ministry. Until recently historians, perhaps as a direct result of the women's movement, have subordinated consideration of the parent–child relationship in early modern times to that of the husband–wife. Many contemporaries, however, would have agreed with Dod and Cleaver that the essential division in the family was that between the 'Governours' (husband and wife together) and 'those that must be ruled' (children and servants). Moreover, although it may be true that in France this relation was, even in the seventeenth and eighteenth centuries, seen in terms of the child's duty to his or her parents rather than the parents' obligations to the child, in England this was far from the case. In both societies, however, the imperative to such obligations came from God in the first instance, not from the needs of the child.[25]

The Relative Importance of the Concept of the Family in France and England

A society accustomed to think in terms of communal responsibilities and obligations, in terms of relationships, developed the concept of the family. Today, when it is individualism which rules and the fulfilment of individual potential which seems all-important, it is often difficult to grasp the original meaning of family.

England, a Protestant country, was characterised by doctrines of marriage and the family which attributed to them great importance in the Christian life. This was as true of puritans who denied the sacramental nature of marriage as it was of others who remained ambivalent. Yet in France, where the sacramental nature of marriage was never seriously challenged in the national Church, the importance of marriage and the family were generally belittled. The Le Playist concept of the family as the 'moral cell' and the skeleton key to social harmony was not a noticeable part of the French tradition before the nineteenth century. Such an important difference between the Anglo-Saxon and the French philosophies of life and society is obscured if we emphasise, as do many historians, the family as an institution. French writers sought to hold up the celibate life as the ideal. Marriage was necessary for the propagation of the species and control of social life: often the impression given is that it is a regrettable necessity and that the state of marriage offers but a slight access to grace.[26] The catechistical writings of the time reinforced this traditional teaching on the purpose of marriage. Bishop Bossuet's catechism for Meaux diocese provides good example:

> For what purpose should one marry? In order to multiply the children of God. What other purpose can one have? To remedy the disorders of concupiscence. What obligations does marriage confer? To unite with one another, and, through charity, to support one another, patiently to bear one another and all the pains of marriage; and to attain salvation by giving a holy education to one's children.[27]

Bossuet concludes that one of the evils which must be avoided in marriage is its use for the gratification of sensual lusts.

Even while acknowledging the 'grandeur and dignity of marriage', French churchmen emphasised the impossibility of 'happiness' within marriage. Indeed, marriage could only succeed if almost impossible preconditions were met. Adrien Bourdoise, of the parish of St Nicholas-du-Chardonnet, described the elevated standards required of those aspiring to head a household (that is, a male about to enter into holy matrimony): he must be able to govern and instruct a family and set a good Christian example to his wife; he must be assured that his wife will prove a good helpmeet in this task; he must feel inclined to help prepare his wife and children for heaven. Robin Briggs makes the apt comment: 'The parallel with the union of Christ and the Church may have dignified marriage, but it also provided a quite inappropriate model of other worldly perfection'. It was a state in which one could not succeed unless one had already achieved sanctification. The devil was seen as lying in wait for the newly married and he used:

> his agents, who are the witches, magicians, and enchanters. … Note that the devil's hostility to these young plants is particularly directed to preventing them having children. … When every-thing is joyful at the wedding, the devil seeks to trouble the feast, and convert the blessing into a curse, therefore it is necessary to make use of the ecclesiastical blessing against his design …[28]

The French clergy who wrote on the topic were generally uneasy when dealing with family relations. Unlike their English counter-parts, these preachers and pastors were excluded from marriage, officially barred from sexual relationships and from paternity and the responsibility for the upbringing of children. Bourdoise even stated unequivocally that clerics must divorce themselves from their native families:

> I do not think a cleric can go to paradise if he lives next to his parents … if you have taken the tonsure and your relatives ask you to help with their affairs … say boldly to them: I am dead. I can do nothing for you. … The worst air that a cleric can breathe is that of his native region.[29]

Such men could cope with community but not with family. Misogynism mingled with an unrealistic belief in the sexual purity of young girls. Women bore the burden of guilt for the Fall. They and their inherent passions remained a lure for contemporary men also. Children were 'obstinate embodiments of original sin'. Paternal authority within the family was emphasised in their writings because the father could control these troublesome mem-bers and also stand for the family as a whole. The obligation for the priest to deal with other members would be minimised. French ecclesiastics drew back, however, from conferring spiritual

importance upon the father. He was responsible for holding
family prayers but for no other spiritual functions. The household
was not spiritualised in early modern France.

Patriarchy

None the less there does seem to have been a steady increase in
the Church's interest in domestic life between the fifteenth and
the eighteenth centuries, which has been charted by J.-L. Flandrin.
There was also a change of emphasis during this period. The
earliest manual studied by Flandrin sketches a picture of highly
formal relations between husband and wife, in which the husband
becomes a replacement for her father, almost. He has the duty to
guide and form his wife and, when she fails, to chastise and even
beat her. This was in accordance with the customary laws of
France: the compilation of Beauvaisis in the thirteenth century
put it thus, 'It is lawful for the man to beat his wife, without bringing about death or disablement, when she refuses her husband
anything.' But a spiritual dimension is added in the late sixteenth
century by Benedicti. She sins if she does not obey his commandments. 'She must do nothing against her husband, to whom she is
subject by divine and human law.' He, for his part, 'is obliged to
correct her' because 'according to the Scriptures the husband is
the master of his wife'. By the eighteenth century the duty of correction has disappeared. There is some evidence that by this time
the wife is seen as the restraining moral force within the conjugal
relationship. Notwithstanding changes in emphasis, there was a
clear intention to use the union to shape individuals according to
the precepts of Christianity as perceived at that time.[30]

The power of the father over the children was extremely clearly
defined within French law. It appears that the authority and power
of coercion which fathers were entitled to exercise by law over
their children and grandchildren actually increased from the
sixteenth century onwards. While Jean Bodin's plea that fathers be
allowed the power of life and death over their children was not
satisfied, fathers maintained absolute control in other respects.
Children could neither enter binding contracts (such as loans or
marriages) nor make wills (even with the father's consent)
because they had no absolute right in property, even over their

own persons. In the written law provinces, these rules applied unless either the father formally emancipated his children or they reached exalted official positions. Elsewhere, the applicability of the rules was variable. For example, in Brittany a man remained dependent on his father until the age of 60 or until he married with the parent's consent, yet in Berri marriage spelt independence at any age and all unmarried children became independent at 25, and in Montargis all unmarried children achieved independence at 20. The Crown and even the French Church were keen to reinforce patriarchal control, resisting in no small way the attempts of the universal Church to free children from parental control when entering a marriage contract. French ecclesiastics stressed that, while parents sinned if they forced children into marriages against their will and interest, children no less sinned mortally if they disobeyed their parents. There were seen to be restrictions on the authority of the father, under the superior authority of God. God it was who determined whether a child should marry or remain celibate or follow a religious vocation. This was not the father's prerogative. This accepted, it was the parent's duty to see that a child was prepared for the estate to which God had called him or her, and the child's duty to follow this way obediently. There were marked similarities here with the English Protestant teaching regarding vocation.[31]

We should not over-emphasise the strength of patriarchy within this French 'family' however. Envisaging the father as an independent, free-acting individual is a mistake. The reverse side of the inability of children to make contracts and wills was that fathers themselves did not alienate property because it belonged to the family. Under the *restrait lignager*, 'A landowner must not alienate his land without the consent of his expectant heirs unless it be a case of necessity, and even in a case of necessity the heirs must have an opportunity of purchasing'.[32]

In England, while a father's control might be no less powerful in France, patriarchy was a matter of precept and pragmatism rather than law. Ecclesiastics and laymen joined to support the power of the father over his children, which was in general the power of the purse, property and preconditioning rather than the law court. Alan Macfarlane went some way towards explaining the basis of this distinction when he described the distinctions in the ownership of land between peasant and non-peasant societies. In France

land was owned not by a specific individual but by the family corporation. This does not seem to have been the case in England.
The fact that, under common law, property was inherited by the
eldest son in cases of intestacy has obscured the fact that there was
no *birthright* for children in either the freehold or copyhold property of their parents. In theory they could be left penniless. Even
where property had been put in tail to the descendants, such
entails could easily be broken and, moreover, did not always devise
property to family members, let alone children. After 1540,
'Fathers may give all their estates un-intailed from their own
children, and to anyone child.' This absence of a birthright left
children less protected by law than their widowed mothers and it
left them even more dependent than their French counterparts
upon the good will of their fathers. Technically speaking, children
were not even disinherited for they had no right to an inheritance.
Blackmail, posthumous or otherwise, was a powerful incentive to
filial obedience even when threats were rarely executed.[33]

There was a good deal of softening of the legal definition of
parent–child relations in contemporary English writing, of course,
and an assumption that, in normal circumstances, property would
be passed to children and their descendants. It is entirely possible
that this moderate approach to the authority of parents over their
children was a direct response to contrary tendencies in contemporary society – preachers and authors strove to prevent one
section of the community from following the letter of the law.

Seen against such a background, the importance of both Robert
Filmer's *Patriarcha* and John Locke's *Two Treatises on Government* as
works of family theory seems less than it might otherwise have been.
True, *Patriarcha* sketched a family in which the father had enormous authority, so that he was almost a god on earth; and true,
Locke argued that marriage was a contract which produced
common interest and property but no power of life or death over
the wife, and that children came under the power of the father only
in a temporary and limited way until they were adult. These were, by
the standards of the day, extreme positions. Filmer's definition of
family relations was as radical as that of Bodin. Yet there was a huge
spectrum of theoretical writing in between these positions, which
we are unwise to ignore. There was lively, and well-documented,
debate concerning the nature of the husband–wife relationship
which came down as often in favour of 'partnership' as of 'patriar-

chy'. Even Filmer, in his little-studied 'In Praise of the Vertuous Wife', stressed partnership in family government and parental rather than male power.[34] Equality, of course, was not at issue.

There is a marked contrast in the attitude of English Protestant writers on marriage and the family and the attitude of French ecclesiastical authors. In England the family life and relationships of the people were centrally important to their lives as Christians. They were modelled upon a particular interpretation of Scripture and the role model of the Holy Family. The family itself had developed religious responsibilities. The opposite seems to have been the case in France. Marriage and the family were grudgingly accepted by most. Salvation occurred in spite of family life rather than within it. French authors sought to limit its fall out – emphasising the need to avoid sin and to remain subject to the Church's authority. Marriage and parenthood could be made to serve a Christian purpose but had to be carefully controlled. In part, this contrast may have been attributable, as John Bossy urged, to the fear of Protestantism within the French Church, which led to a reaction in its teaching on celibate and married states and, hence, on the family. In part it may be attributed, as Briggs appears to argue, to the French clerics' remoteness from family life and problems and to their fear of setting up alternative spiritual authorities. The English clergy had rejected celibacy and embraced family life with a vengeance. As a profession, the English Protestant clergy were bound together by complex family and kinship ties. As preachers and pastors, they remained sensitive to the everyday pressures upon their congregations. None the less they would have drawn back from any suggestion that the spiritual functions of the household replaced or detracted from the importance of the minister's role as pastor. (And in both England and France there was always an insistence that the power of the husband and father, while in some ways analogous to that of God where secular concerns obtained, was always, in cases of conflict, overridden by the supreme and absolute authority of God and his Church.) For somewhat different reasons, they too, on occasion, found it convenient to deal with fathers of families rather than other family members and to elevate the role of the household head.[35]

It is perhaps unsurprising that the teaching on the family in colonial America initially closely mimicked the teaching of the English preachers. The American settlers from Europe, and especially those from England, carried the same cultural and spiritual baggage. Benjamin Wadsworth's comment in the *Well Ordered Family*, that 'The great God commands thee to love her. How vile then are those who don't love their wives' (p. 25), and his conviction that this duty of mutual love should none the less be subordinate to the love each individual felt for God, belongs very much in the tradition of English Protestant writing on the conjugal relationship. Similarly, the obligations of parents towards their children were those of giving food, shelter and protection when they were young, and preparation to make their own way in the world in later years. The law in New England reinforced this theory. New Englanders were as prone to support the corrective role of both husband and parent as were Old Englanders and as careful to urge that it be moderate chastisement that they offered. 'The gentle rod of the mother, is a very gentle thing, it will break neither bone nor skin; yet by the blessing of God with it, and upon the wise application of it, it would break the bond that bindeth up corruption in the heart.' Nevertheless, the local circumstances of emigration and settlement did affect the attitude to the family and its importance within the community. It added 'baggage'. Some of the early settlers emigrated as a result of religious and political persecution but many were the victims of economic dislocation, who settled as indentured servants. There were many who were land hungry. There were also deported paupers and convicts. It is possible to describe the pattern of colonisation as that of hierarchical communities of households, each subject to a pseudo-patriarchal system of authority on the English model. The circumstances of settlement, however, intensified the urgency of communal activity and the co-operation of households in serving the 'commonwealth' and, therefore, the interdependence of households and assertion of communal control over household behaviour. It permitted some speedily to found families and households who, within the societies they left, could not have expected so to do. Within early colonial America also, however, there were profound differences of settlement and, therefore, in the relative exposure to and receptivity of conventional teaching on the family. The society of New England, with its small, nucleated villages based on the existence and preservation of private property, fostered communal co-operation and responsibility for development, village and church policing, and hierarchical relations in the family as in the community. Even here,

though, preachers met with a relaxation of formal deferential relations between parents and children, which they felt reinforced
desirable authority relationship. There was much more local variation in the middle colonies. Parts of New Jersey and New York
were characterised by communities based on landlord and tenant
farmers. Pennyslvania and Delaware developed along very different
lines from New England: here the majority of the population did
not live in nucleated villages but were diffused in dispersed home-
steads radiating out from regional market towns – as a result, there
was much less possibility of communal intervention in family life.
Yet some groups – for example, the Quakers and the Germans in
Pennsylvania – did develop as corporate communities with considerable control over their membership households. The Southern
Colonies were not characterised by communal settlement at all.
Even family life was rendered unstable by the extremely high death
rate and unbalanced sex ratio. As a result, it was the large plantation which became the permanent centre of Southern life, unregu-
lated by outside agencies and tending towards more developed
individual competitiveness.[36]

Co-residence in small households seemed the natural way to
organise the settlements in the New World, even where biological
families were not numerically important. For example, the Massachusetts Bay Company ordered the deputy governor, John
Endicott, to deploy the male indentured servants into artificial
households:

> For the better accommodation of businesses, wee have devyded
> the servants belonging to the Company into severall famylies, as
> wee desire and intend they should live together. ... Our earnest
> is, that you take spetiall care, in settlinge these families, that the
> chiefe in the families (at least some of them) bee grounded in
> religion; whereby morning and evening famylie dutyes may bee
> duely performed, and a watchfull eye held over all in each
> famylie to be appointed thereto, that so disorders may be pre-
> vented, and ill weeds nipt before they take too great a head. It
> wilbe a business worthy your best endeavours to looke unto this
> in the beginninge.

Here at least it was the authority relationships that existed in properly ordered households rather than the biological relations which

were valued. They were thought to be readily replicable despite the absence of nuclear family units.[37]

The desire to bring all persons within household governments is especially evident in seventeenth-century America. There was an attempt to place bachelors and maids under household discipline. So in 1638 Massachusetts ordered every town to 'dispose of all single persons within their towns to service, or otherwise' and Connecticut forbade any unmarried and servantless young man to keep house 'without consent of the towne where he lives'. There was similar legislation in Plymouth in 1669. Moreover, these laws were enacted. For example, 32 offenders were brought before Middlesex County Court in October 1668 and ordered to live in families. Some reported back to the court that they had complied with the order.[38]

One problem facing the historian of the family must be the extent to which a 'theory' of the family can be deduced from the 'law' surrounding marriage and the family. In America, the nature of the evidence is such that it is often difficult to distinguish 'theory' about the family and practice. In many cases the colonial societies were reading and acting upon literature which emanated from the Old World rather than producing their own corpus. However, work done recently on legislation in the colonies suggests that patriarchy was urged. This was to be a patriarchy of older, property-owning males. 'Their rule was not exclusively, or even primarily, over women. They ruled also over lower-class males, who were patronized and expected to act in what would later come to be thought of as feminine ways.' So the courts in both North and South punished heads of household for not exercising this patriarchal role and asserting proper authority over wives, servants and children. In the South, household heads were ducked for failing to control servants; in the North, tithingmen were appointed to maintain family order and report negligent heads, and on the statute books were laws which threatened repeated child disobedience with the death penalty.[39]

Marriage and Household Formation

What has been said so far, should suggest that in England and New England the emphasis was upon the roles of marriage as a 'hospital for lust' and the biological family as a nursery providing education for children in Christian values and vocation. It was primarily a spiritual household, and relationships within it were to conform to spiritual guidelines. Contemporaries also had other material and temporal concerns. Who should be allowed to form a household? The answer had importance not only for order within the local and national communities but also for the future of other members of a given 'family'. It might determine the continued subsistence of the father, mother and children left on the farm as well as the future marriageability of siblings. The theoretical underpinning of marriage as it has come down to us has emanated from those parts of Europe where the simple nuclear family was most common and where marriage normally marked the founding of a new household. Marriage as it evolved may not have been easily accommodated in the peasant life of southern and western France, for example.

In sixteenth-century and northern Europe there was remarkable unity in marriage law. Civil marriage was unknown. The Jews married according to their own rites. The rest of the people lived under Catholic rule and Catholic rules. Marriage, according to decrees of the Council of Florence (1439), was a sacrament, representing the union between Christ and His Church. It was designed for procreation and the education of children and was, therefore, an indissoluble union. Free and mutual consent was stressed as the basis of union. There were, however, impediments to ecclesiastical marriage (that is, a wedding performed according to the rites of the Church in the church or its porch). Certain of these were prohibitive: church weddings were forbidden in Lent and Advent; they were unavailable to those who stood unabsolved of sin – that is, excommunicated; the groom might not marry the sister of his late wife. In cases where these rules were inadvertently disobeyed, the resultant marriage was regarded as irregular but indissoluble. In other words it was a valid marriage. Other impediments were absolute and disruptive: if the rules were infringed the resultant marriage was no marriage. These impediments included those against partners who were under age; those who were unbaptised; those who were already married; those who had taken religious vows; infringements of the rules of consanguinity and affinity between biological and spiritual relatives (one could not marry one's godparent); those resulting from adultery, violence, rape or substitution. Some of these rules guarded against the perceived evils of incest and promiscuity; others against exploitation and violence. Still others protected the identity of ecclesiastical marriage as a sacrament, an outward and visible sign of an inward and spiritual grace.[40]

If none of these impediments applied, a marriage was valid if the parties consented to the union. Even servants could marry without their master's or lord's consent. Parental consent or that of the master or lord, while desirable, was not essential. The stance of the Church in this regard was dictated by traditional Christian teaching regarding marriage and its meaning and, also, a determination to counter undue influence by parents and kin upon the young couple. It led, however, to problems because the Church was not set apart from but part of society. It recognised that what was legal might not be what was advisable. There was acknowledgement that a marriage undertaken against strong parental opposition was in no one's interests, least of all the young couple's. In 1469 the Bishop of Norwich advised Margaret Paston against her marriage to the bailiff, Richard Calle, because by acting against her mother's opposition she had forfeited her assistance in future. But the contract was flawless and the marriage valid. There was recognition that 'peasant marriages' and secret or clandestine marriages, while binding, cloaked young couples against both pastoral and parental influence of a desirable as well as undesirable kind. In Catholic Europe measures against secret marriage were decisive. In 1563 a decree of the Council of Trent actually invalidated marriages not performed in public before a parish priest. In France, however, this decree was not regarded as sufficiently far-reaching. In 1556 Henri II had decreed, in the first French civil legislation on family issues, that parental consent must be secured for 'boys' up to the age of 30 and 'girls' up to the age of 25, on pain of disinheritance. At Trent the Cardinal of Lorraine proposed that marriages be declared invalid where the curé had no proof of parental consent for males below the age of 28 and women younger than 16. In the event, the Decree Tametsi did act against clandestine marriage by ordering three readings of banns in the parish of origin on three consecutive Sundays, the participation in the marriage ceremony of the parish priest of one of the parties and two or three witnesses, and the compulsory registration of marriages by the curé. The effectiveness of the decree lay in the declaration that all other marriages were nullified. But the requirement for parental consent was denied. As a result, the Decree Tametsi was never accepted in France. The English did not go even so far. The *Reformatio Legum* of Edward VI's reign would have made clandestine marriages illegal and invalid but no such decree was promulgated. Nevertheless, the canons of 1597 and 1604 more strictly regulated the issue of licences and the conduct of church weddings: thus the Church emphasised the sanctity of marriage, the canonical proprieties of its performance and the need for ecclesiastical solemnisation. In the early seventeenth century the English church courts were using the canon law to stamp upon clandestine marriage. The common law reinforced this tendency towards the acceptance of church weddings as the norm by making certain property rights dependent upon proof of a church wedding. It is doubtful, however, whether by Elizabeth I's reign 'marriage' truly meant 'marriage in church' as Martin Ingram asserts, because historians, even those dealing with court records, simply know nothing about the prevalence of peasant marriage among the unpropertied. The sources which they use are those which are concerned with the propertied, be they aristocrats or artisans, or the errant children and servants of the same. Even the clandestine marriages that did appear before the church courts were those, celebrated by clergymen, that in some way offended against the canons. People who simply cohabited were more difficult to trace. The lives of the few or the many who dwelt in hovells supported by oak trees, or in mere caves, totally escape the eyes of today's scholars even as they were ignored as irrelevant by our forebears in Church and State. By the seventeenth century, Protestant preachers were emphasising that the parents should take the initiative in arranging marriages for their children, while always bearing in mind the inclinations and needs of the same. But this was advice given to, and perhaps heeded by, those of the middling sort.[41]

In many respects, somewhat ironically, marriage in 'Protestant' England was less tampered with than in traditional and Catholic France. In England the marriage liturgy remained substantially that of the Use of Sarum. Marriage remained a sacrament and there were only minor tinkerings with the impediments to marriage. The Table of Kindred and Affinity, prepared for Archbishop Matthew Parker, was in use from 1567 down to 1907. The sole novelty was that marriages were only prohibited in relatives to the third and not the fourth degree. Marriages not conducted in church remained valid marriages. The flirtation with civil marriage during the Interregnum was but an interlude.

In northern Europe in early modern times the male came of age when he became independent. His independence in some parts of Europe was marked by the founding of a family, the formation of a separate household or 'economic unit'. In peasant France it was marriage that often secured emancipation from the father's absolute control. It was unthinkable that a household should be created without the wherewithall to support it. Marriage without means was to be deplored if a new household had to be formed. Marriage was, therefore, in most social classes in northern France, England and the American Colonies, associated with maturity. The truth of this statement might seem to be undermined by the fact that legal ages for marriage were low: in England, 12 for girls; 14 for boys. But, whereas it was legal to marry young in all the societies under discussion, where marriage marked the foundation of a new household such youthful union was discouraged. It occurred generally in royal and aristocratic households, where young couples co-resided with their extended families, and most notably among heirs and wards. Under normal circumstances a couple must be able to support a new household economically and to run it appropriately.[42] William Whateley recommended that a young man proposing matrimony should have 'some honest calling, and will and ability to walk in the same faithfully, that reason may tell them, through God's blessing, there shall be something gotten to maintain a wife, though not richly, yet sufficiently'. Living with the parents of either spouse after marriage was considered inadvisable. Christians found it difficult to place an outright ban on marriages among the poor. Some, like Philip Stubbes, wanted to raise the minimum age for marriage in order to halt marriages among the economically dependent. In 1589 legislation was enacted to prevent the building of cottages without at least four acres of land to support the occupants: a house must be attached to the means of independence. The social and economic organisation of the household, and expediency, not legal prohibitions, were, however, of the most assistance in limiting poverty-stricken unions. Those in service or childhood were in practice forbidden to marry and live within the household. Young people recognised that marriage without money was unwise. Yet, in the 1590s, Poor Law overseers refused to admit into their villages strangers intending to marry local girls, or with children, who might prove to be a burden on the parish. In the seventeenth century, parish officers and ministers in parts of England at least did act contrary to the law of the Church and seek to prevent the poor marrying: thus, a Dorset minister wrote of Anne Russed in 1628, 'she hath no house nor home and very like to bring charge on the parish, and therefore will hardly be suffered to marry in our parish'. The church courts stood by and watched, doing nothing to enforce positively the Christian view of marriage as the free and consental union of individuals within the law of consanguinity. The ever-increasing problem of clandestine marriage, of course, threatened such attempts at family, communal or Church regulation of the formation of new households, and is in some instances a measure of the failure of 'theory' to become 'practice'.[43]

Conclusion: Prescriptions for the Family

In the sixteenth and seventeenth centuries prescriptions for family life were a feature particularly of English culture and the New England societies which grew out of it. In France, the issue of family was much less central, seemingly viewed as a necessary evil rather than as an asset to society. These prescriptions should not be confused with the lived-experience of families in these societies; the extent to which they were the expression of reality as opposed to ideology is debatable. The purpose of family and the nature and importance of family roles, as perceived in the literature and law of the period, were informed by the religious culture of the time, by the historical development of the family as a social institution, and by external factors such as the political, social and economic organisation of the states concerned.

3. The Descriptive Family – 1: The Wider Family

In this chapter there will be an attempt to disregard the prescriptive writings of contemporaries and to examine real families in early modern society. This intention to discount theory will only be breached where there appears to have been a conscious effort on the part of people to obey prescriptive ideology.

The work of the historical demographers had suggested that throughout Europe and North America 'families' lived in households which were small in size and based upon the nuclear family of husband, wife and children with the addition of house servants. American were distinguished from European households by the relative youth of wives and their consequently longer period of child bearing, which produced somewhat larger households than were usual in France and England. Until the eighteenth century, rates of infant mortality were lower in the colonies. Otherwise the pattern of living was similar. We know, however, that this picture was subject to wide variation. Many of the population lived in different types of household. We know from our discussion of 'theory' that it was appropriate for Church and State to emphasise the importance of the household. Acknowledging all these facts should not prevent us seeking to establish whether the 'family' was, for early modern people, equivalent to the household and, if not, what it did constitute.

In Britain we are fortunate to have at our disposal the papers of a sizable number of, what shall we call them? families, houses, lines. The very preservation of such collections should suggest something to the historian: the importance of the 'history' of the family concerned, to its members, at any time during its existence. The contents of such collections are not exclusively concerned with property or other legal matters. Often the members appear to have saved all of their incoming correspondence. The letters and papers are of invaluable assistance to us as we seek to trace what family meant to these people. It is unfortunate that for France relatively little of such material has survived and/or been worked, although there are large numbers of printed collections of letters and memoirs from the eighteenth and nineteenth centuries.[1] For North America the survival of such evidence is patchy and, again, relatively unworked.

This type of information, even in Britain, exists only for a few families situated at the top of the social hierarchy – those belonging to royalty, nobility, gentry and professional classes. For the remainder of society – perhaps as much as 90 per cent of the population – historians find themselves in a desert environment. There are very occasional data oases which permit them to look inside individual homes and into particular relationships and, more commonly, smaller oases enabling them, for example, to characterise household composition or formation in a given community.

To a great extent the families treated in detail here are drawn from the middle and upper echelons of society. In the event, this may not be as disadvantageous as was once thought, because of the impact these classes were to have upon the development of the family as a concept throughout modern times. While the Stones may have damaged the perception of England's 'Open Elite', and undermined our confidence in the efficacy of the 'aristocratic embrace', it must be remembered that families, even in the upper echelons of society, were living, breathing entities and not static institutions. The Smyth family of Ashton Court near Bristol, for example, was a farming/craftsman family in the fifteenth century; a merchant family in the sixteenth century and a landed family from the seventeenth century to the present day. Such families developed. Family forms, experiences and relationships in this family and throughout society might be arranged on a continuum. For this reason, almost imperceptible differences between families at varying social levels might be more common than the dramatic changes so longed for by historians. Moreover, some of the features of aristocratic families might have been echoed, even deliberately aped, in families lower down the social scale.[2]

Aristocratic Families

Let us start with the families of the aristocracy, broadly defined. In Britain this would include the peerage and the gentry. It has been suggested that this group accounted for no more than 2 to 5 per cent of the population, although it was, by definition, an extremely influential percentage. The French aristocracy is said to have accounted for the same proportion of the overall population, although its characteristics were somewhat different. In France, tenure of public office often involved automatic ennoblement. Public service in army or bureaucracy was oft rewarded in this way. Offices, and the titles which accompanied them, were commonly sold. So in France, as elsewhere in Continental Europe, there were large numbers of aristocrats who could not support an aristocratic way of life. In Britain this was not so typically the case, despite the Stuart monarchs' foray into venality of offices and titles, because of the widespread practice of primogeniture. 'In England' writes M. L. Bush, 'the paucity of corporate privileges made landowner-ship and life-style of prime importance in the identification of aristocratic status, while the tendency for privileges to pass by primogeniture safeguarded against the mass production of impoverished cadet lines'. In North America different conditions prevailed. An aristocracy was exported from Britain to the original colonies and a native 'aristocracy' grew up of families who, while without title, undoubtedly lived an élite life-style dependent upon successful exploitation of resources in land and trade and the support of 'society'. These differences in the composition of and conditions of the aristocracy did have an impact upon the way family life was lived. In each of these cases, however, the probability of fluid family forms and experiences seems self-evident.[3]

Kinship was the primary bond of early modern society. This was as true of early modern France as it was of Britain and North America. This said, relatively little is known about the nature of the bond or the way in which it operated. It may well be that the kinship network of the French aristocratic family was, in general, less extensive than that of the English equivalent. In England there were relatively high nuptiality rates among younger sons and daughters, partly as a result of the strict settlement which, after 1650, made provision for all children before their birth, and partly as a result of the propensity for younger sons to follow careers which provided them with the means to found a household. No such pattern was evident in France, where younger daughters were encouraged to enter convents and younger sons frequently died unmarried. This said, kinship was so important in France, even in the seventeenth and eighteenth centuries, that, when an individual fell from favour, his or her 'family' fell also.[4] More positively, a study of the household of François Duke of Anjou shows how the Seigneur du Fay, Nicolas Hennequin, owed his appointment as a principal financial secretary to his well-placed relatives.[5] Ministers, merchants and magistrates intermarried in seventeenth-century Massachusetts. A 'great tangled cousinry' bound eighteenth-century aristocratic Virginian society together. These differences apart, the dividing lines between simple or nuclear family, household, kindred and lineage in these societies have been drawn on the basis of somewhat inadequate data. The evidence, however, suggests that, while whether family members were affectively close to one another depended upon individual circumstances, families had evolved mechanisms to protect the life of the family, very broadly conceived indeed. It certainly contradicts the statements made by Lawrence Stone, admittedly aimed at the peerage, upon which so many modern descriptions of aristocratic 'family life' depend: 'Since marriages were not based on prior attraction and since children saw so little of their parents, the institution of the family was held together by law, custom and convenience rather than by ties of sentiment or affection. The Tudor family was an institution for the passing on of life, name, and property' and this changed only gradually. Moreover, although family vendettas in Elizabethan England and political alliances based on family connection indicate 'some feeling of loyalty towards the extended family', it would be 'unwise to lay too much stress on the role of the clan in seventeenth-century society.' When he wrote these words, Stone had little acquaintance with family papers except marriage and property settlements, yet his analysis has become the classic description of family life or the lack of it among the aristocracy. The family for him is, on the one hand, identified with the household and, on the other, with the line.[6]

It seems that the conclusions that the Stones reach concerning the nature of the English aristocracy and the 'strategies of indirect inheritance', which they show 'were evolved to deal with the problem' of disruption of the line 'and to save the principle of family continuity, are less contentious than the top-down approach to the family that they adopt. Few would wish to contradict this analysis, although they might suggest that the strategy was less successful than the Stones argue. But this entrée into the family, which derives from a concern with patriarchy or substitute patriarchy (i.e. matriarchy or widowhood) and patriarchal relations (which in its turn derives from reading sources generated at that level), means that historians rarely examine relationships from other perspectives and that information pertaining to them is only arrived at incidentally. What attitude did younger sons and daughters have to the 'family' strategies that Stone and others describe? What relationship did daughters have with their mothers? What was the nature of family life? What did it mean when a relative pleaded: 'I am your kinsman, your friend and must be your neybor … and so I do expected bothe your tonge, your hande and your harte reddy to assiste me in all honest acctions'? It may be that the evidence does not survive for us to answer all these questions in as much detail as we would wish. Yet we must ask the questions if our answers to fundamental questions such as: what functions did the family fulfil? are to produce anything other than a description of strategies employed by patriarchs.[7]

Bagot of Blithfield

We shall begin with an English family, that of Bagot of Blithfield. The Bagots, although of importance in Staffordshire county and national life, were not of the peerage and not possessed of enormous landed wealth. According to Baron Stafford, irked by the Bagot attempt to claim greater antiquity than the Staffords, the Bagots had always been vassals to the Staffords and bore a name derived from 'Bag o' oats'! In the Bagots, therefore, we may be facing a family intent upon emphasising kinship, upon cultivating it, as a means of extending and consolidating influence within the county and the country. They were certainly not unusual in this or in their obsession with the family name, coat of arms and

Bagot family tree – simplified

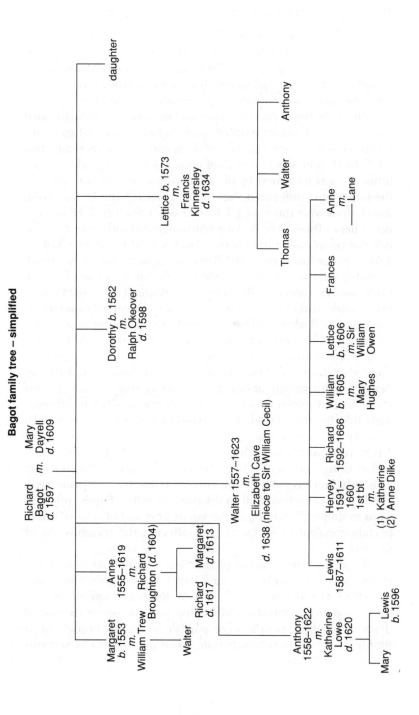

memorials. 'The genealogical tree' write the Stones 'was ... more than merely a symbol of pride in family ancestry. It was essential to the elaboration, generation after generation, of the incredibly complex contingency plans which were so carefully incorporated into the strict settlements.' The family was developing inter-actively as the Bagot role in county and national life grew. Richard Bagot (d. 1597) was a sheriff of Staffordshire, a deputy-lieutenant for the county, a commissioner of array and also for recusants and a J. P. In 1565 he was said to hold estates worth 300 marks, but his influence was increased by his appointment as crown steward of the important confiscated Paget estates in 1583 and by his strong associations with the young Earl of Essex's Staffordshire proper-ties. These offices gave Bagot a patronage and influence that was not commensurate with his own landed wealth. George Talbot, Earl of Shrewsbury, regarded Richard Bagot as the 'most knowl-edgeable man in the shire'. This is underlined by the compara-tively low-key career of his elder son, Walter (1557–1623), who presumably suffered from his family's association with overween-ing Essex, and whose role in national life was rather more mini-mal despite his continuing influence in Staffordshire as J. P. and as M. P. for Tamworth and despite his connection through mar-riage with the Cecils. The Bagot letters are unusual in offering detailed information about a sixteenth-century family at this social level. Collections of correspondence tend to be distress-ingly thin for this period. The correspondence for the sixteenth and seventeenth centuries permits us to trace all manner of family relations, both within and without the Bagot household, and to bring into focus other 'households' and families en route. This may help to counter the current tendency to equate 'real' family with household and to discount all other 'family' relation-ships as simply pertaining to the kin or line, and of relative unim-portance except in so far as they affected the transmission of property.[8]

The precise composition of the Bagot household may always remain a mystery to us. Richard Bagot and his wife Mary (née Dayrell) had two sons, Walter and Anthony, and five daughters, Anne, Margaret, Dorothy and Lettice and one other. At various times all of these people were part of the Bagot household at Blithfield. We know relatively little about the number of servants who dealt with them.

The Bagots, on closer inspection, bore many of the marks of a feudal family living in a still feudal society, riven by lawlessness, armed rebellion and religious division. It is clear from the letters that 'Father Bagot' was regarded as patriarch of a family which included not only his sons and daughters, their spouses and their children, but also his sisters and brothers and their children and so on, whether or not they were co-resident, stretching to a cousin-hood of almost unbelievable and untraceable proportions. A true patriarchy exists when the authority of the patriarch is supreme and is not replaced, on marriage, by the authority of the husband. The Bagot letters demonstrate in an enthralling manner how a conflict between the authority of a family patriarch and of a spouse might develop. They also demonstrate that this situation showed little or no sign of changing during the period 1565 to 1630. While concentration upon the co-resident nuclear family household of husband, wife and children has its merits, it does obscure from view the importance of a different 'family', at least in the upper echelons of society.[9]

Richard Bagot had a younger daughter, Lettice, who married into the Kinnersley family of Tixall. Her father-in-law, Anthony, determined to rule both his own wife and the young couple, Lettice and Francis. At first Lettice and Francis seem to have been relatively content, except in their resistance to Father Kinnersley's attempts to control the place of their abode. Her earliest claims upon her own family were when Anthony Kinnersley tried to make her and Francis live at Leigh Parsonage instead of Badger. The resourceful Lettice persuaded her married sister, Margaret, to offer the two of them board and lodging. In 1605/6, Lettice, whose own father was now dead and whose brother had taken his place as 'patriarch', appealed to her brother for assistance. The couple now lived at Badger but Anthony Kinnersley persisted in felling timber on their land. A quarrel ensued between him and his son, Francis. Walter Bagot, who, as head of the family, held the marriage agreement, intervened – first to ask Anthony to stop fell-ing the timber and then, when he discovered that he was in the right, to implore submission from Francis 'to avoid strife'. In a huff, Anthony commanded Lettice to take her son, Thomas, who was in his grandfather's household, back home; she asked brother Walter to take the boy himself and look after him. Walter obliged. Then two years later Lettice and Francis had a quarrel and she, now 30 years old, again appealed for assistance against her husband's authority from her brother, the head of the family. This, we should note, was a household in which she did not live, indeed had not lived for many years, yet its head, Walter Bagot, was still regarded as head of the Bagot family and in a real sense responsible for its members, married and part of another household or not. Lettice expected Walter to negotiate a settlement for her and her children so that she could live apart from her husband and his mother. For many years afterwards, Lettice and her husband partook of an unsettled, tempestuous relationship, in which he was aided and abetted by his co-resident mother and she by her brother.[10]

Another sister, Dorothy, had problems of a different sort. In 1598, Ralph, her husband, the son of Roland Okeover, died and it was left to Walter to inform Ralph's father of the fact. He conveyed the news, adding that his sister, the widow, who had been left well off, wished to repay his debts (presumably to Roland) and hoped to keep their daughter, 'little Doll'. Okeover senior seemed less bothered by this and more by the retention in Walter Bagot's hands of the 'great indenture of the Okeover entail', presumably handed over on the marriage settlement of his sister, which proved the inheritance of the Okeover lands. Bagot's close connections with the Okeover family persisted.[11]

The marriages of Walter's sisters and the connections these brought with them proved of lasting concern to the Bagots of Blithfield as they sought influence in the county, although they often helped little in the long run. Although Dorothy's marriage to Ralph Okeover certainly produced a daughter and Lettice's marriage to Francis Kinnersley sons and daughters, none of these appear to have survived their parents to inherit the property. Bagot worked hard to obtain the wardship of Humphrey Okeover, heir to the Okeover estate, in order to keep the profits of that estate, and influence over it, in the family, 'the great blesinge of many children which it hath pleased god to bestowe upon mee hath enforced me humbly to requier your honorable bounte may supplye the want in my habilitie' to support them. Ultimately this bid failed. In the seventeenth century the Aston, not the Kinnersley family held Tixall. Margaret Bagot had married against her father's wishes, to William Trew, and she had a son, Walter. Anne, Walter's elder sister, had married well, to Richard Broughton, who received Essex's favour, acted as Richard Bagot's agent and friend at court and became Chief Justice of Wales and a member of the Council for Wales. This marriage brought assistance and influence. The fact that there were two children, a boy and a girl, of the marriage was of relatively little direct importance to the Bagot patriarchs. Indeed, among the elite in England as a whole, indirect inheritance where a sister's son or the son of a mother's brother came into the patrimony was infrequent throughout the period 1500–1740, rarely rising above 5 per cent of the transfers by inheritance, although it rose sharply after that date, reaching 12 per cent in the 1760s and 1770s.[12]

Bagot's responsibility for the family extended further than his married sisters and their children. The obligation extended to his godchildren, who were likely to call upon him for assistance and to receive it. He was asked by Lord Lumley personally to negotiate the marriage of his nephew, who was also Bagot's godchild.[13] The responsibilities which godparentship brought with it were many and important. (Walter Bagot continued the tradition of supporting two of his godsons, Walter Edge and Walter Hamersley, at Oxford.[14]) It, like parenthood and guardianship, could be used to further the network of influence. This said, there is little indication that concerns about land, influence or interest *determined* the obligations which Bagot felt towards his kin, spiritual or biological, or the calls which they felt able to make upon him.

In the case of the Verneys it has been alleged that 'the existence of an authoritarian father figure was by no means a guarantee of harmony and good will among the members of the family' as individual family members jostled for position, sacrificing personal integrity and mutuality along the way. The Bagot example shows another dimension of patriarchy in operation, in which the patriarch acted tactfully but decisively to protect the interests of close and distant natural and spiritual kin who were not part of his household. [15]

The Obligations of Kinship

Some historians have sought to compare the relationships between kin (especially those between a patriarchal or matriarchal figure and another) to the relationships of patron and client.[16] It is frequently true, in all these societies, that persons of position used it to the advantage of their kin. For example, Catherine de Medici was able to obtain offices for her cousins, the Strozzi, who had been close to being her surrogate brothers.[17] Anne d'Este acted as mediator for her relatives with Henri IV. The parallel, although real, should not be stretched. The patron–client relationship was forever shifting; the familial relationship much more enduring. The patron was not obligated to assist a client – the service was offered as a favour. The patriarch, however, be he brother or father or uncle, was seen as having an obligation towards his kin. It was assumed that because Sir William Cecil was Walter Bagot's uncle by marriage he would act to further the interests of Bagot and his friends.[18] Unmarried sisters frequently kept house for their bachelor brothers.[19] It was a brother's role to care for his siblings in the event of the father's death. Thomas Barrington argued to his father, Sir Francis Barrington, in 1624, that some further provision should be made for his daughters by a former marriage 'if I should not live to provide for them nor theay have a brother to care for them'.[20] Sir Edward Aston had promised his mother on her deathbed that he would 'show the love of a father unto my sister Astley's daughter Elizabeth'.[21] This was not a role peculiar to the well born. In the strange case of Joan Bridges of Rochester, Kent, in 1646, it was assumed that the brother, a baker, had control of his sister once her father had died, and, furthermore, that his suspected action in burying her alive was both unnatural and motivated by greed.[22] In the Paris region, during the *ancien régime*, both uncles and brothers were frequently named as guardians of children who had lost one or both parents. Moreover, if a sister became pregnant or was the object of slander, it was the brother, in the absence of a father, who began legal action. [23] The settlers in colonial Maryland also subscribed to this view. When Robert Marston inherited his father's estate as sole heir it was with the proviso that he supported his two brothers until they were eighteen, one sister, Elizabeth, until she was sixteen and another, Mary, for so long as she acted as his housekeeper.[24] In England, Ralph Josselin noted with disapproval the case of a brother whose sister was put onto the parish: 'he said all in his hande was spent. £50 and all her clothes etc; he said that he would turn out the 4 children … he seemed to me void of brotherly and natural affection'.[25] So, Ralph Verney, when his father died, assumed responsibility for his five unmarried sisters and three brothers, even though he was living in France and they in England.[26] So, Anne Clifton, the recently widowed wife of Robert Clifton of Nottingham, in 1518 upbraided her brother, Henry Clifford, later first Earl of Cumberland, for being neglectful of her:

> Right wyrchypfull brodere, I hartyly recowmawnd me unto yow, besechyng yow to be gud brodere to me, and haffyng gret marvell of yowr unkyndnes, that ye wold not be here yowr selfe at thys time, nor nowne for now for here hays bene all my husbandes hukkylles[27] & broders and I hayd nobody to speke in all my cawsw bot myself ... evere gentylwoman myght hayfe trustyd to helpe of hyre broder ... I pray you that ye and my sister[28] wyll speke to gyder & take yowr beste counsell & advyce qwat ye cane do for me.[29]

This does not appear to have been peculiar to the aristocracy although it manifested itself most dramatically amongst the great and powerful. We know that in French urban society, in the sixteenth and seventeenth centuries, the widows of notaries were surrounded by kin who may well have limited their freedom. At a time when the relatives of one's dead husband were behaving much like hyenas attending a lion's kill, freedom to make personal decisions may have been the least of a new widow's worries![30] Widows expected their own kin, and especially the most influential of them, to chase away the marauding hyenas. If no kin were available, the plight of the widow was sorry. 'I am in the hands of potent men. Men skilful to destroy & subtill men, who lay traines to ruine ye widow and fatherles', moaned the widow, Katharine Austen, in 1664. 'A woman without Alliance of the family to help me. Yet O God help me and make me over come those bands that do environe me'.[31] Although there may have been exceptions, membership of one's spouse's 'family' appears to have ended on his death. At a time when so many marriages were curtailed by early death (over a third of first marriages among the peerage between 1588 and 1641 were cut short by the death of one partner within fifteen years), this situation occurred with some frequency. Until remarriage, the widow reverted very positively to her natural family allegiance, even if she maintained a separate household, as Anne Clifton wished to do. This was in sharp contrast to the position of any children of the marriage, who were still very much part of the husband's 'family', often to the grief of the widow.

If the relatives of the widow were expected to shield and protect her in her newly vulnerable condition, the concerns of some husbands and those of the husband's relatives after his decease were all for the offspring of the match. In sixteenth-century England, lower down the social scale, it seems that husbands encouraged their wives to think of remarriage in the event of widowhood. This was especially the case where young children were involved. Several Abingdon wills of the period before 1570 referred with equanimity to this prospect, and in other cases widows as executors were given considerable discretion to protect their children and their inheritances. After 1570, however, there was an unmistakable trend in the opposite direction, particularly in the case of men of wealth and/or social standing. This spread to all social ranks later in the seventeenth century, 'these testators made certain that their wives should take none of their wealth into a new marriage by inserting a penalty withholding or reducing the wife's share of the estate if she remarried.'[32] There appears to have been a parallel movement in France, although conclusions have to be based again upon somewhat flimsy evidence.[33] In Bordeaux, testators displayed a strong desire to protect their surviving spouses either for so long as they remained widows or for life, while acknowledging the possibility of remarriage. This may well have been because of the detailed legal provision for widows, widowers and heirs of the line that was maintained in French customary law. Of which more later.[34]

Widows were themselves only too aware of the implications of remarriage. Katharine Austen, a 29-year-old London widow, with three young children, found that the financial penalties in her husband's will precluded her remarrying for seven years after his death. When this period was over, in 1665, she considered remarriage but decided against it for a variety of reasons: her attachment to her dead husband's memory and the family to which she had been 'grafted'; the sacrifice of her reputation; her concern to protect the inheritance of her daughter and two sons. If she lost her legal powers, by remarrying, she would not be free to rebuild her children's fortunes. She was still a widow when she died in 1683.[35] Widows like Judith Barrington were keen to make marriage settlements which protected their children by former marriages, and others, like Lady Jane Bacon, retained control of their children's marriages when they themselves remarried.[36]

The close relations maintained between married women and their natural families deserve attention in this context. Lady Anne Clifford exchanged letters with her daughter on a regular and frequent basis and preserved links with her children and grand-children over great distances in the mid-seventeenth century.[37] Elizabeth Masham (wife of Sir William Masham and daughter of the Barringtons), Margaret Denton (Sir Edmund Verney's wife), Mary Dayrell (Richard Bagot's wife), Anne Bagot, Anne Lane (daughter of Walter Bagot) and Elizabeth Cave (wife of Walter Bagot) all maintained close contact with their own families. There is a good deal of evidence to the effect that marriage settlements were negotiated with such future contact to the fore. Mary, Countess of Warwick, gave as one of the chief reasons for accept-ing Thomas Barrington as a match for her niece, Anne Rich, the closeness of the family home to the Rich's family estate in Essex.[38] Sir William Meux was keen that his daughter Jane remain near him: 'I had rather match her w[i]th lelss estate neere mee than w[i]th a greater farr of'.[39] In part this is, of course, suggestive of the affecton felt for family members and the wish to retain the social and recreational network which family provided in a locality. A marriage should extend not contract this network. It also indi-cates anxiety: a married daughter far away is a vulnerable creature, who may be ill treated by spouse or in-laws and yet be relatively defenceless. This applied especially to daughters, but to sons also. Lettice Kinnersley wrote to Walter Bagot of the projected marriage of her eldest son, Tom, to the sister of Baron Wolrich of the Exchequer, who would bring £1000 with her. Lettice, however, would not have him marry for money alone but where he would have good friends.[40] Hence the need to win over the family of a spouse.[41] Proximity reduces the risk. The considerable geographic endogamy characteristic of marriages in France, Britain and North America was in part cultivated by parents and in part the natural consequence of the webs of connection woven around the social life of both young and old. We should not be surprised to find that in Bayeux in the early eighteenth century, for example, 63 per cent of brides came from that town or the hinterland parishes.[42] The contrary behaviour of royal personages, who often married overseas and yet married kin, is the exception.

One should not be drawn into arguing that the relationship between one nuclear family and another, linked by close kinship but not co-resident, was disinterested and based entirely upon affection, of course. Families were linked in a network of mutual subsistence relations both inside and outside the co-resident household. The Ferrar family (of Little Gidding) was one family which, like the Cliffords and the Bagots, maintained close family relations whether co-resident or not. For example, when Richard Ferrar's wife became pregnant in 1627, at a time when Ferrar was effectively imprisoned for debt, it was to his mother that he wrote thus:

> I am at this time inforced (by my wife her grett belly) to beccome a petitioner to you (this beinge a tyme of some more then ordenary expence) for a payre of ould sheetes (which my wife shall much want for soome uses at her tyme of delivery) As alsoe for a cheshire chese which may serve us soome tymes for our first and second course ...

Cupboard love bound technically independent 'families' to other families within the kin network even more than it does today. The extent of such dependence might vary from family to family and from time to time in the life of a family, but it was of great importance in an age when access to material goods and services was much more restricted than today.[43]

Was there a marked contrast in the behaviour of urban families? In the case of the children of the aristocracy the kinship network interlinked with other forms of connection to bind together families who 'lived' far distant from one another and yet remained in quite close contact. Correspondence, county and court supplemented the ties of cousinhood. For their social inferiors, it might seem that mobility, more often than not, meant collapse of the kinship connection and that urban growth made the nuclear family withdraw into itself. For example, half of the bridegrooms in seventeenth-century Bordeaux were immigrants. Of the remainder, 22 per cent came from the surrounding countryside; 56 per cent from elsewhere in the South-West and 22 per cent from other parts. Brides were less mobile but still were 29 per cent immigrant; in Bayeux, 31 per cent of the brides were immigrants. Figures for other towns and cities in Britain and France are no less dramatic. In other words, if you were young and wished to marry in seventeenth-century towns and cities you had to be willing at least to look at matches with foreigners, which were outside your own family's purview. Your family became equated with your household and consisted of husband, wife and offspring. But this was a tendency, not a rule: for example, if one moved to London one might leave one set of kin behind only to make acquaintance with another.[44]

When a child from a family in England and Wales whose land was held by knight-service was orphaned, as in the case of the young Mary Blacknall of Abingdon, he or she became a royal ward and potential prey to other families, who saw her as a desirable marriage partner for one or other of their number. It was much more difficult for her/his kin to assert familial control where a wardship was involved, although in practice a few wardships were granted to close kin. Thus, for example, John Crofts of Ketton in Leicestershire was granted the wardship of his brother's son in 1570 and John Vowell, an alderman of Haversham West, was granted the wardship of William Warren, his step-son. This system of feudal marriage was specific to England and Wales and aroused astonishment in Europe. By the sixteenth century the English Crown had abandoned the practice of imposing a marriage upon a feudal widow, although persuasive powers were exercised and licences to remarry issued for a fee. Contemporaries bewailed the decline of family influence in such situations. 'O merciful God! what innumerable inconveniences come by selling of wards for marriage, for lucre of goods and lands.' In thirteen-year-old Mary Blacknall's case the claims of four of her own relatives were fought off, when Sir Edmund Verney purchased her wardship as the bride for his eldest son, Ralph. In such instances the influence of the child's family was early countered by that of the guardian's family. This may in the end have been advantageous for both parties to the marriage, as their 'interests' coincided more precisely. But this was not always the case. For instance, Lady Stanhope bought the wardship of John Hotham and controlled his education in Cecil's household before marrying him to her daughter. The marriage, however, was a disaster and John Hotham packed his wife off to her relations. Humphrey Okeover was brought up as a ward of Elizabeth and Walter Bagot from babyhood and 'married' to their daughter when both were 'inphants'. Humphrey, however, eagerly renounced all this when he reached 14, 'the age of consent', and married another cousin, a Cheyney. It has been claimed that the system of wardship encouraged child marriage in this class, either because parents sought to marry their children to avoid a possible wardship situation, where family influence on the marriage would be prevented, or because feudal guardians married their young wards off to the highest bidder at the earliest opportunity. In fact the percentage of child marriages among the peerage fell from 21 per cent between 1540 and 1599 to 12 per cent between 1600 and 1659. The extent to which the revival of feudal marriage in England and Wales, at many social levels, affected the role of the family in marriage negotiation is still a matter of debate. Lawrence Stone, who overstresses the cold and materialistic approach of the English aristocracy to the marriages of their children in the early modern period, attributes the abolition of wardship, at the Restoration, in part 'to a growth of novel ideas about personal autonomy, and in part in order to restore control of marriage to the family, and to remove this form of inheritance tax upon the elite'.[45]

The emergence of a national marriage market in England in the seventeenth and eighteenth centuries in one sense also posed a threat to continuing protection of the partners to a marriage by their 'family' of origin. Certainly a social round of dinners, balls, races and music parties permitted careful chaperonage of the young of both sexes but it was, from the family's point of view, a poor substitute for the tightly-knit social round which had preceded it.[46]

Matriarchy

The figure of the matriarch, although more shadowy, may have equalled that of the patriarch in importance.[47] (The opportunities for matriarchy were socially circumscribed. Fewer women survived to have grandchildren lower down the social scale. Family strategies mattered considerably less when there was less property and wealth and fewer generations involved. But this does not exclude the possibility of its occurrence at other social levels.) It was often a senior female who controlled the tuition and the introduction to society of young women in the family. For instance, Lady Joan Barrington, of the prominent upper-gentry Essex family, exercised considerable power and influence both within her household and without. She was particularly active in helping arrange the marriages of her grandchildren and of the young people to whom the family acted as guardian. For example, in September 1629 the father of one of her sons-in-law suggested to Joan Barrington the attractions of a particular match for Joan Altham, lamenting that the girl's parents had shown so little interest in it. Although he leaves the decision to God and her parents, Francis implies that Lady Joan should use her influence.[48] Later, Joan Altham's mother, Elizabeth, wrote to her mother explaining why there were problems with the match. Elizabeth suspected that little generosity would be shown by the young man's family and that only that which was formally agreed upon would be given.[49] As matters developed, Elizabeth sought her mother's views on the matter.[50] The negotiation fell through. In 1630 negotiations for a match with Oliver St John were accompanied by like deliberations between mother, grandmother and uncle and were successful. When Elizabeth proposed meeting with her mother, Lady Joan, to discuss the match, she said that this was so that 'sum conclution of this busynis' might be made.[51] Similar involvement by the dowager Lady Joan is apparent in the match-making surrounding Jane Meux. Even more striking is the way in which her widowed son, Sir Thomas, looked to both mother and father for consent when proposing a marriage with Lady Judith, also a widow with children. This was no mere formality. Judith made every effort to gain Lady Joan's approval. Doubtless the existence of children on both sides made such consent doubly important. Thomas assured his parents that Judith was not seeking provision for her own children at the expense of his own either by her or by his former wife.[52] Letters from a younger son, John, indicate that during his adulthood, and at a time when Joan was the dowager, he sought his mother's assistance and approval in all manner of matters.[53] These letters certainly indicate the matriarchal position held by Lady Joan Barrington within the family both when she was married to its head and when she was widowed. She was regarded by her own siblings and their families as having a lasting obligation towards them also. Richard Whalley, her brother, trusted his children to her on his death: 'Good madame even for Gods sake when I am dead (as I cannot live longe) remember my children are of your bloode and bee their mother and defender.' Two years later he was still alive, albeit again close to death, but his pleading had been to good

effect. His daughter Mary had become part of his sister's household – he asked more: 'whom I likewise beseech you to bestow in
marriage' and 'good maddam keepe her from overmuch libertye
& fantasticke new fashions'.[54]

Contemporary correspondence and autobiographies also demonstrate how, in some cases, arranging family marriages was the
preserve of adult women. The widowed Countess of Warwick controlled the marriage of her three nieces by marriage, including
that of Mary Rich to Henry St John and that of Anne Rich to the
Earl of Essex.[55] Anne Bacon appears to have arranged the
marriage between her son, Nathaniel, and the widowed Lady Jane
Cornwallis in 1613.[56] In her turn, Lady Jane Bacon negotiated a
match for her son, Frederick Cornwallis.[57] When a match for him
was projected with one of Lady Judith Barrington's nieces, it was
with Lady Judith that correspondence was conducted. In 1610
Jane Throckmorton was betrothed to her cousin, Lewis Bagot, heir
to Walter, much to his father's displeasure. It was her step-mother,
Lady Jane Skipworth, who persuaded the girl to break off the
engagement and who communicated with Walter Bagot.[58] Jane
caused more trouble in 1621 by a courtship with Simon Rugeley,
then a student at Cambridge. On this occasion it was Simon's
mother who visited her son and obtained from him a promise to
do nothing without his father's consent, and not to go near the
gentlewoman again on pain of disinheritance.[59]

It might be inferred that widows had more power than wives in
the matter of marriages. However, in the case of the Barrington
family, the approval of Lady Joan and Lady Judith was sought even
when there were senior male relatives available for consultation.
Taken as a whole, this evidence contradicts the common assumption that fathers and, in their absence, male relatives controlled
marriages. There is no reason to assume that the involvement of
women became less acceptable lower down the social scale.[60] The
activity of women in the marriage market was regarded as normal
and not as subversive either of patriarchy or of the social order.[61]

It would be unwise to conclude that such matriarchal power was
necessarily either cherished or inevitable. Lady Rachel Russell, for
example, in 1685/6 assumed the role of family match-maker but
grudgingly.[62] While Mary Ferrar appears to have been very much
involved in such matters, the Bagot wives, while active and with
close family relationships, do not appear as matriarchs in the same

way. Indeed, Lettice Kinnersley specifically asked that her mother, the widowed Mary Bagot, not be troubled by her marital plight.[63]

While strengthening the argument for the existence of matriarchy by showing how powerful these women could be in the pursuit of family strategies, such evidence also demonstrates the significant role which close relatives, wider kin and friends played. Dorothe Randolph, close friend and relative of Jane Bacon, helped identify potential suitors for Frederick Cornwallis and expended much time and energy in the quest.[64] When the match with Lady Judith Barrington's niece came to nothing, Lady Judith continued to assist in the hunt for an appropriate heiress.[65] In the Skipworth examples, male as well as female relatives were involved.[66] On one occasion Walter Bagot was called in by Eleanor Cave, the wife of one of his wife's brothers, to negotiate a marriage settlement for her daughter to Mr Egerton.[67] On another occasion Sir Hugh Beeston was proposing a marriage between his son and one of the Cave daughters and Eleanor asked Bagot to appoint someone to view Beeston's properties and also to nominate a formal participant in the marriage negotiations.[68] For the aristocracy, marriage was a family affair. Patriarchs and matriarchs were expected to play, and played, a pivotal role but both male and female relatives and friends assisted.[69]

One of the central problems involved in dubbing the wife, sister, mother or grandmother as a matriarch is whether the 'power relations' implicit in the term adequately describe the relations between children and their mother, grandchildren and their grandmother, brothers and sisters with their sister. Is it an absolute monarchy, albeit benevolent, or no monarchy at all? Contemporaries certainly acknowledged the reality of the 'governance' of such senior women. It was common in royal and aristocratic circles for young women to be placed under the government of women: for instance, Lady Jane Grey was sent to the household of Queen Catherine Parr. For many young newly weds, too, the authority of the mother-in-law was a reality. Lady Judith Barrington looked forward to the prospect of one of her family 'come under your [Lady Jane Bacon's] government'.[70] Lettice Kinnersley believed that her husband's mother was responsible for the deterioration of her relations with Francis. Intriguingly she made no complaint of her mother-in-law's authority – only of her abuse of it. The same might be said of Edward Aston's relations with Lady Lucy, his wife's mother.[71] They did not live in the same household but he claimed that Lady Lucy exercised a malevolent and powerful influence over his wife and their household. It was her 'custome' 'to malice her husbands kindred, her sons wives and her daughters husbande and that in so high degree that the divill himselfe would not devise matter of moare dispite'. 'Truly my Lady Lucy her selfe is the cause of my wives discontentment for she never goaeth … to Charlecott but she is the woorse on quarter of a yeare after.' As a result of her machinations, his wife had refused to 'suffer ether my sisters, brothers or any of my fathers old servants to continew at Tixall'. Although he had promised his dying mother to care for his niece and his cousin 'nether regarding that they weare my kinred, nor my mothers request, wold never be satisfyed affirminge that besse astley did teacher her children foolishe [ways] and besse aston was the monger of all the newes and secrets of Tixall all over the contrey'. To cap it all, there was a humiliating debacle in which she refused to have his niece, Jane Aston, 'one descended from Sir Edward Aston', in the house, while giving a roof to servants who had declared that they would put out the master's eyes. Could he be expected to tolerate being made 'a chylde, a bole, a poopett and a subiecte to my lady lucys malice'? Penetrating behind the dramatic allegations of ill-treatment, treachery and tyranny, one can discern the underlying structure of authority relations within the wider families of the lesser aristocracy. The authority of the older generation of women in a family was acknowledged and accepted but, like all authority, it should be benign and used to achieve family harmony. A family, like a house, when divided against itself could not stand.

If there was a matriarchy then it, like patriarchy, was frequently softened by close and affective family relations. There is a deal of evidence suggesting the powerful relationship between grandparents and grandchildren in landed families. The affairs of the younger generation directly affected the transmission of the inheritance and also the influence of the family, and because of this parents deferred to the patriarch and matriarch, who in effect exercised final authority when it came to marriage settlements and so on. But this concern for the transmission of property was tempered, indeed governed, by natural affection and anxiety. So Thomas Barrington, when seeking his father's approval for the marriage with Judith, wrote: 'For my present daughters, I beseech you rest confident, that I intend an assurance to them allso & greate reason, that unlesse that be otherwise provided that somwhat may be certain to them to trust unto' in the event that they have no other help. It was also extremely common for grand-children to live in their grandparents' household: love, affection and family interest intermingled. Lady Joan Barrington brought up many of her grandchildren. Of Lady Joan's granddaughter, her mother, Lady Judith, wrote 'Your daughter Lucy with her duty longes to be now at home with you quickly before she forgett her coort relation of St Georges feast where shee attended the kinge all daye & can tell brave stories ...' Her sons, who were in their grandmother's care, were to be dealt with as firmly as Lady Joan wished: 'use your authority to chide them'. In 1628 Thomas asked his mother to send for his son Oliver because 'he lookes ill', adding 'I am much bound to you for your loving care of me & mine & desyre it in particular to this poore child, who I hope will be quickly refresht by Gods blessing when he is neear your affect-ionate & tender eye.'[72] On occasion, Lady Joan reported problems with the boys' health, which indicated both her concern and the shared responsibility for their welfare and education: 'that the poore boyes sett at schoole, without any fire this cold weather, which I much feare will prove dangerous to them for Gobert hath gotten a cold & hath 3 or 4 times bledd a good quantities, so that if there be no other course taken for them I would wish youw to have them away or send them to some other schoole'.[73] Lady Anne Clifford gave a home to her grandson, John Tufton, second son of the Earl of Thanet, for about ten months before he went to Eton. From then on he spent many of his vacations with his grand-mother at Skipton, despite having to travel first from Eton and then from Oxford. She doted on him: when he visited in 1663 she recorded in her diary, 'where I now kissed him with much joy a little before supper'.[74] This especially close relationship with John was echoed by her love and pride in her other descendants.[75] When her grandson, William Crompton, died she recorded his precise age – 8 years, 3 months and 18 days old, adding 'He being a childe of great hopes and perfection, both of bodie and minde'.[76] Simonds D'Ewes spent a good deal of his childhood in the household of his maternal grandfather, whom he adored.[77] Lady Alice Fitton could scarcely contain herself with joy when her daughter Nan gave birth to a daughter in 1598: 'I long to hear

exceedingly how you both do ... I long to hear how all things
about your new charge goeth ... And we can do you any good let
us know it and it shall be done ... God bless you and yours and
send us all merry to meet.'[78] Close relations between grandparents
and grandchildren extended down the social hierarchy. For
example, the clergyman, Ralph Josselin, and his wife had their
daughters and grandchildren to visit them and sometimes the
grandchildren stayed for some weeks on their own.[79] Jemimah
Bourne, aged widow of Immanuel Bourne of Ashover, Derbyshire,
made detailed bequests of property as a dowry for a granddaughter, Jemimah Stafford, and income from property for several other
of her grandchildren.[80] Abraham Sanderson by his will of 1652
even gave the care of his youngest daughter, Mary, into the hands
of her maternal grandfather.[81] Alan Macfarlane has argued that
only rarely did grandparents live to know their grandchildren and
experience a relationship with them. Whereas it is probable that
the opportunities for such relationships diminished the further
down the social scale one went, the evidence for their rarity is
dubious. The chances for such a relationship would depend not
only upon the social and occupational group but also upon the
birth order in the family of both children and grandchildren.[82]

Sometimes the young children of the heir would be brought up
almost as siblings of the siblings of that heir. For example, Ralph
and Mary Verney's eldest children were born and raised at
Claydon in the same household as his sisters and brothers, at least
one of whom, Elizabeth, was born after Ralph's eldest child. This
mixing of the generations and of authorities within aristocratic
families presumably caused some little confusion concerning the
precise nature of relationships. In 1654 Lady Anne Clifford wrote
of the birth and baptism of her greatgrandchild John: 'And my
daughter of Thanett was there at ye birth and christening of this
first grandchild of hers. Soe as he suckt the milk of her Breast
many times, she having with her nowe youngest child, the lady
Anne Tufton, being about nyne weeks old.'[83] It also confuses
historians: children at this social level often did not live with their
parents.[84]

The fluidity of the co-residential household was built into the
structure of aristocratic families. Not as peripatetic as royalty, the
aristocracy none the less spent a good deal of their time travelling
around, whether to court, to town or to the homes of their rela-

tives and friends. It was by no means only the men who absented themselves from the so-called nuclear household. When parents went away 'on business' or for pleasure they might entrust their children temporarily to relatives.[85]

Its would-be monarchical tendencies perhaps emerged most evidently when co-operation broke down within the family. A mother or grandmother, like a father or grandfather, would call upon her status if her influence were seriously challenged. A wise matriarch or patriarch never allowed herself or himself to be placed in such an invidious position. This said, there were apparently frequent challenges to the authority of the older generation. When push came to shove, a son or daughter would often place love or personal preference over 'duty' to a parent or grandparent or subscription to some 'family strategy'.

Siblings

Surviving collections of correspondence indicate the close relations which often existed between siblings and which persisted when they moved away from the household. These relationships were not necessarily good but they were important. Good relations among the Bagot children, the Astons, the Ferrars and the Barringtons need to be set against the portrait of envious relations among the Verney brood. We first see Richard Bagot's sons when Walter, aged 20, and his younger brother, aged 19, are entering Merton College, Oxford, in 1577. It was very common at the time for male siblings to attend school (either at home or away) and college together and to chamber together. Walter's own sons, Lewis, Hervey and William, were to do the same in the early seventeenth century. They attended Oxford with two other local lads, Michael and Walter Biddulph, who were accompanied by 'Wat Edge' as their servant and co-student.[86] At school and university wider kin relations might be cemented. A cousin of Walter and Anthony, William Saunders, had recently been in Oxford and the youths appear to have expected to see him there, but he had, it transpired, already gone down. In the early seventeenth century, Oliver Cave, the son of Walter's brother-in-law, was at university with the Bagot sons as, for a brief time, was cousin Astley's son. In 1609 Hervey promised his father to urge his 'brother-in-law',

Thomas Broughton, husband of his sister Frances (at the time only 12), to work harder. This tendency for the sons and cousins to be educated in tandem persisted throughout the seventeenth century also. For example, Thomas Martindale was both 'bed-fellowe and forme-fellowe' of his cousin Timothy Hill, at school in Cheshire, at university in Cambridge and Glasgow. They even intended to go as chaplains to the Indies together until young Martindale's preaching let him down.[87] While being educated, young men laid the ground for their own future influence in rela-tionships with kith and kin as well as local neighbours. Such an education might be short but it was often followed by a period at the Inns of Court, which extended this situation. Anthony Bagot's career at Oxford was short. In 1578 he seems to have spent a brief time at a Junior Inn of Court, Warwick Inn, and moved from there to Cambridge to attend the young Earl of Essex, a student at Trinity College, Cambridge. Part of a young man's reason for being at college was the connections he might make there; if, along the way, he picked up an education, so much the better. Anthony certainly had a tutor of his own, even as he served Essex. By this time he was part of Essex's incipient household. Yet he maintained his close natural family links, writing frequently to his father and supporting the Bagot interest in the Essex household and at the royal court. Walter also attended Warwick Inn. His mother sent him shirts and garden seeds.[88] His father urged more frequent letters.[89] Walter became a representative of Bagot inter-ests with Lord Burleigh. Burleigh is described in the letters as Bagot's 'nuncow'! Eventually Walter married into the Cecil kin-ship connection. For many of England's young élite, spending their adolescence and early adulthood in school, university, inn or another gentleman's household, offered a degree of independ-ence from the patriarchal household and a chance to try one's wings, at a time when lack of inheritance, and perhaps inclination, precluded the taking of a wife and establishment of a separate household. Lewis Bagot, who never saw eye-to-eye with his father, Walter, expressed himself quite frankly on this point in 1610, saying that he had been a long time in London because he lived there more contented than at home.[90] Sometimes, as with Lewis, this period of exile from a household led to, from the patriarch's perspective, unwelcome signs of independence and neglect of overall family strategy. Lewis was threatened with disinheritance if he went ahead with what was considered to be an inappropriate marriage. He submitted.

Sons out of the household retained links with that household and continued to support the family. Once they founded households of their own, these links were somewhat weakened but not destroyed. Anthony Bagot continued to keep an eye on his sister, Anne Broughton, despite his own marriage and establishment of a separate household.[91] There is some evidence that the strength of such links was dependent upon the physical proximity of the various parties. Mary Josselin's relatives, for example, lived too far away to figure very largely in the lives of her own children, and a good many of Ralph Josselin's uncles were too distant to have much contact with him.[92] Nicholas Ferrar, who lived with them, was like a father to his nieces. On the other hand, our knowledge of links between kin often depends upon their physical separation and the existence of written correspondence. Much later, the diary of Anne Lister reveals her close relations with an uncle with whom she elected to live.[93]

Parents who were literate frequently corresponded with married children. Their relationships with individual children varied in intensity. In the case of the Fitton family it seems that both Edward Fitton and his wife Alice had a warmer relationship with Anne than with their flirtatious daughter, Mary, who was so carried away by her life at court that she failed to correspond with her parents. Sir William Knollys, son of Francis, was commissioned to look after Mary while she acted as Elizabeth's maid of honour (a duty which he singularly failed to perform). Nevertheless a worried Mistress Fitton begged Anne for news of her sister: 'If you hear anything of your sister I pray let know, for I never heard from her since.' When Mary was disgraced (because she had been impregnated by the Earl of Pembroke) and expelled from court, her parents tried unsuccessfully to persuade Pembroke to marry her. In the event Mary gave birth to a stillborn boy and went to live with her sister Anne for a while. Her chances of a marriage were not totally destroyed. She later married William Polewhele Esquire of Perton, Staffordshire and, on his death, John Lougher. The letters between the older Fittons and their married daughter Anne are couched in that odd combination of formality and familiarity which characterised so much of early modern correspondence and which is liable to be misinterpreted by historians. 'Nan

Newdigate' writes Edward, and signs himself 'Ed. Fitton' or 'Thy truest friend'. But, in the body of the letters he declares 'thus longing sore to see thee' or 'Your mother will needs send Frelan and I send nobody but my own heart which ever shall be with you wheresoever my body is.'[94]

The relationships of married sisters with sisters and brothers and with their parents emerge very strongly from the Bagot correspondence. It is important to remember that these are the relationships which the physical distance between family members has preserved for us. They probably represent the tip of an iceberg. Anne Broughton, Margaret Trew and Lettice Kinnersley maintained an active relationship through letters, visits and gifts. Anne, especially, corresponded with her family, probably because she lived further away but also perhaps because she had shared companionship with Walter and Anthony when they were children together, practising their signatures and otherwise pestering their father, Richard. When Dorothy Okeover was widowed, Anne Broughton offered to come to Blithfield to comfort her.[95] Anne assumed that her parents, both mother and father, would not only be interested in the national and society news she conveyed in her letters but also in her personal activities.[96] Her husband, Richard Broughton, kept his father-in-law informed about Anne's health.[97] She was concerned about Walter's health in 1600 and sent him affectionate and practical advice about looking after himself.[98] In 1603 she felt sufficiently close to Walter to request the use of his coachman to take Richard Broughton, who was ill, to receive treatment at Bath.[99] Dorothy Okeover returned to her brother's house when her husband died, and spent at least some time there. Lettice, who lived closest, presumably only felt the need to communicate by letter when she was forbidden to travel abroad by her awkward husband. Mary Bagot, their mother, was still in close contact with her own sister, Frances Dayrell, and her mother, Dorothy Dayrell, in 1570 and with her half-brother, George Saunders, in 1568, who sent her a 'sugar loaf'.[100] This brother was evidently on some terms of familiarity with other family members, for he sent thread and needles to 'Mistress Margaret', one of the younger Bagot daughters. Such bonds are clearly shown to have been prevalent elsewhere. For instance, Constance Fowler, the married sister of Herbert Aston of Tixall, was close to him. He had encouraged her to correspond with Katherine Thimelby to relieve her loneliness while he was serving Charles I in Spain. They became very friendly and Constance energetically promoted a match between her beloved brother and Katherine, prompting her brother to negotiate terms.[101] Winifred Thimelby, Katherine's sister, was Abbess of a convent of English nuns at Louvain. She became involved in discussions with her brother-in-law about the vocation or otherwise of her niece, Gertrude. The daughters of the Barrington family retained contact with one another as their households moved from London to Essex and back. Lady Jane Cornwallis/Bacon took into her household Hercules Meautys, son of her brother and sister-in-law, Sir Thomas and Lady Anne Meautys.[102] She also lent them money. In the early eighteenth century, Elizabeth Coke wrote frequently to her brother, Sir Thomas, about his household and family, over which she had charge, signing herself 'your real affectionate sister and faithfull servant E. Coke'. He endorsed her letters 'Sister Betty'.[103] Ralph Josselin kept in contact with all three of his sisters who lived to reach maturity, Mary, Dorothy and Anne, and felt considerable obligation towards all. His sister Anne was even on a Christmas visit to the Josselins' house when she died in 1673.[104] Also, lower down the social scale and in the later seventeenth and early eighteenth century, William Stout, bachelor householder, maintained a close and appreciative relationship with his older sister, Elin, and his mother.[105] Familial and social relations were underwritten by practical support and interdependence. The Bagots relied on relatives in London to buy and send them provisions.[106] There was a good deal of moneylending between the various households. Elizabeth Bagot's brother, Cecil Cave, relied on moneylending for his living and combined business with family feeling when he made loans to Walter and Elizabeth.[107] Ralph Josselin mentions lending money to his older sister Dorothy and her husband, despite his own pressing demands, and giving them 'such old things as wee any wayes could spare'.[108] Walter Bagot's Beaumont cousin (on his mother's side) felt no compunction about requesting the loan of six geldings with a man to bring them to Leicestershire and care for them for the Leicester assizes in both 1610 and 1614.[109]

There is evidence, too, that married brothers maintained links after they ceased co-residence. Continuing links with his younger brother, Leonard, led William Stout to offer a home to one or two of Leonard's eight children 'when they were between two and five years of age' and to provide the second son, William, with a good education. William kept on his business for the preferment of Leonard's children and, against his better judgement, because he did not think his young namesake cut out for trade, took William on as an apprentice 'and confined myself more than I am inclined to, in order to instruct him and observe diligent attendance'. Leonard and his wife thought this his duty for 'I should not turn him off after so long being with me.' When sister Elin, who had been William's housekeeper, died in 1724, however, Leonard reciprocated his brother's services by sending his second daughter, Jennet, 'to keep my house till I was otherways provided'. William Stout's household offers an excellent example of how a family would create and support a household consisting of an artificial 'family' for reasons of mutual advantage to all close family members, be they co-resident or not. Bachelor Stout, spinster sister Elin, widowed mother Elizabeth, two infant nieces or nephews and an adolescent nephew composed the household. Marriage did not form this household. Family maintained it.[110]

Adam Martindale lost physical contact with his second brother, Hugh, who married a papist and went to Ireland, but this same brother urged his father, in letters, to send Adam to be apprenticed to him as a carpenter. Adam's knowledge of the affairs of his other brothers was reasonably detailed. His brother Henry married and lived in Warrington and his eldest brother, Thomas, came to a formal agreement with his father to take over part of the estate and dwell there with his wife and children. In 1644 both these married brothers, with their families, took refuge in the garrison at Warrington. When Henry died, in 1652, Adam described him as 'my dear brother'. He recalled that Henry 'was a most kind brother to me', who had, on Adam's release from prison, 'bare in clothes and money', 'furnished me handsomely at his own charge, thoughe his owne circumstances were then but hard'. This had been 'an extraordinary courtesie'. He also recorded the death of his eldest brother, Thomas, in summer 1663, although with less evidence of emotion. Thomas had been a hard drinker and Adam had reservations about him, although he was an 'honest man'. None the less, Thomas made Adam, along with two cousins, a feoffee to see to the rights of his wife and children. Perhaps importantly, there was a re-forming of the natural family in the grave. Thomas was buried, by the sides of his mother and father and his sister Jane, near the Dial in Prescot churchyard.[111]

Higher up on the social scale we find Philip Gawdy constantly appealing to the family feeling of his elder brother, Sir Bassingborne. 'We wer made both of our metall and framed in our moulde ...'. His love for Bassingborne could be 'compared to the love that was betwixt David and Jonathan which was exceding the love of women', and indeed equalled his love for his wife Bridget ('Bid'). This was a reciprocal relationship, in which Sir Bassingborne was the 'authority' figure but to which Philip also contributed 'favours'.[112] The Ferrar brothers shared a similar relationship.

It does not seem that the English upper and middling classes were alone in maintaining strong links between married children and their parents and siblings. Edmé Rétif sent his son, Nicolas, to live in Vermonton to live with the boy's eldest half-sister, Anne (who was godmother to Nicolas), and her husband, Michel Linard. Later, Nicolas was sent to study at Bicêtre under the supervision of Thomas, his half-brother. When Nicolas went to Paris he stayed in the house of another half-sister. Eventually he was handed over to the care of his eldest half-brother for two years.[113]

All this evidence suggests that there were close relations between siblings even after they ceased co-residence and that there were authority relations between siblings also. This subject had received strangely little attention from scholars, despite the fact that we know that in many families adolescent and teenage children lived alongside infants and toddlers and were used as child minders and educators.

Family Relationships and Co-residence

In England, as the censuses and household listings show, elderly married couples and widowed people fairly infrequently actually lived with their married children. It has been estimated that it happened in about 5 per cent of households over the period 1599–1800, that it occurred more commonly in the wealthiest households (which alone were capable of supporting so many adults) and that, when it did happen, the older couple was generally still in charge of the household.[114]

But, as we have seen, co-residence, while important, did not define the limits of relationships between family members. Indeed, the failure of married couples from consecutive generations to dwell together permanently may tell us more about the limits of the household economy than the limits of their mutual concern, and more about their practical common sense than their coldness and indifference. Moreover, *short* periods of co-residence with parents were not uncommon in the early years of a marriage and may have had an impact upon the formation of relationships. The fluidity of the co-residential household is not adequately captured by the census.

The Dissolution of the Nuclear Family: the Widow

Scholars have accorded some attention to widows – first, because they are one of the only categories of women who emerge from the shadows as real people, because of their legal identity; secondly, because they appear relatively powerful as the 'heads' of households in the absence, however brief, of a deceased male. Thus regarded, they become part of the dirigist approach. While this is perfectly valid, the behaviour of widows, provision for them and attitudes towards them may reveal a good deal about contemporary kin bonds. The part which the widow-led household played in the family cycle is also worth consideration in its own right.

There is some debate about the incidence and causes of widowhood in the early modern period. Widowhood was indubitably very common in England and France during these times of high mortality. On average, one fifth of households in any single English community were those of widows, although there was a considerable deviation from this mean.[115] A tendency, in some communities, to place widows in almshouses or as lodgers in other households may, in some cases, reduce the value of household analysis.[116] There would also be at least some widows who dwelt in rooms in their children's households. Widowhood was as common among the French, although housing arrangements were sometimes very different. This incidence has been explained in several ways. The high mortality rate among men was not entirely down to natural causes. Men *were* more vulnerable to plague and other disease. In seventeenth-century England women enjoyed a slightly higher life expectancy than males. The tendency in both England and France was for females to be younger than their spouses by a few years. In Nantes, records survive of 107 marriages ending before 1660 through the death of one spouse: in 71 cases the male died; in 36 the female.[117] In the plague epidemic of 1603, in London, the ratio of male to female deaths was 6:1.[118] These, however, are very general statements and, when we probe a little further, we discover that mortality rates were highly class-specific. It was more common for marriages among the peerage, for example, to be dissolved by the death of a wife than of a husband. High mortality rates among aristocratic women seem to have been associated with childbirth and, especially, with intervention in childbirth. The rate of such deaths actually appears to have increased after 1750 as male medics began to assist female midwives.[119] Widowhood, and especially widowhood which lasted into old age was, in contrast, extremely common among the poor and in towns. In Norwich, in 1570, a listing of the poor gave twelve times as many widows as widowers over the age of 61. Some 88 per cent of the men over 61 were married whereas only 25 per cent of the women were married. Over two-thirds of these married men had wives who were younger than themselves by ten years or more.[120] But there were sex-selective forms of mortality also. In 1644, for instance, at least 900 noblemen's wives from the provinces of Burgundy, Bresse and Berry were widowed in the campaign in Germany. England's involvement in foreign campaigns also took its toll among aristocracy and lower social orders alike. When William Trew, husband of Margaret Bagot, prepared to go to France with the Earl of Essex in 1591, he wrote to his father-in-law, Richard Bagot, in expectation of death 'this voyage'. The disturbances of the Frondes caused considerable loss of life among menfolk. Mortality rates among combatants in the three English Civil Wars of the mid-century were high, estimated as 20 per cent over all, comparable with mortality rates during the First World War. The most recent study gives a figure for English and Welsh troops of 84,830 dead.[121] The low sex ratio in England, especially characteristic of urban areas, is normally attributed to male vulnerability to disease and a penchant for emigration among males, rather than to fatalities of war.[122] In peacetime, it was common for men to settle their disputes through mortal combat.[123] At all levels of society interpersonal violence was common, and, because almost everyone carried a potential weapon – a knife – frequently resulted in injury or death. In France, it is alleged that 936 gentlemen were killed in duels during the regency of Anne of Austria alone. Duelling did not reach England until the late sixteenth century, and for the period down to the Civil War was kept in check. It became a serious problem among the upper classes after the Restoration.[124]

All these features rendered widowhood part of the anticipated experience of a young woman, and the attempt to find a second marriage partner less certain of success. The practice of marrying girls to older men, which seems to have been common in seventeenth-century France, may well have swelled the number of young widows. In England such marriages did occur among the upper classes but scarcely with such frequency as to make an impact upon the total picture.

Widowhood was, therefore, commonplace in England and France. The North American colonies were characterised by much more diversity. A high sex ratio has been seen as characteristic of the colonial experience in what are now the United States and Canada, producing often exceptionally male-heavy societies, but the ratio differed from colony to colony as a reflection of the phase of that experience. Women were more scarce in seventeenth-century Virginia than in Massachusetts, for example, and more scarce yet on the New England frontier. Yet some urban areas had a surplus of females.

Demographically it might seem that, as a result, widowhood in the male-heavy colonies would be rather more rarely a lasting condition. In which event, one might expect higher rates of lasting widowhood in the towns which did have a low male to female sex ratio. But in general we would expect the American experience to contrast quite sharply with what we know of the French or English. For example, in Nantes, widows were much more likely to die without remarrying than were widowers.[125] There are many examples of extremely lengthy widowhoods in both France and England.

In fact, differences in the mortality rate in the various colonies may have had a modifying effect upon this picture. The data provided by both John Demos and Philip Greven suggests that in New England disruption of marriage by early death was rare and consequent lengthy widowhoods equally rare. The average marriage ended with death when the wife was 63 or the husband 70 and the

average eldest child of the marriage in its early forties.[126] This
picture is very different from that painted by the Rutmans for
Middlesex County, Virginia. Here median first marriages ended
when the wife died in her late thirties or the husband in his late
forties. The controversial finding that female mortality rates here
were higher than male made little difference to the overall picture
of disrupted marriages. Remarriages were extremely common.[127]
Some historians, however, doubt the mortality rates established for
New England and, therefore, the prevalence of lengthy and uninterrupted marriages. Certainly Linda Auers Bissell's study of
mobility in Windsor, Connecticut, throws doubt upon it by showing that 32 per cent of sons inherited land by their sixteenth birthday and after the death of a father, which compares with Virginian
incidence of orphanhood of minors.[128] The debate can only be
resolved by more detailed reconstitution of families.

The chances of becoming a widow varied demographically,
then, both within and between these countries. But did widows
share much other than the state of widowhood? Widows were not
an interest group in the same way as were clergy or master masons
or retailers. As we have indicated above, widows, of whatever class
and in whatever country, possessed in common a certain vulnerability. The extent and nature of this vulnerability varied enormously, however, from social group to social group and from
country to country.

The law regarding inheritance in these three countries in part
defines that vulnerability. Montaigne expressed it well when he
wrote: 'The estate is not properly ours, since by a civil ordinance
and independently of us it is destined to certain successors.'[129]
Inherited property belonged to the descent group, and even the
bestowal of acquired property was hedged with rules to protect
the interests of this group. In Bordeaux, among the upper and the
middling sorts, marriage contracts which spelt out the descent of
property, both inherited and acquired, were usual in the seventeenth century. Far less common was testation. For the majority
who died intestate, in the absence of a carefully worded marriage
contract, inheritance would have been governed by the various
customs. For example, the custom of Bordeaux was that where a
male died intestate, unless the marriage contract stated otherwise,
his property of whatever type would be divided up equally between
his heirs. Even if he made a will, the custom dictated that he must

leave all his inherited property to his direct descendants or, if he had no heirs, give two thirds to his nearest consanguine kin. Property which had been acquired by him could only be freely testated if he was celibate or had a childless marriage; if there were direct heirs of the marriage then these inherited the *acquets*. Protection of the wife, as widow, became a concern for the man with whom she formed an alliance or common project and for her own lineage. Women were safeguarded by the dotal system and by their own inherited property. During the marriage the husband administered and had the use of the wife's property, including the dot. If he predeceased his wife, she could mortgage the estate for return of the dot. If she died first, the dot became part of the husband's *propres* to support the children of the marriage. By the middle of the seventeenth century it was accepted that property acquired during the marriage would be enjoyed by the surviving spouse for life and would then pass to the direct descendants. After 1528 the surviving spouse would also be able to claim a specified amount of the estate. Noble women were allowed, in addition, an annuity out of the estate. The dotal principle was affirmed by the marriage contracts of the time. In France such customs were regionally specific and it is hazardous to extrapolate from one instance to another. None the less, the dotal system, which was characteristic of much of northern and western France, and the support of it by the marriage contract, typical of southern France, was sufficiently common for it to be characterised as a general rule. It acted to protect the woman's lineage property by encouraging a husband to administer it well, by restoring it to the woman and her heirs or by returning it to the line of origin. It was comparable to the system widely prevalent in England among the upper classes. Yet there were forms of household in France which, if centred on the conjugal relationship, none the less viewed the relationship between the couple and the property in a very different way. Slightly more than 12 per cent of all marriage contracts in Bordeaux and its surrounds in the 1640s established *communautés familiales*, in which all the adult kin members held the property, of whatever kind, in common. The institution was most common in the hinterland among peasants but during the seventeenth century the custom was also adopted in the town by about 10 per cent of those marrying, whether merchants, artisans or officials. Originally, in the fifteenth century, the woman's property was often merged inextricably into the communal property and in only 36 per cent of the contracts was there provision for her at her spouse's demise. There is evidence to suggest that by the mid-sixteenth century this was beginning to change, and by the mid-seventeenth century contracts contained provision for the breakup of the *communauté*, and detailed instruction for the return of the dot, a share in the acquired property and a right to an *agencement*.[130]

Until relatively recently historians would have argued that in England there was a sharper social divide in the provision made for women. Widows of the upper class, of whom there were few both as a proportion of women in the class and as a proportion of the total population of women, were best provided for. Despite an overriding concern for the transmission of property by primogeniture, law, custom and family feeling made sure that widows were well cared for and their financial contribution to the partnership (as a dowry) acknowledged and protected. As we have seen, this family feeling was as often that of the woman's natural family as that of the family onto which she was 'grafted' at marriage. Walter Bagot refused to continue paying instalments of his daughter Anne's dowry until her husband made satisfactory jointure arrangements for her widowhood.[131] According to the former orthodoxy, however, married and widowed women lower down the social scale were not well provided for and were entirely defenceless because the common law offered them no protection and no rights.[132] The absence of marriage contracts of the detailed type common in France for the unions of the middling sort seemed confirmation of this argument.[133]

It still appears that the elite married and widowed woman was well provided for. The aristocratic widow had restored to her, as of right, any lands and property which came to her as her inheritance. The tendency for the male line to die out and for freehold estates to pass in their entirety to co-heiresses is well illustrated by the Fitton–Newdegate genealogy. Women, moreover, frequently inherited leasehold land and other moveable property.[134] Statute law also gave her a right to a dower of a third of her husband's freehold (and some types of copyhold) estate. In fact, among the upper classes, this right was normally waived in favour of a jointure arranged in the marriage settlement. The groom's father would offer other arrangements for the support of the couple, which would then be negotiated by the bride's relatives. The initiative lay with the parents of the bride and groom. For example, Richard Bagot suggested that his younger son, Anthony, on marriage would be given an annuity of £40 and his prospective bride, Katherine Lowe, would be given a house, which Bagot had recently had built (presumably with this in mind). The house would become her dower house. The jointure itself was often increased during a successful marriage. Because it involved a contract, the jointure was defensible not in the common but in the equity courts. (The common law denied a married woman's legal identity and, therefore, any contracts she made were rendered null and void). The ratio between the portion (the dowry given the groom by the bride's father) and the jointure itself appears to have risen during the period. Historians seem to agree that the ratio rose from 5:1 in the early seventeenth century to 10:1 in the later half of the century. Lawrence Stone calculated that a bride who in 1550 would have a jointure settle upon her of between £200 and £250 for every £1,000 of her dowry would only have £100 settled upon her in 1700.[135] R. B. Outhwaite suggested a rise of between 12 and 13 times over the period.[136] This inflation may have been as much due to the rising cost of land (the portion or dowry would normally be used to purchase land to provide an annuity) as to the extremely low sex ratio in the late seventeenth century which placed wives in a poor bargaining position.[137] None the less, as Lloyd Bonfield has pointed out, the true value of the jointure depended on the number of years by which a widow survived her spouse.[138] After 1650 the development of the 'strict settlement' enabled a landowner, while preserving the patrimony for his eldest son, or the closest male descendant of that son, or his daughters as sole heiresses, to provide security for his bride and adequate provision for all the younger sons and daughters. It was a family settlement. Usually this meant that the widow was given a dower house and a life annuity from the estate, and daughters cash sums to endow their marriages. At first, in the seventeenth century, younger sons would be given a share in the estate for their lives only and accorded annuities, but by the eighteenth century they were more usually given capital.[139] In fact, landowners and their heirs quite frequently broke the settlement to make a new one which was in their mutual interest and made different provision for their wives and young children.

Our understanding of provision for married women and widows of the 'middling sort' has, however, been considerably modified of late. This is, in part, because we now have an improved understanding of the legal system and its implications. We know, for example, that relatively little land passed by primogeniture from father to eldest son and we know that both written law and custom reserved provision for widows. Whereas ecclesiastical historians and historians of equity law have long been aware of the continued importance in the lives of ordinary men and women of jurisdictions other than the common law, they have only recently begun to make other historians conversant with this fact. In the early modern period several different laws ran and, whereas a married woman was undoubtedly in a state of coverture in the common law courts and therefore without rights and property, married women did have legal identities in the ecclesiastical and equity courts which could be and were defended. More important, study of wills, acts of probate administration, and court records have revealed that women of quite modest means did make marriage settlements to protect their own property and that of children born of previous marriages and did actively defend these settlements. Sometimes these settlements were formal treaties of marriage, such as those made by the London middle classes in the late seventeenth and the eighteenth centuries.[140] Lawyers offered women, both single and widowed, advice on protecting their property, their separate estate, suggesting a range of different instruments which could be used.[141] Women, it has been discovered, were active in litigation concerning their separate estate in the Court of Chancery. The expense of prolonged litigation in the court restricted its use to reasonably well-to-do-women. Even so, over half of women litigants were the wives of professional men and merchants, yeomen and husbandmen and the size of the marriage portions and jointures involved were low compared to those accorded aristocratic wives. (The portions ranged from £40 to £3,000; the jointures ranged from £12 to £200 per annum.)[142] For the rest, the simplest and most common way of making a marriage settlement was by entering a common bond either to pay a specified sum at a given date or to pay portions to the wife's children by previous marriages, or to leave the wife a certain amount on her widowhood. Six per cent of clerical wills proved in Lichfield diocese between 1550 and 1700 made specific mention of either a portion or a jointure or both; this does not exclude the possibility that other bequests to wives were not pre-arranged jointures. Amy Louise Erickson has shown how widows, commonly the executrixes of their husband's wills who applied in the courts for probate (a widow was automatically granted the administration in cases of intestacy), defended their marriage settlements by listing property reserved for herself and/or her children as expenses to be deducted from the estate before bequests were paid. Her suggestion that perhaps ten per cent or more of administrations involved payment of marriage settlements seems reasonable in the light of the Lichfield data from wills them-selves. And it makes clear that labourers, husbandmen and yeomen, possessed of insubstantial estate and, perhaps, fortunate to marry someone with a little independent money, had to make provision on marriage for their wives and widows. Some of the bonds taken out guaranteed the wife a sum of money for her per-sonal use during the husband's lifetime and her right to make a will. Marrying widows were particularly prone to enter bonds to protect their and their children's future livelihood. During her husband's lifetime, should he break the terms of the bond, the sureties of the bond (but not the wife) could sue him in the common law courts and obtain redress for the wife; on his death, the bonds reverted to the widow as moveable property and she could sue for their satisfaction herself under the common law. As we shall see, there are indications that such settlements constituted a bone of contention in some marriages but they offered the wife some power as well as security.[143]

Where colonial parents survived until their children were of marriageable age they commonly sought to direct their children's marriage decisions and to negotiate the terms of the marriage con-tract. The same was as true of seventeenth-century Maryland and Virginia as it was of New England. However, parents much more frequently survived in New England than in the two southern col-onies. As girls married much younger than men, it was more fre-quently the case that the bride's than the bridegroom's parents were involved in such negotiations. The child's portion was, in such circumstances, commonly granted the child on marriage. Testation normally involved only nominal bequests to children who were already married.[144]

In some of the areas of North American settlement women were in a much stronger bargaining position when it came to provision both for their married life and for their potential widowhood, and the common law courts of the colonies allowed them to use this bargaining power to good effect. Where an antenuptial agreement existed to this end, a woman was permitted to administer and use her own property during marriage – by the common law courts. John Phillips and widowed Faith Dory drew up the following contract in Plymouth Plantation in 1667:

> The said Fath Dory is to enjoy all her house and land, goods and cattles [? chattels], that she is now possessed of, to her owne proper use, to dispose of them att her owne free will from time to time, and att any time as she shall see cause. ... The children of both the said parties shall remaine att the free and proper and only disposal of theire owne naturall parents, as they shall see good to dispose of them.[145]

Of course, Faith, as a widow who had inherited property and with it the responsibility to provide for the children of her first marriage, had every reason to wish to exercise complete control over this. Such colonial contracts were not unusual and did not always involve widows.

The courts of the colonies lent their support to yet another device which undermined the principle of *femme covert*. They permitted postnuptial agreements which tacitly acknowledged the separate legal identity of wives. These agreements marked either separation or reconciliation of spouses – commonly they ordered that partners should not meddle in one another's affairs. In one such case – that of Richardson v. Mountjoy in Virginia – the courts acknowledged that the woman involved thereby became *femme sole* and could henceforward make contracts. This would not have been tolerated in either France or by the common law in England. Perhaps these concessions to the legal independence of colonial women were necessary if widows were to rejoin the supply of marriageable women.[146] Dr Gampel has shown how the equity courts provided protection for women's property in seventeenth-century Maryland.[147]

Certainly 'marriage and remarriage was a way of life' in seventeenth-century Virginia. Mary, born in 1637, married George Keeble and had seven children before she was widowed at 29 years of age. In 1666, shortly after George died, she remarried to Robert

Beverley, at least four of her young children alive. She and Beverley had five children. When Mary died, in 1678, aged 41, Robert almost immediately remarried to a widow, Katherine Hone. Her husband had died but recently. The Hone goods were already in the Beverley home before the inventory of them was taken. When Beverley died, in 1687, Katherine again remarried, this time to a widower named Christopher Robinson with four children. Such examples can be multiplied.[148] The need for such a chain of marriage and remarriage must be set against the demographic statistics for Middlesex county if it is to make sense. In the late 1660s there were some 90 white households in the county, by 1687 there were 142, and by 1724 there were 260.

The evidence may point to a greater dependence in England than in France upon testation as a means of provision for widows of the middling sort and, indeed, for the family in general. In France, unlike in England after 1540, there was no freedom of testation where inherited property was concerned. There was some individual initiative where goods and chattels were involved. Certainly, in Bordeaux, while the marriage contract was used universally, much less recourse was made to the will. A fifth of the adult population made wills. There was, in the will-making population, a distinct bias towards the propertied and well-to-do. In circumstances of intestacy, custom governed inheritance. While a similar although not so pronounced bias in the English will-making population can be observed, there was a more marked reluctance among the English population to allow law and custom to determine descent. This may have been because, in France, the custom actually favoured equal partible inheritance, unless a marriage contract specified otherwise. The laws of testation insisted that property devised by will should go to the direct heirs of the will-maker or largely to close consanguine relatives. He or she was allowed to favour one child over the others but not to their total exclusion. Primogeniture was enforced only among the nobility. A desire to provide for the whole family out of one's estate, however humble, is apparent in both England and France. This principle was enshrined in French law but not in the English common law. The will, in France, then gave the testator an additional opportunity, that of dividing the property unequally among the heirs. Of those who chose to make wills in Bordeaux, half clung to the principle of equal partition and there was only a propensity in the opposite direction in the sense that fathers slightly favoured sons and mothers daughters.[149] A parent might give additional reward to a child who had cared for them in their old age and infirmity or a financial punishment to an ungrateful child. The wills also allowed more specific and individual provision for widows, either by giving them life enjoyment of the estate or by making them general and universal heir. The French wills which do exist may reflect a desire among some people to modify slightly the rule of law and custom. In England, however, the will was the chief instrument available to the man (or woman) who wished to care for an entire family and who could do so appropriately only by avoiding intestacy.

In England all adult men and single women of free status, who were in full possession of their senses and living within the law, were entitled to full testamentary powers. As we have seen, some married women secured the formal consent of their husbands to make wills during their spouse's lifetime. There was considerable freedom in the testation of goods and chattels from the middle ages onwards, although this freedom was curbed by custom. The moveable goods or personality were held to include both leases and bonds. The custom of *legitim*, whereby the widow without offspring inherited one half of her husband's moveable goods after his debts had been paid and the widow with offspring inherited one third, occurred throughout England until the sixteenth century. As the personality constituted the entire estate or the largest part of the estate of most husbands and fathers, this was a very important guarantee of the welfare of widows and children.[150] Thus in 1504, John Brown of Knotting, Bedfordshire, asked that all his goods be divided into three equal parts, of which one was to be retained to fulfil his testament, one was to go to his wife, and one to his sons and daughters. The part for the children (the child's part) would normally be administered by the executors, often the widow, until the child or children came of age. Under the custom of *legitim* the will itself may often have been a disposition of the soul's or testator's part only and, therefore, rendered highly unreliable as evidence of the concern a man was showing for his family's future or indeed as evidence of his family's composition. Certainly, in the later period, when it is believed that the custom had fallen into disuse in the south, wills became longer and more detailed. There is, however, some doubt about the currency of the custom after 1500.

By Elizabeth's reign it had ceased to be enforced in the Province of Canterbury although there is evidence that it was observed in the City of London in the early 1700s and in Wales in the 1690s. It continued in force in the Northern Province into the 1690s. Even where *legitim* was not formally in force, however, it may well have been used as a rule of thumb by willmakers and by the ecclesiastical courts who had to arbitrate in cases of disputed inheritance or intestacy. There is some evidence that the church courts were conscientious in their attempts to see the widows and children of the deceased fairly provided for, seeking equitable jurisdiction of an estate whether or not a will was left. Indeed it has been suggested that widows were frequently allocated more than twice their customary entitlement to a third. In the reigns of Charles II and James I Statutes of Distribution were passed which enabled a widow to claim a third part of an estate as of legal right if there was an heir and a half of the estate if there was not, suggesting that the confusion surrounding the rights of widows and children was acknowledged and considered unsatisfactory.[151] Perhaps it was felt that other members of the family were unfairly disadvantaged by the generosity of the courts towards widows. The right to thirds in cases of intestacy (which were the majority) remained until 1856.

Judith Ford's recent study of willmaking in Bedfordshire before 1540 demonstrates how testators used the will and devices such as the *use* to provide for their families.[152] At this time, freehold and much copyhold land were held to descend according to primogeniture or by locally accepted custom such as gavelkind or borough English. It could not be devised by will. This makes wills prior to 1540 an extremely unsafe indicator of property provision for either spouse or family. In general, only leasehold property finds mention therein. But, in practice, this rule was circumvented by a medieval device called the *use*. This enabled property owners to provide for all of their offspring even where primogeniture was the rule. It transferred the legal title to the property to named trustees (feoffees to uses) who held it and administered it for a third party or parties, who were frequently named in the last will or in a statement. Sometimes such uses are referred to in last wills and testaments of the period.

I will and bequeath to Alys my wiff all my purchased lands and tenements and all such as be named ... in my new dede of feoffment weith meadows isis pasturys closys rents ... and all my other land and tenements beyng in feoffment in eyton ... of her liff and after her decease to remayn all holey ... unto John Cutlatt my sonne.[153]

In 1536, by the Statute of Uses and the Statute of Enrolments, this right to devise land by use was abolished in order to prevent loss of revenue to the crown by evasion of feudal dues. This move was met by outcry – enforced primogeniture and restriction of individual choice was not welcome – and the resulting Statute of Wills of 1540 in fact permitted testation of almost all real property under the common law. Those holding land by knight service (that is freehold land) might will away two-thirds of the freehold estate, reserving only one third to the heir and any dower settled on the widow. Other property could be freely bequeathed according to the will of its owner. As it is now generally agreed by scholars that most English land was held not by freehold but by copyhold or leasehold, in effect this Act spelt freedom of testation of most landed property, saving only the widow's dower rights in a third of her husband's freehold property or, where one existed, her jointure and the heir's third.[154] There were, however, a multiplicity of local and manorial customs governing the rights of widows, widowers and children in the partition of property, freehold, copyhold and leasehold.

Inheritance was a complex business in England. The labyrinthine paths of the system of multiple jurisdictions – common law, customary law, equity law, ecclesiastical law, manorial law – have only just begun to be trodden by historians. They bewildered contemporaries too. Probate of the estate was in the hands of the ecclesiastical courts which had in theory no jurisdiction over the transmission of freehold property but did have jurisdiction over the disposal of personalty (including leasehold as well as moveable property). In these courts ancient custom (such as that of *legitim* described above) guided practice. Contracts and settlements made to protect the property and other rights of married women and of their offspring from previous marriages were not recognised by the common law courts (who denied a married woman a legal identity) but could be, and were, successfully defended in equity courts such as Chancery and the ecclesiastical courts.[155]

A real problem, therefore, faces the historian studying strategies for family provision in the early modern period in the precise

status of the chief source of information – the will and testament.
It is rarely clear whether a will restates common law and customary
provision for relatives in addition to making specific additional
bequests. Unless it does so, the will represents only a part, and perhaps the smallest part, of any family strategy. On occasion, the
books granting probate administration can be used to augment
our knowledge of such a strategy but even this information is partial in the extreme.

English use of the will to provide for the future of wife and
children did not, of course, imply that the testator regarded with
equanimity partition of a small-holding or business. When Thomas
Ferebe, a well-to-do Cirencester mercer, died, in 1611, he left his
son George nothing but a 'black mourning suit'. In this case his
younger son, Anthony, who was carrying on the family business,
was to have the bulk of his fortune when proper provision had
been made for the widow. In the event, the widow, Elizabeth,
seems to have gone to live with her son Thomas and his wife,
Bridget, and remained in their household for the next 23 years.
When Ferebe made this provision for Anthony, however, he took
into account the fact that George was a parson with a livelihood
secured.[156] Even where a younger son was not the sole heir, it was
very common for younger children to be provided with property
which had been accumulated by purchase specifically to form
their inheritance, to be granted annuities – sometimes for a term
of years until they had received an education or apprenticeship –
or, in the case of daughters, a dowry. A widow's provision might
consist of the use and administration of the estate during the
minority of the heir (as was the case with William Stout of
Lancaster's widowed mother); of an annuity on the estate for her
life; of the use for life or viduity of apartments in the family house.

In America it appears that the courts were very active in protecting the rights of the wife and widow. For example, in Plymouth
Colony the laws provided that the courts could overturn a will that
did not provide adequately for the widow, especially if she had
brought property into the marriage or had increased the prosperity of the family by her hard work. In 1663, Widow Naomi Silvester
had her portion increased because she had been 'a frugall and
laborious woman in the procuring of the said estate'.[157] Rights of
separation and divorce were also allowed women in the colonies,
but not in England or France. Not only did women bring success-

ful divorce cases in Massachusetts between 1639 and 1692, they were granted generous settlements by the courts and allowed to keep their dower rights. In the South, separations were frequently formalised and maintenance payments to wives ordered. Whereas we must be careful not to exaggerate the incidence of divorce and separation, it is important to recognise not only that they occurred as a result of female initiative, but also that they were legalised by the courts and that these same courts offered protection to the women involved.[158] The knowledge of this protective attitude may have encouraged women to sue for divorce or separation; in England, judicial separation was normally male-initiated. Yet, as Roger Thompson argues, the principle of *femme covert* was not destroyed over-night. Until the early eighteenth century the wife's parents could initiate divorce proceedings: her father possessed legal identity and could fight her corner for her.[159]

Historians are still debating the question of the widow's independence and economic role in eighteenth and nineteenth-century America. Against the interpretation offered by some, that Colonial and Revolutionary Era women knew little of business and public affairs, acting at best as 'deputy husbands' when their men-folk were absent or dead, should be set the mounting evidence that widows played a substantial economic role, that argues for their earlier apprenticeship during married life.[160]

From the perspective of a married male testator, and indeed of his dependents, the use of the will had definite advantages. If it were drawn up, as so many wills appear to have been, within days, even hours, of death, it could make provision in the light of current circumstances. From the widow's point of view, however, it offered a very different kind of protection from that of the marriage settlement. The marriage settlement was a negotiated agreement by the groom's relatives and the bride's relatives. Her kin had her interests at heart; they offered protection against her husband should that be necessary. The will did no such thing. It declared the intent of the testator – the provision he elected to make for his family was between him and God and, where appropriate, the common, customary or ecdesiastical law. Both French and English evidence indicates that the married male often placed his relationship with, and responsibility towards, the children of the marriage above that with his spouse. The conjugal relationship was then placed above his other kin relations.[161] This meant that any provision made for the widow in a will was made after provision had been made for the offspring and, indeed, was often made to secure the future of that offspring. Her potential destitution and her defenceless position took second place.[162] If she had protected herself by an antenuptial contract or a bond she might have to defend this in open court.[163]

We have already referred to the role of marriage in the successful transmission of property from one generation to another. The role of testation was also of extreme importance. Marriage contracts or settlements and last wills and testaments provide us with much of our information about marriage. While the context is important, it is necessary to avoid our view of marriage being distorted by these legal documents and provision for the next generation. After all, we in the twentieth century make considerable provision for our descendants and the law insists that widows and children have a claim upon the estate, and, quite often, such provision is made by a formal will characterised by lack of emotion, yet no historian would claim on this basis that coldness characterised twentieth-century family relations or that marriages were made in order to transmit property to children. This said, this last function of marriage was of great importance at many levels of society in France, Britain and North America in the early modern period. Robert Wheaton has described the extreme care that master craftsmen, merchants and parlementarians of seventeenth-century Bordeaux took to protect their children's future.[164] Each and every eventuality was anticipated in the marriage settlement drawn up between the Chevalier Bernard de Montferrand, Baron of Landiras, and the Demoiselle Marie Delphine de Pontac, who came from a family of eminent parlementarians. If there was male issue, one son would receive half of his father's property and 36,000 livres from his mother. If there were a daughter, but no sons, by this or any other marriage, then the daughter would receive half of her father's estate and her husband would bear her father's title. Provision was made for whichever spouse survived the other. If the wife survived the Baron, she was to receive, in addition, 2,000 livres a year from the estates, and rooms and furnishings in the Château of Landiras appropriate to her station as dowager.[165] Lorena Walsh describes how fathers in seventeenth-century Maryland, on occasion, sought to provide for the widow and keep the family together by carefully designed will strategies.

One wealthy planter left his sons considerable acreage on the frontier but ordered that they not leave their mother to settle it until they reached the age of twenty-five. Edward Bowles bequeathed his estate to his son, Edward, but stipulated that his mother be maintained in the family home 'with sufficient meat, drink and apparrell with one room to herself and a good bed and chest'. Robert Marston, sole heir to his father's land, was to have his two brothers live and work with him until they were eighteen, maintain his sister, Elizabeth, until she was sixteen and support another sister, Mary, for as long as she kept house for him.[166]

What else did widows share other than a certain vulnerability? Preoccupation with power relations and with the widow's legal vulnerability and, indeed, invisibility must not be allowed to obscure other issues. Just as the family may be said to have its own cycle, and marriage, so did early modern widowhood. And just as all families, even when they were nuclear families with 2.4 children, did not experience family life in the same way, neither was the experience of all widows identical. We would not dream of implying that simply being a child or a father could provide the basis for meaningful comparison, why should being a widow?

As our study of family relationships has shown, widows had once been wives or even other men's widows, and before that unmarried daughters, and they were often mothers of young children. They carried with them, into each of these new 'statuses', a baggage of relationships. As we have seen, when they became wives with households of their own they maintained relationships with their family of origin, with siblings and parents. The same happened when they entered widowhood. In addition, they carried relationships with in-laws and with their own children. How far were they still regarded by their kin, their late husband's kin and their children as authority figures? How far were they now simply treated as dependants? Studies of widows have not progressed sufficiently far for generalisation. However, it is possible to study some particular widows to highlight the importance of these issues.

The autobiography of William Stout (1665 to 1752) tells of his father's and mother's marriage in the England of Charles I and of their partnership in management of a yeoman's estate. They had acted to improve that estate specifically for the support of their sons. The father and mother were interdependent. She was a good manager, essential to the efficient running of the household. She kept the house, helped in the fields and prepared produce for market. He was a good farmer. She trained the girls; he trained the boys.

When Mr Stout died, his wife without hesitation decided to continue to run the farm for the benefit of her eldest son, Josias. In this she was not unusual. Among Stout's aunts were several widows who ran farms in order to support young families. On the surface, Elizabeth Stout appears as a strong, even formidable, mature woman – a veritable matriarch. If we probe a little further this impression is somewhat dented. Elizabeth acted on her own initiative in keeping the farm but she did not regard herself as sufficiently skilled in husbandry to organise the farm in more than a general supervisory capacity. This had never been her function and she had not been trained to fulfil it. Accordingly, she followed the advice of the overseers of her husband's will and appointed William Jenkinson as her farm manager. Her prime task was that of ensuring that her sons were educated to perform this managing function in later life. Josias and Leonard worked on the farm under Jenkinson until they reached the ages of 24 and 20 respectively. Her husband and she had purchased land to create an inheritance for Leonard, and during this first phase of her widowhood Elizabeth organised work on this land to provide a working farm for the youth. Elizabeth followed the wishes of her late husband in binding William apprentice to Henry Coward. Her actual day-to-day work differed little from that she had done as a wife, except that now her children were teenagers. She was now, however, the figure of authority in the household, the one who made the decisions.

This phase of widowhood represented Elizabeth Stout at her most powerful within the family. It ended when her son Josias came of age (which may have been at the age of 25). Elizabeth began to act as housekeeper for him. Hers was now a servicing role rather than that of head of the household. This truth was modified only by Josias's memory of her authority and his affection for her. Eventually Elizabeth became too old and infirm to do the job adequately. First of all he elected to lease the farm out and went to stay with his brother Leonard. This experiment collapsed and mother and son returned to the farm to run it with the aid of servants. When Elizabeth could go on no more she advised middle-aged Josias either to hire a servant or to marry a wife. He was accustomed to obeying his mother and went ahead and married a wife.

The third phase of Elizabeth's lengthy widowhood began when Josias brought his new wife into the farmhouse. Strong-willed Sybill was determined to be mistress in her own house; Elizabeth found it difficult to adjust. Even as Josias's housekeeper she had been used to being the one who gave commands. The arrangement lasted only a year. Desperate for peace, Josias asked his brother, William, to look after their mother.

Elizabeth spent the remainder of her days in the household of her unmarried son and daughter in Lancaster. After seven years, at the age of 84, she died.

It would, of course, be foolish to claim that Elizabeth Stout was a typical widow. For many widows the period of headship of the household might be absent (if her children were grown) or truncated. For others, there would be no acting as housekeeper for a bachelor son. A widow was not necessarily a mother and, even where she was, mothering might have been a thing of the past. None the less, Elizabeth's life does demonstrate that a widow's life was characterised by phases. Her period of relative power and authority might not only be ended by her own remarriage; it depended upon the ages and circumstances of her children and, of course, upon the relationship that she had established with them during marriage and was able to maintain afterwards. There are occasions in the life of Elizabeth Stout when one is tempted to ask: will the real head of household please stand up? For much of her widowhood Josias was the titular head of household and would have appeared as such in any listing, yet the experience was very different. On the other hand, at times Elizabeth's power and authority as a widow, even during the early phase, was hedged by her husband's express wishes, by the strategy which she and he had evolved as partners, by his legal pre-arrangements, by the advice of the overseers and by the temporary nature of her position as head of household.[167]

What is known of widows elsewhere suggests the importance of this approach. Widows led highly diverse lives, as one might expect, because they belonged to diverse socio-economic groups. There can be no blanket assertion that widowhood offered opportunities for independence, self-sufficiency and social freedom.[168] Thus only 56 per cent of the widows of London aldermen in the second half of the sixteenth century remarried, and a third of the widows were economically active in widowhood; whereas the widows of poor craftsmen, labourers and porters appeared as supplicants for charity or as spinners, weavers and servants. Widows became dependent upon unrelated friends and neighbours.[169] Even when such opportunities were a reality, they might rapidly disappear if a widow elected to remarry. There is some evidence to suggest that it was need which pushed widows into remarriage and that some would resist it for as long as possible.[170]

Higher levels of mortality, in both metropolis and provincial towns, than in villages may have led to differing widowhood and family experiences in urban and rural communities. Widowhood in villages may have come in the twilight years of a marriage. In London more than half of all marriages lasted ten years or less, paralleling the disruption rates of some American colonies.[171] As widows and widowers over the age of 50 rarely remarried (17 per cent of all London widows fell into this age bracket but probably far more widows overall), the age of the spouses (and their children) at which a marriage was disrupted by death was clearly of great significance for the future experience of that family.

The image of the powerful and independent urban widow has been severely dented. The widows of London craftsmen and tradesmen were inclined to remarry because it was difficult otherwise to continue their business and obtain a livelihood. Thus, in Lyons, where it was relatively easy for a woman to continue her husband's craft or trade, 25 per cent of widows remarried, while in London 35 per cent did so. Moreover, the median interval before this remarriage was only 9 months. Of 70 London widows who inherited print shops between 1553 and 1640, 50 disposed of them either immediately or within four years. Only about 5 per cent of widows seem to have exercised their right to take on apprentices.[172] The economic and legal conditions hedging widowhood could have a profound effect upon the way in which individual widows and their dependants experienced it.[173]

The Dissolution of the Nuclear Family: The Widower

The position of the widower has been rather neglected. If what has been said above about the concern of the woman's kin to protect her is true, then the concern of the male to protect his descendants is even more demonstrable. The law made it easier for him to do so: he had the use of his wife's lands and other property during his life, provided that they had had direct heirs. She was not permitted to will away any land or property that she had brought to the marriage or acquired during it. But it is worth remembering that there were constraints upon the behaviour of a widower as well as upon that of a widow. As late as the 1880s, an innkeeper who married a new wife less than a year after the death of his first received 'rough music' at midnight. A certain loyalty to the dead spouse was expected.[174] Nevertheless, widowers were more liable to remarry and to remarry quickly than were widows. In England the exception to this rule appears to have been in London, where widows of all but the most well-to-do men rapidly remarried.[175] In France, rates of female remarriage were but half that of men in their 30s and 40s. Only young widows (in their 20s) remarried as frequently as males. Why? In the old adage, 'To thrive, thou must wive' may lie part of the answer. For a man to run a successful household, especially one containing minor children, would be considered difficult if not unthinkable, whereas a woman could run a household efficiently with the help of servants. A widower with young children wanted a wife who would manage the household and care for him and his offspring. He did not want a mature or elderly woman with children of her own. James Fretwell's grandfather had taken his three daughters' interests into consideration when contemplating remarriage. He tested the attitude of two suitors towards these children. How much more important was it to tread warily where a widow with children was concerned. It was Catherine Girardin of Villenoy's children by a former marriage that had caused her formal separation from Jean Plicque in 1694; when they began to live together again they agreed to put out these step-children to service.[176] Several seventeenth-century autobiographers left their homes when their fathers married widows with children – Arise Evans, Ralph Josselin, Josiah Langdale, Lodowick Muggleton. Sometimes this may have been an arranged removal to lessen friction between children and step-parents but, even if so, presumably few fathers wished to have to go to such lengths to achieve domestic peace.[177] Widowers, then, did not, as a rule, select their partners from among the pool of available widows. There is a little evidence to indicate that widowers were keener to remarry when they had young children, although it is open to alternative interpretations. Where the children were teenagers and able to assist in running the household, the need for a new wife was less acutely felt. But the presence of someone else's teenage children in a home would surely have deterred all but the most ardent or desperate suitor! A study of remarried people in the seventeenth and eighteenth centuries revealed that 48 per cent of widowers remarrying had done so within a year of bereavement, whereas 37 per cent of the women marrying were in this position. The length of widowhood, for both men and women, increased with the age and number of their children.[178]

When the household was disrupted and then re-formed on a second marriage there were potential problems for all concerned, not least the children of the first marriage. In both England and France the maternal grandparents seem to have been especially concerned to protect the children of a marriage when it was their daughter who had died. Thomas Dondaine, maternal grandfather of the five daughters of Marie, first wife of Edmé Retif, threw up his hands in horror on their behalf when Edmé came to him with news of a proposed second marriage. He acted promptly to make an inventory of the joint property of his daughter and son-in-law in favour of the five girls. The second marriage took place and the four older step-daughters were eventually expelled from the house. They were almost grown up, and so used to independence that they resented their step-mother's attempts to exercise authority over them. None the less, their father did not take their part, neither did their father's sister, who was introduced as an impartial arbiter. It was their mother's father who assisted those of them who were not yet old enough to marry or make their own way nor young enough to adapt to their step-mother.

> It is the older girls who cause all the trouble. ... I have been asked to give the eldest in marriage, the match is advantageous, but I hesitated; yet I will marry her off. The second girl wants to go to the town to serve an apprenticeship; she shall go. My father-in-law Dondaine has asked for the third one; I will give her to him. He already has the fourth, therefore I shall keep here only the youngest, who is of an amiable character and, besides, is only a child. ...These are all natural arrangements.[179]

The position of uncles, especially the mother's brothers, was important in such cases also. For example, Ralph Josselin disciplined his sister's children when their father died. Thomas Raymond, when his father died in 1622, was cared for by his maternal uncle, William Boswell. Thomas was his heir. First Thomas attended boarding school with his younger brother. Then, aged 15, he was 'consigned to a lawyer to better my writing and learne the places and manner of the citty'. Finally, at the age of 20 he joined his uncle's household. This is not to say, however, that the care of an uncle would necessarily compare either physically or emotionally with that of a father. Raymond reported that his lot was then one of 'long waiting and short meales'.[180] Maternal uncles had traditionally been very important in medieval life, often assuming the wardship of their nephews and nieces.[181] When a wife died, it seems that her family obligations died with her. In 1679, Michel Messager had been selected as guardian for the Regnier children but he protested that he was only their half-uncle through his wife, 'who having just died, he was no longer anything to them'.[182]

In sixteenth-century England, 30 per cent of marriages involved widowed persons; in the mid-nineteenth century, this had reduced to 10 per cent. In northern France in the early eighteenth century, 30 per cent of marriages still involved widows or widowers. This statistic alone points to the contribution widowhood made towards complex family forms in the early modern period.

Family Strategies

How was the family provided for on the dissolution of the household? Were there developed strategies? In order to throw some light on this issue, 100 of the clergy wills for the period 1560 to 1700 were examined in some detail. The clergy concerned came from the professional class but varied greatly in their wealth and social origin, from the gentleman farmer to the husbandman. In 17 cases the marital status of the cleric was unstated; 62 recorded that they left behind them wives. In all cases specific provision was made for this wife. Of the testators, 9 were widowers and 3 of these left minor children; 3 had married widows and had step-children; 2 had had two wives; 12 had never married. Only 15 of these wills mentioned living grandchildren; 6 left children who were minors, which is suggestive both of the relatively advanced age of most of these clerical will-makers and also of the stable and secure family lives which their children had enjoyed.

Of course the will was used as an adjunct of the common-law provision for wives and children and direct descendants. Where the property descended under common-law rules to the heir, there was no necessity for the testator to mention this property or compulsion to make additional provision for that heir. Where there had been no marriage settlement containing a jointure, the widow would be entitled to a third of her husband's freehold lands during her life. Where there had been a jointure, there may not always have been a necessity to include mention of it in the will. Property and goods that had been devised to other relatives before the death of the owner were also not entered in a will. It has been established, however, that will-makers were generally anxious to make good provision for their families, through the last will and testament, as part of making a 'good end'. Certainly these clerical wills permit us to comment on the type of provision for wives and children and to observe the range of kin that received some notice. Their usefulness is limited, however, by the partial information that they contain concerning provision strategies. The absence of the mention of the eldest sons in most of these wills is indicative of the fact that the common law and custom had already devised a strategy for their future. The testator was left to work out a plan for the remainder of his family. This plan was often a flexible one, which might change with changing circumstances. 'Brother' wrote John Hill, Rector of Elford, 'I may have often occation to alter the porcons of money given to my sisters children'.[183]

These clergy were concerned for the future of their wives. While some historians have suggested that there was a general change in such provision between the sixteenth and seventeenth centuries, there seems little evidence of this here. Many bequests were conditional. In 1646, one cleric left his wife his whole estate for her life but it was not hers to dispose of. On her death it would go to their daughters. As late as 1681 a clergyman left his wife some leased tenements and lands in Worcestershire that on her death would revert to their son and his two daughters. This may have been less irksome to a widow than the stipulation, when there were no heirs of the body, for the estate to revert to a sister or a brother or a cousin and their descendants, as happened in two cases, one in the sixteenth and one in the late seventeenth century. Another clergyman, who died in 1689/90, had purchased land specifically to support his wife, but in the event of her death it was to pass to his three sisters and then to the children of one of them.[184] These widows had the use of the property and the houses built on it – no inconsiderable advantage – but they were not 'propertied' women who would bring divisible estate to a second marriage. There were exceptions. Jane Broxholme was to be able to dispose of her bequests on her own death. The wife of one well-connected late-seventeenth-century cleric, 'acknowledging all too little to recompence the portion she brought mee in marriage and the love and care she hath expres'd towards mee ever since', was to be able to dispose of half of the estate on her death 'at her will'.[185] When Nicholas Hallam of Shirland died, in 1625, he willed his land in Nottinghamshire to the use of Jane his wife, specifying that on her death she could dispose of it at will, despite the existence of an unmarried daughter.[186] But in a number of wills a further marriage was deemed to have the same effect as death. Thus, in 1597, a wife was to have the use of the estate but if she married again her seven minor children were to have their portions out. In 1690 we read that a clergymen gave his purchased land to his wife, with the condition that if she married it would revert to his sister.[187] In 1634, a clergyman ordered his two sons to pay their mother £12 per annum for her natural life, in addition to 'all the linen in the house which she brought as her dowry and the chest they are stored in'.[188] In 1647, a wife was bequeathed a third of the estate and some rents. The testator advised her in the will to allow her brother to farm the land and pay her rent of £5 per annum, but he left this to her discretion.[189] There is some suggestion in the wills that at least some of the clergy were using the 'thirds of the estate' as a rough rule of thumb for deciding their bequests to wives and children, but sometimes it was a half share.[190] In 1581, another cleric willed 'that my master Sir John Zouche shall have the governinge of my wife Katheren Asheton my last wyfe & rule her for my lyvynge accordynge to his good wyll and pleasure trustinge also in his worshipe that he wylbe good unto her' – a bequest somewhat difficult to interpret but interesting as a comment on the expectation that there would be more than one conjugal relationship in a life-time and on the equation of a wife with a piece of property to be bestowed at will.[191] One clergyman, who died in 1629, was not so much worried by the prospect of his widow's remarriage as of her dishonesty. He had married a widow with a son. He returned to her all the household stuff that was her former husband's, £6 13s 4d in money, his two best pigs and some stock. This was only to be given her if she dealt well with the executors – presumably by not demanding restoration of the £100 she had brought to the marriage, 'for whereas I had with my sayd wife in marriage above an hundred pounds I have disbursed it all & more for the building of her house & the use of her sonne Thomas'.[192]

Sometimes the testator was not free to dispose of the estate as he willed. In one case it was stated that the land was to be divided between the wife and the testator's brother 'according to thintent and meaninge of Edward Kinaston my late father his last wyll and Testament'.[193]

The wills indicate that the clergy regarded it as the duty of a husband to provide for his wife as long as she remained his wife and not that of another. As a widow she remained responsible for the education and support of their mutual offspring. Wives were commonly chosen as executors (either alone or with others) and as responsible for the minor children. For some, this responsibility was considerable. George Dunne, Vicar of Sheriffhales, for example, left his wife with four sons and five daughters, all apparently minors, and a large number of tithe debts to collect to pay their bequests.[194] The wills display the concern of the clergy to provide for their entire family. In at least 18 of the 62 wills of married clergy, the testator appears to use purchased land and/or houses accumulated specifically to make provision for his wife and children on his demise.[195] On occasion, their intention to protect the children against the possibly disadvantageous consequences of their mother forming a new household with a second marriage is clear. Daughters as well as sons were bequeathed land, money and goods, including seed corn and animals. Minor children and unmarried children had first call upon the estate. One cleric had purchased land for the use of his wife and then of his younger son. The elder son presumably came into inherited land and his 'grandfather's chair'. Jeremy Morrell, whose education had been 'a great charge unto mee', was given but 12d and his two brothers and four sisters 5s apiece.[196] But there were unconventional methods of disposing of the estate. One clergyman, in 1649, gave his sons and daughters cash but divided the land equally between his grandchildren and appointed a grandson executor. And there are many reminders that not only land and tenements were of importance to descendants. One clergy wife retained their feather bed, hemp sheets and a winding sheet; on her death (after use of the sheet) these were to be given to her son, Thomas. Books went to clerical sons and occasionally to wives. Personal clothing was given to both children and servants.[197] Tithe ewes, lambs and calves were typical bequests to grandchildren.[198] Where there were no sons, daughters would inherit. Married daughters frequently received silver or rings, cash or items of stock. Unmarried daughters, marriage portions varying from a pittance to a plum. One clergyman managed to provide two daughters with £150 apiece and a further daughter £200. Another could muster only £10. One younger son had a dower house that had cost over £200 to build and a further £240 in dower, and a daughter had a dowry of £200 when she married a London grocer.

On occasion, there was an attempt to exercise authority over children through the widow and others. Thus Alice was to have 20 marks 'provided that see be ruled hir mother, hir brother Henre Latimer and her uncle Frauncis'.[199] Elizabeth Orgell was to receive household stuff 'and if she will be dutifull and obedient to her mother in deportment & carriage, then I doubt not but that her mother will augment her portion accordingly'.[200] Ann Hallam's portion of £120 was to be reduced to £20 if she married against her mother's wishes.[201] William Orton, Rector of Sheldon, Warwickshire was determined that his four minor sons should be trained up for the church, and spelt out in great detail a financial plan for their support during a university course.[202] Thomas Buther, Rector of Arley, made equally precise plans for the apprenticeship of his grandchildren.[203] This type of provision can be seen as evidence of male testators restricting the freedom not only of their children but of their widows; but, equally, it demonstrates the careful forethought which these husbands and fathers exercised and their anxiety to make matters as simple as possible for the surviving spouse. Edward Bennet, Rector of Kirk Ireton, wanted his children to be educated and apprenticed but he modified his plan with the words 'if her power & abilities will serve', not a comment on his widow's intelligence but on her financial circumstances.[204]

More unusual was the determination of a testator whose child was as yet unborn to name the baby Jolyan – if his wish were obeyed the child would receive £20, otherwise the sum would be divided equally between the other two sons![205]

Clergymen also mentioned kin who did not live with them but were accounted part of the family. In almost all cases these were either the testator's own kin (children, brothers, sisters, aunts, uncles, nieces, nephews and their spouses) or the descendants of the children of the couple (granddaughters and grandsons and their spouses).[206] Robert Freeman of Ashley had contracted to keep his daughter and son-in-law for three years and he made provision in his will to fulfil this 'bargaine'.[207] Occasionally those mentioned seem to be quite distant kin: for instance, the nephews of one clergyman were bound to provide a kinswoman and former servant with a home.[208] Another cleric, unmarried, used his estate to provide a marriage portion for a kinswoman, and another made bequests to a servant who was also a kinswoman. Other unmarried testators left their estates to sisters or brothers, nephews and nieces and, in one case, grandchildren. There was a concern to be specific about the inheritance route where there was no heir of the body. For example, a testator split his estate into two, bequeathing half to his wife and half to his brother. The grandson of a second brother was to inherit the house when they both died. Some of the testators made provision for every eventuality: Jane, the wife, was to receive a tenement; should she die, his niece, Martha, was to enter into the tenement and, after 12 months' possession, pay £100 out of it to another niece; if, however, Jane remarried, all the premises, apart from Jane's jointure in them, would go to two trustees, who would put the two nieces into the lease. Another willed his farm and the house to a nephew and sheep to his sisters, sister-in-law (using modern terminology), nephews and nieces. But some did not think beyond the moment. One gave his 'nagg' to his brother, a ring to his sister and the residue of the estate to his mother.[209] Perhaps anticipating trouble, one cleric willed that his sister should have £200 out of the estate or £400 if payment was delayed beyond three months. This same sister's four children were to have £100 apiece. The man's horse and his clothes were bequeathed to his sister's husband and his library to his nephew. Each servant was to have a year's wages. The wife was left with the residue, although some part of this would go to his sister if his widow remarried.[210]

Does this mean that the clergy were so obsessed with property at the expense of family that they were willing to bequeathe this property to distant and unimportant kin just to keep it 'in the family'? I think not. The evidence suggests that the clergy were preoccupied with the needs of their family members. First call upon the land and goods they had acquired belonged to their immediate dependants – wife and children, especially minors. If the wife died, the said property was to be used to provide for their children according to their need and, failing children, for the testator's close kin – brothers and sisters and their offspring and, very unusually, parents. The same applied if the wife married – for she would now become part of a new household and could not alienate or jeopardise provision for the offspring of the first marriage or the kin. The family therefore was not restricted to the simple family household or even to offspring who had married and left that household, but included other kin, especially siblings. Although some unmarried clergy did leave small bequests to non-relatives, especially servants who were members of the household, such bequests were rarely significant and rarely acted to exclude relatives. There is some evidence that the clergy deliberately accumulated property to provide for their widows and younger children in order to give each a livelihood and not over-partition the original inheritance.

The clergy concerned were not only concerned to provide for relatives. Yet family often formed the bedrock of both social and work relations. This might involve both the nuclear family and the wider network of kin. It is well known, for example, that clerical sons frequently followed their fathers into the Church in this period. In some dioceses as many as 25 per cent of serving clergy were the sons of clergy. The web of clerical connection, however, was extremely complex, to be traced through binding together much more distant relationships – of cousin, uncle, brother-in-law, grandson and godparent – as well as those of direct descent. Immanuel Bourne, Rector of Ashover in Derbyshire, served in the diocese of Coventry and Lichfield in the 1630s with two brothers, Elisha and Nathaniel. Their father, Henry, was a Northamptonshire clergyman. Immanuel's sons and grandsons also took orders. Philip Ward was the brother-in-law of two Derbyshire clergymen. The chain then spread to Loughborough. This, of course, is interesting but it becomes more so when we realise that these relationships were maintained and strengthened through both work and social contact. These men met together in professional meetings, lent books to one another, attended college together, introduced their sisters, daughters and cousins to one another, gave patronage to one another. The daughters and sisters of the clergy met few people of equivalent social and educational standing. The daughter of the Vicar of Chebsey was apparently expected by her father to marry his successor: 'My will is that my daughter Mary shoulde be maried to the vicaridge of Chesbsey ... att the oversight of my executors ... and if it happen that my daughter Mary be not maried unto it, that then my will be that she shall receive £60 per annum after my decease'.[211] The wills are full of bequests to local clergymen, whether or not they were kin. While this is not the place to discuss the linking of 'kith and kin', we should observe it and note that, when a testator drew up his or her will, kith formed part of the obligation acknowledged.

Wills, then, do provide some evidence of family strategy although this evidence is partial and difficult to read. Of course, one should not conclude that all social and occupational group-ings, even in England, behaved as the clergy did, although a sample of other wills from the same region produced broadly simi-lar findings which support the suggestion that people used wills to partition their estates to care for *all* family members and modify the effects of primogeniture.[212] As Michael Massey, Rector of Berrington, directed his executor in 1618, he was to administer 'to the benefit of his children' and 'that more special regard by him be taken of the weaker sorte of my sayd children for that some of them (god be thanked) are well enabled with strength and compe-tent giftes to get theyr own liveinges and to be an ayd and stay to theyr weaker brethren'.[213] A detailed examination of clerical wills does demonstrate that the inheritance plan relating to one cat-egory of family member (for example, the widow) should be viewed in the context of total family strategy. The will-makers seem to have tried to use their resources intelligently to supply the antici-pated requirements of all their dependants and friends. A capital sum might be destined to form a daughter's dowry, but be put out to loan during her minority to yield interest to support a son's education. A library might be bequeathed to a son or nephew if he 'become a University schollar & attaine to ye degree of Batchelor of Arts', but if he does not he will not need it and his widow shall dispose of the library as she thinks fit.[214] If a widow remained solitary she would need financial support and a home; if she remarried she would no longer need this but their children would need even more protection. Historians should not be led to regard such provisions as penal, they were merely prudent. As the comments of one husbandman, in 1581, concerning the 'ditts wychid doo woo'[215] indicate, family planning was always circumscribed.

Kinship and the Simple/Complex Nuclear Family

There is evidence from all these societies, and from across the social hierarchy, that 'family connections' were stressed and cultivated. Perhaps it was easier to build up an extensive kinship network and draw a handsome family tree if one were a Montmorency or a Howard, a Bagot or a de Montferrand, than if one were a master baker or humble farmer, but kinship connection still mattered. So we see the 'dynastic' family looming large in Nottinghamshire wills both as beneficiaries and as executors, supervisors and bondsmen.[216] So we see the historian of Myddle taking great care to note the kinship connections of its inhabitants because these bound the village society together.[217] So we see the peasant family of Edmé Rétif maintaining connections with distant cousins. Nicolas Rétif, as an infant, was shown to the first cousin of his grandfather, Pierre. As a ten-year-old, Nicolas met his 'two Gautherin girl cousins', who were the daughters of a sister of his father's mother. 'Marie, the fair eldest girl, was to be married; she came to tell her uncle of this'.[218] So we find, in the common parlance of the time, that peasants, merchants, professional and aristocrats used the epithets of relationship as they addressed one another – 'good day, cousin', 'cousin Jean', 'sister Joan', 'father-in-law Dondaine', 'brother Bagot'. So we see the grocer, William Stout, recording the complicated tree of his familial relationships. So we see gentleman Walter Bagot, very tactfully intervening in the dispute between his sister and brother-in-law Kinnersley on the one hand and Father Kinnersley on the other. His interest was in serving his kin, yes, but also in serving the wider interests of the family of Bagot by preserving good relations with both sides. In some parts of France the interests of all parties were best served by bringing within the household more than one nuclear family. For example, the marriage contract of Bernard de Faux, peasant, and Marie Drouilhard, widow, set up in the late 1640s a household in which all was held in common, consisting not only of Bernard and Marie but also of the bride's two children by her former husband, the groom's widowed father, the groom's brother and his wife and their children.[219] But family outside the household was cultivated and esteemed in both England and France. For example, when John Jemmat was offered a living at Melbourne by Sir John Coke in 1640, he declined because 'it will be no wisdoeom for me to remove from the sight of my kinred & ancient acquaintance to setle amongst them that are strangers unto me, where the meanes of mayntenance are in themselves incompetent and the accessions only arbitrary, so that when my charge is certaine my meanes shalbe uncertaine'. He considered it particularly foolish to move his wife and children north during winter weather 'where we have our acquaintance yet for to make'.[220]

In France, England and the American South this emphasis on the kin group clearly enabled families to continue to function when key members died.[221] Reminding people of a kin relationship was a reminder of a mutual obligation. Searching out one's kin was perhaps all the more important in an age when hybrid complex families were so common. Cousin marriage was very frequent among southern planters in the period down to 1815, binding disrupted families close together. In Salem, Massachusetts, 42 per cent of merchants were in business with relatives.[222] The need for such links was evident in France. In Bordeaux, 23 per cent of first-time brides recorded in the marriage contracts of 1640–47 had both parents still living; 42 per cent had only one parent and 35 per cent had lost both parents; 58 per cent of apprentices (aged between 15 and 18) had lost their fathers and 38 per cent were orphans. More than a third of marriages resulted in no living issue.[223]

When a parent died it was not enough that he or she had left a will or that property remained to be distributed. Kith and kin surrounded the bedside of the English when they died, to hear their will for the surviving family.[224] The probate of wills was a family affair. Arrangements had to be made for the care of any minor descendants and for the carrying out of the provisions of the will and of the law. In a study of the area around Meaux it has been shown that a guardian (commonly the surviving parent) and an administrator were appointed by a family council of relatives and neighbours, normally four on the maternal side and four on the paternal, all usually male. The appointment of a guardian was vital if the parent remarried. In England, the executor of a will, its over-seers and the guardians of any minors were normally specified within the will and testament itself; in cases of intestacy they would be appointed by the court, presumably from amongst self-presented relatives and friends.[225] Once again the surviving parent was commonly the guardian and far from infrequently the execu-tor. When a widow remarried the guardianship would transfer automatically to the step-father; in a conscious attempt to balance interests an administrator was selected from among the deceased parent's relatives. Not all relatives welcomed the prospect of caring for young relatives, with all that implied in terms of expense, trouble and possible inter-generational and family con-flict. It is interesting to see how the provision of care for orphans was debated within a wider context of the needs of other nuclear family households within the kin group. In 1698 the five Philippes children of Barcy were left orphaned. First of all their great-uncle, aged 69, excused himself from their guardianship, then their uncle, then another great-uncle – aged 60 but with five minor children and a pregnant wife of his own, then another great-uncle, who claimed he was only their uncle by marriage. Finally a cousin drew the short straw, the relatives rejecting his excuse that he had four young children and was illiterate, with the words that this was 'of no consideration in view of the poverty of the minor children, whose incomes were inadequate for their food and upkeep'. Actual care of the children, especially the younger ones, was not infrequently given to the person, not necessarily a relative, who would agree to care for them with very little financial support in return for minimal interference from the relatives.[226]

Conclusion: the Importance of the Lineage Principle

The evidence we have surveyed indicates the continued import-ance of the lineage principle in both England and France and probably in America too. This principle certainly pertained to property but it also governed family feeling, responsibility and relationships in a way that historians have not recognised. This is because we tend to see property and its accumulation, consolidation, preservation and transmission as the guiding force in these societies rather than as the means by which contemporaries provided for their families. For some, property may have become an end in itself, sacrosanct, inalienable, at whose altar the lives and happinesses of individual relatives could be sacrificed without compunction. But the evidence suggests that these were exceptional cases indeed. And while marriage occasioned a tension between the lineage principle and the immediacy and reality of the simple family, in practice this was resolved through reciprocity, rather than battle, and the shared interest of husband and wife in the children of the marriage. What we have discovered about the incidence of disrupted marriages in all three societies, however, indicates that the simple nuclear family was, in a large minority of cases, really the complex nuclear family. Complexity was not only the result of custom. So in France, for example, we might be looking at a figure of 25 per cent of hybrid complex families even in an area where multinuclear families were far from the norm.[227] Once again, the lineage principle became an issue as spouses and children looked to their wider kin for support.

4   The Descriptive Family – 2: Co-Resident Relations

The Precarious Family Household

The characterisation of the simple family household as a source of security, identity and stability not found elsewhere in the early modern world now seems far less certain. The nuclear family was precarious and such families were frequently being disrupted by death, desertion and discontent. Against the idyll of the lengthy marriage and stable family that may, in the seventeenth century, have been prevalent in rural areas of England and France and even in some of the American colonies, must be set a picture of the brief unions, frequent and rapid remarriage, and mixed families that characterised some urban areas, especially London and Manchester, and certain of the colonies, and were not infrequent elsewhere.[1] The imminence of untimely death was keenly felt by the young throughout past centuries, its occurrence not taken for granted. A mother in Burwash, Sussex, reported to her rector in 1870 'that she had overheard her little children talking in bed, & saying what shd they do if mother went, who would bake the bread for them, father cldn't …'[2] For a young lad in Stoke-on-Trent in the early 1900s, childhood memories were of the small sister upon whose dead form he gazed, the straw thrown on the cobbles outside the door to muffle the sound of the horses and carts during his mother's final illness, and the sight of his bereft father unable to sit down for dinner with the family without crying, for a long while after his wife's passing.[3] Even when lengthening life expectancy among those who survived the first years of childhood theoretically made a stable and extended family experience probable, the ever present problem of putting bread on the table pulled in the opposite direction. In other words, there were tremendous economic pressures upon the extended existence of the simple family as a co-residential unit, that could rarely be resisted despite close 'family' ties, so that, even where death did not divide them, families could not stay together.

Whereas the demographer may be content with establishing the total size of a household, because it provides the key to determining overall population size and structure, the historian is concerned to establish the experience of living in that household. Clearly, relationships within a large minority of households between the sixteenth and nineteenth centuries were not uncomplicated. The 'simple family' became complex when step-parents and step-children and their baggage of kin and connection were introduced into the picture – this was true whether the household remained small or became large through such change. Whether the early modern family cocooned its members from the world outside, by providing for their emotional and physical needs and protecting them, depended to a great extent upon its ability to absorb changes brought about by death, remarriage or widowhood, and the mixing of step-children. Added to this must be the extent to which other relationships were allowed to intrude upon the co-residential biological unit. These might be internal relations, such as those with servants or co-residing kin, or they might be external relations with kin and friends and community. Disruption of the nuclear family had potential implications for the control of children and of their behaviour by parents, implications which may have undermined, in practice, the importance of the ideal of patriarchy.

In the light of these observations, it seems that the preoccupation of scholars with the patriarchal or even the matriarchal relations of the household must be related to a picture of rather more domestic complexity than has usually been allowed for. In this chapter several tasks will be attempted simultaneously. The first will be to describe the 'household system' of social organisation. The second will be to indicate relationships within this system, for example, between husband and wife, between parent and child, between siblings, step-children. The third will be to evoke the complexity introduced into such relations by relationships with step-children and step-parents, servants, in-laws and community. We must not lose sight of the problem of distinguishing between the household and the family and determining the roles and relationships within each. Our increasing awareness of the complexity of family and household relations in England and France may well have the effect of modifying the contrast that some historians have observed between the Old and the New Worlds.[4] It may also lead us to question the usefulness of the socio-economic concept – the household – as a prism through which to view the family.

The Formation of Households

In the preceding chapter we have seen how the 'line' provided lasting support for large numbers of people of all social groups, especially women and orphaned minors, whom the nuclear family failed. Such failure was most apparent at the moment of the household's dissolution, but could threaten at any time. None the less, the experience of living in a nuclear family household (although not always one headed by one's own natural father or mother) was common to most people in England and the American colonies and to large numbers of people in France for at least a part of their lives, and relationships within such a household demand our attention. Once again, the aim here is to examine actual contemporary relationships rather than to include prescriptive material.

The problem facing the historian of the early modern, or indeed the modern period, is often perceived as one of typicality. Either one describes individual households, which may be regarded as idiosyncratic in the extreme, or one settles for a composite picture of 'the early modern family' or household. In, for example, Pierre Goubert's excellent *The French Peasantry in the Seventeenth Century*, one meets no actual peasant families/households or individual family members, only 'the humble day-labourer', 'ordinary peasants', 'well-off peasants and farmers', 'mothers', 'women' and 'boys and girls'. Such composite pictures of the people of the past and their domestic relations are indeed tempting but we should beware of them. The statisticians have revealed the dangers of the meaningless mean and the mysterious median, but the average man, woman, peasant, noble is no less dangerous a concept. If we elect to describe past social organisation in terms of a statistical framework heavily dependent upon the mean, then we should be careful to temper this description with the departures which actual families and households made from this mean. While every historian wants to be able to offer an accurate description of the 'typical' family, he or she should not be discomforted when this proves elusive or even illusory. Analysis of statistical data relating to some 700 households of working people in East Smithfield in the 1890s, when it was coupled with a very detailed knowledge of the households themselves, revealed that few, if any, of the people or households involved precisely matched the 'average' household in every respect.[5] We should be comforted that examples of contemporary relationships are extremely valuable and not 'anecdotal'. Charles Booth, the nineteenth-century social investigator, was wise when he observed that statistics are required to lend proportion to the detailed personal observation of the way life was lived. The historian of the family, also, should strive to achieve this balance.

In England, throughout the early modern period, and amongst all social classes except the aristocracy, a new household was established as a consequence of first marriage, although not always immediately. When Anne Fitton (aged 12), daughter of a knight, married John Newdegate (aged 16) in 1587 the young couple, a maid and two serving men lived with her father and mother for the first nine years of their married life 'of free will and without haveing paye allowed'. For part of this time John was away from home receiving an education. Only in 1596 did they leave her home to set up an independent household.[6] Even among the aristocracy there were many who set up new households when they married, or wished that they had. In 1606, when a marriage between Lewis Bagot, Walter's heir, and the daughter of Edward Beresford was mooted, her father wanted them to live alone.[7] Lettice Kinnersley fought hard, if ultimately unsuccessfully, to keep her household separate from that of her husband's parents. When young people were able to marry was in part a feature of demography and in part a feature of the wealth of their natural family, because to be able to set up a household one had to have access to adequate material resources. Demographers have posited mean ages at marriage of 26 for women and between 27 and 29 for men throughout the second half of the sixteenth and the whole of the seventeenth centuries. There was a great deviation from this mean, however. In aristocratic households, where co-resident extended families were more common and where, in any event, there were material resources available for additional houses, the age at marriage was more likely to be younger. Quite often, however, marriage in such households was not coincident with setting up a new household. Remember that Walter Bagot 'married' his wife's ward, Humphrey Okeover, to his young daughter, but this marriage was never consummated and no household was ever set up. This differential between aristocratic and other families was also presumably greater in the years 1540 to 1599 than in the Stuart period: 21 per cent of peers and their heirs had married before they were 17 in the earlier period; 12 per cent between 1600 and 1659.[8] Child marriages may also have survived into the late sixteenth century in some relatively isolated communities in the North West (Lancashire and Cheshire, for example) and South West, but cannot be said to have predominated.[9]

In many respects the situation was comparable in France. Marriage was associated with *ménage*, and the ability to gather together 'a cradle to rock, a pot of gruel, wheat flour in a box, white salt in a jar' was the test in lower Brittany just as in England. The average age at first marriage seems to have increased from a low of 25 for men and 21 for women in the late fifteenth century. In some areas of France, in the seventeenth century, the average age of women at first marriage was as high as 27, and in the eighteenth century often plateaued at 28. This has been attributed to the overall population growth, which produced downward pressure on wages and encouraged later marriage. We should also take into account the fact that many people remained single. It was common in the South of France, for example, for younger sons either to live all their lives as bachelors or to marry very late. And women could only marry if they managed to gather together an appropriate dowry.[10] Yet, as we have noted, it is far from clear that the simple nuclear household was the norm throughout France, and there were some notable exceptions to the rule of household formation on marriage, particularly in the South.

In a rural community young people were heavily dependent upon their parents for the wherewithall to marry. This was much less so for those who left their parental home early, to seek their fortunes independently, or for those who dwelt in the towns and cities. In the seventeenth century girls in London often married early, partly perhaps because there was a high male to female sex ratio in the capital. There were, however, very deliberate attempts to curtail this tendency to early and financially unstable marriage. In 1563 the age of termination of apprenticeships was statutorily fixed at 24 in all corporate towns and cities, thus confirming the slightly earlier effort, in London, to halt 'ouer hastie maryages and over some settyng upp of householdes of and by the youthe'.[11] In France, we are led to believe, financial impediments to early marriage were generally respected until the eighteenth century. There were, in the villages, large numbers of single people. By the eighteenth century, however, it seems that more people entered marriage without the necessary material support, and the number of legitimate children being abandoned increased as a consequence.[12]

Remarriage and the Household

Large numbers of marriages, however, were not first marriages. Perhaps 30 per cent of marriages in early eighteenth-century northern France were second weddings for one or both partners. The figure was as high in sixteenth-century England but declined thereafter. Such marriages did not, in normal circumstances, create new households. Instead they formed, very quickly after the disruption of one household by death, hybrid complex families occupying, in many circumstances, the existing house of one or other of the spouses. Relatively rarely did widower and young children share a household and their grief for very long. Widows and young children were more common, but even widows remarried frequently and often quickly after bereavement. Nicholas Lhoste and Nicolas Le Riche drowned in the Marne in 1720: both their widows were remarried within six months.[13]

When testators made provision for their widows in the house that was now to be occupied by a son or daughter and spouse, it was customary both in England and the colonies to make very clear that this widow's apartment was to be a separate enclave and not part of this household. This worked to both parties' advantage. The new master and mistress were not subject to the interference of the erstwhile mistress; the widow was not subject to the authority of the child, who now headed a household. A woman wants at all times to be mistress in her own household, went the French saying of the sixteenth century. In the Stout example, we have seen just how awkward and intolerable it could become for a widow who was used to authority, when a competing daughter-in-law entered 'her' former domain. Indeed, the situation could not be maintained.

The House

It should be observed that the new household in England and France frequently occupied an existing house. This may seem an obvious point to make about a society where fathers and mothers passed down all their property, including houses, to their children. Even in the Americas, once a group had established a settlement they were loth to move and passed down their property from generation to generation. The population of Andover and Dedham in New England, for instance, as of the Chesapeake settlements in the south, was remarkably static in the seventeenth century. The result for a community was fascinating, for family lines oft failed. Think for a minute of Myddle in seventeenth-century Shropshire. Richard Gough's *History* is often seen as a record of families within that parish. In fact it is no such thing. It is a record of the occupants of church pews. These pews belonged not to individual families or households but to actual houses.[14] Even when the household changed and the house was occupied by people with little or no relationship to the earlier occupants, the pew was associated with that house. Community identity and the source of continuity was with the house and land and not with the family or its economic embodiment, the household. There were occasional disputes revolving around this issue.[15] When a new house was built in Myddle, permission was sought to erect a pew in the church nave.[16] In his classic *Families in Former Times*, Jean-Louis Flandrin confuses this usage with the use by the aristocracy not only of the patronymic but of titles such as 'Earl of Clarendon' or 'Duke of Buckingham'.[17] In France it reached an even more exaggerated form than in England. The

Bordeaux magistrate, Pierre de Lancre, wrote at the beginning of the seventeenth century of the practice in Lambourt, where 'the most beggarly men and women in the villages style themselves lord or lady of such-and-such a house, and these are the houses that each one has in his village, even though they be no more than pigsties to such an extent that they usually abandon their 'cognomen' and the name of their families, and the women even abandon the name of their husbands, to take the names of their houses'. The house conferred status upon its occupants.[18] In the Basque regions the parish priests entered details of the 'houses' as well as the people in their registers.

While this point remains valid, it is as well to remember that, just as families and households were unstable through death and economic disaster, there was often a certain impermanence about the place of habitation or the viability of a particular household. The acquisition of land or a trade or a profession did not guarantee a smooth passage in life or the continued ability to support a family. During the English Civil Wars and the ensuing period, for example, Adam Martindale and his married brothers moved their households around quite considerably. Both Henry and Thomas Martindale moved their families and household goods into the garrison at Warrington. Adam could not take possession of the Vicarage for some time because the widow of his predecessor laid claim to it and its contents; he and his wife and two young children 'tabled' in the house of John Bentley until this became so intolerable that he began to 'keepe house at the vicarage'.[19] During the wars, he and his family had to flee the house with their best goods to escape the troops.[20] In 1655, Martindale bought a house and leased a tenement as 'provision for my poore faithfull wife ... if she overlive me'.[21] At the Restoration, at Michaelmas 1662, Martindale was ejected from his living and removed his family 'to a little house at Camp-greene', hardly knowing from where the means of subsistence would come. He thought he would have to sell the house and land he had bought in 1655, but charity, the income from teaching private pupils, income from wheat and rye and his wife's skill as a negotiator enabled them to make ends meet. 'The 10 poundes my wife wrangled out of my successor, together with a table, formes, and ceiling, sold him for about 4 pounds more, together with the rent detained by the other gentleman, after paid me, made up some 20 pounds more.' Then, in 1664, he had to work away from his family to make ends meet. He was employed by the Houghtons at Preston as a tutor: he 'taught one weeke and went home the other'. The pay was good and he almost moved his family to Preston. Instead, in May 1666, the family removed 'to a part of the house belonging to Mr Joseph Allen ... in Rotherston'. Here they were 'straitened for roome' and there were 'some inconveniences falling out (as is usual) by two families under a roofe'. After three years they moved to a new house that belonged to a near neighbour. But Adam's work took him to Dunham, some distance away, where he roomed when the 'family' (i.e. that of his master) was in residence. In May 1674, to be nearer to Dunham, he moved his family to a house at Millington, where they lived until 1681. It is certainly true that the uncertainties of Martindale's situation were partly owing to his particular characteristics – those of an ejected Nonconformist minister. None the less, when one is dealing with such times of uncertainty as the English Civil Wars, the Frondes and later the Revolution, and the unsettled conditions of the English colonies, one has to expect that the ideal scenario of stable formation and maintenance of a household by a married couple was not always attainable even by those who initially looked well set up in life. Even for those who remained untouched by civil strife, movement in and out of poverty was common enough, sometimes following the life-cycle and sometimes the less predictable vagaries of life.[22]

The Partnership of Husbands and Wives

The common aim was to set up a household. Among the French bourgeoisie and the peasantry, the desirable attributes in a wife were those of a good wife and mother. But just what those were varied from class to class and from region to region.[23] Most of the evidence for the French peasantry derives from observations made by travellers in the early nineteenth century. In the Creuse, for example, country girls were 'sought after by the young men on the basis of their reputation as good labourers, as hard workers and as painstaking with regard to the interior of the house'.[24] These observers paint a picture of a society in which husbands and wives lived separate working lives and in which wives were often held in contempt.

The wives are the first servants in the household: they plough the soil, care for the house, and eat after their husbands, who address them only in harsh, curt tones, even with a sort of contempt. If the horse and the wife fall sick at the same time, the Lower Breton peasant rushes to the blacksmith to care for the animal and leaves the task of healing his wife to nature.[25]

In the mountains of Auvergne,

The women are saddled with all the work of the household: they milk the cows, and make the butter and cheese; furthermore they go to bed later and get up earlier than the men ... A man would think himself dishonoured if he went out just to fetch water. These rough countrymen have for their womenfolk that profound disdain and despotic contempt typical of all savage peoples; they regard them as their slaves; their own tasks are to feed the animals, to thresh the wheat, and to go, if necessary, to the local market; apart from these occupations, nothing will rouse them out of their natural idleness.

On the basis of such evidence Edward Shorter felt able to conclude that on the French farm, 'man and wife got along in quiet hostility and withdrawal'.[26]

Whereas Jean-Louis Flandrin and Edward Shorter accept these observations as accurate descriptions of the husband/wife relationship within the peasant household from the Middle Ages until the mid-nineteenth century, with only minor reservations, Martine Segalen is much more cautious. 'A hasty traveller, unfamiliar with the local languages, Victor Hugo's brother judged whatever was told him about local customs in terms of his own moral code, and on the basis of knowledge deriving generally from a specific social category, that of the 'notables', who also tended to reproduce a particular ideology.'[27] Thus peasant wives worked with their husbands in the fields, but this scandalised the bourgeois.[28] Absence of differentiation between the work done by men and women in the household economy was seen by Hugo as a feature of poverty and was deplored. 'In the poorer families' of Lower Brittany 'they work in the fields and undertake all the arduous tasks.' But in some parts of the country there was a sharp division between men's work and women's work, which observers from the cities thought no less odious.

Martine Segalen's evidence suggests that husband and wife worked in partnership on the farm and that we should look beyond the moral overtones of the nineteenth-century commentaries. When we examine the French peasant household we should beware of compartmentalising its life between domestic life and the work of production. 'Certain kinds of work are always reserved for women, others are carried out, depending on the region, by either men or women, while a third category, of predominantly male tasks, intermittently or regularly calls upon a female labour force.[29] Women light the fires, fetch the water, do the cooking, wash the clothes, make preserves, sweep, dust, make the beds, knit and sew, care for the children and manage the farmyard and garden. This garden was no 'hearts of ease' and 'hollyhocks' affair. No, it provided food for the household and the farm animals – cabbages and other vegetables and, in the farmyard, poultry, eggs, milk, cheese and butter, pig swill. It was 'a tiny replica of the fields which the man looks after' requiring daily and arduous labour. Men chop the wood, prepare the soil, tend the vines, manage the cows and horses, and on winter evenings make baskets and do repair work around the house and farm. But there is a complementarity about the work of man and woman on the farm. The man chops the wood, the woman lays and lights the fire. And there is also interchangeability and co-operation. Both men and women prepared the bread. In some places it was the wife who managed, as well as milked, the cows. Although the work of a shepherd was traditionally male, there are many references to shepherdesses. The work of dairy production customarily belonged to the women, yet in central France it was the men who took the cattle to the summer pastures and made the cheese. The man might lead the oxen and the woman guide the plough harnessed to it. Men and women joined together at harvest time, picking and treading the grapes together, bringing in the cereal crops. Men tended to handle the heavier implements – the scythe, for instance – while women used the sickle. In the winter both men and women were about the house more and men did more of the work associated with food preparation. 'The degree of co-operation, and the amount of feminine contribution to the work on the land depended on the composition of the households and the particular stage of its evolution, on its economic level, on the time of year, and finally perhaps on cultural models...' In Brittany there was a distinction between the women who were driven by necessity to work side-by-side with their husbands in the fields and the 'mistress of a large farm who never went to the fields. Her husband, her servants, and her sons were sufficient to work the soil. She kept house, that was her job.'[30]

When we look at the evidence for the contribution made by wives to the rural household economy in early modern England or the colonies the similarities are striking. The amount of physical work done by the wife would depend upon the prosperity of the farm, the number of daughters and female servants. In other words, the wife might have a managerial or a labouring role in those areas which were accepted as wife's work. Elizabeth Stout, in the late seventeenth century, was 'not only fully imployd in housewifry but in dressing their corn for the market, and also in the fields in hay and corn harvests, along with our father and servants'. When she became a widow she 'was employed in looking after her servants in the feilds and dressing her corn and going to market with the same as she usually did. And she also kept a woman servant to do the hardest house service and harrow work, hay and shear in harvest, so that the family and concerns were managed in good order as could be expected.' Adam Martindale's wife, Elizabeth, was accustomed and willing 'to keepe a little stock of kine' to supplement her husband's income as minister and teacher.[31] Anne Ailwey sold large quantities of cabbages from her cottage garden.[32] The books of husbandry incorporated practice into theory.[33] For a well-born woman, the task was set against a background of considerably more leisure and was perhaps largely one of household management. Phebe Bliss complained that her marriage, contrary to her mother's assurances that she would 'live like a lady and never need fetch the water to wash ... [her] hand', had not brought such ease.[34] Yet this aspect should not be overemphasised as it also involved producing embroidered textiles, winding yarn, 'giving out corn', organising meals, preserving quinces, preserving sweet meats, receiving rents and keeping the household books, arranging leases, discussing new building projects, making and administering medicines, helping deliver babies and doing work about the house.[35] Indeed, a study of women's diaries in the Stuart period suggests that there were 'fewer class variations in women's daily round of activities than might have been expected'.[36]

There is some evidence that well-born women were entrusted with household and financial management in both England and New England. Despite suggestions that aristocratic wives were 'ornamental' in their role, there are examples of management activity even in the higher reaches of English society. Honor Grenville acted as deputy head of household when Lord Lisle was absent.[37] In America, for example, Samuel Sewell gave his cash into the hands of his wife in 1703/4 'and tell her she shall now keep the Cash; if I want I will borrow of her. She has a better faculty than I at managing affairs: I will assist her; and will endeavour to live upon my salary ...'[38] The wives of both the Reverends Samuel Whiting and Richard Mather had had exclusive management of their secular affairs.[39] Mistress Norton of Nomini Hall oversaw the consumption of 27,000 pounds of pork, 20 cattle, 550 bushels of wheat, 4 hogshead of rum and 150 gallons of brandy in one year.[40] In the 1820s and 1830s Sarah Gayle shouldered considerable responsibilities, not, she thought, well, in the governance of slaves in Alabama.[41] Even where the record is silent regarding the management activities of women, their participation in estate and financial decision making is apparent.[42]

Wives, barred in all three societies from the law and the Church, were responsible for caring for sick members of the family and household. At Little Gidding, Nicholas Ferrar's nieces used a room in the house as a surgery: here they ministered to the needs of the sick from the surrounding villages as well as the household.[43] This tradition was still lively in the eighteenth and nineteenth centuries. Mrs Lefroy, wife of the Rector of Ashe, Hampshire, innoculated 'upwards of 800' of the poor, with her own hand, against smallpox.[44] Even well born and well-to-do women cared for their daughters and others during childbirth.[45] In some cases, wives offered their medical services for a fee to the community at large. Lady Grace Mildmay had an extensive medical practice and manufactured medicines on a considerable scale in late Tudor and early Stuart England.[46] Unmarried and married women, be it in France, England or the colonies, when they were not bearing children themselves, were engaged in the work of midwifery within the community. Their practice was licensed. Midwives not only assisted in childbirth but were used to attest to the virginity of young women and the sexual compatibility of young people. In early seventeenth-century France, substantial numbers of women were applying for annulments of marriage on the grounds of the impotence of their husbands. The *congrès* which assembled to test the validity of the claim consisted of doctors and midwives, who inspected the genitals of the couple and demanded a sample performance of intercourse from the couple.[47]

A wife was expected to work alongside her husband in supporting the family. William Guise could think of no greater praise for his Elizabethan ancestor's wife than that she was 'a very worthy woman and a good housewife' and that 'by her providence the estate was agayne brought into a condition of subsisting' despite over many children – nine – and being 'enforced to live close'.[48] In contrast his own father married as his second wife one who 'to omitt other faults, ... never could be brought to take any care of the house or estate; a gossip, a makebare, a wastall'.[49] William Stout, who had observed the working partnership of his mother and father in their household economy, reacted with some disapproval to the wife of his master in 1680: 'his wife, my dame, was one who took her ease, and tooke noe notice of trade or of anything but indulging her children'. For within the urban environment there was also traditionally a complementarity between the work of husbands and wives. There is some evidence that women were engaged in manufacturing but, in general, especially as the period progressed, men made and women sold. Women, of course, did sew, and often, as in the colonies, combined this work with teaching young girls to sew and to read. In the traditional crafts such as leatherworking, wives of master craftsmen had in the middle ages automatically been entitled to share in the work. So we read that, in 1398, no leatherseller might 'put man, child or woman to work in the same mistery; excepting their wives and children'; that in 1344, 'no one of the [girdler's] trade shall get any woman to work other than his wedded wife or daughter'; that in that same century, in Bristol, 'no person shall cutt, make or sell any kind of garment, garments, hose or breeches ... unless he be franchised and make free ... (widdowes whose husbandes were free of ye said crafte duringe the tyme of their wyddowhedd usinge ye same with one jorneyman and one apprentice accepted'. Wives were often extremely active on the retail side of a business. Even households which plied trades without strong guild protection depended upon the ability of wives and children to sell goods prepared at home. In the seventeenth-century the pinmakers company was said to consist 'for the most part of poor and indigent people, who have neither credit nor money to purchase wyre of the merchant ... [and who] are constrained to imploy [their wives and children] to go up and down every Saturday night from shop to shop to offer their pins for sale, otherwise cannot have money to buy bread.[50] Some women made a distinctive contribution to the household economy by engaging in brewing. Ale formed an important part of the daily diet. The equipment required to make it was relatively expensive and some women managed to supplement their living by selling beer to neighbours, sometimes on the premises. Town by-laws of the fourteenth and fifteenth centuries acknowledged that brewers were women, although they disapproved of the practice. By an Act of Parliament in 1574, the women were forbidden to brew the ale they sold in and outside their houses. Brewing was henceforth confined to breweries run on capitalistic lines. The monopoly of the brewers' was reinforced by the introduction of licensing in the 1620s and 1630s. This tendency for the work of married females to be forced into the retail aspects of the trades is notable throughout our period. Here, also, there were restrictions which forced wives into particular parts of the retail trade. By the end of the seventeenth century there was a strict apprenticeship requirement for women shop-keepers. Mary Keeling was hauled before the court in Nottingham in 1686 'for falowing ye treaid of a grocer and mercer and keeping open shop for on month last past, contra staum, not being apprentice'. The wives of journeymen and farmers turned to street trading and markets. A woman at St Albans set up a market stall to 'sell shirt bands and cuffs, hankerchers, coifes and other small lynnen wares' but even here it was difficult to operate without impediment. The wives of farm labourers, who could afford no shop and little stock, tramped the countryside as pedlars, regraters (sellers of perishable food), and 'hawkers' (wholesalers), to contribute to their guilds and patriarchy was enforced. In a cautious assessment of the economy. This was casual work and often seasonal, obeying the rhythm of markets and fairs. Outside the farming household the distinction between husbands' and wives' work became much more evident during the seventeenth and eighteenth centuries because of the intervention of the guilds and companies and the corporations.

Wives in the American colonies also produced for the local markets – yarn, cloth, cheeses, butter (only the more affluent could afford the barrel churn, which became available after 1760), laundering and ironing, were products and services that wives could and did offer throughout the colonial period.[51] Urban dwellers, while they did run businesses of their own, often did so during widowhood or as adjuncts to their husbands' businesses. For example, Elizabeth Murray Smith of Boston had been a milliner with a small shop before she married a Boston merchant. It was not until his death that she returned to millinery. When she remarried she protected her right to trade through a prenuptial agreement. Grocery shops, delicatessens, bakeries, taverns and inns, and in the eighteenth century, coffee houses, were popular as business ventures among married and widowed women. Occasionally a plantation home would be turned into a wayside inn by an enterprising wife or widow. Women could effectively run plantations in the South, where the jobs of white men as well as women were essentially managerial. There were legal disadvantages to the married woman in business in the colonies which restricted its practice. A married woman could neither sue nor enter into contracts: unless a husband offered support by suing creditors for debt, a married woman was helpless to protect her assets. Although private bills were not unknown to enable individual women to act as *femme sole*, only South Carolina (in 1744) granted married women, as a category, the right to sue for debt. In 1719 Pennsylvania wives whose husbands were away for an extended period or who had deserted them were allowed to act as sole traders.[52]

Historians have argued that the role of French and English wives and widows in trade was considerably curtailed during the later sixteenth and seventeenth centuries as they were excluded from guilds and patriarchy was enforced. In a cautious assessment of the economic role of women in Oxford, Mary Prior has shown how their contribution responded to prosperity and recession, but nevertheless underlines the dampening effects of patriarchy.[53] But, as J. B. Collins has shown, the evidence from Brittany, Normandy and Burgundy does not entirely support this argument. Women, poor, middling and rich, were very much involved in both rural and urban economic life as farmers and linen merchants, laundry women and nurses, servants and property owners, as well as beggars and prostitutes. The regulatory mechanisms of the state and the municipality simply made them more invisible than they had been.[54]

Recent work points to the important contribution made by married and widowed women as pawnbrokers and money lenders throughout Western Europe. In general, women lent small sums of money at interest to help people, often other women, out of domestic difficulties. These loans were short-term and often charitable in intent. As they were normally paid back in a matter of weeks or months, the interest accruing was rarely onerous. Because these loans were informal, involving no legal contract, they effectively undermined the legalistic attempt to prevent married women from acquiring capital by forbidding them to enter into contracts on their own behalf without these husband's consent. Women also invested in mixed portfolios of low-risk, fixed-rate annuities, thus contributing both to the stock of capital available for capitalistic enterprise and to the stability of governments.[55]

Too little attention has been accorded the work in which poor married women engaged. In all three societies the wives of the very poor shared the labour of the fields as well as the household. Wet-nursing was very common in France as an occupation for relatively poor wives: in parts of France children were put out to nurse for several years. Recent work on wet-nursing in England suggests that poor but respectable women were selected by the poor-law overseers to nurse or foster children 'on the parish'. The children nursed by private arrangement appears to have gone to women from a rather higher socio-economic group.[56] Yet even the well-to-do sometimes made unhappy arrangements. Christopher Guise was 'putt to a woman in 'the towne, indifferently antient and of a dry hot complexion and not very plentifully stored with riches, soe that it was noe wonder if there were neglects in my attendance ...'[57]

The homes of the middling people were primitive and comfortless by the standards of today and it may well be true, as is often stated, that housework was much less onerous and much less fussed over than it was to become in the nineteenth and twentieth centuries. Nevertheless, a reputation for sluttish housekeeping was not desirable at any social level in England as early as the sixteenth or seventeenth centuries. Elizabeth Waister of Ryton, Northumberland, accused a neighbour, Alice Fetherstone, in 1608, of being a 'slut that did shit in her cooking pot'. The insult resulted in a slander suit.[58] Segalen notes that the Breton housewife was congratulated for a well-sanded floor, polished brass, waxed furniture, well-kept wardrobes of clothes, abundant hot meals.[59]

Courtship and Marriage

The nineteenth-century observers of peasant life in France remarked on the coarseness of the French women and concluded that French men took no account of feminine beauty when they selected their wives. Such a conclusion sits oddly with the evidence we have of dalliance and courtship among the peasantry, which frequently ended in marriage. Rather, we should conclude that 'beauty' in the eye of the peasant was something alien from beauty in the eye of the nineteenth-century élite.

> On summer evenings, at nightfall, they go out to take the air, sitting on benches or behind a hedge.... First they exchange glances, then casual remarks, then heavy witticisms. The young man shoves at the girl, thumps her on the back, takes her hand and squeezes it in a bone-cracking grip. She responds to this tender gesture by punching him in the back. The young man rubs his shoulder, sniggers half-wittedly, and notes that the maiden has got a fair right hand and would make a pretty solid housewife.[60]

There is no inconsistency here. Few now find it incongruous that both men and women today discriminate between the individuals with whom they will dally and those with whom they will live, yet feel sexual attraction and perhaps even love for both categories! At the same time, we need to be rather more careful about our use of proverbs and sayings as indicators of the opinions of the peasantry in this matter. A twentieth-century postcard bearing the sentiment, 'If you knew, my girl, the pleasure it gives me to kiss you. Your face is so soft, so soft that when I kiss you it seems as if my face is sinking into a pat of butter', certainly uses a farming metaphor, but it is typical of that badinage between flirting youth in which outrageous insult substitutes for sentimental declarations of affection or desire.[61] The women whom they married were thought lovely by their husbands, who, in those parts of France where freedom of choice was allowed, courted them by promenade, dance and embrace and expressed their affection through the exchange of love tokens.[62]

Who made the marriages? The answer to this question might be expected to have some bearing upon the eventual relationship between husband and wife. The evidence with respect to marital choice, as the previous paragraph would suggest, points to a variety of models. In France, where the law gave the parents control,[63] some girls evaded this control by encouraging their preferred suitors to abduct them, relying upon parents' willingness to submit to emotional blackmail. A few others, like the daughter of the engraver, Varin, in 1651, chose to poison their spouses rather than submit to unions they found horrifying. Some others applied for annulment.[64] But most girls were conditioned to submit to their parents' wishes. They saw the rationale of the move and, moreover, were glad to exchange submission to their parents for submission to a husband. For French girls of the upper classes, confinement in a convent by *lettre de cachet* was not a desirable option.[65]

Lower down on the social scale, in some parts of France, as in Upper Brittany or Savoy, young people had considerable freedom of association and even sleeping with one another out of wedlock was common. In the Maurienne Valley, where collective landholding was the norm, it was not so important for parents to control the marriages of their children and there was a long-standing tradition of egalitarianism. In other parts, as in Cornouaille, both the few farming landowners and the farmers and tenants who wished to become landowners pursued a strategy of arranged marriages. Middlemen frequently put the fathers of the couples in contact with one another and made the initial overtures. Sometimes young couples 'find themselves yoked together, without their ever having seen one another' and certainly without the opportunity to discuss the match. It was only among the day labourers that freedom of choice obtained. In some parts of France cousin marriage was common and resulted both in amazing networks of familial relations and in the narrowing of the circle from which spouses might be selected.[66]

Pierre Bourdieu has warned us not to view the 'strategies' of 'reproduction of their lineage and their rights to the means of production' that emerge in a study of the peasantry of Béarn in the Pyrenees as the result of obedience to fixed rules. Here, as elsewhere, families made decisions about marriage according to conditioning, the material circumstances of life, and by family upbringing, what he terms *habitus*. The marriage of each child involved much individual forethought but proven strategies were normally followed, although not without resistance on personal grounds by the young people concerned. Oldest sons, in particular, in this area were both forced into marriages they would not have chosen freely and also submitted to this parental discipline, because it was regarded as so important that the patrimony passed through primogeniture.[67]

Historians have had some difficulty reconciling the expressed wish of English parents to control their children's choice of marriage partners with the evident freedom exercised in practice by many young people. The degree of liberty allowed the young 'depended among other things upon his or her sex, prospects of inheritance and social rank' and may have increased in the seventeenth and eighteenth centuries. Certainly, in the sixteenth century, the aristocracy sought to arrange their children's marriages, and in the seventeenth century expected to have a considerable say in the process, evidence in itself of the importance of marriage in property transmission and in providing security for daughters. It is certainly a mistake, at least when discussing the English aristocracy, to assume that the making of marriage was a matter simply for parents and children. As we saw in the preceding chapter, many different people, including quite distant relatives and connections, acted to further marriage negotiations. The Bagot correspondence illustrates what an important part marriage negotiations for other people's children played in the life of Richard Bagot.[68] Those of the middling sort may have had more freedom of choice than those above them, but even here daughters appear to have been subject to greater control.[69] Lower down in the social scale – among the day labourers in town and country – the young were free to make their own marriages and enjoyed considerable freedom of association. Drinking, dancing and dalliance were the order of the night. Even among the middling sort, the entry of young people of both sexes into service or apprenticeship offered opportunities for them to make their own matches. And many, many adolescents were the products of broken homes, deprived of the advice of parents as well as of material security. Yet, in practice, the extent of control at any social level seems only to have been as strong as the young people permitted. Margaret Bagot defied her parents and married in secret; her irate father had to give way or lose her. Lewis Bagot wished to defy his father but eventually submitted to his parents' wishes when faced with the extreme threat of disinheritance. John Bruen cheerfully accepted the wife whom his father had chosen. John Josselin and Thomas Martindale married without even consulting their fathers and their parents could do little or nothing about it, except whine and lick their wounded pride. Ralph Josselin did attempt to control his daughter's marriage but, when she would not brook this intervention, had to bow to her wishes. Conflict was always a possibility when the parents were adamant that they must be obeyed or when the child would brook no opposition to a love match. Among the élite there were some parents who demanded unquestioning obedience and some who received it. There is some evidence that daughters in particular received more governance in this matter than sons, and through conditioning were more willing to submit. Children shared the concerns of their parents.[70] There are many examples of quarrels. But conflict was in many cases diffused by various strategies, conscious or unconscious. In sensible families the matter was negotiated. The father of Anne Bagot's husband, — Lane, gave his son his 'free marriage' on condition that, when his father died, he cared for his siblings.[71] Parents discussed the various options with their sons and daughters, some even going to the length of Simonds d'Ewes and his father, who engaged in a joint search for a partner for D'Ewes the elder. A suitor made his intentions clear to the young woman concerned and ascertained her feelings before making formal approaches to her parents. Jane Skipworth discussed quite openly the nature of Walter Bagot's opposition to her marriage into the family in an exchange of letters with Lewis Bagot. It was not that the young people had initiated the match nor that they were cousins, but that she did not bring with her sufficient money. She reasoned with Walter but ultimately accepted his verdict and that of her stepmother.[72] Young people bore in mind the desirability of having parental moral as well as material support in their marriages, at the same time as parents sought the happiness of their children in a match that was congenial as well as comfortable. When children acted without thought, parents and godparents would often try to retrieve the situations, as when Lord Lumley asked Richard Bagot to achieve a favourable settlement for Bagot's godson, Lumley's nephew, Richard Rugeley, now that the young people had alienated both sets of parents by a precipitate, head-strong match.[73] Only rarely did a parent, thwarted by a child, cut off relations entirely.

In colonial America also, the selection of a spouse, at least in upper-class families, was made within parameters determined by the parents. The views of women, in particular, seem to have been little solicited although, as in England, the evidence points to parents considering the potential compatibility of the couple emotionally and sexually as well as materially. Refusal of the spouse one's parents had chosen might lead to disinheritance. Marrying without parental consent was extremely difficult: some of the colonies made the father's consent statutorily obligatory. But, once again, most young people seem to have been glad to obey their parents and actively to seek their advice, for the same conditioning process was occurring in the early colonies as in sixteenth and seventeenth-century England. The later seventeenth and eighteenth centuries saw something of a sea change, with more importance being attached to love and attraction, so that as early as the 1690s, Fitz-John Winthrop opined that 'it has been the custom of the country for young folks to choose'. In the colonies, also, much greater freedom seems always to have been allowed the children of the labouring classes.

There is some evidence that in colonial New England sons did seek to evade parental control over choice of marriage partner, however. A study of marriages in Higham, Massachusetts, shows sons prior to 1780 waiting to marry until their fathers had died. There are many possible explanations for this pattern of behaviour: perhaps the fathers would not permit them to marry or refused or were unable to provide them with land sufficient to support a family, or perhaps the sons wanted to exercise personal control over whom they married. It suggests that marriage prior to 1780 was very much an economic decision. However, the evidence certainly does not support the conclusion arrived at by Carl Degler that 'by the last two decades of the eighteenth and the opening of the nineteenth century, a father's influence over a son's choice of decision was much less than it had been before the American Revolution'.[74] Whatever the reason, the practical effect was in one sense to weaken patriarchy well before the War of Independence.

All in all there are no generally applicable rules, whether it be the sixteenth or the seventeenth century, to the amount of latitude which parents allowed their children in choice of life partner, with the possible exception that the children of labouring families had complete autonomy. What is much more interesting is the assumption by parents and the acceptance by most children that this was a decision in which parents and family had a legitimate say, and that marriage was a serious business, not lightly to be entered into. Why was this? Clearly people were conditioned to accept this situation as normal. The authority of Scripture was cited in its support. Certainly the system was thought to ensure the transmission of land and other property in such a way as to support the ensuing generations. Probably the explanation lies deeper than this, though. For most parents did not have to force their children to ask permission to marry. Children acquiesced because the valuable family support system, and not simply their material inheritances, depended upon their acceptance that all decisions were ultimately those of the parents, be he a lord or a goodman and she a lady or a goodwife.

For two categories of person the answer to the question, who made the marriages? would seem to be the couple themselves. Many were marrying for a second or further time. Even here, however, there is some indication that the spouses involved sought the approval of surviving parents.[75] Many had lost one or both parents.[76] Almost 50 per cent of the single women in a sample taken by Vivien Brodsky Elliott had, by the age of 20, lost her fathers. Patriarchal influence was in these circumstances an impossibility. Widows frequently arranged their daughters' marriages but the daughters as frequently migrated away from parental control altogether.[77]

Mutual Expectations

English men and women often married for love, and, even when romantic love did not underly the initial match, lived in the hope and expectation that it would be discovered during marriage. Few relished the prospect of living on terms of mutual hostility and the accounts of unhappy marriages are interesting because they so often reveal that expectations were not being met. If there was a monarchy in the household it was expected to be benevolent, if not constitutional. Lettice Bagot regaled her brother Walter, in September 1608, with the horrors of her married life at Tixall: 'upon satter day last my husband fel out with me for not haveing provistion of beare: I told him of my want of mault abufe three weekes agoue but he would nether provid it him selfe nor allow me money. I borowed of my neghtbores as much as I cold yet for all that the falt was layd all upon me: with maney bitter corsses and the charge of the house taken from mee, and commaunded to medle with nothing: but keepe my chamber: my servants discharged espeshally she that lookes to my children: and is a bout my selfe.' This was not the behaviour she expected from a husband. Indeed the blame was laid on her mother-in-law. 'He wold never be halfe so ile, but for his mother, now her mayde usethe to stand at my dore to heare what I say and then tels my mother in lawe and makes it more.' She knew that her husband's wrath would subside 'but she must have the over seete of all and then shall not I be able to stay'.[78] This little tale of power relations within an elite family, on further examination, reveals something much more interesting. Taken on its own it tells a tale of a violent marriage in which poor Lettice is the victim, Francis the ogre, his mother the wicked witch and brother Bagot Lettice's only refuge, but taken in the context of other Kinnersley-Bagot letters they tell a tale of a marriage which, if not happy, was nonetheless at times a partnership. For in better times Lettice and her husband boarded with Margaret and William Trew in order to avoid the interference of his parents, and Lettice was wont to ask Walter for help to fur- ther Francis's interests. Moreover, Lettice describes a relationship with her husband and with her household which she sees, and expects her brother to see, as unnatural. She expected either Walter or Anthony to intercede with Francis on her behalf and negotiate a settlement whereby she would live elsewhere, in charge of her children, with a mere maintenance. In 1609 she displayed considerable initiative concerning financial matters when she reached desperate straits, asking her brother to arrange a lease to provide £100 for the maintenance of her younger sons (tactfully named for her brothers, Walter and Anthony). She did this, she explained, because 'my meanes is so smale for house keeping, that my husband is weary of taringing heare, but it doeth not much trouble him, my wants and his poore children, which was never greatter then now: and yet I feare, when my corne is goene, it will be wors: which willnot be loung two ...'. Not only is Lettice resourceful, she has a 'family' who will give her practical assistance in time of need. Clearly historians should bear in mind the way in which households interacted with one another on the personal level, when discussing the relations within the nuclear family household. The argument that by the seventeenth century the co-resident nuclear family had already become 'isolated' seems rather premature.[79] In eighteenth-century Massachusetts, 11 per cent of deponents in divorce petitions were kin. Moreover, in several cases wives who were deserted or abused went back to their families for support. Two wives who abandoned their husbands went back to their fathers' houses and one even carried on with other men there. Interestingly, men only very rarely cited their parents' help. [80]

The same seems to be true way down the social scale. Mary Josselin rejected the suit of Mr Shirley because he was 'not loving' and 'would make both their lives miserable'. No more normal reaction could be recorded than that of Ralph Josselin to his experience of love at first sight in the little church at Olney. 'The first Lords day being [October] 6: was my eye fixed with love upon a Mayde; and hers upon mee, who afterwards proved my wife.' Sent a tempting offer of a position elsewhere, 'my affection to that mayde that god had layd out to be my wife would not suffer me to stirre, so I gave the messenger 5s and sent him away'. He proceeded to court Jane both in the house where he stayed and in neighbours' houses and eventually, when he had secured employment and after a brief engagement, they were married. For the Josselins their romantic love led to a long, companionable and certainly for him satisfying marriage. All the indications are that his love was reciprocated. When he was serving as a chaplain in the army, he reported that during his absence 'Abundance of love made my wife grieve.'[81] They cared for one another throughout their marriage. Probably Josselin was drawing on his relationship with Jane when he wrote 'I was wont to see my dear Wife; here to injoy her delightsome imbraces; her counsel, spiritual Discourses, furtherance, encouragement in the wayes of God, I was wont to find her an help to ease me of the burthen and trouble of my household-affaires, whose countenance welcomed me home with joy.'[82] This led to a companionate marriage in which decisions were generally taken co-operatively by man and wife.[83] But for others, compatibility and affection made a partnership viable even when passionate romantic love was lacking.

It is unwise to assume that when the parties themselves controlled the choice of marriage partner, or had a major say in it, the heart ruled the head. In seventeenth and eighteenth-century New England, contemporaries often seem to have decided to marry

without reference to any specific individual. Thomas Shephard
spoke, in his autobiography, of how 'about this time I had a great
desire to change my estate by marriage; and I had bin praying
3 yeare before that the Lord would carry me to such a place where
I might have a meet yoke fellow'. Thomas Walley wrote to John
Cotton 'the last day of the last week I came to a resolve to stay at
home and not to look after a wife till the spring', but to his great
satisfaction 'god hath sent me a wife home to me and saved me the
labor of a tedioiouse journey' to Boston. In 1718, Hugh Hall wrote
to his father in Barbados 'it will be high time for me upon my
return to you, to think of the conjugal state ...'. It was important
that love could develop between the couple, but, that said, economic considerations were uppermost. In the case of first marriages between young people, the parents sorted out the financial
details while the couple concentrated upon the development of an
affective bond. In the case of second marriages or where the
people concerned were older, there was more for the prospective
spouses to arrange. 'Marriage then, or at least a proper marriage,
resulted not from falling in love, but from a decision to enter a
married state, followed by the choice of a suitable person.' Love
was the chief duty of marriage and a period of espousals (engagement) was used as a trial of suitability and nursery of affection.[84]

In the conjugal partnership both partners were dependent, the
one upon the other. The petition of a bedridden London porter,
John Acors, in 1595, demonstrates just how important the role of a
wife could be, especially in old age. The stairs had been removed
from Acors's house 'whereby his wife is barred from his society,
and comfort and hath been so barred this quarter of a year and
upwards whereby he hath not that attendance and looking unto
which a man in his case ought to have but is in great misery his
bed having never been made since the taking away of the stairs,
nor none ever been above with him ...'. He petitioned the vestry
of St Saviour's 'to be a means that he may be placed in [a] house
wherein he may have the society of his wife to help to comfort him
in this his extremity and also to keep him clean and sweet and to
help to relive him in this case of extremity.[85] The vestries were not
oblivious of the usefulness of wives in caring for elderly, incapaci-
tated males without charge: in one case two males were housed
together so that the wife of one could care for both. The convenience of the arrangement notwithstanding, it was the solace

offered by a wife, in contrast to the paid service of an employee, that was valued. This interdependence stretched to the urban middle classes as well. Samuel Pepys's Diary makes frequent reference to his dependence upon his wife for services such as washing, cooking and cap making, which the servant shared in, yet he also relies on her for conversation and misses her companionship when he is away from her.[86] The French showed a similar awareness of the mutual benefits of marriage, which sometimes outweighed the disadvantages of dislike. In 1694 Jean Plicque, a Villenoy vinegrower, and his wife, Catherine Girardin, obtained a physical separation and a separation of property on grounds of incompatibility, but in spring 1695 they appeared before the Chapter at Meaux explaining that it would be 'not only more praiseworthy but much more advantageous and useful to be united in marriage again than to remain separated'.[87]

Records of divorce proceedings would appear, on the surface, not to be the happiest hunting ground for evidence of romantic or, indeed, any other kind of love between married couples. However, they have been used to reveal the understanding which spouses of both sexes had of the marriage relationship and of each other and to indicate changes in this understanding over time. In eighteenth-century New England an increase in divorce petitions suggests that individuals were more willing to break a marriage if it did not bring satisfaction of their expectations, and that society concurred. So in Massachusetts between 1736 and 1765 petitioners never claimed loss of conjugal affection among their grievances, whereas between 1766 and 1786 one tenth of petitions named this as a grievance of note. He 'ceased to cherish her', 'lost all affection for her'; she had 'almost broken his heart' and had 'opposed nuptial happiness'; 'all conjugal affection has fled' the marriage. In 1781 Phebe Bliss, defending, said that she had loved her husband Amos when he courted her but that since marriage his behaviour had been insufferable and she would rather beg or die than live with him again. Amos, on his part, claimed to love her still, despite her adultery. If only she would stop provoking, 'twitting', him, be his 'friend' and 'be in subjection to him' he would gladly live with her again. There are difficulties with accepting this evidence at face value, however. It may be that loss of affection had become acceptable grounds for divorce only in this later period and therefore plaintiffs had never bothered to mention it in earlier petitions. Or it may be that people in the seventeenth and eighteenth centuries expressed love differently. Earlier petitions do mention conduct unbecoming a wife or husband and neglect as grievances, for example, and these can mean many things.[88]

Women clearly expected their husbands to fulfil certain obligations within marriage, no less than husbands had expectations of their wives. When he married, the man agreed to provide food, shelter and raiment for his wife. Seventeenth-century colonial court records reveal that assertions that a man did not fulfil such obligations were regarded as slanderous and actionable. For instance, in Maryland in 1661, Isabella Barnes insulted John Winchester by claiming that he had taken insufficient care of his wife Margaret during her terminal illness. He retorted by producing a witness who had been employed to watch Margaret at nights, who claimed that Margaret had had 'poultry stewed with butter & Currents and she was shifted and tended and hur husband was as kind to hur as any man Could be to his Wife'.[89] In eighteenth-century New England the saying 'to act like a man' was shorthand for supporting one's wife, and failure to do so was accepted as good grounds for breaking the marriage contract, although women were prone to cling on to a relationship longer than men in similar situations. In her turn, the wife pledged good management and service, and if she did not fulfil this pledge this too was grounds for divorce. Her honour also must be unbesmirched.[90] If we look at these twin responsibilities we can see that this was in fact perceived as a partnership for economic support of the family. At its best, these obligations were met as the expressions of mutual loving. Unkindness, as we can see in the Lettice Kinnersley example, had its economic as well as its emotional implications. When the partnership lapsed, the family broke up. In 1786 a Springfield farmer described how he had been deserted by his wife in 1780 and had tried for six years, with his parents' help, to keep together his family of five children. Finally, he had had to give up and place his children elsewhere.[91] Stephen Lufkin, a fisherman from Gloucester, Massachusetts, petitioned for divorce from his wife Tabitha in 1760 and their depositions reveal many of the expectations they had had of the marriage. Stephen argued that Tabitha had wasted his property, committed adultery and behaved in other ways unbecoming a wife. Tabitha alleged that 'he had been an unkind husband, always checking up on her, finding fault, and getting angry, and only giving her to eat the food he liked, whether or not it agreed with her stomach; second he had refused to pay for a jug of cider she had bought in his absence, although she had drunk only water for seven or eight months; third he had argued with her about cloth that she bought for his coat, and had shut her out of the house until she, on her knees, begged him to be reconciled; fourth, he falsely accused her of wasting his goods, for they had had little when they married …'. In her attempt to place the blame for the disruption of conjugal harmony onto Stephen, she cited his failure to support her properly.[92]

The English law, which had a very restrictive definition of legally actionable defamation and did not permit divorce except by private Act of Parliament, makes such evidence much rarer, yet what does exist suggests very similar expectations of spouses.[93] Historians have argued persuasively that a double-standard applied respecting the fidelity of spouses to one another.[94] Men were allowed to sow their wild oats; women were chastised for allowing them. Looking beyond the realm of ideas to that of practice the picture is not always so clearly defined. The English ecclesiastical courts vigorously prosecuted males as well as females who committed adultery. For instance, in February 1600 a husband who had committed adultery and made the woman pregnant was hauled before the Lichfield consistory. The court inquired 'whether he did his penance in a white sheet bare and with a white wand and how many dayes'. Sadler replied 'that he had noe sheete about him nor any white wand in his hand & did do one day of penaunce onlye'. He was sent away to perform his penance in the appropriate humiliating manner and ordered to provide proof.[95] It is also worthy of note that it was the males who were prosecuted and sentenced within the ecclesiastical courts for impregnating their wives before marriage.[96] The same courts insisted that husbands who had deserted their wives return to them to cohabit and support them.[97] The Courts Christian objected strongly to the popular custom of wife sales, which treated the wife as the possession of the husband. In February 1600, Ottiwell Andrew of Eyam, Derbyshire, confessed 'that about Easter last past he being in one Raphe Arnefield his howse in Hefield did buye the sayd dorothie of her husband Michaell Ogden and gave unto his 44s for her which monye he sayeth the sayd Michaell receyved in the presence of' witnesses. For this he was ordered to do humble penance and cease to live with the said Dorothy.[98] On the other hand there is considerable evidence that in France the Parlement of Paris treated errant women much more harshly than men.[99] The difference here may be less one of nationality than of perspective: the Church taking a very different approach to that of the lay authorities.

In some Protestant states divorce became available to both sexes during and after the Reformation period. In England there were those, like John Milton, who argued strongly that divorce should be introduced. The proponents of divorce were always anxious not to undermine the importance of marriage thereby. Where divorce was possible, long-term desertion was the most commonly cited reason, followed by adultery, but divorce was still difficult to obtain. Even where it was available, and notwithstanding the possible operation of a double-standard, women often found that they were in no economic position to seek divorce. A study of Neuchâtel, now a Swiss canton, has shown that very few divorces were petitioned or granted during the period 1547–1706. Petitions arising out of desertion could not be entertained until seven years had passed. Adultery had to be witnessed by two independent persons – this meant that a wife or husband could not confess to adultery and thus release themselves from an unhappy match. Usually, where adultery was alleged, women obtained divorces when their husbands' mistresses produced offspring or, more frequently, men did when their wives had pregnancies when they themselves were absent. After 1706 the number of divorce petitions and grants increased considerably. Desertion and adultery remained the chief pleas. Violence and incompatibility were now accepted as grounds for breakdown of marriage, although normally after several years of official separation. This pattern was not discernible, for example, in contemporary Geneva, where divorces were limited to those petitioned on grounds of desertion and adultery. Divorce was not readily available as a way out of a miserable marriage in the sixteenth and seventeenth centuries. By the eighteenth-century, in some communities, it was offering hope to unhappy couples but more studies are needed before we can judge whether this was the dominant development, paralleling that in the British American colonies.[100]

When it comes to describing the relationship between husbands and wives there are at least as many examples of devotion as there are of detestation. In English women's diary accounts of 21 marriages in the Stuart period, there were 15 'loving and companionable marriages and six unsatisfactory marriages'.[101] This is unsurprising in a real world where husband and wife were often much in one another's company as a partnership in both the natural family and the household economy. Lady Joan Barrington stayed with her husband throughout his imprisonment in the Marshalsea 'and nothing but death shall part thee & me'.[102] Heigham Coke of Suckley, Worcestershire, begged 'Cosen Coke', in 1705, to use his influence to prevent Heigham being made High Sheriff: 'my wife being dead but some monthes agoe, my house this yeare being the house of morning, I hope I may be excused.[103] We read that Adam Martindale's father was so distraught by the death of his wife that his married daughter, Jane, invited him to go to London with her 'and indeed it was great charity ... to give him that diversion'. Poor Martindale the elder became 'much disordered in his head' as a result of his grief.[104] Reports of unhappy and violent marriages and liaisons were no more characteristic of early modern unions than are those reports which provide the staple diet of the modern tabloid press. Indeed, they form part of the many newsletters with which London dwellers plied their relatives: 'At London men and their wives still make dolorous catastrophes of their jarrings: an other woman hath poysened her husband ... Sir Robert Howard hath converted his extremyty of loving lust into as foule a disguise of inhumanyty as he hath putt upon his long kept mistress the Lady Purbeck her fayre face, which (upon a jar between them) he hath made as many crosses upon with his unkind knife as he could find attractive beautyes in her severall features; an unheard of ferocity ...'[105] Little had changed at the close of the century when Sir Thomas Coke's sister, Mrs Fanshaw, reported recounting to Mrs Fanny a story of a miserable marriage and sparking 'a great many storyes of ill husbands and the best wives in the world'.[106]

A good example of a marriage which knew of its ups and downs and yet operated in many ways as a companionate union is that of Adam and Jane Eyre. Adam had a circle of male friends and rarely a day went past when he did not drink at the alehouse with 'the gang', but he and Jane also had a joint social life with other couples (Nicholas Greaves, John Wainwright, Edward Hinchcliffe and John Shaw and their wives) and a few single people. Of one meeting, in February 1646/7, Adam said, 'We mett this day only to be merry, and I spent 2s 0d.' There were also trips to Denby, to Wakefield, to the alehouse, for walks, to hear sermons and to dine out. In October 1647, 'after I came home toward night, my wife went with mee, and we swam the scueball[107] in a pitt' ... This Yorkshire farmer was to be found in Barnsley, shopping at 'Greene shop things for my wife', making 'my wife a place for chickens' and 'blooding' his 'wife in her sore foote, which bled very well'. In her turn, she acted as willing go-between in negotiating a sizable loan from her father in exchange for an increased jointure. But the couple quarrelled, sometimes seriously, about her property, about her immodest attire, about his drinking and bowling.

> This morne my wife began, after her old manner to braule and revile mee for wishing her only to weare such apparrell as was decent and comly, and accused mee for treading on her sore foot, with curses and othes, which to my knowledge I touched not; nevertheless she continued in that extacy till noone.

Finally, at 'diner', he told her he 'purposed never to com in bed with her til shee tooke more notice of what I formerly had sayd to her, which I pray God to give mee grace to observe' ... The situation was serious. She would not allow him to go out bowling; he contemplated separation; she locked him out 'and sayd shee would be master of the house for that night'. Eventually, on 1 January, he formulated a new year's resolution (perhaps a contract) whereby she would 'forbeare to tell mee of what is past, and [he] promised her to become a good husband to her for ye time to come, and shee promised mee likewise shee would doe what I wished her in anything, save in setting her hand to papers and I promised her never to wish her therunto'. Apparently harmony was restored for a time once Adam promised not to touch her property.[108]

What happened when a marriage was not a partnership and became intolerable for one or both spouses? Because formal divorce (with the right to remarry) was not possible in England for any but the very well-to-do before 1857, this does not mean that couples were always trapped within unhappy relationships. Each society offered both sexes redress in specific circumstances. Annulment was possible in the event of bigamy, proven incest or impotence, for example.[109] Divorce was available in some circumstances in the colonies – adultery, desertion, impotence, perhaps habitual cruelty.[110] Judicial separation was, in serious cases, an option in all three societies. In France, a *séparation des corps et des biens* allowed women to cease living with their husbands and to have financial independence if there was physical or emotional cruelty or if a mistress was installed in the home.[111] There were other ways of dissolving a marriage and here it does seem that the initiative usually rested with the husband. He could desert or even sell his wife and the onus was upon the civil and ecclesiastical courts to force him to honour his obligations, and to deny his right to any such initiative. Desertion was evidently quite common.[112] If, after investigation, a spouse could not be traced he or she might be officially presumed dead and the deserted spouse permitted to remarry. Eight per cent of poor women in Norwich in 1570 had been deserted by their husbands. The ecclesiastical courts tried to compel husbands to cohabit with their wives when such cases were brought to their attention and they used economic penalties to enforce their decisions.[113] The offence was not only against the wife and any children but also against the parish, who were left to support the deserted family. But often such marriages must have been irreparable. Deserters could relatively easily lose themselves in a society which kept poor records. We know that some husbands, faced with what they saw as inadequate wives, often those who had been unfaithful, actually sold them at markets and in public houses. It seems that this form of poor man's divorce was not peculiar to England. It existed, for example, in China, Italy, Scotland, Wales and Ireland. It is, however, difficult to say how prevalent this practice was in England. It may be significant that the period when wife-selling appears to have flourished in England among artisans and the middle-class as well as labourers coincided with the collapse of ecclesiastical authority. Yet, by the 1880s the custom appears to have survived only in the industrial north.[114]

Historians, to some extent misled by late-twentieth-century preoccupations with the position of women and the whole issue of equality, have tended to formulate their assessment of the early modern family in terms of power relations. It is certainly true, as we have seen in an earlier chapter, that theorists accorded the head of household, the husband, the father, power and authority, even though they engaged in many of the same debates about the nature of that sovereignty as contemporary political theorists and practitioners did. It is also true that in unhappy marriages, when husband and wife or father and children were in conflict, appeal was often made by the husband and father to his position of authority and, on occasion, it had the effect desired by him. Yet we now know enough of the early modern family's day-to-day operation to know that the relations of man and wife and of parent and children were rarely so simple as those indicated by such an analysis. In real life situations family members did not spend their lives reflecting on power politics; inequality was not an issue but vocation and relationship were to the fore. Harmony was the goal and religious teaching reinforced the natural fondness for 'peace'. When we see Grace Mildmay coping with her husband, Anthony, who was by turns 'touchy' and 'techy', we recognise an echo of the advice offered by Erasmus in his Colloquies, and by his many successor marriage counsellors.[115] Age and generation helped to fix the relationship between spouses and between parents and children. In peasant France, the aphorism, 'Fille de 15 ans, homme de 30', met with approval although it is doubtful whether the discrepancy between partners' ages was normally so great. Males and females in English marriages were usually separated by only a few years and this was conducive to partnership relations between spouses.[116] Even so, there was established what we today would call a natural authority relation, based on age, education and assumption. Marriages where there was a discrepancy between the social class of the spouses were discouraged in all societies and not only for obvious economic reasons. The mother in households in the Pyrenees, while she did not wish her son to marry downward, equally opposed an upward match with the daughter of an important family, who would enter her marriage with natural authority and thus come into conflict with her mother-in-law. Balance was to be observed. Social endogamy prevailed in all three societies.[117] Everyone had a different vocation in life which was to be fulfilled. This vocation might best be realised when proper and natural balance was achieved in the family relationships. Each member of a family stood in different relation to other family members. The male spouse stood in one relation to his female spouse and another to his children, another to his servants and yet another to his own parents and siblings. Similarly, the female spouse stood in a different relation to her children and, again, her servants, than to her spouse or her parents.

Parents and Children

Until recently, historians were convinced that in the early modern period there was no awareness of childhood as a separate state from adulthood and that harsh, even systematically abusive, treatment of children was normal. Lawrence Stone, Philippe Ariès, Edward Shorter, Demos and De Mause used examples of indifference and cruelty towards children as if they were characteristic of the entire population of *ancien-régime* Europe and the New World. Practices, which were dictated by genuine religious belief, such as baptising infants in cold churches with icy water from the font or binding the babies in swaddling bands, were viewed as cruel rather than possibly misguided. Linda Pollock's work has replaced this thesis, at least as far as England and America are concerned, with one that sees parents as far from indifferent towards the needs of their children as children, and indulging in child-rearing practices which they genuinely believed to be beneficial.[118]

In these societies parents were expected to give food, shelter and protection to their children. Of all the relationships within the family, it was that between parents and children which was 'natural' and comparable with that of the 'bruit creatures' towards their young. It follows that 'politically correct' behaviour to one's children had to be justifiable as 'protective'. Being anything other than protective of one's children was 'unnatural'. But one could not justify absolutely *any* kind of behaviour on the grounds that it constituted necessary correction or protection. When, in 1834, a magistrate described the damage done when N. Weston bound his eleven-year-old daughter to a bed post and whipped her with belt and buckle as 'the most shocking sight he ever beheld', he added 'it was the duty of parents to correct disobedient children, but not to inflict such barbarous punishment'.[119] In France also, we should note that the behaviour of parents towards their children was monitored by society as a whole. It was not considered appropriate that Colbert should thrash his adult son or that Anne de Polignac should beat and kick her daughter in the stomach.[120] The court records of Massachusetts, which have been used to illustrate the neglect and abuse of children, in fact indicate that such behaviour was abnormal and abhorred. Tabitha Lufkin was asked how she could elope with her lover and leave her children behind, and replied that she never thought about them. Susanna Chambers, when she heard her small daughter inform a neighbour that Susanna was in the bedroom with a man, 'unhook'd the door, & called her daughter little Bitch & said she would sacrifice her if she did not get away'. Hannah Wales allowed her four-year-old daughter to witness her intercourse with a lover. The child told a maid-servant that she saw a man 'lay on the bed with her mamma, and she saw her thighs, and the man told her to lay up higher'. When Stephen Temple of Upton raped his sick daughter, who was 'afraid of him and thought I must obey him', his wife forgave him the incest when he promised not to continue.[121] Practices such as infanticide were much less common than was once believed. Incest and child abuse did indeed occur in early modern times but they were as anathema as today. Adam Martindale's description of the trial by neighbours of one case involving an old man, accused of raping a six-year-old daughter of his neighbour, seems very reminiscent of the child-abuse investigations of today: 'an old man had carnally known ****, the daughter of ****, my doore neighbour, severall times ... The child having accused him to her mother, who told my wife, I was desired to examine the child; which I did; and among other questions, asked her whether any body were present, and she answered that my daughter was present once: and as soone as my daughter awaked ... I examined her whether she knew such a man; what manner of man he was; what she saw him doe at ****, and where it was? And she answered to all punctually, confirming to a tittle what the other had said.' The case was taken to the Justices at Bowdon by the child's father. 'A jury of women were sworne to inspect the child wronged' and they proclaimed that she had been raped. Parents took it upon themselves to protect their children's innocence. Neither the behaviour nor the protective reaction was confined to the seventeenth century. Parents disagreed between themselves as to what was appropriate treatment of children. An American woman autobiographer, Abigail Bailey (1746–1815), obtained a divorce from her husband, having tried for years to protect her children from his stern discipline and incestuous impulses. John Richards had to put his wife out of the room when she objected to him beating their son Jack

'for his bad [behaviour] in play'.[122] Although child-abuse legislation did not appear in England until 1889, child abuse was neither
condoned nor covered up. Linda Pollock discovered 385 cases of
child neglect and sexual abuse reported in *The Times* between 1785
and 1860, the majority of which resulted in a guilty verdict.[123]

Children and parents may frequently have been at odds but this
natural tension between adolescents and their parents has to be
seen against a backdrop of love, in the sense of concern and affection as well as duty. There is considerable evidence of the love and
concern English parents felt for their children, whether or not
they died in early childhood.[124] A principal reason for putting children out to wet-nurse, in England at least, was the fear that strong
emotional bonds would be formed too early with a child whose
hold on life was precarious. Lady Anne Clifford was kept apart
from her daughter Margaret for her infancy but thenceforward
became close to her.[125] Christopher Guise was told by his mother
that he was 'a very weake child' and 'though the first borne, yett
not permitted to be nurst in the house or by my mother'.[126]
William Knollys, who stood godfather to Anne Newdegate's first-
born daughter Mary in 1598' advised Anne that he 'should like
nothing that you play the nurse if you were my wife'. 'I must confess it argueth great love, but it breedeth much trouble to yourself
and it would more grieve you if sucking your own milke it would
miscarry, children being subject to many casualties.'[127] Linda
Pollock's study of English and American diaries concluded that
parents fulfilled the following roles in relation to their children –
educative, protective, disciplinary, provisory, advisory, training,
helping. The evidence suggests that from the sixteenth century
onwards there was a clear distinction between punishment and
abuse and, moreover, that parents were not brutal in their discipline. A few parents beat their children but remonstration and
reason were more common by far. Examples such as that of Byrd,
who whipped his co-resident nephew and niece for refusing to
learn to read and, in the girl's case, soiling the bed, are balanced
by the many more instances of parents dealing indulgently with
their children. Grace Mildmay received verbal not physical
reproof from her governess.[128] Henry Newcome, who in 1661
noted, 'w[ha]t a deale of patience is requisite to beare any con-
verse with our little children How peevish and foolish are they!
and what fits doth our heavenly father beare with us in', found

bringing up children was full of anxiety. 'My son D[aniel] in his passion spoke very irreverently and sinfully to me.' Yet his response was not physical chastisement. 'I did desire to deale with him as well as I could to make him sensible of his sin, & I prayed to God to forgive him poore childe.' The matter continued to trouble him to the extent that he had 'a night of much dreameinge. Esp[ecially] how in ye way a lad had angered mee, & I had stricken him with a little sticke in my hand. But I was after much troubled at it, & yt of ye ap[?] came in upon mee. Ye servant of God must not strive. No striker. I was ashamed much at it, but glad w[he]n it was but a dreame. But I desire to take warning hereby.'[129] Some children were sent to their rooms for punishment: for example, when Ann Clifford, at the age of 13, went our riding with someone her mother disapproved of, 'my Mother in her anger commanded that I should lie in a chamber alone, which I could not endure, but my cousin Frances got the key of my chamber and lay with me'. Threats were tried, as with Ralph Josselin when he threatened his wayward son, John, with disinheritance, but a threat made is not a threat executed. Although parents were interested in obedience and in persuading children to certain courses of behaviour, there was little or no evidence that parents sought to break the will of their children. Byrd, a Virginian plantation owner, was angry with his wife when she tried to make their daughter eat against her will. Indeed, from my own reading of Martindale's autobiography it is apparent that he wanted to make it clear to his readers that he had not forced his daughter, Elizabeth, to servant placements which she did not find congenial.[130]

What precisely constituted child abuse as opposed to appropriate physical discipline was then, as now, an occasion for debate. Many conduct books counselled beating as a final sanction; schoolboys and apprentices *were* beaten; the common punishment for many offences was a beating in a house of correction. However, it is also true that some Western societies still have the death penalty and yet deplore any corporal punishment of children. While it may be true that parents in the early modern period accepted as normal far harsher physical punishments than we might in the late twentieth-century, it is nevertheless certain that many parents in England and America treated physical discipline either as abhorrent or as a last resort, and that many agonised over the permissible levels of this 'violence'.[131] That the contrary was true of France by the late seventeenth century appears to rely upon the testimony of a single French traveller that, unlike the English, the French applied discipline early to keep their children in awe of their parents.[132] The paucity of evidence makes it nigh on impossible to discern whether this debate belonged chronologically to the seventeenth century rather than earlier.

Early American diarists, when compared with English, were especially keen to protect their offspring – perhaps because of the exceptional hazards of the colonial environment – and from the eighteenth century were less interested in disciplining and advising their children.[133] Protection was not a simple matter. Both Ralph Josselin and Adam Martindale record accidents which befell them as children; Josselin reports his own children's falls. Fires, wells, animals presented hazards where young children were concerned. Nehemiah Wallington (1598–1658) may not always have known where his children were but he was concerned enough when his daughter, aged three years and eight months, went out with 'a nother little childe to play as wee had thought but it semes my dafter sarah left the other child and went herself so far as the fell'. He went out and sought for her for 'how could wee eate or have sleept that night with thinking what is become of our poore childe, thinking yt maybe is drowned at the wather side or some other mischife hath befallen it'.[134] Any suggestion that fathers were never intimately involved in the rearing of their offspring is thus easily refuted. In 1705 Elizabeth Coke wrote from Derbyshire to her brother, Sir Thomas Coke: 'I must beg leave to give you the trouble of asking your approbation for Miss Betty's being weaned, she having suck'd longer rather then designed ...', referring to the delay in teething which echoed the development of her older sister.[135] Diarists from both sides of the Atlantic, from 1500 to 1900, confided great anxiety about their duty to provide financially for their children and to guide them appropriately.[136] Parents were concerned to prepare their children for adult life. There was an increasing tendency to offer children a period of formal education outside the home, the precise nature of which would depend upon the class of the child and the vocation for which it was indeed. In New England and the middle colonies, from the seventeenth century onwards, it was normal for children of both sexes and all classes, after the age of six, to receive some formal academic education, but it would be unwise to over-emphasise this aspect. In England the accessibility of academic education was much more restricted.[137] Whereas in the sixteenth and seventeenth centuries there is a good deal of evidence of parents using a religious reference point for the correct upbringing of their children, by the eighteenth century this is balanced by a concern for the socialisation of the child.

Children were also expected to be active participants in the early modern household. The extent to which childhood was regarded as a period of preparation for future independence, as opposed to one of work within the household economy, or expected to contribute towards this economy depended to a great extent upon the socio-economic character of the family.[138] Adult children certainly provided a valuable human resource for many farming families in England, France and the Americas. In slave-holding households in the South, however, daughters seem to have been poorly prepared for their future lives as mistresses of plantations. Frequently they married young and appeared shocked at their new responsibilities.[139] The Stout children were important to their farm in late-seventeenth and eighteenth-century Lancashire. The six children of Deacon John Abbot of Andover, Massachusetts contributed between 10 and 29 years of adult service apiece to the family farm (68 years of male labour and 27 of female). One son, Joseph, was at home until he married at the age of 45. What made 'children' willing to offer this labour to their parents? These children received a detailed training or apprenticeship for independent futures as they understudied their parents, older siblings and hired managers. The evidence also suggests that the lack of opportunity or desire to do anything else was at least as potent a factor in their 'decision' to stay as was patriarchal control and/or strategy. Because of the preference for partible inheritance, the children of New England farmers did well enough, although ultimately this subdivision of farms led to lack of economic viability. When family farms ceased to flourish in eighteenth-century New England, some proletarianisation occurred but many families transferred the system to new settlements in Ohio and beyond.[140]

Mothers, especially, set great store by their role. Much of their time was spent bearing children, tending them and educating them. In addition to relying upon their common sense and the experience of their kin (especially mothers), literate English women referred to books of advice (which especially proliferated in the seventeenth century) and even to manuscripts handed down in the 'family'.[141] The advice covered such topics as the value of breastfeeding, which was recommended in even the most aristocratic of families; the use of wet-nurses; the organisation and timing of weaning; the education of the young.[142] While it was important to parents to have children, there was anxiety about producing too many. Elizabeth Turner, in 1672, recorded her fear that she was again pregnant. Mary Holden suggested a diet designed to 'make a man no better than a eunich'.[143] There is evidence that women knew about and acted upon the contraceptive effect of prolonged breastfeeding.[144] Childbearing brought danger of death and the prospect of grief. Too many children brought, for many, much onerous work and premature aging. For some, children tipped the balance between economic viability and non-viability as a household. Yet even those who were forced by poverty to abandon their children often showed evidence of care and concern.[145]

Parents in the early modern period did feel natural love for their children and were aware that childhood was different in kind from adulthood. None the less parents and children lived in a different relation to one another than is the case today. The cycle of pregnancy and child rearing lasted much longer for the married woman of the past. As a result, mothering was not as intensive as it often is today. Wives had also to continue their ordinary chores. Typically, mothers rested for a few days after childbirth – the length of the lying-in period was reduced to a couple of days only among the poor. In America, Indian women spent no time in physical recovery at all. In many cases, therefore, while emotional commitment was considerable, there simply was very little time to spend with infants, except in those families where there was servant labour. Older children were often relied upon as deputy mothers and fathers when babies were born to a family. It might be these siblings rather than the parents who socialised and educated the younger children. As a result, place within the family was probably yet more important then than it is acknowledged to be even today. Very little work has been attempted to uncover the child-rearing practices and attitudes of the poor. Supervision may have been less than in the houses of the middling or upper classes,

morality less certainly taught. When Elizabeth Reve of Wyveton
was examined by the Justices of the Peace in 1605, depositions
revealed that she had had frequent and fruitful sexual liaison with
a parson of dubious character (previously convicted of rape) and
had contrived to 'lye with some other man' once 'in her mother's
house and another tyme in the feild'. When her mother found
that her daughter was pregnant, she sent Elizabeth, with money, to
an abortionist in Saxlingham. Another case before the same
justices indicates the part played in a youthful clandestine
marriage by the father of one of the parties.[146] The use of such
sources may help us to penetrate the families and the family values
of the poor.[147] In the Old World, babies were sometimes wet-
nursed although the advisability of the practice was disputed and
many women of the English upper classes fed their own babies
because of its health repercussions.[148] In the Southern colonies,
some women used African wet-nurses but wet-nursing was otherwise rare in the colonies.[149]

Children also felt affection for their parents and a sense of loss
when they died, to which they lent expression in various ways.
Once again this was not negated by the tensions which existed in
some families between parents and children over some issues.
Love is revealed in the letters of the élite as well as of the middle
classes. The Gerards were concerned for the health of Lady Joan
and Sir Francis Barrington in 1627, wondering 'how you both
brooke this strong weather in the country after so long lying in
the city, I hope you weill both of you be careful to keepe you out
of this sharpe aire so long as it continues this extreme'.[150]
Southern women of the slave-owning classes regarded their
mothers almost with worship.[151] Love also appears in the actions
of children. Adam Martindale, 'as a minister and his sonne', had,
in 1658, given his ailing father spiritual counsel. Adam and his
surviving siblings, 'considering how good a father he had beene',
brought 'him home handsomely out of his own' and entertained
all those who came to escort his 'corpse thence' with 'good meat,
piping hote, and strong ale in great plenty'. The interment of the
corpse and the funeral sermon were followed by 'a rich dinner
prepared at a tavern for the kindred, and so many more as a great
roome would receive'. This was extraordinary. In addition, 'as are
usuall at ordinary burialls', 'for all the rest tag and rag store of
such provisions'.[152]

Harmony in Simple and Complex Households

Harmony in everyday life was secured by bringing these relationships into focus, accepting them and making them work to the family's advantage. This family, while it was at its most evident and persistent in the household, embraced much more than the co-resident nuclear family. It is when the relationships of those who co-resided became discordant that the place of this unit within a wider set of relationships is liable to come into the historian's view. So, Lettice Bagot Kinnersley, faced with disharmonious relations in her marriage, could look legitimately to the Bagot 'patriarch' for a restoration of harmony. While we have more evidence of relationships of obligation within this wider family for the élites, there is no evidence that it did not exist to some degree throughout the social spectrum, as is shown in eighteenth-century Massachusetts and the nineteenth-century frontier settlements.

For the people of central and southern France, the problems of living together in harmony were rather different. 'In Limousin, in Perigord, in Rouergue, in Provence, in the area of Nice, and in Corsica, apparently in most of the central and southern regions of the kingdom, there existed a sufficiently significant proportion of families with complex structures to make one question the normalcy of the conjugal family.'[153] When two or more couples (and their children) lived together, who had authority within the household? Who managed the farm? Who controlled the children? Who decided what was to be done and by whom in the house itself and in the part of the farm which in England and northern France was seen as the wife's preserve, when there were two or more wives? The problem for the historian is magnified by the fact that there were many different kinds of complex household, some of them regionally specific and linked to inheritance patterns. In some areas families might hold and farm land in common yet live in separate domiciles. 'In the north of France, the *commaunité* was usually limited to the nuclear family; in the Pyrenees, Languedoc, and Provence, *commaunités* were formed as stem families, uniting parents and one married child; in central France they were often the basis for joint families.'[154] *Commaunités* which were joint families and which held in common not land but only personal and acquired property were common in seventeenth-century Nivernais and were associated with sharecropping rather than land ownership. In other words, they were families no longer 'concerned about the inheritance of land for their sons and marrying out their daughters, but ... labour-sharing domestic groups held together by commercial agreements or even unwritten understandings'.[155] Peasant landowners still formed *commaunités* but these were stem families rather than joint families. A study of the region in 1820 shows that there was considerable regional variation in the distribution of household types even within a département (the proportion of stem house-holds ranged from 12 to 22 per cent and of joint households from 1 to 7 per cent) and that nowhere did the percentage of complex households exceed 30 per cent. None the less, this study indicates that complex households had a tendency to dissolve into simple households at a certain stage of their development so it is uncer-tain just what percentage of households in this area passed through a complex phase. What is certain is that more marital units were in complex households. In 1820 there were 1,109 households in the Morvan and 1,855 marital units. Although only 16 per cent of the households were joint, 33 per cent of the mari-tal units were within joint households.[156] This evidence would seem to suggest that adults had to accustom themselves to rapidly changing relationships within the household but architectural evidence may contradict this assumption. Architectural plans of farmhouses in the Jura indicate that within frérèches families of brothers farmed together but kept their families' living arrange-ments separate within the same house, keeping their own kitchens and bedrooms. Here the household economy (based on fields, lumber store, manure pit, cellar and byre) was a common one, but while the families lived in close physical proximity they were dis-tinct in terms of organisation and relationships. This is an intrigu-ing example of the way in which a household could be complex but the families simple! It brings into question the assumption of so many historians that the household and family were coterm-inous and the implicit belief that contemporaries lent little importance to the interpersonal relations of the mother, father and children. Yet in some quite prosperous farms in Finistére, occupied by complex multigenerational families, 'living' as well as working was communal. Perhaps this was more natural where the family was extended upwards or downwards and did not involve solely the co-residence of brothers and their families. A word of caution is in order. Architects design houses for one purpose; their occupants quite often use them for another. We should not assume that people did not create their own divisions in the use of dwelling space or, alternatively, obliterate divisions when they found them inconvenient.[157]

It would be unwise to assume, because complex households of either the multiple or the extended type were less common in England and America than in France, that such households did not exist or that they did not raise many of the same problems when they did exist. It seems to have been relatively common enough for young married couples to lodge with one or other family of origin for a short while after marriage, for example, and the figure of the widow living in the same house as her son and daughter-in-law does appear quite frequently. In Ryton, Co. Durham, apparently quite often in the late sixteenth and seventeenth centuries households achieved amazing and changing complexity. At times, for example, the French household on the high street accommodated two married couples and five young children from various marriages, yet at other times it consisted of a single family of husband, wife and children.[158] Family disruption had both physical and emotional implications. Children of one marriage might be thrust into straitened circumstances by the remarriage of a parent. William Guise's father, Sir William, had first married a member of the Ken family, who had died when William was born. Next Sir William married Elizabeth Walronde, a widow with a jointure. The couple proceeded to have four sons and three daughters. There was, as William commented, no room for him now:

> This plentifull broode by a second venter coming in to stock the house, my Lady Stelenge [widow of his grandfather] tooke my father into her charge and bred him up with her young daughter neere of one age.[159]

Contemporaries were aware of the problems and inconveniences caused by both extended and multiple household arrangements and tried to cater for them by either formal agreements or informal organisational means. For the elderly, some loss of independence and some introduction of uncertainty was implied. Elizabeth Stout moved from household to household during her widowhood yet her situation was happier than most for her children cherished her. Adam Martindale's father, a widower, entered into articles with his eldest son, a married man, to let him have part of the house for development. The indications are that the arrangement was not an especially happy one for Martindale the elder. Farming partnerships between father and son were far from unknown even in the nineteenth century. Freedom of action might be curtailed, as this example from Burwash reveals: 'Sir, says he, I'm partners in the farm with my son and never buy up bullocks nor nothing without consulting him. So I think I'll consult him before I sign this petition.' In Guilford, Connecticut, the 'stem family' pattern of residence was common in the seventeenth and eighteenth centuries.[160]

In some senses both the families and the households of the *ancien régime* were being continually disrupted – death, desertion, physical separation, departure of children when they went into service or trade or married, warfare, economic difficulty, migration, emigration. Yet, in another sense, the household and even the family was in continuous existence. Martine Segalen and Jean Cuisenier have made this very clear. Studies of individual households show how the household was never a fixed unit – its membership changed, its size changed, its structure changed, its character and its prosperity changed. Yet, whereas today, for instance, parent–child relations tend to belong to one short part of the life-cycle of a family – that is, in the early years when a small number of children are born in quick succession – in peasant France the work of bringing up young children stretched over many, many years, as did the relationships that went with it. This was true of English families, also, until the mid-nineteenth century.[161] In stable households large numbers of infant, pre-adolescent, adolescent and married offspring might live alongside the conjugal couple. In a poor craftsman's household, however, children spent less time co-residing with their family because there was no means of material support therein. Complex relations (in the sense of differing types of parent–child relations) were less evident here. In yet another household, relations were made complex by first and second marriages and co-resident step-siblings.[162] Yet this type of complexity seems scarcely to have disrupted the demographic rhythm of some households, whatever it may have done to its emotional experiences. Nicole Picard had her eighth, ninth and tenth children in 1739, 1741 and 1744, at intervals of 2 years 2 months, and 2 years 9 months, but during this period she was widowed twice and remarried twice.[163]

Servants

Households encompassed not only members of the simple nuclear family but also servants. Servant-keeping was widespread throughout the social hierarchy in early modern England, France and the English American colonies. There is some evidence that it was rather less prevalent in the colonies than in the Old World. For example, in Bristol in 1689, 13 per cent of the population were classified as servants and two-thirds of households had no servants at all.[164] Various studies have shown how servant labour was commonly used as a substitute for, or supplement to, child labour. For example, when Adam Eyre married Jane in 1647, the first requirement was to find a maid – he was unable to 'table with my wife' until he had arranged for one of the daughters of a local man, John Greaves, 'to come and live with my wife'. But servant-keeping was more than a matter of providing labour within the households of the independent. It also offered a service to the servant in terms of training, subsistence, connections and patronage. In the early modern period a servant was defined as a dependant who lived in the household of another. As Cissie Fairchilds has explained in her stimulating study of *Domestic Enemies* in *ancien-régime* France, a servant was not, at this time, necessarily or even primarily one who scrubbed and cleaned for a living. Chaplains, clerks, tutors, governesses, armed guards and grooms, ladies and gentlemen in waiting, and so on were as much 'servants' as were the kitchen and chamber maids. As was the case with so many epithets of the early modern era, 'servant' described a relationship rather than a job of work. Adam Martindale described his period as tutor to the children of Mr Shevington of Eccles in the period preceding the Civil War thus: he 'sent for me to teach his children, and to read prayers in his family, and this was either all (or the main substance of all) that I undertooke; but afterwards he put such varietie of businesse upon me, and involved me in such trusts about his housekeeping ... that sometimes I have not gone to my naked bed for a week together'.[165] Servants, like widows, were a highly heterogeneous group, bound together by the nature of their formal relationship with the master and/or mistress of the household. In some cases one's servants might be drawn from one's own class – as, for example, the young men and women who became part of noble households, receiving an education and an instruction in noble living. Such might even come from the master's or mistress's own blood stock – a poor relation or even a not so poor relation. While many scholars have assumed that it was relatively rare for households to include collateral kin as servants, the evidence from early censuses is rarely clear. Kin did not necessarily bear the same patronymic as the married couple who headed the household, and might well not be ident-ified as kin in an official return. They might also be step-relatives or half-relatives. It may be true that only about 4 per cent of apprentices were bound to masters with the same surname, but the precise implications of such information are unclear. For that 4 per cent this was an important experience. Moreover, the assumption that only those who bore the same surname were 'significant kin' should at all costs be avoided.[166] The term 'servant' also describes Mr Rhodes, the young chaplain to Lady Margaret Hoby, in the sixteenth century, and Richard Lowe, chaplain to the Coke household at Melbourne. Bishops' house-holds were often hosts to young scholars who were technically 'servants' – Bishop Morton of Coventry and Lichfield, for instance, gave a place in his household to George Canner, a blind boy of humble parentage from Lancashire. Canner's education at grammar school and, later, at St John's College, Cambridge, was financed by Morton. Eventually he was made curate of Clifton Campville, Staffordshire.

The position of servant was, for most of these people, a tempor-ary one. The period of service varied enormously. Mary Greaves served Adam and Jane Eyre for barely a month before a replace-ment had to be sought, but Richard Gough acted as clerk to Robert Corbett for many years until he inherited property in 1661. Immanuel Bourne spent a much shorter time in the household of Sir Samuel Tryon before marrying the lady in waiting of Lady Tryon and setting up a household of his own in Derbyshire. For many of these individuals, though, when they did set up house independently it was as a result of the recompense for their service that they had received from the master and mistress. So Bourne, Lowe and Canner received what historians of patronage call 'preferment' but what historians of the household should regard as the equivalent of the recompense or dowry paid to so many servants in addition to, or in lieu of, payment for their services when they departed the household. Richard Gough recounts the tale of

a poor weaver named Parks, who lived in Newton on the Hill, he had eleven children, all baptised by Mr Kinaston;[167] at the baptizing the tenth or eleventh Mr Kinaston said (merrily) 'Now one child is due to the Parson',[168] to which Parks agreed, and Mr Kinaston choase a girle, that was about the middle age among the rest, and brought her up at his own house, and she became his servant; and when she had served several years, he gave her in marriage with thirty, some say sixty pounds portion to one Cartwright, who lived beyond Ellesmeare, and had an estate to balance such a portion.[169]

In the France of the sixteenth to mid-eighteenth centuries, while wages were theoretically paid to servants, it appears that in most cases no actual money changed hands. A servant received board, lodging, clothing – all his or her needs – and lived in a style not far below that of the master, mistress and their children. When the servant left the household he or she was recompensed. In England wages do seem to have been paid in at least some cases.

One of the richest sources for the lives and conditions of female servants in the seventeenth century is the account book of Joyce Jefferies, a gentlewoman. At any one time Joyce employed up to three female servants. Their pay and their status varied. For instance, in July 1639 Anne Davies was paid 40s a year and Elyzabeth Hackluit 60s. By contemporary standards, these girls were treated well. Joyce Jefferies paid for medicines and for doctor's visits to her maids, despite the expense involved. She gave the maids spending money when they attended the fair at Hereford and paid for quite comely clothing for them ... 'paid Mawdeline Mawris my coock maid her first half yeares wages due November ye last day 1641, 11s. I also gave her 2 yeards of red cloth for a wast cote – cost me 5s'. At the New Year the servants were given gifts. One of the maids, Elyzabeth Hackluit, probably

came from the home of an industrious craftsman or husbandman who endowed his daughter with a portion to be paid to her
on her marriage. In June 1640, Joyce Jefferies noted that she
'paid Mrs Elyzabeth Hackluit alias Russell 6 months use for 100 li
which her father turned over to me, to pay her, for the portion
he gave her' – a sum of £4. On 9 July she recorded that she 'paid
Mr William Russell, confectionary, in full paiment of one hundred pownds, being the portion which Mr Thomas Hackluit of
Knitley gave his daughter ... in marriage to Mr William Russell:
the other 60 li he received before'.[170]

Anne Davies's position is less clear. She was paid less than
Elyzabeth. Yet, when she married in May 1641, her erstwhile
mistress treated her handsomely enough. 'Anne Davies wedding
gowne which I gave her, she was married to Joshua Ailwey on
Whitson, Thursday 1641. Imprimis paid Mr Henry Meredith
mercer in herifford 3 li for 12 yeards of fine black silk mohere at
5s a yeard, for 17 yeards of fine black silk bon lace to dresse her
gowne at 4s a dozen – 6s 4d.' This gown also required quantities
of buckram, taffeta and yards of satin trimming. Perhaps even
more important is the fact that Joyce maintained her close relationship with Anne long after this marriage and removal from the
household. She, for example, 'gave Mrs Tomkins ye midwife at ye
cristening of Mrs Anne Ailweys daughter Beatrice 1s' and recorded
the following payments on the occasion of Anne's own churching:
'gave the coock at Anne Ailwey's churching 1s; gave her maid Bes
then 6d, gave Eliza Acton then 6d, gave Anne Ailwey to by wine then
10s'. In 1644 Joyce bought 250 cabbage plants from Anne. But, perhaps most interesting of all, Joyce looked after the interests of
Anne's first child, Beatrice, who was probably her goddaughter. In
November 1645, 'I gave little Beatrice Ailwey at Horncastle 6d', and
in summer 1646 she entertained the child at her home and 'paid
Dick done for carring from Horncastle to her mother'. Many items
of clothing were also provided for the little girl: 4 August 1642, 'paid
Edward Munckland for making betridge Aiywaies first gowne of red
tamma 16d'; October 1644, 'paid Mr Henry Meredith mercer in
herifford for 3 yeards of fine scarlett barragon at 3s 4d a yeard to
make Anne Ailwaies childe betridge to make her a cote, 10s'. Some
servants in Joyce Jefferies' household were also her godchildren.
For example, Elyza Acton both lived in and was married from her
household. Other godchildren were provided with gifts and help.

This detailed account book helps our understanding of the position of servants girls in a household. Domestic servants were given a wage; they had clothing provided of a standard commensurate with that of the head of household; a dowry might be administered by the household head; wedding clothing might be provided (a parallel with the suit of clothing that an apprentice would receive from his master upon completing his term); the head of household might continue his or her association with the servant after the period of service was over, giving practical help and perhaps acting as sponsor to any children. Even if a young person spent only a brief time in another household, he or she made a relatively intimate connection which might be of considerable emotional and practical value in later life. Both Elyzabeth Hackluit Russell and Anne Davies Ailwey, however, became mistresses of their own households and kept maids of their own.

There are, of course, some peculiarities about the Jefferies' household. It was the household of a well-to-do mature single woman who had no children of her own and may have treated her 'servants' differently because of this. Elyzabeth, Eliza and Anne were perhaps more like her daughters and stood in a very different relationship to her from, for example, that of Mary Greaves to Adam and Jane Eyre. We already know from other studies that the conditions of servitude were highly dependent upon the financial and social position of the household and the personality and personal circumstances of the master and mistress. None the less, the Jefferies example tells us much that is valuable about the way in which the household system interacted with the wider community by weaving webs of patronage dependent, for their resilience, not only upon blood but upon service.

Young women went into service in order to prepare themselves for marriage, which they regarded as their ultimate, inevitable and desirable destiny. Fifty-seven young women went out to Virginia in 1621 declaring their suitability for marriage on the basis, often, of their training 'in service'. Some bore their employers' written references. Ellen Borne was 'skillfull in many workes'; Martha Baker was 'skillfull in weavinge and making of silke poynts'; Alic Burgs was 'skillful in anie countre worke. She can brue, bake and make malte & c.'[171] Adam Martindale's sister insisted, in the early seventeenth century, against her parents' wishes, on going to London to seek employment as a lady's maid because then she could cast her cap at a wider circle of male admirers. But many girls became servants quite close to their own homes, immediately transferring their allegiance to the master and mistress. In eighteenth-century Toulouse and Bordeaux most female servants came from peasant families in the prosperous hinterland, where their families could retain boys on the farm but had no need of the labour of more than one or two daughters. In service, both English and French girls widened their circle of male acquaintances. Mary Matthews was not alone in marrying a fellow servant.[172] In service they were trained in housewifely skills appropriate to their own social station, whether that was aristocratic, middling or extremely humble.

For young men from farming communities who sought positions as servants, the situation may have been rather different. In Bordeaux and Toulouse, in the eighteenth century, the male servants came from peasant families in areas where the farms were so poor that families had to send all their children away, male or female. These long-distance subsistence migrants presumably found the towns of the south-west the nearest suitable hunting ground. They hunted not wives but bread.[173]

It would be a mistake to assume that all servants were young or that for all it was but a temporary phase in the life-cycle. In 1664 Katharine Austen grieved for a trusty servant, William Chandeler, 'who had dwelt in my house almost Ten yeares. He served me faithfully.... A long faithful servant is a breach in a family ...'.[174] The case of Anne Ralphe, daughter of George Ralphe, carpenter, neatly illustrates the point that people moved in and out of independence and dependence in seventeenth-century English society. Anne 'was sometime servant to the Lord of Powes, and there she became a papist. Att her returne [to Myddle] shee was maryed to Thomas the son of Francis Jones, of Marton; and had many children by her'. They weren't exactly self-sufficient – one of the children had to be bound apprentice by the parish, which was, in effect, a relationship of dependence or servitude to the parish. 'After the death of Thomas Jones shee went to bee servant to Madam Clifford of Lea Hall, and there she marryed Nicholas Astley an Irishman and a papist.' This second period of service again ended in a life of relative independence when she and her second husband became tenants of Blacke Eavan's tenement.[175]

Servants and Children

There has been some debate among historians about the relationship between servants and masters, especially as compared with
the children of the master, who were also, of course, dependants.
The issue has, it seems, been further confused by the relatively
primitive living conditions of even the most well-to-do English,
French and North Americans in the sixteenth and seventeenth
centuries. It is well known that the very poor lived in cramped and
squalid conditions. In Myddle, in 1701, there was a squatter colony
of 14 cottages. But some squatters lived in even less salubrious
accommodation. One such family lived in a cave on Harmer Hill;
another dwelt in a 'poor pitifull hut built up to an oak'.[176] Less well
known is the fact that, even for those who farmed, a house was
most often a one-room affair with little furniture, which provided
shelter rather than comfort. The house of a sixteenth-century
Breton peasant was a single room, distinguished from the stables
only by the craftsmanship of the woodwork. Yet houses were not
much more commodious or divided in the seventeenth and early
eighteenth centuries. In 1674 the inventory of a cooper in the
Maconnais contained only one room for living and sleeping in – it
contained four beds in good condition and two more not in use.
The probate inventory of a wealthy farmer, taken in 1723,
consisted of one room with a curtained bed and a smaller adjoining room containing two uncurtained beds. Urban houses in
eighteenth-century Massachusetts had more rooms but were of
poor construction. Court records tell of paper-thin walls and
gaping cracks and knot holes in the floors and walls.[177] To keep
warm, whole families, even households, shared beds. The practice
was widespread. In colonial America it may have persisted until
well into the eighteenth century. In Boston, Massachusetts, in
1754, the McCarthy and James families lived under the same roof.
Mary McCarthy, wife of Daniel, shared a room with her two sisters
and a transient, William Stone. It was divulged in court that Mary
and William shared a bed while her sisters slept in another.
Susanna Chambers slept in the same bed with a thirteen-year-old
maidservant when her own husband was at sea. When Susanna
took a lover, the servant, Mary Salmon, continued to share their
bed. Lodgers, too, slept in the same rooms and beds as their hosts.
Captain Peter Staples slept on a bed at the foot of that occupied by

Mr and Mrs Thomas Hammet; this was regarded as unremarkable – only the fact that he leapt into bed with Abigail once her husband had risen from it was cited as grounds for divorce.[178]

Communal sleeping was certainly common in rural areas of England and France until late in the seventeenth century. Celia Fiennes reported that it often became so crowded in Buxton that the inn-keepers would crowd several beds into a room and even make strangers share beds. This was clearly something for a gentle-woman to remark on by this time in late seventeenth-century Britain or France. References in Samuel Pepys's diary suggest that sharing beds and rooms was regarded as exceptional by this time. Indeed, it appears that before the 1560s the practice had died out among well-to-do French people. Noel du Fail reflected, 'Do you not remember those big beds in which everyone slept together without difficulty? ... there slept together all the married people, or unmarried ones, in a big bed made for the purpose, three fathoms long and nine feet wide.'[179] Yet, in seventeenth-century Paris, children often slept two or three to a bed even in homes not considered poor. By the eighteenth century, this was much more rare but not unknown.[180] The Church frowned upon communal sleeping of mixed sexes, for fear of incest, fornication and adultery. It may have had some success in suppressing this, although it was very common for people of the same sex to sleep together whether or not they were related. More efficacious in stopping communal sleeping among the well-off was probably the status associated with possessing more furniture, and especially, expensive beds. Communal sleeping continued among the peasantry of France and seems to have been accepted in some remote areas until well into the nineteenth century. 'Families are large, all the individuals that compose them, without regard to age or sex, sleep all together in the cow stables, on a rough bed covered with woollen sheets which are never washed', wrote an observer of conditions in the Hautes-Alpes in the 1850s. As Flandrin points out, the big bed was often the only comfortable meeting place for peasants in poorly furnished, heated and lit cottages. There was 'a logical correlation between the discomfort of the house and the comfort' of the feather mattress.[181] The prominence of the bed in the life of the house is indicated in French and English inventories of the sixteenth and seventeenth centuries and in American of the seventeenth, although, in the

homes of professional people, merchants and gentlemen, its relative importance decreased throughout the period. Clearly everyone, masters, mistresses, daughters, sons, apprentices and servants,
lived in close proximity in the houses of the sixteenth, seventeenth
and even eighteenth centuries, frequently sleeping together. Even
when, as in the roomy house of the widow of an Inspector of Taxes
in the Macconnais in 1780, there were sufficient rooms to accord
each inhabitant a separate bedroom, the maidservant in fact slept
in a truckle bed in her mistress's room.

Not much day-light was spent in the house, especially on farms.
In many places in rural France the following pattern of behaviour
was found. At five o'clock in the morning those who had not
already gone to the pastures, like the shepherd and cowherd,
would gather together for a meal and a prayer, 'then they went
their ways and did not meet together again until the evening',
when almost everyone was gathered together for supper. In others
there were variants – some laboured before breaking fast at day-
break on a snack taken into the fields; others returned to the
house at midday for a meal; in some places the sexes were segre-
gated for meals. When the household gathered together for
supper, servants joined members of the master's natural family at
table and shared identical food. After dinner, servants and
children joined in prayers and social activities, listening to readings and stories and songs. 'It was a delightful amusement for
peasants and children who had never known more agreeable
entertainments. These conversations and the reading must have
pleased them greatly: we have often had in our house the sons of
the best inhabitants as domestic workers.[182] It is certainly true that
people lived in rather primitive conditions and that the forms of
conviviality encouraged communality. Yet to assume that this
means there was no hierarchy of relations within the households is
going too far. By the same count, those children who slept with
their parents in the big bed should have been treated as equals; yet
to assert this, in the face of overwhelming evidence to the contrary, would rightly be regarded as an absurdity. In a house where
space and material possessions were shared and privacy was hard
to find, there may have been even more attention to defining relationships in a rigid manner.

Cissie Fairchilds, won over by the arguments of those historians
who have traced the development of the companionate marriage

and affective family in the seventeenth and eighteenth centuries, and its concomitants, private family life and the ideal of domesticity, has argued that there was a sharp contrast between the place of the servant in early eighteenth-century France and England. By this time, in England, the élite in particular were living private lives, but the French were still very much public people, who set little store by family, domesticity or privacy. Whereas in England there was an increasing sense of domestic privacy and decorum and the correct demeanour of 'master and mistress' and 'servant', in France servants still lived on terms of considerable familiarity with their household heads. While architectural drawings demonstrate that there were distinct quarters for servants in French châteaux and great houses, in fact servants spent their days in close society with their masters and mistresses.[183] Pardailhé-Galabrun's illuminating discussion of the reconstruction of Parisian housing arrangements suggests that the picture was not quite so clearly defined. The tendency to 'spread out' vertically may have introduced degrees of privacy into family life, for example.[184]

Flandrin claims that it is an anachronism to reduce the early modern family to the father, mother and children. On the contrary, it is a misunderstanding of the data to conclude that the people of those times did not accord a separate and considerable importance to the 'natural' family as opposed to the household – a form of social and economic organisation which they, from our point of view confusingly, often called the 'family'. The household included the family, as we understand the term, but it was not synonymous with it. The master and mistress had obligations towards their servants of a moral, economic and religious character. They had a duty of Christian love towards them. But these obligations were not tempered by the natural human love a parent feels for a child or vice versa *except* on those occasions where a servant was also kin. Contemporaries realised this but historians appear to find it more difficult to accept. Thus when Ralph Josselin's eldest sister, Mary, came to live with Jane and himself in 1644, a spinster of 21, she is said to have 'come under my roofe as a servant', but he promised that she would not be treated as such: 'my respect is & shall be towards her as a sister'. After eight months she went to live in the household of the Harlakendens. Adam Martindale was under no illusion that he stood in relation to his master as a child.

He was very high and tyrannical in his carriage toward me. Many a time hath he chidden me severely for not doing such worke as he required of me, (as perhaps copying over a lease into a great booke, or his letters to his factor at Burdeux) within a time limited, when he himselfe, by employing me about other businesse, had made it impossible; and were I never so innocent, I must not answere for myselfe, for if I did, he would presently hit me on the teeth with this, that servants must not answere againe; urging that text Titus ii. 9, in the most rigid sence.... His sonnes also which I taught, (especially the elder), gave me great occasion for exercise of patience, for they were just like him; and so encouraged by their parents and flattering servants, that I would almost as soone have led beares, as take the charge of such ungovernable creatures.

Such comments do not belong only to the mid and later seventeenth century. Katherine, daughter of Lady Lisle, in 1539 was gratified that her new mistress treated her as if she were a daughter rather than, as she anticipated, 'but as her woman'.[185] So, much of the evidence cited in support of the view that servants were treated as children is in fact prescriptive in nature – it is what French and English moralists commanded masters and mistresses to do in order to use the household as a form of social and religious control.[186] Yet, in the wording of such advice to masters and servants lies evidence that it was necessary to persuade both to treat the interests of the other as one's own – servants tended not to regard a master as a father or a mistress as a mother; masters and mistresses did not 'care' about the future, the morals, the churchgoing, the behaviour of their servants and did not cherish them as children. The fact that cases of sexual exploitation of female servants by their masters was common and *far* more frequent than incest reinforces the point.[187] When John Reeve of Exeter put his servant, Anne Barker, in a truckle bed at his bed's foot and used her 'constantly and familiarily every week' he was not treating her as any child of his.[188]

All the evidence, eagerly cited to demonstrate the lack of division between children and servants in the households of the sixteenth to eighteenth centuries, is certainly tempting. But it is distracting rather than convincing. There was a hierarchy, for example, at the dinner table of the French farmer that precisely reflected the difference in status of household members: at the head were the master, in place of honour by the fire, and, by his side, the housewife, who was responsible for bringing the dishes she had prepared to table; then came the children ranged in order of their ages 'which alone determined their rank' [not their sex], 'then the oldest of the ploughboys and their companions'; then those who tended the vines, after whom came the cowherd and shepherd'; 'finally the two servant girls concluded the number'. These two servant girls sat at the foot of the table under the direct gaze of their mistress, 'from whom they could not hide any of their movements'. They were in her charge and would be disciplined by her.[189] The ranks (and family roles) of husband and wife, children, male and perhaps female agricultural labourers and female domestic servants are thus clearly differentiated, and, within each rank, age not gender determines place. To conclude that servants were treated as children would be precipitate – all shared the same food but to have done other would have been too complicated. The table itself was usually a make-shift affair and the room too congested to permit separate seating arrangements. When it came to after-dinner entertainment, the servants shared this household activity but they were introduced into the group as outsiders. Just as in the nineteenth century, the servants themselves had a hierarchy. On French farms the male servants were ranged beneath the chief cowman, the female beneath the 'maitresse servante'.[190]

Moreover, periods of service in any one household were frequently brief. It has been estimated that in England half or more of farm servants, the largest category, remained in a single employment for a year or less. A common (but by no means the only) term for apprentices was seven years. Other types of servant contracted for briefer periods. Elizabeth Martindale served in at least three, probably four, widely dispersed households in her short life (c.1648–1673), after receiving an education both at home and at school in Warrington and Manchester.[191] In addition, when one term of employment ended, she spent some time in the household of her maternal grandmother, Elizabeth Hall, after whom she had been named. Sometimes these experiences were happy, sometimes not, but it is difficult to argue that they were an adequate substitute for the constant 'family life'. When they did approach it, it was thought worthy of comment. Thus, Adam Martindale observed that when Elizabeth was taken mortally ill in her last employment at Weeford, near Lichfield, 'her master and mistress tooke great care of her, as if she had not beene a servant but a child'. That it was more common for servants to be sent home when they were ill is suggested by Ralph Josselin's attitude to his servant girl, Jone. When she was ill she was sent home to her mother *post-haste*.[192] And Elizabeth, notwithstanding the attitude of her master and mistress, 'was desirous to come home'. Adam and his wife, also Elizabeth, spent a good deal of time and effort and consultation with their daughter to find her a congenial and safe placement.

The structure of households in certain of the early American colonies seems superficially similar. American labour needs, apart from in New England, were answered to a great extent by servants in the seventeenth and eighteenth centuries. But servitude initially was rather different from that in the Old World. Whereas, in England, servants were of many different kinds and included dependent kin and also people from the same social backgrounds as their masters, this was not so true of the early days of the colonies. In Bristol, Plymouth Colony, in 1689, for example, 90 per cent of children were living in their own homes, suggesting that service was not regarded as a way of removing adolescents from their families during the 'difficult years'.[193] Here children supplied labour needs and were supplemented by servants. But servant exchange was no more prevalent in the Chesapeake. Elsewhere in the colonies, servants were imported in some numbers. Broadly speaking, in the seventeenth century, England was the great provider. These servants were sought out by merchants and mariners eager to meet demand in the colonies for indentured labour.[194] They represented a cross-section of British society and, it appears, came from among those migrants who had already been uprooted from their villages and towns by shortage of work or parental death and had thence found their ways to the city ports. Emigration was not part of their long-term strategy. It was thrust upon them, occasionally by kidnap. A Bristol City (England) ordinance of 1654 spoke out against the 'inveigling, purloining, carrying and Stealing away of Boys, Maides and other persons and transporting them beyond the seas and there selling or otherwise disposeing them for private gaine and profitte'. More benign were the efforts of the Virginia Company to export wives for the settlers.[195] While most Southern colonists used white indentured servants to fulfil their 'manual' labour needs before 1680, some African slaves were employed. It seems that both categories of 'servant' were treated alike; there were, for example, sales of white indentured servants as well as black; the two groups lived together and sometimes intermarried. These colonial servants, black and white, were never part of a family-based household system. Masters were the exploiters of labour, servants the exploited. Both masters and their dependants were immigrants, with short life expectancies. The masters were quite often bent upon making their fortunes through tobacco and then returning to England – the establishment of long-term families and households was not a priority. Houses were crude wattle and daub structures. None the less, servants and masters lived together in much the same way as in the Old World. The servants planned, on their freedom, to set up for themselves, but life-spans were short and the male to female sex ratio high. It was not until the end of the century, when life expectancy had risen significantly because of acquired immunity, and the sex ratio had become more balanced, that earlier and longer marriages and larger families became a reality.[196] By this time, white indentured servitude was being replaced by dependence on black slave labour.

In practice, servants were servants and were treated as such, either benevolently by the benevolent or harshly by the harsh. Masters and mistresses could both hire and fire, buy and sell in a way that was impossible where children were concerned. Ebenezer Parkman, minister of Westborough, Massachusetts, 1724–1782, recorded in his diary his stream of unsatisfactory employees. Robert Henry was hired in 1726 at a rate of £3 per annum to do the farming; Parkman was able to dismiss this blundering incompetent after three months. Then he bought a slave for 74 pounds but Maro soon died. Then, in 1738, he bought a fifteen-year-old indentured servant from Ireland. When this boy attempted to rape Parkman's thirteen-year-old daughter, Mrs Parkman refused to stay alone with him and Parkman sold him to a neighbour.[197]

In the late seventeenth and eighteenth centuries many American households exchanged female servants. The habit of 'kin-related' households exchanging female labour was marked, paralleling earlier developments in England.[198] Such were essentially 'house servants', often helping in production, and not to be confused with land servants.

Black Slavery

The existence of black slavery in the American colonies introduces a further complicating factor into the structure of the American household yet it also helps to elucidate the nature of the relationship between indentured servant and master. It is commonly accepted that slavery was introduced because black slaves were cheaper than white or black indentured servants, who became more expensive to hire once their period of indenture ended, and because poorer living conditions could be enforced once servants were unfree. For the same reason, the possibilities of hiring convict labour were explored. In other words, masters wanted to make their relationship with servants even more exploitative than it had been, rather than to introduce a newly exploitative situation. Slave-owning in the eighteenth-century South was extremely widespread, although it did not affect the household structure of the 50 or so per cent of the white population of the South engaged in purely subsistence farming. Perhaps 40 per cent of households in the Chesapeake region had three or more slaves apiece, and some in the Piedmont region of Virginia had large numbers of slaves. Large concentrations of slaves were not common, however, except in the rice-growing areas of South Carolina.[199]

Little or nothing is known about the slave families themselves, who lived on the plantations, before 1760. High mortality during the passage over and after, and an enormously skewed sex ratio, acted as inhibitors to the establishment of families. In the Chesapeake, in particular, slaves lived in male groups on isolated plantations and had little opportunity to meet and form relationships with African women. Those African women who survived the hardships of the trip were often infertile, an infertility which was exaggerated by poor diet and age. This situation righted itself by the eighteenth century: infant mortality reduced; the sex ratio became balanced through natural forces; Africans were born into slavery and accommodated themselves to forming relationships within it. The black native-born population in the Chesapeake exploded because young slave girls formed sexual relationships in early puberty and started their child-bearing years very early. Parents seem to have tried to steer their daughters into relationships with slaves who stood in high standing with the 'big house'. It was, however, difficult for slaves to live regular family lives based on any idea of a co-resident household. White law did not recognise slave marriage. Slaves were property and husbands and wives or parents and children could be, and were, sold away from one another. Because small children were normally kept with their mothers for convenience's sake (the plantation owners' convenience), slave family life became matrilineal in emphasis. The mothers, and not just the fathers, were polygamous. The plantation household economy, therefore, changed the traditions of West African family life with which the slaves were acquainted, to new patterns of relationship and co-residence.[200] There were, of course, slaves in the northern colonies. Perhaps because of the much smaller numbers they were treated more humanely. Marriages between slaves were recognised and often solemnised by a minister of religion. None the less, families were disrupted by owners at will.

There has been considerable debate about the long-term development of the black family under slavery. There have been those who have argued that the black family was never a viable institution because the law of slavery made it weak and ineffective. There were a very limited number and range of decisions that could be taken within the family. The instability of the family forbade the development of companionate marriage and led to widespread sexual promiscuity and cold relations between fathers, mothers and children. There were, however, a wide variety of conditions in which black families developed, and some plantations nurtured real family groups.[201] In sharp contrast are those studies which portray a remarkably stable black family forming predominantly two-parent households which strove to act as traditional and authoritative nuclear families. Black slaves regarded marriage as an important institution, limiting procreation and existing to control the behaviour of offspring.[202] One major area of debate remains the extent to which the plantation owners destroyed or maintained the slave family. Fogel and Engerman argue that masters valued the family as a means of control on the plantation and, as a consequence, did not exploit female slaves sexually as much as had been thought, or engage in breeding slaves, which would have resulted in only marginal economic benefit. But census evidence suggests that some eastern slave-owners did breed slaves for the market.[203]

More work on the experience of the slave-owning household is required if we are to penetrate the true relationship between slaves and slave-owners. For example, in her excellent study of black and white women of the old South, Elizabeth Fox-Genovese notes that Sarah Gayle formed a deep attachment to a former slave of her father and his family, observing, 'she saw nothing contradictory between her deep affection for – and emotional dependence on – people whom she proposed to hold in perpetual slavery and her acknowledgement of their ability to take care of themselves as well as her'. Again, her devotion to some slaves contrasted sharply with her irritation with, even contempt for, others.[204] Both love and hate crossed class lines. Slaves, who by prescription belonged to the 'household', might either be drawn into or cast out of the 'family'. We must, however, proceed beyond the concept of power-relations to lay hold of the full meaning of family life to all its members.[205]

Economy

Some historians maintain that the family changed quite fundamentally in response to economic change.[206] Some even argue that the response was a conscious, deliberate strategy pursued by 'families'. Few would contest that the family, or at least the household, was, to a degree, responsive to economic factors. However, the co-resident family was not a mere reflection of the economy. Economic determinism must be avoided: individuals and the families in which they lived were subject to other influences – cultural, sensual, emotional, psychological, religious. Moreover, any suggestion that families (or their heads) sat down and planned a strategy is dangerous. First of all, 'strategy' and 'plan' imply a route towards a known goal. What was this goal? Secondly, do people plan rationally in this way? Thirdly, what is the evidence that they, having planned, act out such a strategy rather than respond in an ad hoc way to changing circumstance? Fourthly, where is the proof that their actions are dictated exclusively or primarily by economic considerations?[207]

Certainly, as the household system was underpinned by productive resources in terms of both property and human capital, then the historian of the family must also be interested in the nature and organisation of those resources. If, as I have argued, co-resident families were more interested in harmonious living than in power

conflict, the organisation and success of the household economy
was of considerable importance in achieving this end. Obligations
of an economic nature were laid upon all family members. Recent
studies have demonstrated that the term household covers a multitude of, if not sins, then variations on a theme of domestic production. The several regions of British North America possessed highly
distinctive labour systems which were, none the less, encompassed
by what we call households and they called families. In the South
this was based upon, first, indentured white servitude and, second,
black slavery, always assisted by family labour; in New England
upon family and, secondarily, upon wage labour; in the Middle
Colonies – New York, New Jersey, Pennsylvania and Delaware –
upon a mixture of immigrant servant and slave labour with family
and wage labour; and in the Caribbean colonies upon African
slaves.[208] So we cannot legitimately speak of a Colonial American
system of household production – there were differences by region
and by locality. In England, household production, be it of farm or
workshop, depended first and foremost upon family labour, including that provided by step-children and collateral kin, and secondarily upon indentured, native-born wage labour. This in itself
suggests that there were considerable numbers of people who did
not work within their own households but in other people's.
Studies of early modern France indicate a much greater diversity in
household organisation than in England. Households, especially in
Northern France, often resembled the English nuclear family
household, but in the South, household structures included those
of related adult couples co-residing in order to work their land and
reap its profits.

In England the proportion of the land held by people who
could be classified as small property owners diminished sharply
over the period 1560–1914, from around 50 per cent at the turn
of the sixteenth century to 30 per cent at the turn of the
seventeenth, 15 per cent at the turn of the eighteenth and 10 per
cent at the turn of the nineteenth. These were the owner–
cultivators, whose farms could not have supported, and were not
expected to support, any other than the household in occupation. In North America the proportions were reversed: 'freehold-
ing families controlled seventy per cent of the land and, except in
the South, represented a similar proportion of the population.[209]
There were tremendous variations in the amount and value of the

land held and lifestyles experienced among American free-holders, but even poor farmers were not dependent upon the wealthy for their bread.[210] These figures in themselves would suggest that in England the proportion of families that could have lived in a 'traditional' manner was in quite rapid decline over the period 1560–1914, whereas the proportion in America was much higher, although regionally differentiated.

Everything was not cosy down on the French farm, traditional and predominant though it might have been. By the nineteenth century as many as 40 per cent of Frenchmen, albeit still often encumbered by seigneurial obligations, were accepted as being proprietors. Share-tenancy or metayage persisted in many areas (the central highlands and the lands adjoining them) until the late nineteenth century, when it became restricted geographically. Simple tenant farming predominated in Picardy, Artois, parts of Flanders and Normandy, the Ile de France and the Pays de Beauce, and, in the nineteenth century, prevailed over metayage in many areas. But many French 'farms' scarcely merited the name: they were scattered small-holdings barely capable of maintaining a nuclear family. In Picardy, during the time of Louis XVI, the Intendant had informed the government that the 'farms were exceedingly minute; that farmers paid what they owed usually in grain and as a result there was only just enough corn left to feed them'. This led to a degree of semi-proletarianisation. It meant that the number of the French who could be enclosed within the comforting arms of the traditional household was also much less than the figure of 40 per cent proprietorship might suggest.[211]

In England, the rural economy was based upon agriculture and industry. Probably all farming households produced some goods – clothing, linens, baskets, furnishings – but far from all produced enough for all their own needs and far fewer produced for the market. In an age of relatively primitive technology it was both easier to diversify one's economic activities and less necessary to specialise, on the one hand, and more possible to alter the balance of one's activities as circumstances dictated, on the other. Moreover, as so many youths were apprenticed to various crafts or trades only to inherit farms of their own, there was a natural mixing of agricultural and craft interests in rural households at whatever social level.[212] In colonial British America, where farmers were, in general, prosperous and fully occupied in farming, before the

Revolution material requirements were met from within the household, through local markets or from imports.[213] In France, households were also involved in both agriculture and manufacture for family consumption or for highly local markets.

The proto-industrial cottage system took root in England in the seventeenth century and was ever-increasing in importance during the eighteenth.[214] Defoe observed as early as 1728 that 'in the manufacturing counties you see the wheel going almost at every door, the wool and the yarn hanging up at every window, the looms, the winders, the combers, the carders, the dyers, the dressers, all busy; and the very children, as well as women constantly employed'. This was thought to provide both the means of subsistence and population growth. 'Predominantly, the first phase of industrialization had been based on the extensive exploitation of family labour', but the years 'between 1770 and 1850, witnessed a final Indian summer for the human-powered handicraft mode of production', which overlapped with the development of factory production.[215] The organisation of cottage industry has been so often and so well described that there is no need to do more than refer to it here.[216] The putting out system did not spread to the Americas until after the War of Independence. By the 1800s up to 40 per cent of farmers in older settlements depended upon outside work or craft production within the household to preserve the family farm.[217] Reorganisation of the rural household's economic activities around manufacture was even slower in France, where it was not widespread until the mid to late nineteenth century.

The traditional rural household was already under siege in much of late seventeenth and early eighteenth-century England – by which time fewer people were farmers and even fewer lived by farming alone. Already many so-called farmers were producing goods for a capitalist entrepreneur and their economic activities no longer obeyed the rhythms of harvest.[218] But, while eventually the American and the French household also fell under siege, the time lag was very considerable. Here the proportion of families motivated by the desire for self-sufficiency today and the livelihood of their offspring tomorrow, by the passing down of land and stock and the work of all co-resident family members towards that end, was throughout our period much higher than in England.

It seems that such an analysis raises more questions about the family than it answers. True, cottage industry may have

permitted rural dwellers far down on the social ladder to maintain households and co-resident families – delaying their proletarianisation. In Leicestershire, in the early eighteenth century,
framework-knitting was still a journeyman occupation and a late
age at marriage obtained. From 1730 capitalist organisation was
introduced, resulting in slow proletarianisation and changes in
the family. The prosperity which marked the years 1750 to 1815,
it has been argued, produced radical changes in family form.
Marriages took place early. There was a noticeable rise in marital
fertility. Births tended to be crowded into the early years of marriage to minimise the period during which the wife was incapaci-
tated and during which there was a strain on family resources.
But when a stagnation of the national economy set in after 1815,
the birth rate stabilised. The severe depression after 1825 had
even more dramatic results. Families actually restricted births.
There was considerable migration out of Leicestershire. Fewer
marriages took place and there was a rise in illegitimate births.
Women and children entered the labour force in greater
numbers. Families lived together in order to maximise their
resources. Those Leicestershire framework knitters who
responded to capitalist organisation of the industry in the 1730s
by marrying earlier and producing more children were taking
advantage of new economic circumstances to become independent householders at a younger age. However, many of the demographic features identified as proof of rational economic
decision making within the family have a more natural explanation. First households in English society were established on
marriage – prosperity and perhaps a decrease in emphasis upon
skill and apprenticeship permitted the workers to marry earlier
and form households. They did not need to *organise* their family
plan – it was quite natural to have more children in the early
years of a marriage and fewer surviving ones later. Similarly, the
drop in average household size was commensurate with a later
age at marriage and household formation. The organisation of
production allowed women and children to participate and to
remain within the house. These were instinctive responses to subsistence pressures, which differed in extent rather than kind
from those pertaining in earlier communities depending upon
farming alone. Sometimes they were uncontrollable responses –
for instance the number of surviving children was not entirely in

the hands of the father and mother. The changes, in themselves, tell us nothing of change in familial relationships or obligations, only of changes in economic relations.[219] We know, for example, that close family relationships and even economic obligations could be, and were, maintained without co-residence or participation in a household economy.

The 'Modern' Co-residential Family

The remit of this chapter has been to examine the relationships within the co-residential family in the early modern period, laying especial emphasis upon the lived-experience in so far as the record allows. It seems appropriate, however, to reflect upon the possible implications of these findings for the future study of the so-called 'modern' or 'new' or 'middle-class' domestic family of the late eighteenth and nineteenth centuries. This is important because it allows the historian a new perspective upon the modern family.

One of the chief focuses of family history has been the middle-class family, which is said to have emerged in Britain in the eighteenth century and elsewhere in the early nineteenth. The pattern of this development, as it has been described by historians, shows remarkable if superficial similarities. Attempts to encompass whole sections of society by over-arching theories are fraught with difficulties. The dominant interpretations – the compartmentalisation of the lives of the middling classes into the 'public' world of work and the 'private' world of the family; the role-division of males and females within this overall framework according to the 'separate spheres' paradigm so well articulated by John Ruskin – largely ignore the differences in structure, role-play and definition, life-style and ethos between various groups within the middle classes, except as rather inconvenient exceptions to the rule. This is true even in the case of sophisticated studies.[220] It is perhaps significant that the size of the middle class is extremely uncertain.[221] Moreover, the class system of America was not the class system of England, and neither was equivalent to the class system in France. And, even within these societies, the term 'middle class' or 'middle classes' has indeterminate meaning. Whereas in England, for example, 'working class' or 'working classes' are synonymous with 'manual working class' and describe those who work thus for their living, the 'middle class' is not descriptive in the same way. Lowly clerks are middle-class. Salaried school teachers are middle-class. Parish clergy are middle-class. Manufacturers are middle-class. Bankers are middle-class. Some of these are employers; some are employees; some have property; some do not; some are separated from the working classes by income; others are barely so separated. Families like the Potters and the Booths were on more than nodding terms with the aristocracy. Their clerks (Jesse Argyle and George Arkell) and associates (Ernest Aves and Hubert Llewellyn Smith) belonged to a rather different social milieu, except when they mingled with the Booths and Potters. The increasing economic specialisation of the period, and its accompanying social fragmentation, make it impossible for scholars to write with confidence of a single middle class. American historians have argued that their society was a two-class society – bipolarised between a business class and a working class.[222] Others have criticised this stance, claiming that, while the middle class did not have a collective class position, it did deny persuasively the role of class in determining economic and other change and exalt the role of individual agency.[223] We would not expect to find uniformity within such a class. Because of this we need to be especially careful not to emphasise similarities at the expense of very real differences both within and between societies.

In seeking to understand the development of the family it is helpful to adopt a rather different perspective than most of the recent work. We should, rather, see the eighteenth and nineteenth century 'family' as an institution which grew out of the early modern co-residential household and its ideological underpinning. The family did not stand still as an institution. It responded to economic, social, religious and cultural change. As society became more complex so the family displayed a wider variety of types, distinguished from one another by occupation, income, class and culture. The changing nature and organisation of production forced many changes on the nature and organisation of reproduction and consumption. But the process was often much more gradual than historians, bent upon demonstrating 'change', would allow. Older structures persisted, in all these societies, well into the twentieth century in some sectors.[224]

Historians have felt able to use studies of late nineteenth-century farming families in all three countries as illustrative of early modern practice. Why? Because this way of living in families survived. An early modernist is less liable to be swayed by the assertions of modern historians that certain practices and behaviours are novel.[225] The family as an institution, even where change was most felt, carried forward with it existing characteristics. For example, eighteenth and nineteenth-century religious and moral teaching about the family and the roles, within the family, of its members bears a striking resemblance to that of the preceding centuries. To deny this fundamental similarity would be a mistake. We should resist generalising about families among the middling sort until those features which historians have identified as most important in changing the family were themselves generally present.

Although historians of the modern period commonly employ the language of class to describe the family, this does not seem to be particularly helpful when it obscures rather than illuminates the important differences between families, in the interests of highlighting a few known similarities. Neither the epithet 'middle class' nor the concept of 'separate spheres' within a public/private divide helps us to such an understanding. By way of illustration: we know that, among successful manufacturers and businessmen in early nineteenth-century Britain, there was a tendency physically to separate residence and workplace. When prosperity disappeared or was at risk, home and workplace were again brought together. A relatively new way of life, which involved physical separation of home and work, gave way once more to the traditional rhythms. In America, the urban middle classes, also attached to a cult of domesticity, did not find it necessary to desert the city and town centres, and the class segregation and public/private divide are not as marked as among some of the more affluent sections of the English middle class.[226] While American historians have identified the same call to middle-class Americans to keep home and work separate, it seems that the largest number of adherents to this creed occurred among the lower middle classes, 'families of farmers, ministers, lawyers, small-scale shopkeepers, boarding house keepers, small printers and writers', who had least *experience* of such a separation, indicating that ideology and experience did not always match.[227] For large numbers of so-called middle-class people in England, separation of home and work was never a reality, a possibility or even a desirability. Until the 1850s, as many of the people of England and Wales lived in the countryside as in towns. Many of the rural middle class were farmers. In their households, throughout the nineteenth century, the 'farm' was the focus of all activity, whether we see the roles within that homestead as 'gendered' or not.[228] There was no real sense in which women dwelt in a private world and men in a public. My own memory of a North Staffordshire farm, as late as the 1950s, is of the farmer and farmer's wife and their children involved in the day-to-day 'farming' enterprise, with a division of labour, real though it was, which suggested little of the 'public/private divide'. Day to day, the farmer's wife was as intimately involved in marketing, dairying and poultry management as her seventeenth-century forebears, and her work was every bit as close to 'nature' and hard manual labour as her husband's. The same is true of the many small business enterprises of the period. If there is a useful concept of 'middle-class identity', then it is not to be found as a single definition of domestic or work arrangements. We should beware of creating a paradigm middle-class family where none existed.

What is missing is a typology of 'middle-class' households. If such could be constructed, it would then be incumbent upon future scholars to quantify how many families 'fit' the various categories and thus determine whether or not one family type predominated at any one time.

Any attempt to create a typology of English middle-class families is bedevilled by the preponderance of material – 'family histories', 'business histories', autobiographies and biographies pertaining to the upper middle classes. The representatives of families who made their money from manufacture, big business, stockbrokering and investment, and work in the Empire and distant foreign parts, appear time and again as the cast of modern studies of the middle-class family – the Booths, Potters, the Cadburys, the Nightingales, the Frys, the Stephens, the Wilberforces. Until historians look in more detail at other middle-class families we can move little further. What I offer here are a few contrasting family structures which pertained in families which historians would define as 'middle-class' – a first step towards constructing a typology.

A Provincial Shopkeeper and Schoolmaster in Eighteenth-century Sussex

Thomas Turner (1729–93) and his wife, Peggy Slater, lived in East Hoathly, Sussex. Thomas was formerly the village schoolmaster and clearly a man of some education. His business languished during the Seven Years War but prospered again after 1763. Thomas's diary tells us a little of what he expected from marriage and what he received. Clearly he had high hopes of the married condition. In June 1755, just over a year after his wedding and in the wake of a disagreement with his wife about her movements, Thomas reflected on the state of marriage.

> Oh, was marriage ever designed to make mankind unhappy? No, unless by their own choise its made so by both parties being not satisfied with each other's merit. But sure this cannot be my own affair, for I married, if I know my own mind, intirely to make my wife and self happy; to live in a course of virtue, and to be a mutual help to each other.

The first glimpse of their married life together is of Peggy reading aloud to him, *Clarissa Harlow*, during August 1754. Almost a year later Peggy wanted to go to Lewes and Thomas had words with her about it. He was in despair.

> Oh what am I going to say! I have almost made as it were, a resolution to make a sepperation by settling my affairs and parting in friendship. But is this what I married for? How are my views frustrated from the prospect of an happy and quiet life, to the enjoyment of one that is quite the opposite.[229]

Yet, two years later, despite poor relations with Peggy's mother (described as 'a very Xantippe' with 'a very great volubility of tongue for invective'[230]), and Peggy's own very poor health, Thomas was able to write:

> This is the day on which I was married and it is now three years since. Doubtless many have been the disputes between my wife and myself during the time, and many have been the afflictions which it has pleased God to lay upon us ... but I may now say

with the holy psalmist, 'It is good for us that we have been afflicted'; for, thanks be to God, we now begin to live happy ...[231]

In July 1757 Thomas bewailed Peggy's decision to visit Lewes at the very time when he needed to be away on business. 'I have several journeys to go next week, which I must postpone, on account of her absence. But alas! what can be said of a woman's temper and thought? Business and family advantage must submit to their pride and pleasure.' On further reflection, he thought that this applied to men also, 'but most people are blind to their own follies.'[232] There follow, however, references to their attending dinners and sermons together, to their carousing together, to them sharing a horse, and to his constant distress at her ill health. But by October 1758 he was once again bewailing his married lot, that he had no one to share his innermost thoughts and worries about trade.

> Oh how happy must that man be whose more than happy lot it is to whom an agreeable company for life doth fall – one in whome he sees and enjoys all that this world can give; to whom he can open the inmost recesses of his soul, and receive mutual and pleasing comfort to soothe those anxious and tumultuous thoughts that must arise in the breast of any man in trade!

When Peggy died, in June 1761, Thomas's tribute to her is somewhat different. Had his earlier complaints been exaggerations of the moment or was he simply not speaking ill of the dead when he wrote:

> In her I have lost a sincere friend, a virtuous wife, a prudent good economist in her family, and a very valuable companion.

and in August,

> Almost distracted with trouble: how do I hourly find the lost I have sustained in the death of my dear wife! What can equal the value of a virtuous wife? I hardly know which way to turn, or what way of life to pursue. I am left as a beacon on a rock, or an ensign on a hill.

The next March, after a visit carousing with his father-in-law, Thomas exclaimed again:

> I could see a sufficient difference at my arrival at my own house between the present time and that of my wife's life, highly to the advantage of the latter. Everything then was serene and in order; now, one or both servants out, and everything noise and confusion. Oh! it will not do. No, no! it will never do.

And in November 1763 he once more confided in his diary, 'What afflicts me is the loss of my dear Peggy.... For want of the company of the more softer sex, and through my over much confinement, I know I am become extreme awkward, and a certain roughness and boisterousness of the disposition has sexied on my mind.' He had become morose and antisocial. He shunned the company of other women, he wrote in 1764, 'for really there seem very few whoes education and way of thinking is agreeable and suitable with my own'.[233] By the end of the year he had changed his mind, and toyed with the idea of courting another wife. He settled upon a young woman at Chiddingly. He referred to her as 'my charmer, or intended wife, or sweetheart' and was clearly besotted. 'I had the opportunity, sure should I say the pleasure, or perhaps some might say the unspeakable happiness, to sit up with Molly Hicks, or my charmer, all night ...' His estimate of her is interesting: 'Well, to be sure, she is a most clever girl.' 'I certainly esteem the girl, and think she appears worthy of my esteem.' As the courtship progressed, in the spring and early summer of 1765, he took stock:

> The girle, I believe, as far as I can discover, is a very industrious, sober woman and seemingly endued with prudence, and good nature, with a serious and sedate turn of mind. She comes of reputable parents, and may perhaps, one time or other, have some fortune. As to her person, I know it's plain (so is my own), but she is cleanly in her person, and dress, which I will say is something more than at first sight it may appear to be, towards happiness. As to her education, I own it is not liberal; but she has good sense, and a desire to improve her mind, and has always behaved to me with the strictest honour and good manners – her behaviour being far from the affected formality

of the prude, on the one hand; and on the other, of that foolish fondness to often found in the more light part of the sex.

Content, he married this daughter of a Lewes yeoman farmer on 19 June 1765. And there the diary ended.

The Life-cycle of the Family through its Generation: the Cadburys

In some cases the varying typology of the family can be traced within the generations of a single family. The household of the family of Richard and Elizabeth Cadbury, in Birmingham in the early 1800s, was the archetypal family enterprise. The Bull Street building was both home and workplace; the enterprise was run by both husband and wife along lines reminiscent of early modern practice. Elizabeth helped with the business and stood in for her husband when he was absent. She bore ten children in fourteen years and cared for them and the household while Richard devoted most of his attention to the business. The children, boys and girls, helped out as and when required and were trained for their future roles within the family enterprise. Wider family and friends, especially from within the Quaker community, provided socio-economic and religious comfort and support.[234] Change came with increased prosperity. In 1812 the family bought a second house, in rural Edgbaston, which, while it was run by Elizabeth, housed the children, their pets and servants, but formed only the occasional residence of both parents. Prosperity seems to have reduced the call which the business made upon Elizabeth's time but her contribution to the enterprise was still crucial. It was not until 1829, when their eldest son, Benjamin, married and took over the business, that both Richard and Elizabeth retired from public life to a new home in Edgbaston with three unmarried daughters. This 'life-cycle' of the family, expressed in terms of the nature and location of 'productive' and 'retailing' work as well as of reproduction and care within the residence, was observable in the career of Benjamin and his wife Candia. They brought up a family of six daughters and one son in the Bull Street household, moving to suburban Edgbaston only in 1840. His brother, John, lived with his first wife over their tea and coffee shop on Bull Street. When, in 1832, he married a second time, to another Candia, they began married life over the shop, but after the birth of a child they moved into a small house close to John's parents in Edgbaston. Here they raised five sons and a daughter. The classic statement of the public/private divide is apparently contained in the words of this daughter, Maria. 'Home was the centre of attraction to us all, and simple home pleasures our greatest joy.' 'Our home was one of sunshine' but 'our father was greatly occupied with business and town affairs and other interests and he had very little time during the week, for enjoying his garden.' The supportive role of the wife was emphasised by the physical distance of the home from the workplace. The business was still, however, a family affair: the work of the women ensured that the men could work successfully; family members still provided most of the managerial personnel; ownership, investment and profit belonged to the family. That residence away from the workplace signified withdrawal from a particular type of work seems evident from the behaviour of the Cadbury women and children. The division of roles among family members which had been evident in early modern enterprises was now accentuated by geography. The youngest child of Richard and Elizabeth, Emma (b. 1811) married Thomas Gibbins, of the Birmingham Battery Company, in 1837. For as long as they lived close to the works in Digbeth, Emma played an active role in the business, but removal to Edgbaston spelt for her, too, diminution of this role. The daughters of Candia and Benjamin Cadbury, remote from the business enterprise, substituted involvement in substantial philanthropic work. Some authorities believe that gender and class alone informed individual identity within these families. Undoubtedly they played an important part, but place in the family was still crucial: wives were helpmeets not dependants; children (boys and girls), until they reached a certain age, were dependants.

An Upper-Middle-Class London Family – with a Bohemian Cast

Another family type, this time of a more idiosyncratic variety, is represented by that of Linley and Marion Sambourne in the later nineteenth century. Linley (b. 1844) was a cartoonist for *Punch*. His father had been in trade, his mother belonged to a family of musicians from Bath, the Linleys. He brought to his marriage, in

1874, an annual income of £650, a comfortable but not excessive amount. His wife, Marion Herapath, was seven years younger and the daughter of Spencer Herapath, a prosperous London stock-broker, with interests in railway construction in Argentina and Brazil and in scientific subjects through membership of the Royal Society, the Statistical Society and the Institute of Civil Engineers.

Spencer Herapath's family was large (nine children) but Linley and Marion had only two children, Maud and Roy, born within four years of the marriage. Unlike her mother, Marion was not fully occupied with the production and care of the children. The nurse and the children lived on a separate floor and took a house in Kent each summer. It was not until they were much older that the children became the centre of the family's life.[235] Then both parents enjoyed the company of their children and were con-cerned about their progress, both social and academic, and health.[236] Linley fostered his daughter's talent for drawing and, in such a household, it was not seen as an idle pastime of 'feminine' character.

The pattern of the young couple's life together emerges from the pages of Linley and Marion's detailed diaries. Linley worked from home. This was a leasehold house in the Phillimore Estate, Kensington, a development built to house the affluent profes-sional classes. Basement, groundfloor, and three floors above – each originally had two rooms apiece.[237] All was decorated accord-ing to the precepts of the Aesthetic Movement. Although he did other work, Linley's chief source of income was *Punch*. He belonged to a team of artists who met together for dinner every Wednesday evening to discuss the work for the next issue, which had to be delivered to the engravers by Saturday morning. The rhythm of work was uneven: hard labour on Thursdays and Fridays; an active sporting and social life for the rest of the week. He had no studio. Instead, his easel stood beside the south-facing window in the upstairs drawing room, with a portable gas lamp and engraver's globe to hand. When he worked it was all-absorbing: 'Up at 7:45 worked hard and fast on drawing much pushed finished 11:00 p. m. Exhausted. Bed 12:00.' Marion corroborated his long hours. She could not participate in his work but she was concerned with it. One minute she was anxious about him overdoing it, another she was agitated about his dili-tariness, 'Wish Lin would get more forward with work'; another she was basking in the reflected glory of his accomplishments; another she or other family members and servants were dressing up and posing for the photographs which he used as models for his cartoons; another she was 'calling', or holding 'at home' days for callers, as she maintained a social circle which supported their livelihood as well as their life-style.[238] Her role as hostess and party/dinner companion to Linley expanded once the children were grown but contracted after her daughter, Maud, married. The importance of maintaining an active social life was much reduced once her husband's career was established and her daughter had found a husband. Linley amassed a huge collection of photographs and cuttings for use in his work, which absorbed his attention and irritated Marion. 'Lin at those everlasting photos' ... 'More of those hateful photos, Lin wastes time, late with work.'[239] She shared a social life with him – attending dinner parties and dances (especially in June and July) and visiting the theatre – but he also belonged to all-male societies, such as the Garrick Club, from which she was excluded, and which frequently kept him away from home in the evenings. A good deal of her time was spent in housekeeping – directing the three servants in their work of ordering the household, deciding what food would be eaten and how it would be prepared, shopping (largely in department and book stores but often to buy delicacies for dinner parties and occasionally to buy household supplies) and supervising the accounts.

If Linley haunted the clubs, Marion maintained extremely close relations with her mother and father, who lived a few hundred yards away from Stafford Terrace. Marion spent her first confinement in her parents' house at Upper Phillimore Gardens. Almost every day thereafter she visited them, often having lunch or tea. Her parents gave help and advice and gifts of money, food and drink. Maud and Roy were indulged by their grandparents. The month of September, when Linley visited Scotland for the shooting, was normally spent by Marion, Maud and Roy with her parents at Ramsgate. She spent many weeks of each year at Westwood – perhaps as much as a quarter or a third of the time. Communication with Linley was maintained throughout. He would come down and sleep for a few nights, return to London for a while, come back to Westwood for another night or two. Daily letters kept them in close and affectionate touch.

Throughout the 1880s Linley's elderly and widowed mother spent a good proportion of her time at 18 Stafford Terrace. She seems to have stayed with them for the three winter months from Christmas, and often to have spent a month or so with them during the summer. Frances Sambourne was 'entertained' with trips to the shops, invitations to lunch and tea and so on. She helped out with the children, acting as babysitter. But there was constant friction between her and Marion because 'Mrs S will interfere'.[240] By 1889 Marion was at breaking point: 'Mrs S rubs me (as I evidently do her) up the wrong way & we both hate each other.' Eventually, in 1892, rooms were taken for Mrs Sambourne at Edwardes Square. Interestingly, Marion then regularly spent time with her mother-in-law, taking her out for drives and supplying her with delicacies.

Most of Marion's siblings founded their own families. Their choice of partners was governed by the social and residential circle not only of their parents but of one another. For instance, Spencer Herapath the younger married Ada Oakes, who lived near to his parents; Edgar Herapath courted Sophy Fletcher, one of the earliest graduates of Girton College, Cambridge, who was the sister of Tabby Herapath's husband, Hamilton; Conrad married Effie Boehm, daughter of the successful sculptor, Joseph Edgar Boehm, to whom he was introduced by Marion; Jessie Herapath married Hamilton Langley, a business connection of her father in Argentina; the youngest sister, Ada or Tabby, married George Hamilton Fletcher, son of the founder of the White Star shipping line, who was well known to her father.[241] Linley and Marion's own daughter, Maud, married the son of one of their social circle, Leonard Messel, a wealthy stockbroker.

Marion's sister, Annie, provides us with an example of rejection of family. Annie Herapath (b. 1854) had married a solicitor, William Furrell, who was much older than herself, when she was 17. There were two sons and a daughter of the marriage, but after nine years William divorced her on grounds of adultery with two correspondents. Annie and the two boys went to Australia to make a new life away from the social disgrace. The daughter went to boarding school on the Isle of Wight. Annie abandoned her sons to an orphanage in Adelaide and returned to London. Although her mother continued to keep in contact, Annie was ostracised by the family. Her chosen route was unacceptable.

The Lower Middle Class

The society into which H. G. Wells was born was a world apart. His mother, Sarah Neal (1822–1905), was the daughter of a Midhurst innkeeper, George Neal, and his wife, Sarah Benham. Their inn stabled the relays of horses which pulled the London–Chichester stagecoach. An uncle drove the coach. When Sarah's father died he left the family (a widow, son John (17) and daughter Sarah (31) – Elizabeth having died in her early teens) with a mortgage on the property and a good deal of debt.

Sarah the elder was frequently ill and during such times her daughter, Sarah, tended the inn and provided meals for her father. In 1833 George came into some property and sent Sarah to a finishing school in Chichester for three years. Here she learned handwriting, reading, sums up to 'but not quite including long division', a little elementary geography and history but not French which was an 'extra', and a certain 'early feminism' associated with the claim to the throne of the young Victoria of Kent.[242] From thence she went into four years' apprenticeship as a dressmaker and hair-dresser 'to equip herself more thoroughly for that state of life into which it had pleased God to call her', in service as a lady's maid.

> By nature and upbringing alike she belonged to that middle-class of dependents who occupied situations, performed strictly defined duties, gave or failed to give satisfaction and had no ideas at all outside that dependence. People of that quality 'saved up for a rainy day' but they were without the slightest trace of primary productive or acquisitive ability. She was that in all innocence, but I perceive that my father might well have had a more efficient helpmate in the struggle for life.[243]

She served, first, in the house of Captain and Mrs Forde and then in the house of Miss Bullock at Up Park, Petersfield. In 1851 a bachelor gardener joined the household. He, Joseph Wells (1827–1910), was five years her junior and, as one of eight children, the son of Joseph Wells, chief gardener at Penshurst Place. The courtship between Joe and Saddie was interrupted by her mother's serious illness in spring 1853, her father's death in August and her mother's dementia and eventual death in November 1853. But on 22 November the two were married in London.

Togetherness did not last long. Joseph became under-gardener at Trentham, Staffordshire; Sarah stayed with relatives, sometimes visiting him. Eventually he obtained a job and cottage at Shuckburgh (Shugborough?). In her diary Sarah said she was 'very happy and busy preparing for my new home' and, later, 'The Saturday laborious work I do not like, but still am very happy in my little home.' Her son later described her as 'that sort of a woman who is an incorrigibly bad cook'. Then Joe was sacked and he and his wife and new baby obliged to 'leave my pretty home'.

Joe contemplated emigration but, perhaps because of the impending birth of another child, decided to remain in England. A cousin, George, who owned a small china and crockery shop in Bromley, offered it to Joe on reasonable terms. 'My father antici-pated his inheritance of a hundred pounds or so', spent all his savings and reserves and bought the business with its stock. They moved in on 23 October 1855 and within days suspected the worst, 'very unsettled. No furniture sufficient and no capital to do as we ought. I fear we have done wrong.' 'This seems a horrid business, no trade …' 'November 8th. No customers all day. How sad to be deceived by one's relations. They have got their money and we their old stock.'

Poverty and his upbringing forced the Wells apart:

> he had been brought up in a country home with mothers and sisters, and the women folk saw to all the indoor business. A man just didn't bother about it. He lived from the shop outward and had by far the best of things; she became the entire household staff, with two little children on her hands and, as the diary shows quite plainly, in perpetual dread of further motherhood.[244]

There were no servants or nursemaids and Sarah was the dom-inant influence upon the children as a result. 'No nurses and gov-ernesses intervened between us.' Joe sold little but turned his passion for cricket to good effect as a professional bowler and cricket instructor. This broadened his social circle to include neighbouring banking families.

The picture of Sarah Wells toiling alone in her house, 'engaged in a desperate single-handed battle with our gaunt and dismal home, to keep it clean, to keep her children clean, to get them clothed and fed and taught', aided only by the occasional presence of a char named Betsy Finch, while her husband, Joe, spent his time in the shop or, more often, playing cricket, is belied slightly by a more detailed description of how they used their time. 'My father would get up and rake out and lay and light the fire, because she was never clever at getting a fire to burn, and then she would get breakfast while he took down the clumsy shutters and swept out the shop. Then came the business of hunting the boys out of bed …' then cleaning the house without benefit of vacuum cleaner or O-Cedar mop. 'My father usually bought the meat for dinner himself, and that had to be cooked and the table laid in the downstairs kitchen' for the midday meal to which the boys returned. While Joe was out delivering, Sarah had to be on hand to serve customers. 'Customers bothered my mother, especially when she was in her costume for housework; she would discard her apron in a hurry, wipe her wet hands, pat her hair into order, come into the shop breathless and defensive.'

Retrospectively it seemed that Sarah 'in those days was just the unpaid servant of everybody'. The family were also insensitive to her feelings. Her dinners met with outright criticism. She was left alone to wash the dinner dishes, repair and make clothing, prepare tea, put the children to bed and deal with correspondence. Her husband spent much time during the day chatting with customers and reading, and after supper spent his time at The Bell. Her son believed her to have lived in a world of innocent reverie, of retreat from the reality around her. 'She was resolved that to the very last moment we should keep up the appearance of being comfortable members of that upper-servant tenant class to which her imagination had been moulded.' Her son was instructed never to let it be known out of doors that they had no servant. The children must not play with common children, from whom they would learn bad language. The royal family provided vicarious living. The Queen 'also a small woman, was in fact my mother's compensatory personality, her imaginative consolation for all the restrictions and hardships that her sex, her diminutive size, her motherhood and all the endless difficulties of life, imposed upon her'.[245] Her son, Herbert George, was destined for greater things than his father and duly sent to Mr Morley's Commercial Academy to train to become a clerk – preferably, if his mother had her way, to a draper. The household broke up in 1880. In 1877 Joe Wells broke his leg very badly and could no longer support the family. Miss Bullock inherited Up Park and called upon Sarah to become her housekeeper in 1880, leaving Joe and the boys in Bromley. She remained there as a highly ineffective housekeeper until her ignominious dismissal in 1893. Herbert George spent much of what we would term his 'childhood' as an apprentice draper living over the shop in Windsor, as a pupil teacher in a second cousin's establishment in Wookey, as a visitor at the hotel run by Uncle Tom, his mother's cousin, and as an apprentice chemist.

A London and Provincial Coaching Family in the Nineteenth Century

Anne Nelson, widow, lived at The Bull, Whitechapel Road, Aldgate, in East London in 1812. She also had interests in several other London inns and was in partnership with a number of coaching businesses. The business was extensive and at one time she held a monopoly of the busy East Anglian route. If historians of coaching are anything to go by, she was not the only woman thus involved. She was 'one of those stern dignified magisterial women of business, who were quite remarkable and a feature of the coaching age, who saw their husbands off to an early grave and alone carried the peculiarly exacting double business of inn-keeping and coach proprietorship and did so with success'. Her grandson recorded in the 1880s both 'her regal form' adorned in 'choicest black bombazine' and the family nature of her enterprise. 'For years, unaided, she alone held possession of this Eastern Road, different friends and members of her family residing at the principal towns along its route.' She was defeated only by the coming of the railways.

Three sons and a daughter were born to Anne and survived to adulthood. Robert managed the coaching business which operated from the Belle Sauvage, near the Fleet prison, into the west, south-west, north and east. John assisted Anne at The Bull and took over the inn at her death. She was still alive in 1826. In 1812 her daughter, Rebecca, married James Haxell at Grey Friars, Newgate. He was a Suffolk man who may have been an ostler at one of the London coaching inns. Possibly Rebecca and James helped with a business in London at first, but by 1817 they had been set up by Anne at a farm called New Place, near Ipswich, to supply the horses required for the coaching business which they helped to run. Ten children were born to James and Rebecca Haxell prior to 1832. At first the family lived on the farm, but by 1822 they had removed into Ipswich where James and Rebecca had to be on hand to run the coaching office. They continued to maintain the farm but did not live there. The coming of the railway hit the Haxell business hard, although they responded flexibly enough by timetabling their coaches to meet the incoming trains.

The children appear to have spent a good deal of their youths with their maternal relatives in London. The six girls were all educated at Ipswich schools and Elizabeth, at least, learned French and German, Latin, music, and drawing. When the time came for the Haxells to set up in trade, family tradition proved strong and at least two sons and three daughters continued in the coaching business, although one son emigrated to Australia and others went into drapery and leather businesses.

Elizabeth, born in 1819, married Herbert Cotton, a tenant farmer (b. 1800), in 1834. He came from respectable Suffolk stock and had been born on a small farm owned by his mother's family. Herbert was born at Grange Farm, was brought up to farm and took the small-holding over when his father died. He bought land of his own, inherited property from his grandfather, and by 1841 was tenant of his grandfather's old property, Amor Hall. On 20 September 1843, when the harvest was safely gathered in, he married Elizabeth.

The Family of a Tenant Farmer in the Nineteenth Century

Elizabeth Haxell was 23 when she and Herbert Cotton married in 1843. He was about 43, a well-established, reasonably prosperous bachelor farmer, set in his ways, and with a closely-knit circle of male friendships. She brought with her to the match a large family network. From the start, her home was the workplace. It contained Herbert's office, from which daily farm business was conducted; daily callers were farmers and agricultural associates, whom she was expected to entertain; her kitchen was open to the farm labourers; the dairy under her supervision. She and Herbert had a close relationship despite the difference in their ages and backgrounds. She always addressed him by his first name. They attended church together with the family, visited the theatre and galleries. She read to him in the evenings 'as usual', modifying her choice to suit his tastes. Each Tuesday they went to Ipswich together and, after following separate paths in the morning, met up for late dinner together at the Great White Horse. She was not restricted by him socially. For example, she went out for walks in the neighbourhood and in London and on their frequent holidays unchaperoned. Remarkably, he, a devoted member of the Church of England, treated her religious enthusiasms with great tolerance, even when she flirted with Catholicism and entertained large numbers of nuns and priests in the house. And within the household she exercised considerable independence. It was she who chose schools for the children, selected servants, paid bills, took the doctor to task for negligence, sorted out the children's problems, organised activities for the children. But Herbert was a fond and involved husband and father. There is no sense here of the stereotypically remote and stern Victorian Papa.

Both Herbert and Elizabeth took a very active role in the upbringing of their children. Certainly they had nursery maids to assist, but their daily activities were their parents' concern. They took the children out for frequent drives and to accompany Herbert on business. There were also many exciting day trips, such as the excursion to Edmonds' Royal Menagerie in December 1854. There were also many opportunities for enjoying life together on the farm: the little ones were taken to see the lambs, the older ones to watch the threshing machine in action; there were romps and games of cricket and battledore in which Elizabeth participated; the new fashion of croquet was taken up. Music, dancing and riding were introduced to all the children at an early age. The children were encouraged to extend their social circle outside the family confines: Elizabeth took them to visit her friends' families in Ipswich and seems to have held more or less open house for their own friends at Amor Hall.

13 August 1861: Tuesday. Edwin Edwards, H. Miller, E. Bates, E. West and Walton Turner came to stay with our boys. 14th. With the boys. Saw them play cricket. Archery and fishing each

day and sometimes had to prevent their quarrelling and played cards with them in the evening. They stayed the rest of the week.[246]

Alongside this picture should be set that of Elizabeth and Herbert's concern for the children's health, welfare and future prosperity. References to placing money in their savings banks, for example, remind us of the supposed propensity of the middle classes to 'save' for the future.

The early education of the Cotton children took place at home, where they were taught by Elizabeth. All the children, boys and girls alike, attended boarding and day schools in Ipswich from a quite early age although Herbert's income would have allowed a governess. Boarding was convenient for Alice but did not restrict parental access to and interest in their eldest child. Moreover, their grandfather lived nearby and kept an eye on their progress. Many a Tuesday Elizabeth called upon her Alice, sometimes taking with her the younger children who were not yet at school. When there were family get-togethers at James Haxell's home in Ipswich, Alice left school 'to pass the evening with her grandfather'. When Elizabeth heard from her father that Alice was ill, she visited the school every day for a fortnight to see the child, the doctor refusing to allow her leave of absence. Eventually, Elizabeth could tolerate this no longer: 'as Mr Hammond still refused giving leave for her removing and believing the child was taking unnecessary medicine, I sent for a warm carriage and took her home with me.[247] In January 1855 Elizabeth was expecting her fifth child and it was time for the two boys, Bertie and Allan, to go to school. Perhaps learning from experience, Herbert and she chose a secondhand cab especially to take the boys daily to Ipswich. Her second daughter, Evelyn, began school in Ipswich as a boarder when she was about seven and a half. She was home sick from the start, and scared her parents by walking home the three miles from Ipswich and turning up unannounced on the doorstep. Elizabeth changed her school and made arrangements for her to attend as a day pupil. The education of the youngest daughter, Blanche, followed the same pattern from the age of seven. In 1859 the boys had been moved to Queen Elizabeth Grammar School, Ipswich, and from then on the diary is crammed full of references to the help Elizabeth gave them with their homework.

6 February Monday. Arranged mineralogical specimens. Evening helped boys with their lessons.... Sunday. At home, Helped boys with Scripture lessons; 27 March 1859. In the garden and helped with boys' lessons.... Other days in the garden and helping boys with lessons.... Helped boys with maps and lessons; 11 September 1859. Wednesday afternoon with boys studying Latin.

In 1863, at 15 and 16, the boys left the grammar school. Bertie took a crash course in French and went to study for a term in a French college south of Paris. In the autumn of 1864 he joined his brother, Allan, as a pupil of Mr Burrell, an Ipswich clergyman. Allan left to study law at Norwood in 1865 and passed his preliminary law examination in 1866. In 1872 he was admitted to the Law Society and practised as a solicitor until his death in 1917. Bertie settled down to life as a country gentleman for a while, but then studied medicine at Norwood and entered the Army Medical Service. In his old age he retired to live with his unmarried sisters. None of Elizabeth's children married.

The birth of a delicate baby girl, Ethel, in January 1855, brought with it private grief and anger. Grief that Ethel died when she was just a few weeks old, from convulsions; anger that Doctor Hammond had taken two hours to attend her in her last illness. 'I have no record of a few days following, for they were of great sorrow', she wrote in her diary. Then a seaside holiday for a fortnight in Felixstow allowed the family time to come to terms with their grief. In July 1856 another girl, Blanche, was born. She was suckled for four months and then weaned.

Alice left school at the age of 16 and spent ten months in France learning the language and widening her horizons. When she returned it was to take up a place as her mother's constant and close companion. In 1864, for example, she accompanied her mother and Bertie to France; Herbert was a poor sea-traveller and declined to go.

During the period of the diary, the Cottons set about modernising their timber-framed farmhouse – constructing an extension, hanging paper, buying carpets and new furniture, collecting luxury items to embellish the rooms. Elizabeth also spent much time and energy creating a garden. Accommodation in the house was far from commodious for such a brood. Five bedrooms and two attics provided sleeping and retiring room for master and mistress, five children and several servants. There is some suggestion that Alice had a room to herself and that the boys shared one room while the younger girls shared another. Mrs Marskall, the housekeeper, had special responsibility for the children and may have shared the younger children's room. There does not appear to have been a nursery.

At about the same time, Herbert spent considerable sums modernising the farm building and improving the farm. It may be that the dairy was, for the first time, separated from the house in 1854.

Elizabeth's diaries throw considerable light upon the importance of her wider family, both to herself and Herbert and also to their children. The first diary (which ends in 1863) demonstrates its enormous influence; the second suggests a decline in this influence as the older generation died and the generation of Elizabeth's four brothers and five sisters became more absorbed in establishing their own families. Rebecca Haxell died some time prior to 1850 and James Haxell died in 1854. Elizabeth's Uncle George died in 1867. Uncle John, who had frequently entertained the Cottons when they went to London, died in 1868. Anne and Margaret, Elizabeth's sisters, spent much time at the Cottons' house. There were somewhat strained relations with sister Kate Nelson. Contact with the family of Edward and Arabella Nelson was diminished when they purchased a country home for their family. Elizabeth's closest relationship was with her sister, Rea, and family. Henry Page, her husband, was a city businessman. The Pages spent holidays abroad. Elizabeth maintained close relations with her nieces, Emily and Fanny, when relations with other members of her extended family were declining.

Agenda for Future Research

These descriptions of eighteenth and nineteenth-century 'middleclass' families form the bare bones of a typology as part of the agenda for future research. Historians must assemble many more such case histories before we are confident that we know all the various categories of family life and experience and can safely embark upon ascertaining the prevalence of particular forms. It may well be that sources other than diaries and autobiographies can be used to demonstrate family experience as well as to quantify: for example, the census may serve to indicate how many wives and children worked; inventories may yield information about the use of domestic space; wills, the relationships between family members.

It is clear from even a cursory examination of a few middle-class families that there is a discrepancy between the imagined 'middle-class' family and these families. Issues of definition and enumeration remain pressing. We need to know, also, how the fragments of the middle class relate to each other and to the social hierarchy, and the ways, if any, in which these relationships are informed by family experience. For instance, how did members of small tradesmen's and craftsmen's families regard their membership of the middle-class? Were they all, like Mrs Wells, painfully anxious to conceal their impoverishment from the world in which they moved and to promote the image of a servant-keeping household? How many such families maintained servants? Why did Charles Booth regard servant-keeping as the mark of a middle-class household? Were members of the lower middle class able to keep home and work separate? Were they interested in so doing?

Put plainly, this book argues that the family was no less important or independent than class, nationality, gender, education, age or any other of the variables commonly employed in historical explanation in informing the values, beliefs and behaviour of people in times past and present. 'Family' was not simply the vehicle for transmitting social norms and values to individuals; it formed its own values and accepted behaviours, which undoubtedly interacted with and drew from others, to shape its members. The true importance of family history lies not in showing the family as a reflection of contemporary society and economy but in showing it as an agent in society, in some senses more potent than class or gender or education. It can convey existing values and behaviours; it can transform; it can enable its members to select from the menu before it, whether in terms of career, life partner, moral standards, social conscience or religious belief. That the family acts within a class context is undoubtedly the case. Contemporary dismay at the death of the family reflects our subconscious awareness of its importance as an active participant in the creation of a stable society.

Conclusion: the Co-residential Family

Household and simple nuclear family were not necessarily synonymous in early modern times; although there were some households which consisted of nothing but a simple nuclear family. Looked at in another way, many biological families, given the economic means, saw it as their goal to constitute the basis of an independent household. This has not been the case in all human societies – a mere glance at the economic organisation of the American Indians shows this to be true.[248] It is the historians' misfortune that we can see most easily, and at closest quarters, middling and upper-class families within households, so that we are liable to assume coincidence. On closer inspection, however, we are becoming acquainted with other kinds of family, who did not constitute independent households and who were not necessarily co-resident.

We are becoming more conversant with the idea that work alone did not give people an identity and that removal of 'work' from the household might yet leave a strong and influential family. In such a situation the woman might not 'go out to work' and her public role might be restricted, but this did not make her 'powerless'. Moreover, in middle-class families, even in the modern period, there still was a 'household' which included, but was not synonymous with, the co-residential family. Middle-class wives 'worked' in households which included dependent servants as well as children and they felt that this was important in defining their status as 'middle-class'.[249] We are also becoming much more aware of the hybrid 'complex' household, in which there were biological relationships but not exclusively those of either the nuclear or the extended family, and in which lines of authority were much more complicated than any label of patriarchy might suggest.

5. A Day's Work for a Day's Victuals: The Families of the Very Poor

In the agrarian societies of the early modern period it was possible to persuade oneself that the 'ideal' of the family preached in the pulpit and enforced in the courts bore some semblance to reality. If there were lapses, even serious ones, then it was still conceivable that the fallen might rise again. The tensions caused by political and social change, growing urbanisation and the drift of labourers away to the towns could at first be submerged by the overall dominance of the 'household system' in which both those of the middling sort and their dependants were housed and controlled. But there came a point when the traditional household became not the rule but the exception. In an urban environment it happened even earlier than in a rural. In Britain it was not so much industrialisation as proletarianisation that was the vital ingredient in this mix. In France it was not so much industrialisation as the replacement of a pre-market by a market economy based on competition and conflict. In the United States, to these ingredients were added the disrupted lives of myriad immigrants.

Production within the household ceased to predominate in all these societies but at widely separated periods of time. Britain, France and America all had to face the concomitants of this development but, again, at different times. Whereas, in parts of Britain, the household was relatively unimportant as the unit of production and, therefore, employment by the late eighteenth century, such developments had not occurred in France or North America until the late nineteenth. As a consequence, the household was present in France and North America to perform its other traditional roles much later than it was in parts of Britain. Yet we should bear in mind that even in nineteenth-century England 'Family employment, recruitment and training of labour characterised most of the factory textile trades throughout the century', even when domestic industry itself was not present.[1] In rural areas the traditional household persisted as a feature of the economy.[2] In these circumstances the sharp differentiation between home and work identified by other scholars was not observable.[3] Moreover, much 'service' and 'craft' work still did occur in the household. The areas of employment accessible to married women narrowed in the late eighteenth and nineteenth centuries but work of many kinds was available at home.[4] Nevertheless, with the advent of the factory system, more rapid urbanisation and the proportionate decline of agriculture in economy and society, in all these countries, the numbers of persons without 'households' accelerated. In America particularly, immigrants were drawn from other communities entirely and recruited to the new industries. These people were released from the control, imperfect though it had always been, of the traditional household. People with no means of independence were yet freed from dependence and the controls which went with it. If these people had any sense of identity with a family it was fostered by biological or sexual links and its strengths were anathema to the rest of society.

So it is that, while one is able to draw remarkably close comparisons between the working-class families in these societies, this comparability is considerably reduced if one, for example, compares the situation on a chronological basis. As I shall argue in this chapter, the nature of the working-class family was determined by the presence or absence of a large urban proletariat and extreme urban poverty and overcrowding. By the close of the nineteenth century, when such were present in all the societies under discussion, one is struck by the comparisons rather than the contrasts in working-class life. Having said this, one has continually to be aware of the precise context in which the working-class family lived its life.

Freedom without Bread: the Demise of the Household System

The societies concerned faced this situation with a sense of trep-idation. The poor themselves did not relish freedom without bread. Later in this chapter we shall encounter examples of wage earners trying to replicate their old family and kinship networks and recreate their 'economies'. The rich and middling were at a loss to find ways of reimposing control over the men and women who had once not only worked for them but also lived with them. Sometimes there are examples of early industrialists seeking to build the traditional way of life in the new and far from traditional environment. The paternalistic employer was the patriarch. The workplace was gathered up into a pseudo-household, in which workers doffed their caps in deference to the employer's family. Workers were provided with model housing and all manner of facilities, schools, shops and so forth, close to their place of work. The example of Saltaire, in mid-nineteenth-century Yorkshire, is pre-eminent. Here Titus Salt planned and built a new factory with a new town to support it. This town was, over a period of twenty years or so, supplied with cottages, Conregational and Wesleyan places of worship, elementary schools, baths and washhouses, a public health system, alms houses, a factory canteen offering meals at moderate prices, clubs and reading rooms, an art school and a park. (In Massachusetts, Samuel Slater purchased land for male household heads to work in return for the labour of their dependants in his mills.[5]) Patrick Joyce has argued that paternalism of this kind persisted in some industries and some areas throughout the century.[6] But the old relationship of interdependence between master and men was in some cases and some places beyond recovery. No doubt many among the upper middle classes were as bereft by developments as the workers: the relationship of interdependence and deference which had existed had been considerably more comforting than that of antagonism and alienation which now pertained, and there is evidence that many employers tried to regain it.[7]

The demise of the household system forced the middle classes back upon the central importance of the biological 'private' family. Stephanie Coontz describes how, in the United States, the middle classes enveloped themselves in a mythical world, where success or failure was the result of personal character. The central prop of this mythical world was the concept of 'the formative role of a nuclear family built upon universal gender roles and emotional commitments to home life'. The details of these roles and commitments varied between the countries we are treating, of course, but broadly speaking the belief of the middle classes was the same in all. The family or the absence of it explained success or failure. Poverty was the result of the parents' failure to teach good values and appropriate work habits, to impose moral and physical discipline. Infant mortality was the direct result of maternal ineptitude. Poor budgeting, drink and neglect of housekeeping skills led to undernourishment, filth and degradation. The revival of the family would lead to the obliteration of all these evils. In the United States this 'cult of domesticity' appears to have made the middle classes resist any suggestion that reforms should be set in place to end social injustice. The British were rather less committed to laisser-faire liberalism. Minimal, and sometimes not quite so minimal, intervention was necessary to restore the health of the whole body social.

While it is rewarding to draw together the points of similarity, it is equally important to observe the important differences in socio-historical context which informed various middle-class and intellectual responses to the 'working-class family'. Sometimes this marked a distinct break with tradition. For instance, probably the most important contributor to a social theory of the family in the nineteenth century was the Frenchman, Frédéric Le Play (1806–82), a mining engineer and pioneer in the development of élite technical education. Unusual among Frenchmen, who had previously given little attention to the family's importance vis à vis that of other institutions, Le Play, from 1855 onwards, presented a comprehensive model of the family's role in society, which included detailed studies of the father/husband, wife/mother, child, and the unmarried relatives therein. His work, as we shall see later, profoundly affected the reformist movement of the late century in France and did not go unnoticed by social investigators and reformers in late nineteenth-century Britain.[8] Le Play's work, however, arose directly out of concern for the establishment of social order, in its turn arising from the French Revolution of 1830. A Catholic and a conservative, he has, however, incorrectly been dubbed a Conservative and Reactionary. His *Ouvriers européens* (1855) was a work of thoroughgoing empirical research, which sought to understand precisely how society in the past had functioned within a comparative framework. Thirty-six mono-graphs of individual families throughout Europe, set within detailed case studies of the communities in which they lived, and arranged according to a taxanomic scheme, provided the basis of his analysis.[9] While he lauded specific attributes of the past he did not regard the Middle Ages as a halcyon world to which return was possible or desirable. Rather, he wished to learn from the past in order to provide new solutions to new social problems. Thus, unlike French traditionalists, he regarded the family as the 'moral cell' of society, its primary unit, and suggested reforms of the family to provide stability in society. After 1856 Le Play turned away from empirical investigation to teaching the 'truths' which emerged from his studies. He acted as adviser to Napoleon III and carried out a number of studies of proposed legislation. His own record in promoting new laws was poor: the National Assembly rejected the only law – significantly, that to introduce the freedom to will one's property as one wished – out of hand.

Le Play, like the Vicomte de Bonald, responded to a social insta-bility arising not from industrialisation (not, as yet, apparent in France) but from a corruption of the *ancien régime* which had resulted in the social isolation and vulnerability of workers in the family, the workplace and the local community. De Bonald, a Res-toration conservative, was one of those who saw the family as pro-viding the continuity which would preserve social order. Le Play took over his idea and remodelled it as a direct consequence of his investigations. It seemed to him that the destruction of paternal authority in the family by the 1789 inheritance laws (which had introduced compulsory equal inheritance) was responsible for the breakdown in the social harmony. The situation could be reme-died if the Anglo-Saxon pattern of freedom to bestow property according to personal dictates were adopted in France. 'The head of the family, bound by no single law or custom, freely following his heart and his conscience, finds the solution in each case by drawing on his profound knowledge of his property, his pro-fession, his clientele, and by studying the character of each of his children; he can divide his estate equally among his children if each is capable of putting his share of the inheritance to good use; otherwise, he can keep the family's wealth intact, to everyone's advantage.' 'Freedom of testation tends to assure that land, businesses and workshops are all distributed in ways which suit the local requirements of the soil, climate, and the genius of the race.'[10] Love and affection among family members and the perceived economic needs of individuals within the family would inform inheritance decisions and guarantee social as well as family harmony.

Probably the best known, but not well understood, part of Le Play's theory of the family is his observation of three categories of family: the patriarchal, the unstable and the stem. This observation came in a later work, *La Réforme sociale*, of 1872. In the patriarchal family, the household governed by the head or father is the focus of the family's life. All members share in the family's well-being but there is no room for independent development or mobility. The father 'presides at the creation of a new household – it is equally he who determines who will be invested with the new authority'. Contrasted with this is the unstable family which 'now dominates the working-class populations subject to the new manufacturing system of Western Europe' and is multiplying among the bourgeoisie who practise the forced partition of property. In the unstable family, in which individuals are not responsible for their relatives, individual mobility is possible but so is pauperisation. The third type, '*la famille-souche*' or stem family, is favoured by those with good sense. 'This organisation associates with the parents just one married child. It establishes all the others with a dowry and they enjoy a degree of independence denied them in the patriarchal family.'[11] Le Play believed that the free people of Europe naturally gravitated towards this latter pattern because it allowed for mobility and yet preserved the good aspects of continuity and support.

Leaving aside the debate about whether the family types which Le Play claimed to identify from empirical research were prevalent or not in France, his preferred solutions for social disharmony clearly emanated from a society where small property-holding was becoming more and not less a feature of society. What he suggested would already have seemed a nonsense in early nineteenth-century England, for example, where the poor had no possessions to bestow, the craftsmen had no property and pauperisation was already widespread. A pronounced Anglophile, Le Play seems to have ignored some of the more prominent problems faced by that society. An analysis of a still largely agricultural Europe was to prove deficient for contemporary England and for the rest of Europe in the future. Yet he also articulated some views which were to inform the middle-class approach to the ideal family in England and America as well as France. The family is the protective agency. The degree of 'protection' it offers each individual is greater than that provided by any other tutelary institution because it results from 'human nature's most powerful instincts' and works through feeling and morality, not regulation and compulsion.[12] He preached the ability of the family, through love and affection, to impart bourgeois values of privacy and domesticity, responsibility and thrift to its members.

It is noteworthy, however, that the problem in Britain and the USA was perceived by many to be one of inadequate housing and environment, not a defect in the inheritance laws. Replace the housing which prevented family life and all would be well from thereon. The New York Association for Improving the Condition of the Poor (AICP), founded in 1843, put it clearly enough: 'What they are ... they are made to a greater or less extent, by circumstances over which they have but little control; and vain will be the effort to elevate their character, without first improving their physical condition.'[13] Throughout Britain, inspectors were deluged with complaints about the sanitary state of the towns. In 1850 the Superintending Inspector of the Dudley General Board of Health received so many such complaints that he simply could not note them all down. Readers of *The Times* correspondence columns on 5 July 1849 must have been jolted by the painfully written letter it contained from residents in the slum courts of the Church Lane and Carrier Street quarter of London:

Sur, May we beg and beseach your proteckshion and power.... We live in muck and filthe. We aint got not priviz, no dust bins, no drains, no water splies, and no drain or suer in the whole placey.... Sur we hope you will let us have our cumplaints put into your hinfluenshall paper, and make these landlords of our houses and these comishoners ... make our houses decent for Christians to live in. Preaye Sir com and see us, for we are living like piggs, and it aint faire we should be so ill treated.[14]

The people who lived in such appalling conditions certainly wished for better and were dismally aware of the impact which such a hostile environment had upon their lives. But the rich who observed them, while often moved to genuine compassion, were often also moved by loathing and fear of contamination and its consequences. If the poor were forced to live as pigs in sty and trough then their morals would be those of the yard, their abundant offspring an encumbrance upon the 'farmers' purse, their disease infectious, their noise disruptive, their smell unbearable and their potential for rampage a cause for concern. The poor would cease to live like pigs if their tumble-down sties were replaced with improved housing and environment. The re-creation of the poor in the image of the rich offered the best prospect for social and economic progress. Living in a clone of the middle-class house would force the poor to live like middle-class families, disciplined and moral and civilised.

The Conditions in which the Urban Poor Lived

Make no mistake about it, the problem perceived by the concerned middle classes was not a small one. A majority of the population, certainly in urban areas, lived in a fashion more suited to pigs than people. The comparison and contrast lies in the proportion of a nation's working population living in big cities and thus affected. We must constantly be aware of the uneven rate of urban growth. Some cities, like London in the 1880s, were full of street folk, while others, like Leeds, were not. Workers and their families were packed, layered and compressed like geological strata into the made-down houses of the wealthy, or crowded into such accommodation as the speculative builders were willing to provide; and in a low-wage economy that offered precious little. The trend towards higher densities, already evident in the late eighteenth century, became more strongly pronounced from the third decade of the nineteenth. Infilling on a colossal scale took place: the origin of the ubiquitous back-to-back, the perilous backlands of urban Scotland, the claustrophobic courts and alleys of Birmingham and Liverpool, the Rookeries of London and the dank and dreadful cellars of Manchester. Thomas Beames expressed the fundamental fear: 'Our argument is that the Rookeries are among the seeds of Revolution; that taken in conjunction with other evils, they poison the minds of the working

classes against the powers that be and thus lead to convulsions.'[15]
The 'homes' which the poor inhabited were frequently torn from
them by the processes of commercial redevelopment, railway construction and 'urban improvement', so that Gareth Stedman Jones
has estimated that 100 000 people were displaced by street clear-
ance in London between 1830 and 1880.[16] This all further aggra-
vated the problem of the poor, which gave rise to so much concern
in Victorian Britain.[17]

One observes the same features in the cities of France and
North America. Mid-nineteenth-century Paris may have been, in
many respects, a medieval city but it was displaying a physical
deterioration consequent in part upon an invasion by the poorer
classes. 'In the very heart of the busiest centres of industry and
trade, you see thousands of human beings reduced to a state of
barbarism by vice and destitution.... The governments are rightly
apprehensive.'[18] At this time buildings were multi-occupied by a
mixture of classes in the heart of Paris. Many degenerated into
slums of the worst kind, 'infested hovels', which seemed to breed,
in the body politic as in the body corporeal, disease and disorder.
In mid to late nineteenth-century Boston the immigrant Irish were
initially housed in the vacated houses of the well-to-do, 'till houses
once fashionable ... become neglected, dreary tenement houses
into which the families of the low paid and poverty smitten ...
crowd by the dozens.'[19] Then came speculative and shoddy new
building, designed to cram as many one-roomed apartments as
possible into narrow, sunless plots. The compiler of Boston's first
Atlas gave up his attempt to map the areas of the city inhabited by
the poor Irish as 'too full of sheds and shanties'.[20] Cellar-dwelling
and overcrowding, non-existent sanitation and ventilation and
extremely high rents were as much a feature of late nineteenth-
century Boston as they were of Liverpool or Manchester in the
early nineteenth century. By 1850, 586 cellars were inhabited in
Boston – at least one of these held 39 people every night. If
residents of the slums in Britain found the stench from the
middens intolerable, so that it made them physically sick in the
mornings, and brought water up from the well that was full of
dead cats, then so did the residents of the Irish quarters of Boston.
After 1825, New York also was increasingly a city of overcrowded
tenements, one-time family houses, converted stables and ware-
houses.[21] At the end of 1864, 500,000 (out of a total New York

population of 800,000) lived in tenements and 15,000 in cellars and basements.[22] Hell's Kitchen, the New York Council of Hygiene divulged, was the site of three slaughter houses, a varnish factory, a distillery and a hides-and-fats plant, jostling for space with residential tenement blocks.[23] In 1899/1900 Lawrence Veiller set up a cardboard model of an entire East Side tenement block to prove that in New York 'the working man is housed worse than in any other city in the civilized world, notwithstanding the fact that he pays more money for such accommodations than is paid elsewhere'. In its 39 tenements dwelt 2,781 individuals, with 264 water closets and not a single bath tub between them.[24] Throughout the nineteenth century the fear of epidemic disease and riot panicked the urban American middle class. As in England, though later in the century, this eventually led to a sanitary reform and supervision.

There were features of urban working-class life which were noted and identified as alien by contemporaries. The poorer elements among the working class constituted 'a roving, itinerant, and unsatisfactory class, whose filthy and vicious habits have long remained a social problem difficult to deal with.[25] Overcrowding was appalling. The 'respeckfull servants' of the Editor of *The Times* observed that 'the great men of the Suer company' 'would not beleave that sixty persons' slept at 12 Carrier Street every night. Random inspection of ticketed houses in parts of Scotland failed to uncover the true proportions of the problem.

> Even now the offenders manage, despite the vigilance of the police, to evade detection, for no sooner do the officers enter one or two houses in a tenement, than the others are signalled to, and the inmates of the overcrowded houses steal out into the stairs and passages like ants swarming out of an anthill before the police have time to go half through the tenement.[26]

Living in 'nuclear families' in such a context was out of the question. What was true of London and Liverpool was as true of New York, Philadelphia, Chicago and Boston in North America and Paris and other large cities in France. The Committee of Internal Health acknowledged as much of the Broad Street Area of Boston:

> This whole district is a perfect hive of human beings, without comforts and mostly without common necessaries; in many

cases huddled together like brutes, without regard to sex, or age, or sense of decency; grown men and women sleeping together in the same apartment, and sometimes wife and husband, brothers and sisters, in the same bed.

One district of New York in 1894 had a population density of 986.4 people per acre, approximated elsewhere only by Koombarwara in Bombay, which had 759.66 persons per acre in 1881.[27] Indeed, one might argue that the conditions of life of the poor in all the major cities of Britain, France and North America differed only in the relative size of the slum quarter. Separation between the sexes was impossible, let alone separation between families. The idea of privacy was foreign. It was not simply that houses were ill- or unfurnished, unheated and lacking in amenities of any kind. The morality which flowed from a middle-class life-style built upon economic stability, responsibility and comfort was alien here. Neglect of marriage, fluidity of relationships, illegitimacy, failure to maintain support relationships with their children when the parents separated, prostitution, incest, absence from the 'home', were natural in such an environment. A study of Bridegate and Wynds, 'the Alsatia of Glasgow', in the 1880s is indicative. Here the population had been halved between 1871 and 1881 but the remaining population mainly lived in one or two-roomed apartments or common lodging houses. In 1888, 51 per cent of the houses were ticketed for police inspection. In the entire district there were only 105 water closets. According to Russell, the MOH, the area was occupied by a residual population, a third of whom were Irish-born, who lived in social and moral degradation and held the forces of law and order in contempt. Here 22 per cent of all births were illegitimate (against 8 per cent for the city as a whole); abortion may have been extensively practised, or, at the least, antenatal care minimal (a ratio between the slum and the city as a whole of 41:17.5 premature births per 1,000 births was recorded); marriage was unpopular; the mortality rate for 1871–2 was the highest in the city and it had the greatest proportion of acute diseases of the lungs, consumption and infectious diseases throughout the decade 1870 to 1880. Of children born in the slum, 24 per cent did not survive their first birthday; 40 per cent of these infant deaths (as opposed to about 5 per cent in other working class districts) were uncertified, indicating that the children had received

no significant medical attention in their final illness. Life insur-
ance was less commonly afforded in this slum than in working-
class areas of the city (32 per cent insured as against 55 per cent in
another working-class area and 45 per cent in the city as a
whole).[28] When Lynn Lees compared households in London and
Chicago she discovered that there were remarkable similarities
among the so-called households of the poor, notably high proportions of one-parent households, and large numbers of children
effectively growing up on the streets, grubbing for food, because
parents could not offer supervision.[29]

In all three countries during the nineteenth century the cities
were unable to keep up with the influx of population. The housing supply was simply inadequate. This meant that, in the many
towns and cities where single-family houses for the working classes
were the norm, the development of tenements and overcrowding
altered the situation. This change occurred at differing times from
city to city and from country to country. For instance, at a time
when 46 per cent of working families in Bristol lived in one-room
apartments, the great majority of wage earners of Nottingham
lived in cramped and squalid single-family dwellings.[30] Housing in
the growing cities was provided by landlords anxious to exploit
their properties to the full and by speculative builders intent upon
making the maximum profit from their ventures. The cramped
and comfortless quarters they created nowhere encouraged the
poor to live in families.

Inevitably, frustration was felt with the response of the governing classes to what they saw as alien and unacceptable. The middle
classes believed that the poor among the working classes should
live in families like their own, enclosed in households like their
own. The cellar dwellings should be closed up. Overcrowding
should be outlawed. Anti-social practices should be regulated out
of existence. Immorality should go through the window and
middle-class morality enter through the door. The working classes
of the industrial north were a paradigm: here the family economy
was restabilised, by the mid-nineteenth century, on lines acceptable to and reinforcing of employer paternalism.[31] But elsewhere
the working classes and their way of life constituted a problem, not
part of a social cement.

When the 5,000 cellars were closed in Liverpool, the starving
Irish reoccupied as many as 60 per cent of them. In 1865 the

Medical Officer to the Privy Council told how it happened: 'The tenants get at it by raising the planks in the rooms above.'[32] Poverty, and insufficient and inadequate housing, prevented the poor living in neat nuclear households, and simply stamping down upon 'alien' practices was not enough.

In some sections of the working class there was unquestionably a fear of incest. 'There must be three bedrooms' opined one woman '… where there's a family you must have three.' And by the turn of the century there were those who vocally deplored their inability to ape middle-class home life because of their physically poor environment. A male occupant of a back-to-back two up, one down complained thus:

> Every sound can be heard in the next house. We ourselves can hear those next door sweeten their tea – by that I mean we can hear them stirring it up. If the man comes home drunk at night, and uses filthy language, our children pick it up. Now every good wife tries to pick one day for washing. Oh what a time for the poor working man when he comes home! Everything is topsy turvy, clothes horses round the fire, as there is no drying accommodation outside, every table full of damp or wet clothes, because all has to be done in one place. But think what a time the poor woman must have had, smothered with steam and heat from the fire, and having to boil in such quantities. And in the face of this they expect working people to be comfortable. No wonder the publicans prosper.

> This is just one day in the week. Another night the children have to be bathed. Mother generally starts about 7 o'clock, and this means a night of it.

> It disheartens both a man and a woman to have to be crowded with their children in about the same room as you get in the cemetry when you are dead.[33]

But before we jump to the conclusion that the working class everywhere and at every time would have embraced the ideal, we should pause a little and reflect. The question is, was it simply poverty which forbade the poor to live as the middle classes in families, or was there a different culture among the poor, a traditional life-style which would have rejected the middle-class family even had it been a possibility? Many modern scholars, for example Geoffrey Crossick, have argued that the working classes, or at least the élite among them, wished to remain distinct from the middle classes in every aspect of their lives, even when they had the income to support a similar life-style. Patrick Joyce, however, seems to imply that many of the factory workers came from among the class of landed labourers – the agrarian proletariat – and may have had few traditions of independent family life upon which to draw in their new urban environment.[34]

Did the poor adopt the middle-class family when they were given ameliorated physical conditions and, in some cases, improved economic conditions? The problems the historian faces in framing, let alone answering, such questions satisfactorily are manifold. First, adopting the life-style of another class is tantamount to entering that class. Thus, for many working-class families yesterday, as today, living like a middle-class family meant that you could lay claim to being a middle-class family. This change of status was perceived as a step up the social ladder. Even when parents drawn from the working class still identified with their origins, their children may have felt no such identity. So, many of the people who provided evidence before the nineteenth-century commissions of inquiry were interested in improving their own social standing. They were also frequently those members of the working classes who were least separated physically and philosophically from the middle classes. They were those who shared, to some extent at least, middle-class aspirations and who were as likely as the middle classes to throw up their hands in horror at the life-style of the poor and lumpen proletariat. Perhaps their greater proximity to that class made them even more anxious than the middle classes for its obliteration. Whether the historian is justified in accepting their opinions or experiences as 'typical' of the majority of working people is dubious.

Secondly, as the above comments imply, there was not just one working class but many, and, moreover, these classes were forever changing in their character and composition. Le Play had been acutely conscious of the economic responsiveness of the family and of the social hierarchy among the workers. 'Workers can be recognized by certain common traits …; these traits distinguish them from society's other classes. At the same time, workers are far from being equal among themselves.' They could be distinguished, he asserted, by first their occupation, secondly their rank in the worker hierarchy within that occupation, and thirdly their relationship with the men at the top of that hierarchy. It was not simply a matter of relative material wealth. Neither was it simply a matter of housing conditions.[35] Charles Booth's researches in the later nineteenth century showed, through empirical research, how precariously the working poor of London lived and how frequently they moved in and out of poverty according to age, occupation and circumstance. A family might be Class C, D or even E today and class A or B tomorrow. What were the implications? It meant that people who could viably mimic in their lives a lower-middle-class nuclear household one day, occupying a small house with some pretence to amenities, and defining their adult lives by work and their children's by school and play, might, on another, be forced to lodge in the house of others, beg for food and work, clothing and heat and draw their children into the fight for communal existence. How frequently did they have to adapt their conception of 'the primary unit of social life' to suit their economic circumstances? This concept of the precarious and continually changing life-styles of the working poor was new in Britain and was not, in general, shared by contemporaries, but it was none the less full of insight. Booth was also able to show how the various working classes imperceptibly merged into one another, interacted with one another and, on occasion, controlled one another.[36]

Thirdly, the working class was divided into groups not only by income but also by origin, religion, occupation and generation. For much of the nineteenth century the urban population did not replenish itself: enormous population growth was dependent upon immigration from the countryside or from overseas. The immigrants were often young; their very immigration resulted from breaking up a nuclear family; and they brought with them rural and sometimes foreign ways into an urban environment. Fourthly, in assessing the possible effect of environmental change upon the concept and reality of 'family life' we have to consider what other influences may have intervened. For at least some of the re-housed working poor, the deliberate attempts of evangelists and philanthropists to reshape their morality and their mores were a prominent potential influence. Even if the words of preachers and lady visitors did not change the way people lived they may have changed the way they talked about how they lived. And last but not least, it is nigh on impossible to find out in detail how the poor working classes lived at different points in the nineteenth century. The problem is especially acute for the first half of the century.

Penetrating the Family Lives of the Poor: Egerton, Mayhew and Le Play

What I have to say here is, therefore, highly speculative if suggestive. What we do know of the lives of the extremely poor indicates that life was lived in groups larger than the biological family, which were yet highly dissimilar to the traditional household in that they were not defined by hierarchical economic relations. In other words, the groups bore more resemblance to tribal than to household living. The distinctiveness of this manner of living might be regarded as a featured of poverty but it was, none the less, a fact. The people would live together when in a state of utter poverty in interdependence, using their common resources to obtain food, clothing and shelter in cellars and tenements. When living sixty to a room, private life based on a conjugal or nuclear group was impossible. Henry Mayhew has described graphically the lives of the 'wanderers' in mid-Victorian London. These ranged from the vagabond, half-beggar, half-thief, through the pedlars, showmen and harvesters, to the 'mechanic on tramp'. For our purposes, the comparison lies less between the *experiences* of the poor of the different nations than between the *proportions* of the people of each of these nations who shared this life-style.

It is hard work penetrating the family life of the working classes but three contemporaneous although very different writers, Henry Mayhew and Frédéric Le Play, and the remarkable parson, John Coker Egerton, allow us privileged insights into the homes of the poor in the 1850s. I can give just a few examples here. I begin with Parson Egerton.

Contemporaries were aware, as we should be, that nineteenth-century urban dwellers were frequently migrants from the countryside and commented upon the transference of rural values and standards. The landless rural proletariat became the urban proletariat. Knowledge of the domestic arrangements of the poor in the countryside may give us some criteria for the distinctiveness or otherwise of the family lives of the urban working classes. The *Victorian Village* of Burwash, in East Sussex, is particularly well documented for the years 1857 to 1888. Its Rector recorded in his diary much information about the ways of his parishioners, drawing sharp distinction between the parochial aristocracy, the comfortable, independent farmers and the agricultural labourers, whose lives shaded imperceptibly into those of the poor on relief. He was struck by the large number of couples who lived together without marrying. One who was living thus said, 'that she did not know what it was wrong, but that she could not marry him, he was too old: what can one do where the moral is gone ...'[37] Indeed, so eager was he to persuade the poor to marry that he tolerated witnesses to a church wedding who were not themselves married, and was prepared to forego his fee when marrying G. Blackford and Hannah Relf in 1860, to qualify them for assisted emigration.[38] Many of those who did marry had lived together before solemnisation and/or were pregnant.[39] Egerton pointed out their 'sin', but when the alternative to living with a man who would not contemplate marriage was the workhouse, what real choice was there?[40] Outdoor relief was disallowed illegitimate children. This reluctance to marry and bear responsibility for dependants on the part of so many working men infuriated Egerton.[41]

[The granddaughter of Mrs Watson] is living with a man Hyland by name. The girl wants to be married, but the man won't marry her, alleging that he does not want to be burdened with a large family or he is growing old, that is calmly looking forward to throwing them on the parish. It certainly seems almost a premium on illeg. children that a man can have as many as he likes & then when he pleases send them & their mother into the workhouse.[42]

If, from the perspective of the ratepayer, this behaviour was irresponsible and intolerable, such an attitude certainly made sense if one was impoverished.

Married or not, the poor of Burwash lived in simple two-parent family groups. They lived otherwise conventional lives and used the terminology strictly applicable only to those legally wed. For example, when 'thatcher and pig killer' Levi, who was unmarried,

gave information to the census in 1871, he referred to himself as
'widower'. At that time he was living with an unmarried daughter,
Martha (aged 25), a son (19) who was a labourer, and four grand-
children, parentage unknown, ranging from 1 to 8 years of age.[43]
Clearly the Levis regarded themselves as a family whatever the
Church's attitude.

The conditions of poor families varied according to the depth
of their poverty. Some lived in an appalling environment. On
26 November 1860 Egerton called on John Clapson, a 69-year-old
ex-road worker. 'No furniture: I could not sit down. He nevertheless has a great fear of "ye House".' He gave Clapson 1 shilling.[44]
On 24 March 1860 he visited Piper's cottage: 'house not fit for a
horse to live in. The walls in places broken thro' to ye open air.'[45]
Mrs Lee, wife of a hawker, with five children under 12 and another
on the way, opined, 'our's isn't a living, it's only a being'. 'I fear
that she is right,' sighed Egerton, 'Cottage not much larger than a
couple of bandboxes'.[46] A visit to Mrs Collins, on 8 June 1872,
found her 'better, but with a filthy drain right under the house,
how is she to be well. The landlord is a regular screw, & it would be
of little use to ask him to set it to rights, so what is the poor woman
to do ...'[47] Harriet Relf's house was so low that Mr Relf generally
went outside to put his coat on.[48]

Egerton himself showed a good deal of understanding of the
plight of his parish poor, by no means always siding with the decisions of the relief officers. So, in 1876, he quoted a meeting of the
Tilehurst Board of Guardians at which a man was addressed with
the not unfamiliar words: 'We are afraid Master Styles that your
wife isn't a good manager', to which friend Styles made answer:
'Well Gentlemen I don't know nowt about my wife not being a
good manager, but I be quite sure of one thing, she could manage
a good deal more, if she could get it'.[49] The Cramps, eight of them
in all, with the father often out of work and the nine-year-old ter-
ribly ill with rheumatic fever, were not allowed 'the doctor ... on
account of his wages' but 'with a willing heart I left 10/−'.[50] Earlier
his conviction that the illegitimate children of couples since
married should not be allowed relief had been changed by the
argument that reminders of past sin prevented present virtue.

The story of one Burwash family must serve to illustrate some
of the features of the family life of the poor labourer. Egerton
was particularly concerned about the family of John Isted. He

evidently enjoyed talking to Mrs Isted, reporting that he 'staid longer than I meant to'.[51] Each time he visited he left a small dole of money. In 1872 he stayed a long time with Mrs Isted, who was very near the time of her confinement, 'it is very dull for her all day while everybody is out hopping & she is quite helpless in bed'.[52] Isted was a drunk and his wife was continually pregnant. Egerton tried to persuade John to sobriety, with some success.[53] When Egerton visited them in August 1868, a brother, William, had come to call.[54] On another occasion, Egerton wrote in his diary, 'called and prayed with Mrs J. Isted who gave me a wonderful idea of the shifts to which poor people are put in managing. Flour now 1/6 a gallon before baking ...'[55] Mrs Isted reinforced this realisation later in the year. 'Long talk with her and her husband. The shifts which poor people are put to get a living are really wonderful.'[56] 'She let me take down on paper her income & outgoings. It is a sharp struggle.' The budget, which Egerton recorded in his diary, reveals a family that contributed to benefit and clothing clubs, and whose heaviest capital outlay per annum was for boots and firewood. The family's diet consisted of bread, cheese (Dutch), butter, tea, sugar, and a quarter of a pint of milk daily. Egerton was under no illusions as to the contributory causes of their poverty. Isted was paid 13s 6d a week and he drank. Hopping, gathering acorns, harvesting, mowing and keeping two pigs helped to supplement this regular income. Charity raised the income of £45.2.0 to £52.18.0 a year. 'She has been married 15 years next Xmas day has had 11 confinements & 13 children 6 are alive.' In 1869 none of these children was earning anything 'except the eldest who is a girl & does a little hop-tying & a little hop-picking'. She couldn't do much of this though because she had 'to attend to her mother, who is a permanent invalid'.[57]

This daughter was Sally, who in 1870 impressed Egerton as a 'remarkable girl, at 15, and able to attend to all house duties as well as most women'.[58] Her case touched Egerton's heart. In 1872 he wrote, 'How gladly would I put a £10 note into the Savings bank for Sally if I cd spare it, to compensate her for staying at home with her mother instead of going to service & earning something for a future day'.[59] He was aware that circumstances such as these made it impossible for the poor to save towards a rainy day. His chance to help came in June 1873, when he allowed Sally to sleep at the rectory because her parents' new cottage was too cramped for the nine of them (which included a new and sickly baby).[60] This caused adverse comment in the village. 'It shows how little even an act of kindness is to be misunderstood'.[61] The Rector bowed to public opinion: 'Called on Mrs Isted in her new house. 3 beds in one room, & Sally sleeping in ye [kitchen] downstairs. It is too close. Mrs Isted quite poorly'.[62] Later the same year the baby, just 14 months old, died and Egerton contributed towards the funeral expense. Not long after, Sally set up in business as a baker,[63] 'it was excellent bread' and her mother had to remove the next eldest daughter, Annie, from service to look after the family.[64] The business flourished sufficiently for it to be still going in 1880, when her mother took it over, yet Sally still relied upon hopping to supplement her income, as did most of the poor of the village.[65]

Egerton was not without sympathy for John Isted. When he saw him on a Saturday early in July he was 'going up to the village: said he should be back at 7'. 'Wonder whether he was, poor fellow, he has been mowing all the week from 4 a.m. till 8 or 9 p.m. & who can wonder at his wanting a little relaxation on Sat. evg'.[66] None the less he persuaded John to take the pledge and 'to allow his wife to tell me of the first beginnings of any future outbreak'. And he put himself out to intervene to save Isted's job[67] and relocate them into their old cottage.[68] In 1872 John got the sack again and the Rector advised him not to resist but to be submissive and ask to be taken on again. A little later in the same year he observed that Isted as at home with a bad hand: 'times are certainly not very gay with them just now'.

In March 1874 Mrs Isted was recovered from the difficult birth of her fourteenth child and the parish withdrew relief from the family. Egerton, somewhat disillusioned, observed the change in her behaviour. She had 'gone with Farley for a drive to Tilehurst! All this freedom I believe owing to the taking off of the relief. She is now not afraid of being seen about'.[69] By this time Egerton was beginning to realise that Mrs Isted was not as she had seemed. In order to benefit from Egerton's generosity she had tried to disguise her earnings from hopping by adding her work to her husband's and Sally's tallies and pleading lack of income.[70] There was then a sharp fall-off in Egerton's contact with the family.

For most of the nineteenth century the populations of London and other industrial centres did not reproduce themselves.

Charles Booth and others were well aware that many Londoners were not Londoners but rural immigrants. Mayhew, too, noted the importance of immigration, most dramatically among the street-selling Irish.[71] The culture of poverty had a rural aspect of a kind which Egerton evokes so marvellously.

Mayhew's description of the private lives of the costermongers indicates how precarious the family life of the urban poor could be. Whether one married or not depended upon an ability to pay the fees, and whether wives were faithful to their husbands depended upon whether the need for a square meal or some heat was sufficiently pressing. Only one tenth of couples who lives together were married, because the fees were a deterrent. This led to a certain disregard for the legalities of the situation. Living together met with no disapproval in this society. 'There is no honour attached to the married state, and no shame in con-cubinage.' 'As regards the fidelity of these women I was assured that, "in anything like good times", they were rigidly faithful to their husbands or paramours; but that, in the worst pinch of poverty, a departure from this fidelity – if it provided a few meals or a fire – was not considered at all heinous.' The men, however, were not faithful. Young boys were catapulted into sexual unions both by the need to cast off the father's authority and by the associated wish to become economically independent. The young-sters found their mates at dances; it was common to form such a union at the age of 14 or thereabouts. The courtship was brief and marked by inviting the girl to raffles, treating her to 'twopenny hops' and half-pints of beer, and the union formalised by giving her a silk neckerchief. It was common to mark the occasion by renting a barrow for trade and casting off paternal authority. The girls, who may have been responsible for keeping their own families out of the workhouse since the age of seven, were in favour of such unions because 'the life is such a hard one, that a girl is ready to get rid of a little of the labour at nay price.'[72] Though they rarely married formally, the costermongers were jeal-ous spouses. A lad of 15 told Mayhew, 'If I seed my gal a talking to another chap I'd fetch her sich a punch of the nose as should plaguy quick stop the whole business.' The costermongers believed that the women liked it that way: 'the girls ... axully liked a feller for walloping them. As long as the bruises hurted, she was always thinking on the cove as gived em her.' Most of the costermongers had numerous children, but 'chance children' (that is those whose fathers were unrecognised) were rare.

The costermongers were a particular group – members of a tightly knit community in which the work was often hereditary.[73] Mayhew's account of *London Labour and the London Poor*, journalistic, overdrawn and sensationalist though it may be, is invaluable because it demonstrates the variety of family life-styles even among the street folk of London. Le Play's accounts of family life in contemporary Europe (1850s) are anything but journalistic and sensational but a similar variety is displayed. His study of the masons of Paris shows that he was well aware of the differences of life-styles which might be present within a single occupation, let alone within a single community. The masons were drawn from the families of small owner–occupiers in rural communities. They had usually been working on the farm since the age of about six but, if able, chose to become apprentices as an upwardly mobile step. They were taken into the household of a master mason, who wielded firm authority over them, and worked the season in the capital. While there they were able to send savings of between 70 and 200 francs a year home, living more or less comfortably on 60 francs a month. When they reached the age of about 25 or 26 they returned home to live in their native community. The goal of the mason was to return to the small-owner–occupier class, which he did at the age of about 45 if he had been moderately successful in masonry. At the time of writing, Le Play noted sadly, this traditional way had changed. The young apprentices now, as like as not, formed illicit relationships during their time away, spent money on clothes and frittered away money on pleasure. So, short-term liaison had harmed family life, family responsibilities were less acutely felt and the money sent back home became less and less. Moreover, because it was more difficult to become a master mason, jealousy of the bourgeoisie and social alienation had reared their ugly heads among the young masons.[74]

Despite enormous variety, the evidence does seem to point to the poor showing a preference for nuclear family living when economic and housing circumstances permitted. But it should be noted that contemporary observers already had a concept of what a family was and should be, and may well have unintentionally imposed this concept upon what they observed. This said, it is difficult to penetrate the record to discover the real family of the poor. For example, neither Mayhew nor Le Play were interested in the extent to which poor people had close, or indeed any, relations with their wider kin, or, indeed, with the families with which they had co-resided. As a consequence, their record, upon which historians are dependent, is largely devoid of references to such relationships. Historians have argued that this family life was identifiable as 'the working-class family' and in some ways different from that of the well-to-do. Even when a 'couple' lived long enough and mustered together sufficient resources to found a household in a one or two-room apartment, some argue that they and their offspring still maintained an economic interdependence with the neighbourhood, which was unusual in middle and upper-class households. For examples, child care among those mothers who had to work inside or outside the home would be shared with other women and not necessarily with kin; food, when available, would be shared; contacts would be used to secure or supply work opportunities; some economic endeavour would be semi-communal. There would be a high incidence of broken or disrupted families and, as a concomitant, a higher than normal occurrence of matriarchal households. David Garrioch, in his study of non-industrialised but highly urban Paris, notes the difference in child-rearing practices between classes in that city. 'Among working people ... family and community complemented each other in bringing up children.' Parents had the primary responsibility but children were associalised in the street and on the staircase and supervised as much by neighbours as by parents. A laundrywoman's assistant left her three-month-old baby with a neighbour while she went down to the river to wash. A midwife cared for her god-daughter during her mother's absence as a domestic servant. When boys reached a certain age they were subsumed into the neighbourhood 'gangs', escaping the minimal supervision of parents and neighbours. Girls, however, were more carefully supervised than boys and tended to play about the house, stairs and public yard. But, among the well-to-do, 'the local community had little or no part in bringing up children.'[75] Some of the available evidence seems to point to rather different conclusions. The son of a waggoner and a London washerwoman described a similar life but his was an existence in which there was little or no supervision from anyone, parent or neighbour: 'There was two on us at home with mother, and we used to play along with

the boys of our court, in Golding lane, at buttons and marbles....
Father I've heard tell died when I was three and brother only a
year old. It was worse luck for us! Mother was so easy with us.... We
did as we liked with Mother, she was so precious easy, and I never
learned anything but playing buttons.... Mother used to be up and
out very early washing in families – anything for a living. She was a
good mother to us. We was left at home with the key of the room
and some bread and butter for dinner. Afore she got into work –
and it was a goodish long time – we was shocking hard up, and she
pawned nigh everything. Sometimes, when we had'nt no grub at
all, the other lads, perhaps, would give us some of their bread and
butter, but often our stomachs used to ache with hunger, and we
would cry when we was werry far gone. She used to be at work
from six in the morning till ten o'clock at night, which was a long
time for a child's belly to hold out again, and when it was dark we
would go and lie down on the bed and try and sleep until she
came home with the food. I was eight year old then.'[76] Mayhew's
example of a costergirl's childhood shows her lot as different but
not significantly more supervised. 'When quite young she is placed
out to nurse with some neighbour, the mother – if a fond one –
visiting the child at certain periods of the day, for the purpose of
feeding it, or sometimes, knowing the round she has to make,
having the infant brought to her to be 'suckled'. As soon as it is old
enough to go alone, the court is its playground, the gutter its
school room, and under the care of an elder sister the little one
passes the day, among children whose mothers like her own are
too busy out in the streets helping to get the food, to be able to
mind the family at home.' When she is strong enough she either
minds her own siblings or 'she is lent out to carry about a baby'. At
about seven years of age the little girl is sent into the streets to sell.
Her earnings go straight to her parents and, if she has not any
money, she will not dare to go home but sleep beneath acres. The
work day stretches from 4 a.m. to 10 p.m.[77] If we reflect upon these
accounts, however, we are forced to acknowledge that it was
poverty and privation which delineated the different family life-
styles of poor and middling. It might be noted that, among the
well-to-do, the wet-nurse, the governess and the school, the master
craftsman, also shared considerably in the associalisation of the
young, and that we should not allow ourselves to be carried away
by such comparisons into assuming that the relatively well-to-do in

any society were treated to an undiluted diet of parental attention and control. Middle-class children at all levels relished extended stays with kith and kin.[78] The poor did not supervise their neighbours' children without financial or economic recompense. Moreover, Mayhew's costermonger's lad indicated how far neighbourliness and interdependence could be pushed: 'If a feller as lives next me wanted a basket of mine as I wasn't using, why, he might have it; if I was working it though, I'd see him further! I can understand that all as lives in a court is neighbours; but as for policemen ther're nothing to me.'[79] This sentiment must be set alongside the reports of neighbours giving the really poor amongst them some of their unsold cabbages.[80] There might be little resort to the forces of law and order maintained by the state and the city, but a good deal to informal but no less effective group pressure.

The periodisation of childhood and adulthood seems to have varied with the degree of poverty. This was not only important in that boys and girls whom the middle classes would have cosseted and regarded as immature, irresponsible and unable to make decisions, let alone work, were expected to contribute considerably to the total resource of the family; but in that these same 'children' were henceforth placed in a totally different relation to their 'parents' and hastened towards liaisons and parenthood themselves. The childhood of the watercress seller was an aeon away from that of the son or daughter of a skilled worker or a middle-class couple.

> I am just eight years old – that's all.… On and off, I've been very near a twelvemonth in the streets. Before that I had to take care of a baby for my aunt.… Before I had the baby, I used to help mother who was in the fur trade; and, if there were any slits in the fur, I'd sew them up. My mother learned me to needle-work and to knit when I was about five.

Her days were long, cold and miserable – a struggle for food for herself and for her mother and siblings. Her work as a watercress seller was supplemented by doing domestic work for a Jewish family each sabbath in exchange for 'wittals and 1 1/2d'. For her this meant the difference between life and mere existence. As she said, 'I aint a child, and I shant be a woman till I'm twenty, but I'm past eight I am'.[81]

The type of responsibility which the poorer sections of the working class entered into when they became parents thus differed radically from that of the artisans and lower middle classes as well as the middle classes. Even those from among the settled workers had problems. In 1772 a Parisian who discovered that her unmarried daughter was pregnant explained, 'Being engaged in trade, I am unable to stay at home ... and unknown to me they have maintained their liaison until this very day.'[82] Thus, while most parents of the self-supporting working classes may have wished to supervise their daughter's courtships and veto their marital choices, their economic circumstances often forbade them doing so as effectively as wealthier parents. But, for some, the relationship of responsibility between parents and offspring was destroyed completely by the need to make a living. The plight of the flower-seller in mid-Victorian London was probably not unusual: her parents were effectively her pimps. She was sent out onto the streets by her parents at the age of nine. She could not state positively that her parents were aware of the manner in which she got the money she took home to them. She supposes they must have imagined what her practices were. They used to give her no supper if she 'didn't bring home a good bit of money'. When, some time later, she failed to support the family she was turned out onto the streets. Still in her teens, she 'was sick and tired of her life' and deliberately engineered arrest and imprisonment.[83] But to suggest that all parents behaved identically when they became dependent upon their children for income would be simplistic in the extreme. Some responded with kindness, others with oppression. Looked at in one way, the child had an economic power in the family which the middle-class child did not have.

Le Play believed that this lack of parental supervision and discipline was an inevitable concomitant of the unstable family that he saw as characteristic of the working classes. Downward mobility perpetuated itself 'either because the parents are no longer able ... to contribute by saving to the establishment of their children, or because they are left without supervision ... or, above all, because they are early perverted by evil example'.[84] When Le Play attempted to rank the occupations of the working classes in terms of their social value he used, as his criterion, 'the relative aptitudes of these trades to maintain moral order among the families who work at them'. The type of work in which a head of household was engaged determined his family life and his possible contribution to social harmony. There were, moreover, six rungs on the ladder which individual workers and their families might occupy, which in their turn defined their family influence. There was the domestic servant with no household of his own; the day labourer with a household, in the west more likely to occupy rented than owner-occupied accommodation; the job-worker, who had more control over his time and therefore freedom to control his family; the worker-tenant who exploited property belonging to a landlord but for his own benefit – such ranged from small to large tenants, rural to urban tenants; worker–proprietors, who resembled the former with the important exception that they owned their property outright; and finally master-craftsmen – peasants in rural culture; artisans in urban.

Some historians have urged that those children who left their parental homes for independence in the towns (an ever increasing number from the late eighteenth century onwards) still remained part of their original household and contributed to its economy, while others have urged that distance between children and parents dissolved the old economic bond. Le Play's description of contemporary French workers suggests that the old system was breaking down, although not broken, by the mid-century; and it is still possible to find examples of youthful financial commitment to the parental home well into the twentieth century in Britain.[85] In many workers' homes in nineteenth-century Britain young people continued to live at home once they began working. Boys handed over (tipped up) their wages until they reached 18, and thereafter were lodgers in their own homes; girls 'tipped up' their wages and assisted in the house until they married.[86] On occasion, historians have described the relationship between working-class husbands and wives as both economic and opportunist in the extreme. Such see the relations between and the roles of spouses as unrelieved by affection and characterised by violence, perceiving, rather, a division between women and children on the one hand and adult males on the other which sometimes approached outright hostilities and scarcely ever improved upon a ceasefire.[87]

To suggest that even in these so-called family homes life was lived as it would be in a comfortable middle-class home would be foolish. Privacy was difficult. Rooms were marked on plans as bedrooms, parlours or living rooms and kitchens but were, in fact, multi-purpose. An old man described his home in New York's East Side thus:

> Privacy in the home was practically unknown. The average apartment consisted of three rooms: a kitchen, a parlor and a doorless and windowless bedroom between. The parlor became a bedroom at night. So did the kitchen when families were unusually large.... Made comparatively presentable after a long day of cooking, eating and washing of dishes and laundry, the kitchen was the scene of formal calls at our house and of the visits of friends and prospective suitors.'[88]

But there were widely different homes among the poor of all cities and all groups. Mayhew in the late 1850s and Charles Booth in the 1890s gave examples of home life, in the various trades and localities, which differed greatly from one another. Mayhew's observation about the Irish lodging houses falling into two categories – clean and dirty – should be taken to heart. The point is that there was no single 'working-class family type, just as there was no single 'middle-class family'.

Unfortunately the sources which historians can and do use are often highly specific in their reference. They may fail to reveal much about the conditions of the truly poor among the working classes or they may relate to one tiny group. And yet, they are often employed as the basis of generalisations. For example, Olwen Hufton describes the life of a working woman as if she belonged to the generality of the poor, yet this is a woman who was distinctive in many respects – she went out to work although married; her domestic chores were not her central preoccupation; she had possessions to be rifled and resources to 'husband'.[89] Yet we know that there were many women whose families moved in and out of extreme poverty, who had no possessions to steal, no resources to conserve, and a 'passle of brats' to tie them to what resembled a hole more closely than a home. Olwen Hufton's working woman may have had her equivalents in all modern cities and she may been more typical of eighteenth-century non-industrialised French cities than of nineteenth-century industrialised British and American cities, but she certainly cannot be regarded as typical of all married women of the working classes. Other historians draw material from highly specific sources such as police records or murder trials to sketch the home life of the working classes, as if criminality and the working class were co-terminous. Ellen Ross assumes that the family lives of those brought before the Old Bailey for trial were typical of the contemporary London working classes. This tendency to generalise leads even the most intelligent historians astray.[90] Of course, contemporaries were as likely to 'lump' all the poor together as are modern historians. Probably one of Charles Booth's chief contributions to our knowledge of the working classes, although imperfectly executed, was not his poverty line but his acute appreciation of the gradations among the working poor.

One area which has been under-researched is the regulatory role of the working-class landlord or landlady in the domestic lives of the working classes. The letting of lodgings had long been a great industry. In eighteenth-century London, furnished rooms may have been the most prevalent form of housing. At the lowest end of the scale were common lodging houses. Shopkeepers commonly let out one or more rooms and a certain income was required to offer proper lodgings. However, some very poor and cramped families found space for unofficial 'lodgers'. By the mid-nineteenth century it was considered important among the middle classes that each family 'possess' an entire house. Taking in lodgers implied a loss of both privacy and gentility. The middle classes deplored the mobility and flexibility of relationships which accompanied working-class 'lodging' and sought to control what they thought to be its worst excesses. To them, it replaced the responsible relationships of the natural family with the irresponsible ones of a commercialised household.[91] The reality may not have squared with the perception. Taking lodgers allowed many widows of the middle and working classes to re-create households as well as to subsist independently, and permitted married women to use their skills to bring in income while not working outside the home. This was both convenient (especially where there were young children) and status-preserving. It drew the lodgers themselves into households and sometimes into families, providing them not only with creature comforts but also with relationships. It allowed many 'families' to stay together as households.

Charles Booth gives a description of his lodgings in the East End and, specifically, of relations between his landlady and the tenants who belonged, according to Booth's own classificatory system, to different sections of the working class.[92] The landlady displayed, according to Booth, a strong sense of social responsibility for the tenants – she made over a dress for the thirteen-year-old 'drudge' of one of the tenant families; rebuked another child for telling tales; and told the father of one family – a drunk – to mend his ways or get out. The women associated with one another, and the children played together, sharing the goodies available to the better-off. The landlady had authority arising from the power of the purse but she used it to discipline the tenants in responsible ways. This informal discipline from within the working class, broadly conceived, should surely be set alongside the overt attempts of middle-class landlords and building managers to shape the family lives of their tenants. It should also be compared with the role of the caretaker and the concierge. In late-Victorian model dwellings in London the caretaker emerged as someone from the working class who not only kept a building clean but controlled its tenants, sometimes physically, and advised the management on the suitability or otherwise of the occupants. We know that the French concierge was an important figure. There are several ways of looking at this question. Was the caretaker/concierge a communicator of middle-class values to the more unruly sections of the working class, or did he or she have more in common with the landlord or landlady of a lodging house?[93]

Ethnic and Immigrant Families

Booth was also aware that the people of London came from many different origins. On the one hand there were native-born Londoners, on the other, immigrants from countryside and overseas, from Ireland and Poland as well as from rural Essex and urban Glasgow. Like Beatrice Potter, he was wont to contrast the urban working-class family with the rural. We, too, should bear always in mind the various origins of the people of the cities. It would be incorrect to regard only the Unites States of America as possessing an 'immigrant' problem. The cities of France and Britain were melting pots too. Immigrants brought to their new destinations a plethora of different experiences and family traditions. These were adapted to new circumstances as far and as fast as possible. But the need to acculturate new groups was a continuing and continuous problem. One wave of immigrants was replaced with another, often diverse in origin, if not from overseas then from the country. Charles Booth and his associates tried, at the end of the century, to show how some communities in London, for instance the Isle of Dogs, still retained a quasi-rural quality which affected the life-styles of its people. When Beatrice Potter wrote up her case histories of the tenants of Katharine Buildings, in the later 1880s, she was keen to note their origins.[94] Among other things, she noted the still strong rural roots of some families and the links maintained with the folks back home. The child of one single-parent Irish family was returned to Ireland for care; another woman of Irish birth, whose husband worked at the Tower of London, paid a visit back home and returned, Lord luv us, with a number of hens, which she proceeded to keep in the living room! The family links of the Irish were, however, paralleled by similar examples among the Scots and the English in the Buildings. If Beatrice Potter made implicitly derogatory remarks about the Irish, the tenants fixed upon the few Jewish tenants, who felt themselves to be hounded out of the dwellings. She said of a Turk, a Moslem, that he just did not fit in, his ways being so alien from those of the other tenants, and she had to give him notice. There are relatively few detailed studies of the nineteenth-century British immigrant experience, but, in her study of the Irish slums of London, Lynn Lees argues that Irish immigrants more or less successfully adapted the pre-industrial peasant household to their new surroundings. 'Instead of joining the lumpen proletariat in London lodging houses, migrants responded to the city by quickly reorganizing themselves in family units: over three-quarters of the Irish individuals sampled in 1851 lived in households headed by Irish nuclear families.'[95] Very few lived alone, lived with friends or moved into lodging houses. But these reconstituted families differed in important respects from their Irish peasant counterparts. Very few stretched to three generations. Young married couples now set up new households. There were rather more households containing other kin than among the 'native' population but this was not a feature of the Irish household. Lodgers were, however more common than in English households. Matriarchal households were frequently encountered. Some of these features, however, owed more to accident than intent. The single-parent households were often the result of a higher than normal male mortality rate in poor areas rather than an indicator of the absence of family values.

The Americans were faced with an especially problematic situation with regard to the family, although the difference from the British or even the French experience may be one of degree rather than essence. From the start, an enormous variety of family forms and traditions were imported from the Old World and grafted onto the pre-existent forms and traditions of the New, be they those of the indigenous peoples, the Indians, or earlier waves of settlers. To put the problem into perspective: first-generation immigrants made up one-seventh of the population in nineteenth-century America and, yet more importantly, two-fifths of the manufacturing and extractive industry labour force. In some of the big cities, immigrants formed a majority of the working class. But the authorities had no simple task before them. The immigrant tradition was not one tradition but many – and those diverse. Whereas one might generalise and state that girls from immigrant families left home and started work younger than was normal in non-immigrant homes, that women were more likely to be employed, that fertility rates were higher, that a higher proportion of children were engaged in child labour and that fewer households contained non-family members, a closer look at the characteristics of various ethnic groups in America indicates that such generalisations mask enormous variations. Irish women, for example, tended to withdraw from paid labour after marriage whereas German and Jewish women remained within the labour market. The Germans tended to see the family as the focus of socialisation whereas Italians emphasised the social groupings of males and females.[96] Fertility rates among the Catholic Irish were high and increasing, while those among the Presbyterian Scots, the Canadian Protestants and the English Methodists were on the decrease.[97] The extent to which a given community would be faced with such varying patterns itself depended upon circumstance. In Boston, for example, the immigrant experience was heavily Irish and Catholic and it began, really, in the 1840s. Before that date most Irish immigrants had passed through Boston on their way West. After 1840 they settled in the city. By 1855 more than 50,000 Irish lived in Boston and the number from then on remained fairly constant. By comparison, the city housed only about 6,500 Germans, about 2,000 Scots and some 200 German and Polish Jewish families.[98]

The problems of ethnic diversity combined with other trouble-some features of American urban working-class life to create con-sternation in some quarters: the low wages of the employed; the high transience rate (there was population turnover of between 40 and 60 per cent in some cities); and the lack of support networks within the community. Acculturation of immigrants proceeded quite naturally of course, as the new settlers sought to make their way in a new society and the environment played its own part in the formation of new family forms and ways. Nevertheless, accul-turation was insufficiently fast, or even, to satisfy those in authority at community, state and national level. Deliberate programmes of 'Americanisation' were entered into. In New York Jewish children were taught the language and practical civics. The schools and playgrounds were kept open for afternoons, weekends, evenings to keep the immigrant children off the street and away from its corrupting influence. Adults were taught English and civics and trained in domestic skills such as cooking, infant care and clean-ing.[99] Historians tend to enphasise the 'Americanisation' of Emily, the individual, but the Americanisation of the Family was no less, and perhaps more, important.[100] The role of 'service' experience in this process should not be overlooked.[101]

Contrasting immigrant family life-styles with those of the estab-lished community is, however, much less simple than it sounds. Nineteenth-century immigrants were overwhelmingly working-class in origin and destination. Those who became 'middle-class' did so by becoming small, local landlords, shopkeepers or pawn-brokers within their own community.

Interestingly, the strength of immigrant traditions, in one sense a threat to national and community identity, proved, in fact, an asset to those seeking the Americanisation of the people. The household system was still alive and kicking in much of the Old World, although threatened by industrialisation. What we have to say next may suggest that late nineteenth-century urban Americans were more able to adapt it to their new circumstances than were their contemporaries in France and Britain. In a great many cases the immigrants were those who had sought to escape the disintegration of their traditional way of life by transporting that way of life to America. When they emigrated from rural areas they brought with them the household, and they tried to make it work for them as a socio-economic unit in the very different circumstances of American life. The prime importance of the net-work of kinship and ethnicity, both in providing an impetus for and mechanism for migration and in creating a support system for it, should be noted. This had earlier been, as Henry Mayhew observed in 1861 and as Lynn Lees has echoed, a feature of Irish immigration into London as well.[102] Family and kin support sys-tems became more and not less important with the breakdown of other forms of support and interdependence. This fact and the economic circumstances in which the immigrants found them-selves encouraged, indeed forced, the immigrant family to organ-ise itself as an economic unit for the purposes of survival. Situations which seem all-too familiar to the historian of eighteenth and early nineteenth-century Britain occur in late nineteenth-century American cities. The mills contracted whole families to work together, sometimes paying the father the wages for the whole family and using him as a foreman and keeper of order. Whole families engaged in sweated trades, each member of the family working at piece rates. When the family could work together neither in factory nor home, then all its members, where possible, worked and ploughed back their income into the family coffer.[103] In Lowell, Massachusetts, French-Canadian textile work-ers relied upon large families to keep them out of poverty. Here, one child could increase the family income by more than a half and two children could more than double it.[104] Irish families in Boston placed their daughters in service in middle-class house-holds – to the tune of 2,227 in 1850.[105] And indeed the response of most working-class American families, whatever their ethnic back-ground, to poverty seems to have been to produce large families. While the overall American fertility rate fell by 40 per cent between 1855 and 1915, the urban working-class fertility rate sometimes rose significantly. For instance, Massachusetts-born semi-skilled worker families had higher family fertility in 1880 than in 1850. In New York, between 1855 and 1915, fertility among the unskilled rose rather than fell over the period. Michigan figures suggest that fertility among rural workers fell, while that among the Detroit workers increased.[106] Only middle-class ethnic groups, such as the Presbyterian Scots, displayed decreasing fertil-ity rates. One feature of late nineteenth-century family life was the withdrawal of wives from the labour force. This was true of all ethnic and class groups apart from blacks. The absence of large numbers of married women from the labour force might, in the context of the above argument, seem puzzling. But no. Survival required the full-time work of one individual in household tasks not least of which was food preparation. In most instances this would be the wife, although there were cases where a partially disabled child or an unemployed husband would fulfil this role. Jeanne Boydston has calculated that, before the American Civil War, the woman's work inside the home was of more value to her family than that of her work outside the family. Stephanie Coontz has argued that the outgoings on transport, food, clothing and cleaning that would have been necessary to support a wife in work would easily have outweighed any income she could have anticipated.[107] She employs in this argument an estimated average wage of $5.25 in 1905. At home the woman could prepare food, make clothes, clean the house, care for the very young and the very old, organise the lives of her husband and children, and perhaps take in lodgers or do a little sewing to bring in additional income. Her argument is persuasive when one reflects that, of 7,000 working-class families interviewed between 1889 and 1892, more than half made their own bread, and that as late as 1890, in Pittsburgh and associated centres of coal, iron and steel production, half the families grew vegetables and/or kept livestock and poultry, with some 30 per cent being self-sufficient with regard to vegetables, with the exception of potatoes. Add to this the absence of household technology, which made laundering and cleaning excessively onerous tasks even when practised at lower than modern hygiene levels, and the case seems overpowering.

The immigrant household appears, in some cases, to have altered its traditional form. For instance, the extended family became more common in working-class American families in the later years of the nineteenth century. Lynn Lees found that Irish families in London also tended to include lodgers and kin more frequently than did 'native' households. Immigrant households took lodgers not only to make ends meet but to provide support for newcomers in a hostile environment where housing of any kind was scarce. Some desperate families in the Jewish quarter of New York put three boarders in the front room and two in the kitchen, and fount it increasingly difficult to do this as room size shrank.[108] The relative absence of families taking in lodgers in Katharine Buildings in the East End of London in the later 1880s perhaps suggest that this was not a typical practice among the lowest class of self-supporting London families at that time. Only single males showed any propensity whatsoever towards accommodating lodgers. Of course there is always the problem of establishing how frequently householders 'hid' their lodgers from the eye of census enumerator or building manager, but there seems little reason to suppose that they would be more reluctant before one than the other.

Failing the re-establishment of traditional relations between masters and men, and in the face of the collapse of religious influence upon the lives of the poor, societies sought to control these through legislation and private endeavour. At the worst, such legislation brought order out of a potential chaos; at best it sought to impose upon the poor the conception of the 'family' shared by the minority. Looked at in this way, for example, the many acts which tried to limit the employment of children tried to force working-class couples to regard children not as sources of additional income but as dependants, as the middle-class intelligentsia had come to view them. During the middle and later twentieth-century we have come to view such legislation as 'right', as logical steps towards a correct approach to children. Leaving issues of correctness aside, from the point of view of poor people with little or no reliable income, it made no sense at all to forego the income which young children might bring in, and to pose as a middle-class family, able to support and succour all its members below a statutory age. As a consequence, because the poverty which forced people to send their children out to work was not itself addressed, the legislation could do little to bring about a family life among the poor which met with middle-class approval.

Middle-class Homes: Middle-class Clones

The traditional household was of decreasing importance in the modern period. But the advantages of 'using' the biological family as the primary unit of society were not lost on the governing classes. How, though, could this be done? Contemporary observers noted the closeness which did obtain in respectable working-class families, commented on the strength of biological bonds, sought to identify the conditions which were necessary to enable the working-class family to mimic an idealised middle-class institution.

The wage earners of eighteenth and early nineteenth-century British towns and cities did predominantly live in terraced houses (remarkable exceptions were those Scottish and Northern English cities in which tenement housing was widespread), and an interest in improving the health and sanitation of the cities was stirred in the early decades of the century and might have been expected to lead to return to the middle-class ideal of one family, one cottage. Unavailability of land and extreme reliance upon the private sector prevented this. The same constraints did not obtain in the United States except in the very largest cities.

Even philanthropy wore pseudo-speculative clothing in the United States and Britain. From the 1840s onwards, model dwellings companies were active. In this context the American experience was not only comparable with the British but imitative and interactive. A subsidiary company of the AICP (Association for Improving the Condition of the Poor) built a model tenement near Elizabeth and Mott Streets in New York. This contained 87 apartments, two stores and a large hall. Rents ranged from $5.50 to $8.50 a month. It was planned that the project would return a profit of 6 per cent. In the event it was occupied by blacks rather than white workers. It proved neither a commercial nor a social success and the AICP sold it off in 1867. By the 1880s it was condemned as a slum property by the AICP.[109] The model tenement programme did not die, however, as Alfred White's three blocks, built between 1877 and 1890, bore witness. White patterned his first Brooklyn building on Sir Sydney Waterlow's London Langbourn Estate.[110] By 1885, English commercial philanthropic companies were showing a return on their investment and had housed 4 per cent of London's population in what were, effectively, modern tenements. But such attempts barely scratched the running sore of homelessness and overcrowding, and the housing which was provided was scarcely inducive to home-life. Imposing tenemented buildings resembled hospitals, military barracks and penitentiaries rather than comforting and comfortable family residences. They seemed, and were, more designed to perpetuate and accentuate the problems of working-class life than to resolve them. At the same time, what seemed to be single-family terraced houses, on closer inspection proved home to myriad families. The 'model dwelling' provision in New York was far more minimal than in London. However, interest was rekindled in the 1890s by the Gilder Tenements Commission. In 1896 the Improved Housing Council sponsored an architectural competition and eventually formed the City and Suburban Housing Company to build the best design. The president, Elgin Ralston Lovell Gould, was a firm believer in tenement reform as a form of social as well as sanitary control, but his buildings, unlike those of some of the London companies, excluded the lower strata of the self-supporting working class.[111]

Even among those who deplored the effect of the physical environment upon the life-style of the working poor, there was an awareness, by the later nineteenth century, that something more than a Great Rebuilding was necessary. When a 'lady resident' wrote about life in model dwellings in London in the 1880s she observed, 'Life in Buildings as we may say, depends more on the class of inhabitants than on structural arrangements.'[112] But she might also have observed that the type of housing provided for different income and class groups varied in any event, and to some degree reinforced existing differences in 'Life in Buildings'. For instance, one five-floor block of industrial dwellings offered self-contained two or three-room flats, each with a scullery containing 'sink, copper, water-closet and other conveniences', all well lit, painted and kept in good repair, whereas another contained mostly one-roomed apartments, with no facilities other than stoves, and offered communal access to water supply and water-closets at the heads of the staircases. It was not surprising that the former attracted those able to pay its higher rents while the latter catered for those families who could barely support themselves without charity.

Octavia Hill's observations about the unfortunate effect of block or tenement dwelling upon the working population are important, for she shows that the Americans and French were not alone in holding tenement living suspect. She underlines the tendency to a tribal existence fostered by the block: 'a huge community of those who are undisciplined and untrained' produced 'the violence, the dirt, the noise, the quarrels' which were beyond any inspection or regulation to control. These evils were, she thought, entirely absent in small blocks wholly inhabited by 'quiet, respectable, working-class families who, to use a phrase common in

London, "keep themselves to themselves"'. But the rough and vicious could not be 'trained' to live like these in blocks. 'The very same evils are nothing like as injurious where the families are more separate, so that while in smaller houses one can often try difficult tenants with real hope of their doing better, it is wholly impossible usually to try, or to train them in blocks. The temptations are greater, the evils of relapse far greater. It is like taking a bad girl into a school. Hence the enormous importance of keeping a large number of small houses wherever it be possible for the better training of the rowdy....' Gentle life in a block 'only becomes possible when there is deliberate isolation of the family'....[113] At about the same time, in the United States, Charles F. Wingate was inveighing against tenement living as tending towards the 'growth of intemperance and immorality' and the disintegration of the primary moral influence – that of the family.[114] Gould, president of the City and Suburban Homes Company, complained in the *New York Times* of 23 February 1893 that the tenement was a menace to 'the family, to morality, to the public health, and to civic integrity'. As the home was 'the character unit of society' when it was under attack 'we must accept social degeneration and decay'.[115] Model dwellings might counter some of these tendencies but were not, on the whole, to be recommended.

All this may seem to suggest that if the philanthropists of the Victorian period rehoused the working classes they did not do so in a manner conducive to their living like prosperous middle-class families. But it is as well to note the assumptions behind Octavia Hill's criticisms. They are that better housing and improved amenities will not, of themselves, civilise the working poor, and that herding the poor together into a corporate life for which they are ill fitted will brutalise rather than improve their way of living. The biological families of the poor should be housed in isolation from one another in, if necessary, minimally sanitary conditions. Then the middle-class visitor can come in and 'train' the families to live in a civilised fashion. 'Civilisation' is defined by middle-class morality, so this means that they will adopt the middle-class values of family life.

Friendly rent collection was spread by Octavia Hill's writing and example in both England and the United States. In the 1880s Ellen Collins bought and reformed three tenement buildings in Manhattan's fourth ward, using Octavian methods. The Octavia

Hill Association of Philadelphia acquired 179 houses, containing 244 families, between 1895 and 1917 and followed the Hill model of rent collection combined with visiting. 'Observation' of the family was also in vogue on both sides of the Atlantic.[116]

My own study of Katharine Buildings, East Smithfield, in the late 1880s, under the philanthropic management of Ella Pycroft and Beatrice Potter (later to be Webb), indicates the possibilities for a study of working-class family experiences in relation to the pre-scriptive roles of middle-class management. It shows the sincere efforts which these young women put into 'reforming' the family lives of the tenants along Octavian lines. The Buildings were erected to cater for the lowest class of self-supporting labourer, Charles Booth's Class 'C'. Most of the apartments were moderately sized rooms of about 12 ft by 10 ft with no private amenities other than smoking stoves. Indeed, in terms of dimension, they make the notorious 'dumb-bell' tenements of nineteenth-century New York appear commodious. The water-closets and water supply were situated at the head of the staircase on each of four balconies. Laundry and bathing facilities were in the narrow yard at the back of the building, where there was also an opportunity for the children to play. The Buildings also possessed a club/reading room for the men and there were two resident caretakers to clean and maintain order. The amount of room allocated to a family depended not upon its size but upon its income. So, for example, 225 households with 3 or more occupants lived in the equivalent of a bed-sitting room. Some of these households were large: for instance, there were 25 households containing 6 persons, 19 con-taining 7 and 8 containing 8 persons in these cramped circum-stances. While some of the largest nuclear families did occupy the larger two-room apartments or rented additional rooms (2 fam-ilies with 8 children apiece), the assumption on the part of designer and manager was not that if one had more children one had more space, but that if one had more money one could afford to rent more rooms. One well-to-do single inhabitant was allowed to rent approximately seven rooms in the Buildings and convert them for her use by installing a water-closet and convenient features. Other families who felt that they could afford more than just one room were not so fortunate. Their rooms were not linked and were still lacking in private 'facilities', making living like a family difficult. In many cases the individual rooms remained bed-sits even when technically rented as additional bedrooms or, in one or two cases, shops. Real family life, with the possibility of individual privacy and divisions between the functions of rooms, was impossible.

The above study suggests that one should be more than usually careful not to allow the 'house' or the 'room' to define the family. Censuses of all kinds (be they the official census or the informal censuses of the people taken by clergy, philanthropists and social investigators) regard the 'family' as the occupants of an architecturally defined space – be it a 'house', a 'room', an 'apartment' or part of a house. In fact the 'household' even defined in these terms, was extremely fluid. Households might constitute and reconstitute themselves several times within a short period of time (five years), in ways which sometimes were related to life course (as Tamara Hareven and other historians have labelled it) but as often not. A male and a female resident of the buildings met and, having lived together for a while in their two, separated rooms, married and moved into one household. They had children, one, two, three, four. The husband deserted his wife. The wife moved into another, smaller room with her children. The husband lived with another woman who had an older child living with her. The eldest daughter eventually went into service. The wife's mother moved in to care for the younger children while her daughter worked. Poverty forced a couple temporarily into the workhouse. When they emerged the husband lived with one daughter and her family and the wife with another daughter and her family. Illness or disability permanently or temporarily reduced a family to beggary. Rows could turn wife and son against husband and result in the temporary formation of different households. Such examples show that, while 'the life course' did inevitably affect families, as a model for the behaviour of real families it is sadly mechanistic and simplistic. But there is more. A statistical study of Katharine Buildings seems to show that the number of families was equivalent to the number of apartments – normally but not always single rooms. But this is deceptive. First, as I have indicated, 'families' enlarged or decreased the spatial character of their household when circumstances dictated or permitted, albeit that these circumstances were not entirely connected to the stage of life one was in. This was a feature which might be ironed out by the statistician. Secondly, the distinction between different types of household was not nearly as clear-cut as the demographic historians, working almost entirely on the basis of the census, would have us believe. Katharine Buildings looks as though it is neatly divided into nuclear, conjugal, disrupted and single-person households, with a smattering of extended. Certainly the management wished to define the family thus preventing the extension of the household to include lodgers. This was often not the case at all. An older son might live with an aunt a few doors away. A married daughter might hold open house to the rest of her family, who lived in the Buildings in a number of rooms – mother, sisters and their families. The daughters who technically still lived with the mother might spend a good deal of time, day and night, in the home of a more prosperous sister in another nearby dwellings. A couple rented an extra room as a shop but this was, in effect, the bed-sit and independent household of the grown-up daughter. When we bear these examples in mind, the statistics for kin living in the Buildings might seem yet more significant. Fourteen per cent of married women, and even more of the female heads of household (21 per cent) had kin living in the Buildings in what were, technically, distinct households. But it was as possible to live like an extended family in such circumstances as it was when the father lived in one bed-sit and wife and children in another a few doors or a floor away (a household in that the father held the rent book of both rooms). What made distinct 'families' of the upstairs and downstairs of an ordinary terrace house when it was a mother and father and younger children living downstairs and married daughter and family upstairs? Presumably they were distinct to the census enumerator but they were perhaps no less living as an extended family than they would have been, had all three generations lived under the same tenancy. When Beatrice Potter visited a Jewish tailoring establishment in London's East End, she noted that the wife provided diet for her unemployed brother and that one of her daughters, who lived in another place, infant in tow, cleaned her mother's home daily in exchange for a square meal. The child was effectively left to the supervision of the grandparents' workshop.[117] These examples demonstrate relations of dependence which are totally disguised by a mere count of households and analysis of their membership. An anthropological approach to the family is indeed called for.[118]

It would be only too easy to over-estimate the relative importance of the 'model dwelling' experiment in rehousing Britain's poor working class. Even in London and other major cities, only a fraction of the working-class population were accommodated in this way. Many of the new flats were designed for, or taken over by, the lower middle and middle classes. Rents were high and the attractions of living in a 'supervised' environment mixed. Social reformers and philanthropists were often disillusioned by the experiment, and began more and more to postulate other solutions to the perceived problem. It is perhaps ironic that a form of housing and housing management which was, on the whole, rejected by its initiators was effectively taken over wholesale by the state, in its large-scale rehousing programmes of the twentieth century.

Although there were broad similarities between the approaches of the British, the Americans and the French to the cultivation of a proper working-class family by appropriate rehousing, closer examination reveals considerable variations on this theme, dictated by specific local circumstances, national traditions and chronology. For instance, the redevelopment of Paris from the mid-nineteenth century created a crisis for its working classes. New accommodation at high rents priced them out of the city centre and either into overcrowded, high-rent accommodation or into the suburbs. In the early 1880s, socialist agitators and recession impelled both the national and the city government to reconsider their housing policies. An official report produced in 1883 suggested that a return to the mixed housing pattern of the past was desirable – with the working classes living on the upper floors and middle classes on the lower floors of the buildings. Anne-Louise Shapiro has shown how the term 'low-rent housing' replaced 'working-class housing' in a deliberate attempt to end class divisions. There were recognised expedients at work: low-cost single-family dwellings in the suburbs (on the London model) were impractical in a city like Paris, where the working day was long and transport inadequate. But the implications seem clear – given similar housing, the family lives of all will be similar. The national and city governments forbore providing this mixed housing stock although a number of schemes were broached to provide financial assistance to private contractors and encourage building projects. Such schemes met with no success and when the recession receded the imperative towards a comprehensive housing policy more or less disappeared. The Municipal Council did

engage in building a few model homes to inspire private specula-
tors, but in all cases these projects were abandoned. By the end of
the century the ball was back with the private sector. 'There was ...
a sizeable group of social reformers in the private sector who had
mobilised around the question of working-class housing to pursue
a reformist programme which was grounded in a conservative
social ideology and laisser-faire economics.'[119] They, following the
line of Frédéric Le Play, identified the home as the source of all
evils and all good. Edmond Demolins wrote the following in *La
Réforme Sociale*:

> The possession of his home creates in [the worker] a complete
> transformation.... With his own small home and garden, one
> makes of the worker the head of his family worthy of this name,
> one who is moral and provident, aware of this roots, and able to
> exercise authority over his family. He soon forgets the cabaret,
> whose principal appeal has been remove him from his miserable
> hovel.... Soon it is his home which possesses him; it gives him
> morals, it establishes him, it transforms him.[120]

This ideal was realised in individual family homes, not shared
tenements, and the model for the reformers was provided by the
cité ouvrière, a community of worker houses built at Mulhouses in
1853 by Jean Dolfus and lauded by Le Play himself. In this *cité
ouvrière*, houses were built (by a private entrepreneur) in groups
of four. Each had a garden. The houses became the property of
the tenants after 15 years of mortgage payments. 'Bourgeois
reformers thus sought to remake society in their own image.' Like
the model dwellings built by the 5 per cent of philanthropists in
London, these *'habitations à bon marché'* were not charity but a
commercial investment. Unfortunately they failed in their purpose. Those at Passy-Auteuil, for example, with four or five rooms
and a garden apiece, were effectively priced out of reach Parisian
workers. Even the reformers accepted the failure of the experiment. As in Britain, the poor health of the nation provided an
imperative for the authorities to improve sanitation and, thereby,
the standard of working-class homes. But this did not solve the
problem.

Richard Sennett has argued that by the end of the nineteenth
century the middle-class house in North America had become the

focus of 'a new kind of intense family life', just as, in fact, it had already become in Britain for the urban middle classes sixty to a hundred years earlier. In the United States the middle-class house form had changed to create and reflect a separation between the private and public spheres. Individuals each had their own room upstairs; family interaction took place downstairs in the dining room and back parlour and out on the porch; visitors to the house were confined to the front parlour; women and children, and servants, regarded the kitchen as their preserve, separated from the adult menfolk; business was banned from the house.[121] It was not until the early twentieth century, however, that housing reformers in America were able to privatise the poor working-class dwelling in imitation of this model. Contemporaries were, by then, consciously following such a policy of providing single-family dwellings, because tenement dwelling made it impossible 'to obtain necessary privacy for true home life and personal development'. There was a marked reaction against experiments in New York and other cities with what were seen as alien forms of housing. Gould, for example, saw the tenement as something to be accepted only grudgingly. Even the model dwelling was an intermediate stage between 'the promiscuous and common life of the ordinary tenement and the dignified, well-ordered life of the detached home'. The ideal was the single-family detached home, in sharp contrast to the 'promiscuity in human beehives, rendering independence and isolation of the family impossible'. Homewood, Brooklyn, was the answer his company proposed – 250 two-storey brick and timber cottages with all utilities, domestic and communal, provided by the builders. A well-designed public transit system was advocated, to direct the New York population to choose to live outside the downtown area and to encourage other suburban developments.[122] Lawrence Veiller, also, was convinced of the virtues of urban decentralisation to save the family, and saw tenement reform as an immediate and ameliorative action, requiring nation-wide measures, en route to long-term ideals.[123] Working-class housing had to be brought into line with the middle-class family ideal.[124] American working-class housing, like the British, was heterogeneous in character but, in the American mind, family life was associated with occupancy of a single-family home. 'Tenements were perceived as the threat to American culture: building and loan associations were seen as the bastion of single-family homes, owned by their proud and self-reliant residents.'[125]

> The separateness, the sanctities, the privacies of home life can hardly be said to exist in the more crowded tenements.... It is true that many cities in Germany, England, Scotland, and France show a large percentage of one-room apartments, but we do not want to Europeanize our American standards. We are going up, not down; forward to completer, sweeter living, not backward to a reproduction of the sordid squalor of swarming London slums.[126]

Presumably the numbers of American workers who borrowed money for single-family dwellings or even engaged in self-build programmes in the later nineteenth and early twentieth centuries shared this vision. In certain northern American cities self-build seems to have made an important contribution to the stock of working-class housing. Examples abound for Milwaukee and Detroit. In 1892, for example, a railroad car inspector in Milwaukee built himself a house. When John Kreft, a Polish day labourer working for the Detroit Brewery Co., built a house in 1887, at a cost of $340, he sublet part of it to offset the cost. Sixty-three per cent of the home-owning Detroit Railway employees in 1896 do not seem to have borrowed money to finance their house building. These workers appear to have shared the middle-class conviction that the family, dwelling in isolation, was an integral part of the American dream.[127] Mrs McNabb, an Irish immigrant to Philadelphia, on her deathbed at the age of 80, was to say 'I have much to praise God for I haven't a child that is dependent on the day's work for the day's victuals. Every one of them owns a roof to cover him.'[128]

Those Americans who remained absorbed with the problem of the inner cities, as was Jacob Riis in New York, continued to grapple with reform of tenement housing. There was a fundamental similarity and interaction between those American and British reformers who sought to improve not only the buildings but the neighbourhoods in which they were situated, in the interests of furthering the reform of the working-class family. Some, like Gould, neglected this aspect.[129]

Although the emphasis may have differed slightly and the success rate of the American and French dream may have been higher than the British, because of tradition and the relative availability of land, one should not overstress the contrasts. The French working-class suburbs were as characterised by tower blocks as the British; Americans of all classes dwelt in apartments. The British philanthropists, having dabbled with tenement housing, also came down in favour of single-family dwellings, seeking to support and improve on the provision of terraced housing. Much later it was the semi-detached house, two up, two down, which became the symbol of the working-class/lower-middle-class family's existence, not the flat. But despite this preference, in Britain the management system pioneered by Octavia Hill and her fellow travellers was transferred, lock, stock and barrel, along with many of its ideological undertones, to the public-sector housing of the twentieth century.

If by the 1900s, overcrowding in cities was less severe than it had been earlier, there can be little doubt that it still acted as a barrier to the growth of a cult of domesticity among the working class. The struggle was still to provide the physical and economic conditions in which such a family could flourish.

Conclusion: the Imposition of a Middle-class Ideal upon the Working-class Family

The approach of the middle classes to the 'problem of the working-class family' tells us as much, or more, about the meaning of 'family' and 'household' to that class as it does about the working-class family. We should not allow ourselves to be distracted by the middle-class belief that they could and would create clones of themselves by rebuilding and renovating their houses. While difficult, it is possible to penetrate the lived-experience of the poor family in order to recover it in all its variety – distinctly preferable to recovering the wished-experience of the philanthropists and reformers.

Conclusion

Until recently there have been two dominant approaches to the history of the family. The first of these, the historical-demographic approach, suggests that what is important about the historical family is encapsulated in the structure, composition and size of the co-resident household. It has undoubtedly revealed much that is interesting about the form of household units in the past and has suggested questions to the historian which might otherwise have been ignored. Nevertheless, this approach does confuse the 'family' and the 'household'. It accepts that the co-resident census household is the key unit for historical study, yet we need to reflect that this is the 'family' as defined by the census-maker and not necessarily by the people themselves. An example from London in the 1880s underlines the point. Mr and Mrs Moses of Oxford Street, Stepney, were Jewish tailors visited by Beatrice Potter in the course of her investigations for Charles Booth. Their house, two up, two down, was family home, workshop and lodging house. 'The fat jewess seemed to have but a slight knowledge of her trade & spent much of her time looking at the pot of sibber on the fire & seeing after a troublesome grandchild who crawled on the floor.' This grandchild did not live with the Moses but was very much part of the family because her mother, married to a man who drank too much and earned too little, came in daily to housekeep for her own mother and to share their food. Among the other employees were one, perhaps two, nieces of Mrs Moses, and Mrs Moses' brother. 'A loafing-looking man appeared from time to time and gave a hand to the coats. He was brother to Mrs Moses and father to the two girls. He had no work & apparently lived on his sister – taking the coats to & fro to the buttonhole maker & generally fetching & carrying to the family', sharing their meals but again seemingly living elsewhere. There were several step-children on both sides, presumably not living at home, and one of these, Mr Moses' son, had fallen on hard times and was making financial claims upon them. This was a household which would appear in the census as composed of husband and wife and lodger, but closer examination reveals it as effectively an extended household.[1]

The second approach takes the prescriptive literature about the domestic unit and assumes that the family was an experiential projection of this. Prescriptive and descriptive evidence is often read as if it were one and the same. Yet we know that, even when people read and discuss prescriptions for their behaviour, there is frequently a great chasm between ideas and action. Moreover, as we have shown, both secular and religious theorists and practitioners wanted to use the family for very different purposes than did individuals within families. The attempt to use the domestic unit, the household, as an instrument of social and religious control was at times in direct conflict with the desire of individual members of society for a satisfying, harmonious and relatively comfortable life. The values presented in the literature and in the pulpit (sometimes described by historians, rather misleadingly, as 'norms') were not necessarily accepted as either normal or desirable by the families who were at the receiving end. The theorists offered contemporaries small guidance on how wider family relationships should be ordered. A little attention was given to handling complex relations within the co-resident unit. Thus, *A Godly Forme of Household Government* counselled to twice marrieds 'carefully to remember, that they do not displease their wives, or their husbands, which they now have, by overmuch rehearsing of their first wife or first husband', and noted their great duties towards step-children in the capacity of 'stead father' and 'stead mother'.[2] If State and Church wished to focus on the co-resident household as the important unit, it is far from clear that individuals saw the family as limited by co-residence. Indeed, many other aspects of existence dictated that the wider family should be of immense significance even down to the present day.

For both Church and State the household was the important unit. Penetrate it and social and religious control became possible.

Unfortunately historians have also concentrated almost exclusively upon the household, confusing it with family. The view of the family as isolated household, shrinking in functions, is well expressed in much recent literature.[3] Much excellent work of this kind has been done but, if we are to proceed further to an understanding of the nature of family relationships, this must be complemented by different kinds of study.

Recent work has sensitised scholars to the importance of personal relations within the family and led historians to ask new questions and seek out new evidence. The severe criticism levelled at the 'affective' school of family history, which suggested that changes in the feelings of parents towards their children, and spouses towards one another, could be charted via a history of behaviour, has unfortunately deflected interests away from family relationships. If people always loved their children and children loved their parents, and husbands and wives always loved each other, what then is the point of attempting a history of personal relations? Women's history, which has done much to focus our attention on the family – the chief forum for women's lives – has unfortunately tied itself up with the issue of power relations within the family. In so doing it has accepted the premiss that the prescriptive family was the real family, and has locked itself into a self-fulfilling investigation, thus limiting its potential. While not wishing to deny that power relationships did exist in the family, we must look beyond.

Let us take the example of the Ferrar family of Little Gidding, Huntingdonshire, in the seventeenth century, to demonstrate how vital it is for us to examine the experience of real families. This extended family, in its commitment to lay devotion, was certainly unusual but in other ways it was not perhaps so different, except in scale, from many other gentry households. In 1620 Mary Ferrar, long the wife of Nicholas, a London Merchant Adventurer, and mother of his nine children, was widowed. At about this time her sons were involved in the Virginia Company – an enterprise favoured by James I. It appears that she was only too relieved when her younger son, Nicholas, determined, on the dissolution of the company, to retire to form a lay community at Little Gidding. The household little resembled the 'average' unit of which scholars are so fond. It was very large – probably thirty or more members, not counting servants, at one time. For a large household, there were

Ferrar family tree

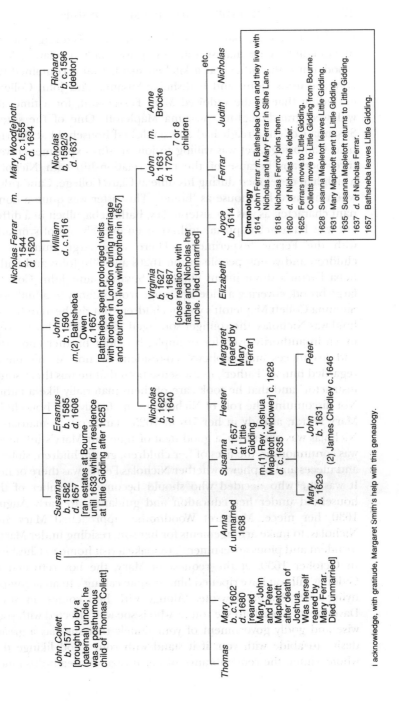

I acknowledge, with gratitude, Margaret Smith's help with this genealogy.

very few servants: a male 'house keeper of Great Gidding' and two maidservants. One maidservant was presumably a relative, Mary Woodenoth; the other was a kitchen maid. It also contained two conjugal units (John and Bathsheba; Susanna and John Collett), excluding that of the widowed Mary Ferrar and, for a time, the widowed granddaughter, Susanna Mapletoft. One of the sisters, Susanna Collett, already had an established household at Bourne, near Cambridge, yet was willing to join in this experimental venture, perhaps because of the close relationship with Nicholas, which had developed during his time at Clare College, Cambridge, when he used her house as 'home'. This sister was quite a dominant character, as was her sister-in-law, Bathsheba, albeit in a different way. Bathsheba appears to have been entirely out of sympathy with the Ferrar 'experiment'. There were large numbers of children and young people in the 1620s and 30s: John and Bathsheba Ferrar's three infant children; Susanna and John Collett's large brood, covering a wide age range from infancy to adulthood; Susanna Collett Mapletoft's young children. But the head of household was Nicholas, the younger son, aged 32 in 1625, who was very much in authority over, for example, his elder brother and sister and his nieces and nephews, co-resident or no. All his nieces regarded him as 'Father', in the sense both that he was their 'soul's instructor' and that he took care of them materially like a father. Not discounting the role of Nicholas in the family and household, Mary Ferrar, already in her 70s in 1625, stands out as matriarch. Nicholas was absent for a good deal of time but Mary's influence was continuous in the lives of her children, grandchildren, siblings and nieces and nephews, whether Nicholas Ferrar was there or not. It was she who decided who should become a member of the household under her education and guidance. In early August 1630, her niece, Margaret Woodnothe, approached Mary, not Nicholas, to make arrangements for her son, residing under Mary's 'prudent and pious government', to make a visit home to Cheshire. In October 1630, at the request of Mary, the boy returned to Gidding 'till you have ripened him to some calling'. In an accompanying letter Margaret wrote, 'Alonge with him comes my sister Davenport ... partly to see you ... who is soe well affected with your wise and godly government of your famely that she has a greate desire to abide with you, if it stand with your good likinge this whole winter, the remembrance of her husband's death dos much afflicte her which she knowes to be a fault but is not able to over maister it' but she 'knowes no better course then to be take herselfe to some godly and well disposed company' 'to be free from that all other distractions'. This gives a whole new meaning to the concept of the unexpected guest! It was Mary who, with Nicholas, shaped the characters of the many grandchildren who shared the home – their parents played a relatively minor role in this regard although they emerge as figures of authority when marriages are discussed and arranged. Initially their grandmother, Mary, led their story-telling in the Little Academy in 1631–2. The records of these sessions demonstrate the wide reading of the Little Gidding women. Each of these granddaughters was trained to manage the household – learning to keep careful accounts and so forth. Three of the granddaughters participated in a rota to relieve their aged grandmother of the burden of housekeeping. They also played a prominent role in running a surgery for the household and locality and in teaching school lessons. At the same time they engaged fully in the religious activities of the family. Several of the grand-daughters also determined to remain single, sometimes against the preference of their parents, who were, however, careful of their children's self-determination. The various conjugal units did, to some extent, share a common life at Little Gidding, acknowledging common authorities, yet there is also a suggestion that they did not necessarily co-reside throughout the period. We know that there were houses on the estate belonging to, and presumably occupied by, individual members. Perhaps the individual nuclear families did have some quasi-privacy within the larger unit. It was also a very fluid 'community' with individuals and couples joining and leaving it frequently. The Ferrar papers also provide us with a rare insight into family decision making. In May 1630 it appears that Nicholas Collett, son of Susanna and John, was requesting to end his appren-ticeship. Nicholas Ferrar was asked for a decision by his cousin. He gave his opinion but seems again to have been approached, per-haps because 'Nick' Collett would not take no for an answer. This time Mary Ferrar, her children, Susanna Collett and John Ferrar (Susanna was Nicholas's mother, John his uncle), and Susanna's daughters and Nicholas's older sisters – Mary Ferrar (Collett), Anna, Hester and Margaret – sat down and deliberated the matter before taking a vote. 'There desire is that God would send opportu-nity and give him a willing mynde to serve out the reste of his tyme in Apprenticeship toward which they will always afforde there prayers in confidence of good success.' More interesting still is the fact that Nicholas thought it necessary, when delivering his final judgement on the matter to his cousin, to say 'I am much more confirmed in my former opinion by the unanimous and free votes of every one whose hands you see before. I assure you I have delivered here judgement with more vehemency & playneness then ever you hearde mee to do which I write that you may not thinke that they have received resoluteness from my authority but have rather added confirmation to my judgements.' Consensual decision making was clearly a reality in some seventeenth-century families.[4]

To the still prevalent arguments of economic and demographic determinism has been added the idea that the prescriptions of secular and religious leaders were followed. Clearly all these influences were important in shaping the family in the past but no one such influence acted alone. It is only by studying the lived-experience of families that scholars will be able to identify what influences were at work therein. Students of the family, from whatever standpoint they have initially approached the subject, have been forced to discuss the relationship of the general to the particular. When real families have been studied, the evidence has, more often than not, modified the generalisations. We should not be led, in our valid desire to generalise about the past and to chart change, to regard such modifications as an irrelevance.

In the early modern period an individual lived family life flexibly. He or she was born into a family and was reared in that family, with or without significant interruptions of apprenticeship, schooling or service, until adulthood, which could be defined by marriage or by age. Ceasing to co-reside with the biological family of origin did not spell an end to belonging to that family; membership of the wider family (including parents and siblings) continued and overlapped with the new family founded on marriage. So it was not only families that had cycles in terms of size, composition and structure. It was also individuals. These individuals carried membership of several families around with them, and with it a number of different family relations – grandmother, mother, daughter, sister, niece or grandfather, father, son, brother, uncle, and various step-relationships. They found their individual identity within these differing relations. No one of these relationships was constant in its import. If you resided with your father and

mother the relationship with them was presumably of more immediate importance than a relationship with an aunt one never saw,
but this situation was fluid. A once important relationship could
fade into insignificance and a previously slight one suddenly
develop – if, for example, one visited a distant relative for a period
or if one became an heir presumptive. It goes without saying, but it
is often not recognised, that personalities had great importance in
family relationships and may have been as significant in formulat-
ing identity as economic or other factors.

The family, then, provided a kind of prism through which individuals were taught to view the world and their own roles within it.
The family did not simply import ideas and behaviours from the
world outside it, or adapt its members to what already existed; it
acted upon ideas and behaviours and in some cases transformed
them; while to some extent bound by ideology, convention, economy and the socio-political hierarchy, it could, on occasion,
encourage a flouting of such restrictions through its commitment
to the well-being of its members. Historians must identify a typology of family forms, and the experiences which united or divided
them, but they must also appreciate the significance for society of
the apparently infinite variety of familial experiences on the one
hand, and the natural bonds which underpinned personal relationships on the other.

This book is an attempt to explore the reality of the wider family
and the narrow co-resident family in the early modern period in
these three societies. In so doing, I have shown how individuals
within the family struggled to achieve a tolerable existence within
the bounds set by their culture – convention, economic and social
reality, religion and law – and by their own and their relatives' personalities, abilities and beliefs. In France, England and colonial
America most families struggled for this in households, albeit not
simple nuclear ones, that stood in sharp contrast to, for example,
native American forms of social organisation.[5] To a limited extent
I have carried this investigation into the modern period. I have
attempted to identify the implications of this study for research
into the nineteenth and early twentieth-century families of the
middling sort, laying out an alternative agenda. In the final
chapter I have considered the ways in which contemporaries
sought to tackle the problems caused by the breakdown of the
early modern household economy. With proletarianisation, a

huge number of people, previously largely contained within households with which they had little or no biological connection, or distributed throughout the countryside in cottage dwellings, were, to the perturbation of the upper and middle classes, let loose upon the cities. To the consternation of the prosperous, the poor did not appear to use the family to communicate 'proper' values and behaviours to the young. The interest displayed in the 'family' life of the working classes by social investigators, reformers and philanthropists, in theory permits us to look at the 'real' family in a much more immediate way than is possible when we look at families in the sixteenth and seventeenth centuries. In fact, however, as we are often reminded, the nature of the sources themselves often obscures the view. I have sought to demonstrate how we can penetrate this barrier and visit the real working-class family.[6] But such a study also draws out what it was about the family which members of the concerned middle classes thought was so crucial.

We cannot study the family in time and space without knowledge of socio-economic and religious conditions, but the family was never, any more than its individual members, a simple reflection of external factors. We ignore, at our peril, the tension which existed between the biological and emotional 'family' and the family which State, Church and economy 'required'. Associalisation was never a simple process. The opportunity is there to explore the lived-experience of families, notwithstanding the obstacles placed in our way by the nature of our sources. When we engage in such an exploration we are able to show how the interaction between family life and factors external to it helped individuals define themselves on the most personal of levels. If some would have wished the family to resemble a bee-hive, producing almost identical bees working in perfect and instinctive harmony to further the interests of the Queen Bee, in reality it was an institution that ensured invaluable variety. It was, above all, an adaptable institution which could and did and does take on a plethora of different shapes in order to further the interests of its members. It was an agent – an active and not a passive force. While it imported information, values and behaviours current in society, it also served as a filter for these imports. It transformed them in the light of family experience and interest. It communicated mutually acceptable ways of living, thinking and believing to its members through both its structure and its personal relationships. Its strength lay as much in the bonds of kinship and physical closeness as in those of economic dependence. Try as they might, external agencies found such a family difficult to control.

Notes

Notes to the Introduction

1. For an illuminating study of families in civil war see Christopher
   Durston, *The Family in the English Revolution* (Oxford, 1989).
2. I wish to thank both Sally Gosling and Margaret Smith for their
   contribution to my understanding of these issues.

Notes to Chapter 1: The World that Slips through our Fingers

1. T. H. Hollingsworth, *Historical Demography* (1969) p. 37.
2. J. Hajnal, 'European Marriage Patterns in Perspective', in D. V. Glass
   and D. E. C. Eversley (eds), *Population in History: Essays in Historical
   Demography* (London 1965) p. 104
3. T. P. R. Laslett and R. Wall (eds), *Household and Family in Past Times*
   (Cambridge, 1972).
4. Ibid., p. 22.
5. Ibid., p. 26.
6. For a more careful consideration of such solitary households, see
   Yves Blayo, 'Size and Structure of Households in a Northern French
   Village between 1836 and 1861', in ibid., pp. 256–8. On Clifford and
   Jefferies, see below, pp. 85, 177–9.
7. David Hey (ed.), *Richard Gough: The History of Myddle*
   (Harmondsworth, 1981).
8. Judith Ford, 'Wills and Will-making ... in Bedford, 1500–1540',
   unpublished Open University PhD, 1992.
9. Peter Laslett, *The World We Have Lost Further Explored* (London,
   1983) p. 91.

10. H. E. Hallam posited a mean of 4.5 or 5.0 for South Lincolnshire in the later thirteenth century and, more controversially, J. C. Russell suggested a mean size of household of 3.0.

11. 4.75 MHS (Mean Household Size) as opposed to around 3.0 MHS.

12. Philip Greven, 'The Average Size of Families and Households in the Province of Massachusetts in 1764 and the United States in 1790: An Overview', in Laslett, *Household and Family*, p. 551.

13. Philip J. Greven, *Four Generations: Population, Land and Family in Colonial Andover, Massachusetts* (Ithaca, 1970); Barry Levy, *Quakers and the American Family: British Settlement in the Delaware Valley* (New York, 1988); David Blake Smith, *Inside the Great House: Planter Family Life in Eighteenth Century Chesapeake Society* (Ithaca, 1980); James M. Gullman, 'Determinants of Age at Marriage in Colonial Perquimans County, North Carolina', *William and Mary Quarterly*, XXXIX (1982) pp. 176–91.

14. Annik Pardailhé-Galabrun, *The Birth of Intimacy: Privacy and Domestic Life in Early Modern Paris* (Oxford, 1991) pp. 37–40.

15. Laslett, *The World We Have Lost*, p. 95.

16. Tamara Hareven, 'The Family Life Cycle in Historical Perspective: A Proposal for a Developmental Approach', in J. Cuisenier and M. Segalen (eds), *Le Cycle de la vie familiale dans les sociétés européennes* (The Hague, 1977) pp. 339–52.

17. M. Segalen, 'The Family Cycle and Household Structure: Five Generations in a French Village', in Robert Wheaton and Tamara Hareven (eds), *Family and Sexuality in French History* (Philadelphia, 1980).

18. A. Collomp, 'Famille nucléaire et famille élargie en Provence au XVIIIe siècle', *Annales, ECS* (July–October 1972).

19. Philip Greven, 'The Average Size of Families and Households', in Laslett, *Household and Family*, pp. 558–9; 551–3.

20. Greven, in ibid., pp. 555–6.

21. E. T. Pryor Jr. 'Rhode Island Family Structure: 1875 and 1960', in Laslett, *Household and Family*, pp. 571–89. Joan Cashin, *A Family Venture. Men and Women of the Southern Frontier* (Oxford, 1991) p. 11, also takes issue with the assumption that southern planter households were nuclear by the early nineteenth century.

22. S. Ruggles, *Prolonged Connections: The Rise of the Extended Family in Nineteenth-Century England and America* (Wisconsin, 1987), *passim*.

23. E.g., J. C. Peyronnet, 'Famille élargie ou famille nucléaire? En Limousin au début du XIXe siècle', *Revue d'histoire moderne et contemporaine*, October–December 1975, pp. 568–82. For the disappearance of the extended family household in Paris see Pardailhé-Galabrun, *The Birth of Intimacy*, pp. 33–4.

24. Louis Merle, *La Métairie et l'évolution agraire de la Gâtine poitevine, de la fin du Moyen Age à la Révolution* (Paris, 1958).

25. Jean-Louis Flandrin, *Families in Former Times: Kinship, Household and Sexuality* (CUP, English Translation, 1979).

26. Jean-Noël Biraben, *Annales de démographie historique* (1970) pp. 441–62; 'A Southern French Village: The Inhabitants of Montplaisant in 1644', in Laslett, *Household and Family*, pp. 237–54.
27. See pp. 97–111.
28. See pp. 187–91.
29. Flandrin, *Families in Former Times*, p. 91.
30. Laslett, *The World We Have Lost*, p. 14.
31. See the economic motivation for the adoption of sixteen-year-old Edward Austen by a kinsman in 1783, Park Honan, *Jane Austen, Her Life* (New York, 1987) p. 25.
32. R. Wall, 'Work, Welfare and the Family: An Illustration of the Adaptive Family Economy', in L. Bonfield *et al.* (eds.), *The World We Have Gained: Histories of Population and Social Structure* (Oxford, 1986) pp. 261–94.
33. See Rosemary O'Day, *Education and Society in Britain, 1500–1800* (London, 1983).
34. Michael Anderson, 'What is New about the Modern Family?', in M. Drake (ed), *Time, Family and Community* (Oxford, 1994).
35. See Lorena S. Walsh, ' "Till Death Us Do Part": Marriage and Family in Seventeenth Century Maryland', and Darrett B. and Anita H. Rutman, ' "Now-Wives and Sons-in-Law": Parental Death in a Seventeenth-Century Virginia County', in Thad W. Tate and David L. Ammerman (eds), *The Chesapeake in the Seventeenth Century: Essays in Anglo-American Society* (Chapel Hill, 1979).
36. See pp. 259–60.
37. Martine Segalen, 'The Family Cycle', p. 254.
38. See pp. 36–7; 267–8.
39. Seymour V. Connor, 'A Statistical Review of the Settlement of the Peter's Colony, 1841–1848', *Southwestern Historical Quarterly*, **57** (1953–4) pp. 38–64.

Notes to Chapter 2: The Prescriptive Family, c.1450–1700

1. See Ferdinand Mount, *The Subversive Family: An Alternative History of Love and Marriage* (London, 1983 paperback edition) pp. 1–7.
2. The debate in 1993 about the social implications of the 'death of the family' has further revealed profound misconceptions.
3. Sarah Hanley, 'Engendering the State: Family Formation and State Building in Early Modern France', *French Historical Studies*, **16** (1989) pp. 8–15; see below for these regulations set in a different context.
4. Richard Baxter, *Gildas Salvianus or The Reformed Pastor* (London, 1656). These extracts, interestingly, come from William Brown (ed.), *The Reformed Pastor* (Glasgow, 1829) pp. 158–160.
5. G. E. Corrie (ed.), *Sermons of Hugh Latimer*, Sermon XXV (Cambridge, 1844) p. 470.

6. See also Sarah Hanley, 'Engendering the State', p. 21

7 David Herlihy, *Medieval Households* (Harvard, 1985) pp. 8–10

8. Ibid., pp. 124–5

9. Ibid., pp. 127–30.

10. C. H. and K. George, *The Protestant Mind of the English Reformation, 1570–1640* (Princeton, 1961) p. 266.

11. K. V. Thomas, 'Women and the Civil War Sects', *Past and Present*, **13** (1958) p. 42; M. Todd, 'Humanists, Puritans and the Spiritualized Household', *Church History* (1980) **49**, pp. 19–34; C. R. Thompson (ed.), *The Colloquies of Erasmus* (Chicago, 1965).

12 C. R. Thompson (ed.), *The Colloquies of Erasmus*, pp. 88–98; 115–27.

13. L. Roper, 'Luther: Sex, Marriage and Motherhood', *History Today*, December 1983, pp. 33–8.

14. John Cotton, *The Covenant of God's Free Grace* (London, 1645); I. M. Calder (ed.), *Letters of John Davenport, Puritan Divine* (New Haven, 1937) pp. 262–6; E. S. Morgan, *The Puritan Family* (New York, 1966) pp. 135–6.

15. S. Coontz, *The Social Origins of Private Life* (London, 1988), p. 85.

16. K. M. Davies, 'Continuity and Change in Literary Advice on Marriage', in R. B. Outhwaite (ed.), *Marriage and Society: Studies in the Social History of Marriage* (London, 1981) pp. 66–7, sees the conduct books as expressing a bourgeois ideal.

17. William Gouge, *Of Domesticall Duties* (1622) Epistle, sig. 2v.

18. Epistle to the Ephesians 6: 5–9.

19. Corrie (ed.), *Sermons of Hugh Latimer*, Sermon XXI, Fifth Sermon on the Lord's Prayer, p. 392.

20. Ibid., p. 393.

21. Ibid., pp. 501, 503.

22. Ibid., p. 536.

23. *endowed*.

24. William Perkins, *Workes* (1613), vol. III pp. 693–4.

25. John Dod and Robert Cleaver, *A Godlie Forme of Householde Government* (London, 1612) p. 30 being a new edition of R. Cleaver, *A Godlie Forme of Household Government* (London, 1598).

26. C. B. Paris, *Marriage in Seventeenth-Century Catholicism* (Paris, 1975) pp. 71–80.

27. J. B. Bossuet, *Catéchisme du diocèse de Meaux* (Paris, 1687) pp. 183–5; cited in R. Briggs, *Communities of Belief* (Oxford, 1989).

28. R. Briggs, *Communities*, pp. 235–76, especially pp. 240–3; C. Maillard, *Le Bon mariage* (Douai, 1643) p. 206, cited by Briggs, *Communities*, p. 242.

29. R. Briggs, *Communities*, p. 253; A. Bourdoise, *L'Idée d'un bon ecclésiastique* (Paris, 1667) pp. 12–14.

30. J.-L. Flandrin, *Families in Former Times: Kinship, Household and Sexuality* (Cambridge, 1979) pp. 123, 126–9; Jean Benedicti, *La Somme des pechez* (Paris, 1601 edition, first published 1584) Bk II, no. 28.

31. Flandrin, *Families in Former Times*, pp. 130–1; R. O'Day, 'Hugh Latimer, Prophet of the Kingdom', *Historical Research*, **65** (1992) pp. 269–76.

32. F. Pollock and F. W. Maitland, *The History of English Law before the Time of Edward I*, 2nd edition (Cambridge, 1968) II, pp. 309, 313.

33. Alan Macfarlane, *The Origins of English Individualism: The Family, Property and Social Transition* (Oxford, 1978) pp. 80–101.

34. Margaret J. M. Ezell, *The Patriarch's Wife: Literary Evidence and the History of the Family* (Chapel Hill and London, 1987) pp. 36–61; Robert Filmer, 'In Praise of the Vertuous Wife', c. 1643; many of the marriage conduct books echo this view – see, for example, William Whately, *A Bride-bush; or, a Direction for Married Persons*, 1623 edition, pp. 17–18, 24, and M. Griffith, *Bethel: or, A Forme for Families* (London, 1633), pp. 320, 326.

35. J. Bossy, 'The Counter-reformation and the People of Catholic Europe', *Past and Present* (1970) **40**, pp. 51–70; J. Bossy, *Christianity in the West, 1400–1700* (Oxford, 1985) pp. 19–26, 122–5; R. Briggs, *Communities of Belief* (Oxford, 1989) pp. 238, 245–8, 274–6; R. O'Day, *The English Clergy: The Emergence and Consolidation of a Profession* (Leicester, 1979).

36. E. S. Morgan, *The Puritan Family* (New York, 1966) p. 65; John Eliot, *The Harmony of the Gospels* (Boston, Massachusetts, 1678) p. 29; Deodat Lawson, *The Duty and Property of a Religious Householder* (Boston, 1693) p. 51; Thomas Cobbett, *A Fruitfull and Usefull Discourse Touching the Honour due from Children to Parents and the Duty of Parents Towards their Children* (London, 1656) p. 94; S. Coontz, *The Social Origins of Private Life* (London, 1988) pp. 76–7.

37. Massachusetts Records, i, 397.

38. E. S. Morgan, *The Puritan Family*, pp. 145–6.

39. Coontz, *The Social Origins of Private Life*, pp. 78–80.

40. R. Pillorget, *La Tige et le rameau: Familles anglaises et francaises XVI e– XVII e siècle* (Paris, 1991) pp. 22–7; Flandrin, *Families in Former Times*, pp. 24–5; R. Houlbrooke, *The English Family, 1450–1700* (London, 1984) pp. 39–40.

41. Houlbrooke, *The English Family*, pp. 68–73; Flandrin, *Families in Former Times*, pp. 131–4; Pillorget, *La Tige*, pp. 32–6; M. Ingram, *Church Courts, Sex and Marriage in England, 1570–1640* (Cambridge, 1987) pp. 133–4, 192–3, 213–17; M. Ingram, 'Spousals Litigation in the English Ecclesiastical Courts, c. 1350–c. 1640', in R. B. Outhwaite (ed.), *Marriage and Society* (London, 1981) pp. 37–42, 45, 48, 55–7; D. Englander, 'Stille Huppah (Quiet Marriage) among Jewish Immigrants in Britain', in *The Jewish Journal of Sociology*, XXXIV (1992) pp. 85–109.

42. See H. W. Saunders (ed.), *The Official Papers of Sir Nathaniel Bacon . . . JP 1580–1620* (Camden Third Series, XXVI, 1915) pp. 37–8.

43. William Whateley, *A Bride-bush*, 1623 edition, p. 175; F. J. Furnivall (ed.), *Philip Stubbes' Anatomy of the Abuses in England in Shakespeare's Youth* (New Shakespeare Society, 6th Series, 1877) 4, p. 97; Ingram, *Church Courts, Sex and Marriage*, p. 131; for the actual coincidence of marriage and independent household formation, see below pp. 131–4. See also Saunders (ed.), *Official Papers of Sir Nathaniel Bacon*, pp. 37–8, for a good example of Justices throwing a 'marrying vagabond' into gaol.

Notes to Chapter 3: The Prescriptive Family – 1. The Wider Family

1. An indication of what material exists for France in the early period is provided in Roger Chartier (ed.), *A History of Private Life*, vol. III (Cambridge, Mass., 1989); see M. Chrisman, 'Family and Religion in Two Noble Families: French Catholic and English Puritan', *Journal of Family History*, 8 (1983) pp. 190–210, for an interesting case study using the papers of the Chantal–Rabutin–Sevigne family.

2. J. H. Bettey (ed.), *Calendar of the Correspondence of the Smyth Family of Ashton Court, 1548–1642* (Bristol Record Society, 1982).

3. See M. L. Bush, *The English Aristocracy: A Comparative Synthesis* (Manchester, 1984) pp. 1–5, 35.

4. Sarah Hanley, 'Engendering the State: Family Formation and State Building in Early Modern France', *French Historical Studies*, 16 (1989) pp. 4–27, especially pp. 7–9; Lawrence Stone, *The Family, Sex and Marriage in England 1500–1800* (1976) p. 126.

5. Mack P. Holt, 'Patterns of Clientele and Economic Opportunity at Court During the Wars of Religion; The Household of François, Duke of Anjou', *French Historical Studies*, 13 (1984) p. 315.

6. Lawrence Stone and Jeanne Fautier Stone, *An Open Elite? England 1540–1880* (Oxford, 1984) p. 110; L. Stone, *Family, Sex and Marriage*, p. 85; B. Bailyn, *New England Merchants in the Seventeenth Century* (New York, 1964) pp. 135–7; Edmund S. Morgan, *The Puritan Family* (New York, 1966) p. 161; Lawrence Stone, *The Crisis of the Aristocracy 1558–1641* (paperback edition, Oxford 1967) p. 271.

7. Stone and Stone, *An Open Elite?*, p. 104; Folger Shakespeare Library, Bagot Collection, la 21.

8. Bagot Collection, la 78, 258, 811; Stone, *An Open Elite?*, p. 78.

9. M. Slater, *Family Life in the Seventeenth Century: The Verneys of Claydon House* (London, 1984) p. 26, deliberately rejects contemporary meanings of the term family.

10. Bagot Collection, la 595, Lettice Bagot to Walter Bagot, 2 February c. 1602; la 596, Lettice Kinnersley to Walter Bagot, 21 March 1605/6; la 120, Walter Bagot to Anthony Kinnersley, 23 March 1605/6; la 568, Anthony Kinnersley to Walter Bagot, 23 March 1605/6; la 598, Lettice Kinnersley to Walter Bagot, September 14? 1608.

11. Bagot Collection, la 105, Walter Bagot to Ronald Okeover, 16 March 1598; la 660, Roland Okeover to Walter Bagot, 12 April 1598.

12. Stone and Stone, *An Open Elite?*, p. 119.

13. Bagot Collection, la 127. For an important discussion of kinship, see David Cressy, 'Kinship and Kin Interaction in Early Modern England', *Past and Present*, 113 (1986) pp. 38–69.

14. Bagot Collection, la 437, Walter Edge to Walter Bagot as 'his patron', c. 1612.

15. Slater, *Family Life in the Seventeenth Century*, p. 59.

16. Sharon Kettering, 'Friendship and Clientege in Early Modern France', *French History*, 6 (1992), p. 146.

17. Sharon Kettering, 'The Patronage Power of Early Modern French Noblewomen', *Historical Journal*, **32**, (1989) pp. 817–41.

18. Bagot Collection, la 856, Sir Thomas Skrymsher to Walter Bagot, 1605.

19. This practice continued in the nineteenth century. See Sheila Hardy, *The Diary of a Suffolk Farmer's Wife, 1854–69* (London, 1992) p. 17.

20. BL, Egerton MS 2644, f. 220.

21. Bagot Collection, la 21, Sir Edward Aston to Richard Bagot, 2 July 1590.

22. Anon, *A Strange and Wonderful Relation of the Burying Alive of Joan Bridges of Rochester in the County of Kent* (London, 1646).

23. Micheline Baulant, 'The Scattered Family: Another Aspect of Seventeenth-Century Demography', in R. Forster and O. Ranum (eds), *Family and Society, Selections from the Annales, ESC* (Baltimore, 1976) p. 114.

24. Lorena S. Walsh, ' "Till Death Us Do Part": Marriage and Family in Seventeenth-Century Maryland', in Thad W. Tate and David L. Ammerman (eds), *The Chesapeake in the Seventeenth Century: Essays on Anglo-American Society* (Chapel Hill, 1979), p. 135.

25. Alan Macfarlane (ed.), *The Diary of Ralph Josselin* (London, 1976) 19.10.1654.

26. Slater, *Family Life in the Seventeenth Century*, pp. 14–24.

27. *uncles.*

28. probably -in-law.

29. Letter of Anne Clifton to Sir Henry Clifford, 6 March 1518, printed in A. G. Dickens (ed.), 'The Clifford Letters', *Surtees Society*, **172**, (1957).

30. Julia Hardwicke, 'Widowhood and Patriarchy in Seventeenth-Century France', *Journal of Social History*, **26** (1992) pp. 133–48; see also Baulant, 'The Scattered Family', pp. 104–16.

31. BL, Additional MS 4454, Katharine Austen's Miscellanies, ff. 65, 69.

32. B. J. Todd, 'The Remarrying Widow: a Stereotype Reconsidered', in M. Prior (ed.), *Women in English Society, 1500–1800* (London, 1985) p. 73.

33. Wendy Gibson, *Women in Seventeenth-Century France* (London, 1989) p. 95.

34. Robert Wheaton, 'Affinity and Descent in Seventeenth-Century Bordeaux', in R. Wheaton and T. Hareven (eds), *Family and Sexuality in French History* (Philadelphia, 1980) pp. 117–21, 127–9.

35. Cited in B. J. Todd, 'The Remarrying Widow', p. 77; will of Thomas Austen, PROB 11/285, f. 338, 15 December 1658; BL Add MS 4454, ff. 79v, 110v, 50; will of Katharine Austen, PROB 11/375, f. 1.

36. See pp. 81–2.

37. D. J. H. Clifford, *The Diaries of Lady Anne Clifford* (Stroud, 1990) *passim*, see especially, pp. 240, 243, 246 for weekly letters, and pp. 119, 127, 133–4, 138, 147, 151, 173–4, 179 for family visits.

38. *Autobiography of Mary Rich, Countess of Warwick*, p. 31.

39. BL, Egerton 2645, f. 54.

40. Bagot Collection, la 607, Lettice Kinnersley to Walter Bagot, 10 March c. 1620.

41. BL, Egerton 2644, ff. 209, 215–19, 220.
42. Mohammed El Kordi, *Bayeux au XVIIe et XVIIIe siècles* (Paris, 1970) p. 125; Jean-Marie Gouesse, 'Parente, famille et mariage en Normandie aux XVIIe et XVIIIe siècles,' *Annales: Economies, Sociétés, Civilisations*, **27** (1972) p. 1145.
43. Ferrar Papers, Magdalen College, Cambridge, Richard Ferrar to Mary Ferrar, 6 December 1627.
44. Wheaton, 'Affinity and Descent in Bordeaux', p. 116; Mohammed El Kordi, *Bayeux au XVIIe et XVIIIe siècles*, p. 125.
45. Joel Hurstfield, *The Queen's Wards, Wardship and Marriage under Elizabeth 1* (London, 1973, 2nd edition) pp. 147–8, 152; Slater, *Family Life in the Seventeenth Century*, p. 13; T. H. Hollingsworth, 'The Demography of the British Peerage', Supplement to *Population Studies*, **18** (1964) p. 20; Lawrence Stone, *The Family, Sex and Marriage in England, 1500–1800* (London, 1977) p. 183.
46. Stone, *Family, Sex and Marriage*, pp. 316–17.
47. Margaret Ezell, *The Patriarch's Wife: Literary Evidence and the History of the Family* (Chapel Hill and London, 1987).
48. BL, Egerton MS 2645, f. 52.
49. BL, Egerton MS 2645, f. 84.
50. BL, Egerton MS 2645, f. 92.
51. BL, Egerton MS 2645, f. 168.
52. BL, Egerton MS 2644, ff. 209, 215–19, 220.
53. G. A. Lowndes, 'The History of the Barrington Family', in *Transactions of the Essex Archaeological Society*, **1**, New Series (1878) pp. 25 ff.
54. BL, Egerton MS 2644, f. 234, f. 275. Whalley paid his sister £40 a year for the upkeep of his daughter.
55. *Autobiography of Mary Rich, Countess of Warwick*, pp. 34–6.
56. Richard Griffin, Lord Braybrooke (ed.), *The Private Correspondence of Jane Lady Cornwallis, 1613–44 ...* (London, 1842) pp. 1–22.
57. Private Correspondence of Jane Lady Cornwallis, Letters CXXXII, CXXXIV, CXXXIX, CXLII–IV.
58. Bagot Collection, la 850, Jane Lady Skipworth to Walter Bagot, 20 September 1610.
59. Bagot Collection, la 771, Richard Rugeley to Walter Bagot, 31 March 1621. Ferrar Papers, Susanna Collett to Thomas Collett, January 1627, once again shows a mother deeply involved in marriage plans for her children, this time the eldest son.
60. Vivien Brodsky Elliott, 'Single Women in the London Marriage Market: Age, Status and Mobility, 1598–1619', in R. B. Outhwaite (ed.), *Marriage and Society: Studies in the Social History of Marriage* (London, 1981) pp. 91, 95.
61. I am grateful to my student Sally Gosling for reinforcing this point.
62. J. M. Mowman (ed.), *Letters of Lady Rachel Russell ...* (1820) pp. 99–100.
63. See Chapter 4 for the dependent position of kin imported into households.
64. *Private Correspondence of Jane Lady Cornwallis*, Letters CXXXII, CXXXIV, CXXXIX, CXLII–IV.

65. *Private Correspondence of Jane Lady Cornwallis*, Letters CXXXII, CXXXIX.

66. See p. 82.

67. Bagot Collection, la. 350 Lady Eleanor Cave to Walter Bagot, 22 September 1606.

68. Bagot Collection, la. 351 Lady Eleanor Cave to Walter Bagot, 1 February 1607/8.

69. See p. 82 for male involvement.

70. *Private Correspondence of Jane Lady Cornwallis*, Letter CXXXII.

71. Bagot Collection, la 21, Edward Aston to Richard Bagot, 2 July 1590.

72. BL, Egerton, MS 2644, f. 297–8.

73. BL, Egerton, MS 2646, 25 February 1633.

74. D. J. H. Clifford, *The Diaries of Lady Anne Clifford*, p. 162.

75. Ibid., pp. 148, 152.

76. Ibid., p. 152.

77. J. O. Halliwell (ed.), *The Autobiography and Correspondence of Sir Simonds D'Ewes, Bart* (London, 1845) vol. I, pp. 2–4, 25–33, 37–38.

78. Lady A. E. Newdigate-Newdegate, *Gossip from a Muniment Room* (London, 1898; 2nd edition) p. 19.

79. Alan Macfarlane, *The Family Life of Ralph Josselin: A Seventeenth-Century Clergyman: An Essay in Historical Anthropology* (Cambridge, 1970) p. 127.

80. Will of Jemimah Bourne, 3 September 1679. L.J.R.O.

81. John Addy, *Death, Money and the Vultures: Inheritance and Avarice 1660–1750* (London, 1992) pp. 9–10.

82. Macfarlane, *Family Life*, pp. 127–8.

83. D. J. H. Clifford, *The Diaries of Lady Anne Clifford* (Stroud, 1990) p. 123.

84. Slater, *Family Life in the Seventeenth Century*, pp. 14, 19.

85. e.g., Bagot Collection, la 32, Walter Aston, 2nd Baron Aston of Forfar, to Sir Edward Bagot, bart., and Mary Bagot from Newmarket, 20 January 1641, thanking them for caring for his little ones.

86. See R. O'Day, *Education and Society in Britain, 1500–1800* (London, 1982) pp. 88–99, especially p. 94. See also Vivienne Larminie (ed.), *The Undergraduat Account book of John and Richard Newdigate 1618–1621* (Camden Miscellany, XXX, 1990) *passim.*; also G. Davies (ed.), *The Autobiography of Thomas Raymond* (Camden, XXVIII, 1917) for Raymond's experiences in the 1620s.

87. R. Parkinson (ed.), *The Life of Adam Martindale*, Chetham Society, 4 (Manchester, 1845) p. 210.

88. Bagot Collection, la 95.

89. Bagot Collection, la 96.

90. Bagot Collection, la 65, Lewis Bagot to Walter Bagot, c. 1610.

91. Bagot Collection, la 45.

92. Macfarlane, *Family Life*, pp. 133–4.

93. Helena Whitbread (ed.), *The Diaries of Anne Lister, 1791–1840* (1988) pp. ix, 6–7.

94. Lady A. E. Newdigate-Newdegate, *Gossip from a Muniment Room* (London, 1898, 2nd edition) pp. 8–9, 18–20.

95. Bagot Collection, la 230.

96. Bagot Collection, la 222, 223.

97. Bagot Collection, la 251, 267, 269.

98. Bagot Collection, la 231.

99. Bagot Collection, la 232.

100. Bagot Collection, la 407, la 777.

101. A. Clifford (ed.), *Tixall Letters* (1815), pp. 124–25.

102. *Private Correspondence of Jane Lady Cornwallis*, pp. xxv, 264, 275–7.

103. e.g., BL, Additional MS 69941, f. 157, Elizabeth 'Betty' Coke to Thomas Coke, 26 August 1705.

104. *Diary of Ralph Josselin*, 25.12.1673.

105. J. D. Marshall (ed.), *The Autobiography of William Stout of Lancaster, 1665–1752* (Chetham Society, Manchester, 1967).

106. For example, Bagot Collection, la 775, la 777.

107. Bagot Collection, la 348, Cecil Cave to Walter Bagot, 29 June 1598; la 349, Cecil Cave to Walter Bagot, 11 September 1599.

108. *Diary of Ralph Josselin*, 20.10.1647.

109. Bagot Collection, la 193, Sir Thomas Beaumont to Walter Bagot, 18 Feb. 1610/11; la 194, Sir Thomas Beaumont to Walter Bagot, c. 1614.

110. Marshall, *Autobiography of William Stout*.

111. Parkinson (ed.), *Life of Adam Martindale*, pp. 24, 39, 109–10, 171–2; see Elizabeth A. R. Brown, 'Authority, the Family and the Dead in Late Medieval France', *French Historical Studies*, 16 (1990) pp. 803–31, especially p. 831, for an interesting discussion of the emergence of the practice of dissecting the corpse so that parts of the deceased could be buried with different members of a family. The practice achieved its greatest popularity during the period 1500 to 1800.

112. BL, Egerton MS 2804, f. 160, 148, 199. I am grateful to Sally Gosling for this reference.

113. Cited in Jean-Louis Flandrin, *Families in Former Times: Kinship, Household and Sexuality* (Cambridge, 1979) p. 45–6.

114. P. Laslett, *Family Life and Illicit Love in Earlier Generations: Essays in Historical Sociology* (Cambridge, 1977) p. 201.

115. P. Laslett, 'Mean Household Size in England since the Sixteenth Century', in P. Laslett and R. Wall (eds.), *Household and Family in Past Time* (Cambridge, 1972) p. 77–8.

116. See Jeremy Boulton, *Neighbourhood and Society* (Cambridge, 1987) p. 129.

117. J. Hardwicke, 'Widowhood and Patriarchy in Seventeenth-Century France', *Journal of Social History*, 26 (1992) p. 145.

118. F. P. Wilson, *The Plague in Shakespeare's London* (1963) pp. 3–4; Mary F. and T. H. Hollingsworth, 'Plague Mortality Rates by Age and Sex', *Population Studies*, XXV (1971) pp. 131–46.

119. Stone and Stone, *An Open Elite?*, p. 95.

120. R. A. Houlbrooke, *The English Family, 1450–1700* (London, 1984) p. 213.

121. Charles Carlton, *Going to the Wars: The Experience of the British Civil Wars* (London: Routledge, 1992) pp. 204–5.

122. D. V. Glass, 'Two Papers on Gregory King', in D. V. Glass and D. E. C. Eversley (eds), *Population in History* (London, 1965);

Roger Thompson, *Women in Stuart England and America: A Comparative Study* (London, 1974) p. 35.

123. T. H. Hollingsworth, 'A Demographic Study of the British Ducal Families', in Glass and Eversley, *Population in History*, p. 359.

124. Stone, *Family, Sex and Marriage*, pp. 93–4.

125. Hardwicke, 'Widowhood and Patriarchy', p. 145; see also Laslett, *Family Life and Illicit Love*, p. 200.

126. Philip J. Greven Jr, *Four Generations: Population, Land and Family in Colonial Andover, Massachusetts* (Ithaca, New York, 1970); John Demos, *A Little Commonwealth: Family Life in Plymouth Colony* (New York, 1970).

127. Darrett B. and Anita H. Rutman, '"Now-Wives and Sons-in-Law", Parental Death in a Seventeenth-Century Virginia County', in Tate and Ammerman (eds), *The Chesapeake in the Seventeenth Century*, pp. 171.

128. L. A. Bissell, 'From One Generation to Another: Mobility in Seventeenth-Century Windsor, Connecticut', *William and Mary Quarterly*, 3rd Series, **31** (1974) pp. 79–110.

129. Donald M. Frame (ed.), *The Complete Works of Michel de Montaigne* (Stanford, 1958) p. 285.

130. Jacques Lafon, *Les Epoux Bordelais 1450–1550* (Paris, 1972) pp. 255–6; Wheaton, 'Affinity and Descent in Seventeenth-Century Bordeaux', pp. 124–5.

131. Bagot Collection, la 613 Walter Bagot to Jane Lane.

132. L. M. Glanz, 'The Legal Position of English Women under the Early Stuart Kings and the Interregnum, 1603–1660', unpublished PhD thesis, Loyola University, 1973.

133. R. Thompson, *Women in Stuart England and America*, p. 164.

134. Lady A. E. Newdigate-Newdegate, *Gossip from a Muniment Room* (London, 1898, 2nd edition), Genealogy A.

135. Stone and Stone, *An Open Elite?*, pp. 73–4.

136. R. B. Outhwaite, 'Marriage as Business', in N. McKendrick and R. B. Outhwaite (eds), *Business Life and Public Policy* (Cambridge University Press, 1986) pp. 21–37.

137. Amy Louise Erickson, 'Common Law Versus Common Practice: the Use of Marriage Settlements in Early Modern England', *Economic History Review*, 2nd Ser., XLIII (1990) p. 31; R. Thompson, *Women in Stuart England and America*, p. 164.

138. Lloyd Bonfield, *Marriage Settlements 1601–1740: The Adoption of the Strict Settlement* (Cambridge University Press, 1983) pp. 117–118.

139. Stone and Stone, *An Open Elite?*, pp. 73–4.

140. Peter Earle, *The Making of the English Middle Class: Business, Society and Family Life in London, 1660–1730* (1989) pp. 194–8.

141. Erickson, 'Common Law Versus Common Practice', pp. 26–7.

142. Ibid., pp. 28–31.

143. Ibid., pp. 31–6; Lichfield data extracted from the author's survey of clerical wills.

144. Walsh, 'Till Death Us Do Part', pp. 133–5.

145. Demos, *A Little Commonwealth*, p. 86.

146. R. Thompson, *Women in Stuart England and America*, pp. 166, 180.

147. G. Gampel, 'The Planter's Wife Revisited: Equity Law and the Chancery Court in Seventeenth Century Maryland', in B. J. Hanns and J. K. McNamara (eds), *Women and the Structure of Society* (Durham, NC, 1984) pp. 20–35.

148. Rutman and Rutman, 'Now-Wives and Sons-in-Law', pp. 155–6.

149. Wheaton, 'Affinity and Descent', p. 123.

150. Amy Louise Erickson, 'Common Law Versus Common Practice', pp. 23, 37.

151. Statutes of Distribution, 22 & 23 Chas II, c. 10; 1 Jas II, c. 17.

152. Judith Ford, 'Wills and Willmaking', *passim.*

153. Ford, 'Wills and Willmaking', p. 145; see John Addy, *Death, Money and the Vultures*, pp. 9–10 for another good example, this time for 1652, of the operation of the custom of York. Interestingly, under this custom, where a woman was assured of a jointure she was held not to be entitled to a third part of the personalty.

154. Alan Mcfarlane, *The Origins of English Individualism*, p. 83; Amy Louise Erickson, 'Common Law Versus Common Practice: The Use of Marriage Settlements in Early Modern England', *Economic History Review*, 2nd series, XLIII (1990) p. 24.

155. See also Erickson, 'Common Law Versus Common Practice', for this complex situation.

156. Ida Gandy, *Round About the Little Steeple: The Story of a Wiltshire Parson, 1573–1623* (Stroud, 1989) p. 35.

157. Demos, *A Little Commonwealth*, p. 85.

158. R. Thompson, *Women in Stuart England and America*, p. 179.

159. Ibid., p. 177.

160. J. H. Wilson, 'The Illusion of Change: Women and the American Revolution', in A. F. Young (ed.), *The American Revolution* (Illinois, 1976), pp. 385–445; Mary Beth Norton, *Liberty's Daughters: The Revolutionary Experience of American Women, 1750–1800*: (Boston, 1980), preface *et passim*; L. W. Waciega, 'Widowhood and Womanhood in Early America: The Experience of Women in Philadelphia and Chester Counties, 1750–1850', unpublished Temple University PhD thesis, 1986.

161. Wheaton, 'Affinity and Descent', p. 129.

162. See also, Baulant, 'The Scattered Family', pp. 113–14.

163. See above (pp. 102–9).

164. Wheaton, 'Affinity and Descent', pp. 112–13.

165. Ibid., pp. 113–14.

166. Walsh, 'Till Death Us Do Part', p. 135.

167. See Marshall (ed.), *Autobiography of William Stout.*

168. Richard Vann, 'Toward a New Lifestyle: Women in Pre-Industrial Capitalism', in R. Bridenthal and C. Koonz (eds), *Becoming Visible: Women in European History* (Boston, 1977) p. 195.

169. Vivien Brodsky [Elliott], 'Widows in Late Elizabethan London: Remarriage, Economic Opportunity and Family Orientations', in Lloyd Bonfield et al. (eds), *The World We Have Gained, Histories of Population and Social Structure* (Oxford, 1986) pp. 123, 124, 150.

170. See above, p. 76.

171. Brodsky [Elliott], 'Widows in Late Elizabethan London', p. 136; Rutman and Rutman, 'Now-Wives and Sons-in-Law', p. 153.
172. Brodsky [Elliott], 'Widows in Late Elizabethan London', p. 143.
173. See above, pp. 97–111.
174. Gandy, *Round About the Little Steeple*, p. 35.
175. Brodsky [Elliott], 'Widows in Late Elizabethan London', p. 123.
176. Baulant, 'The Scattered Family', p. 113.
177. R. Houlbrooke, *The English Family*, p. 217.
178. R. Houlbrooke, *The English Family*, p. 214.
179. Rétif de la Bretonne, *La Vie de Mon Père*, p. 118.
180. G. Davies (ed.), *The Autobiography of Thomas Raymond* (Camden Society, XXVIII, 1917) pp. 19ff.
181. See G. C. Homans, *English Villagers*, p. 192.
182. Cited in Baulant, 'The Scattered Family', pp. 113–14.
183. L.J.R.O. Will of John Hill, Rector of Elford, W.P. 16 January 1621/2.
184. L.J.R.O. Will of John Fisher, Rector of Donnington, W.P. 11 February 1689/90.
185. L.J.R.O. Will of Matthew Fowler, Rector of Whitchurch, W.P. 3 March 1683/4.
186. L.J.R.O. Will of Nicholas Hallam of Shirland, W.P. 3 August 1626.
187. L.J.R.O. Will of Nicholas Hallam of Shirland, W.P. 3 August 1626.
188. L.J.R.O. Will of Hugh Clark, Vicar of Wolston, W.P. 3 December 1634.
189. L.J.R.O. Will of William Bennett, Rector of Morley, W.P. 27 October 1647.
190. L.J.R.O. Will of Martin Delane, Rector of Ashow, W.P. 18 February 1610/11; Will of William Butterton, Vicar of Nuneaton, W.P. 8 June 1626.
191. L.J.R.O. Will of Roger Asheton of Pentrich, W.P. 8 June 1581.
192. L.J.R.O. Will of Robert Bamford, Vicar of Mugginton, W.P. 19 October 1619.
193. L.J.R.O. Will of Edward Kynnaston, Vicar of Rushall, W.P. 14 February 1598.
194. L.J.R.O. Will of George Dunne, Vicar of Sheriffhales, W.P. 12 March 1621/2.
195. See, for example, L.J.R.O. Will of John James, Rector of Avon Dassett, W.P. 30 April 1618.
196. L.J.R.O. Will of Richard Morrell, Vicar of Cubbington, W.P. 27 March 1628.
197. L.J.R.O. Will of Roger Daker, Vicar of Drayton in Hales, W.P. 12 May 1618; L.J.R.O. Will of Jemimah Bourne, W.P. 1679; Will of Richard Garbett, Rector of Enville, W.P. 23 October 1592.
198. L.J.R.O. Will of William Mather, Vicar of Barrow, W.P. 10 September 1638. God-children were also recipients of like bequests.
199. L.J.R.O. Will of Richard Latimere, Vicar of Polesworth, W.P. 17 November 1624.
200. L.J.R.O. Will of Richard Orgell, Rector of Lullington, W.P. 1646/7.
201. L.J.R.O. Nicholas Hallam of Shirland, W.P. 3 August 1626.

202. L.J.R.O. Will of William Orton, Rector of Sheldon, Warwickshire, W.P. 10 June 1628.

203. L.J.R.O. Will of Thomas Buther, Rector of Arley, W.P. 24 June 1598.

204. L.J.R.O. Will of Edward Bennet, Rector of Kirk Ireton, W.P. 19 July 1603.

205. L.J.R.O. Will of John Alsoppe of Atherstone, W.P. 21 September 1582.

206. L.J.R.O. Will of Robert Evans, Rector of Darley, W.P. 30 November 1639; Evans made a bequest to a married daughter in Virginia and her children, and to a daughter in Lincolnshire.

207. L.J.R.O. Will of Robert Freeman of Ashley, 31 October 1606.

208. L.J.R.O. Will of Robert Bamford, Vicar of Mugginton, W.P. 19 October 1619, gave Barbara Hibbert £15 and a home for life.

209. L.J.R.O. Will of George Gamull, Vicar of Chesterfield, W.P. 10 April 1616.

210. L.J.R.O. Will of John Greaves, Rector of Whitwell, W.P. 23 December 1693.

211. L.J.R.O. Will of Humphrey Whitmore, Vicar of Chebsey, W.P. 1617.

212. See, for example, L.J.R.O. Will of William Anorrey of Lilleshall, labourer, W.P. 28 May 1582; and Will of George Alestrey of Duffield, 'yoman', W.P. 15 October 1585.

213. L.J.R.O. Will of Michael Massey, Rector of Berrington, W.P. 1 December 1618.

214. L.J.R.O. Will of John Greaves, Rector of Whitwell, W.P. 23 December 1693.

215. debts which I do owe!

216. Anne Mitson, 'The Significance of Kinship Networks in the Seventeenth Century: South-West Nottinghamshire' in C. Phythian Adams (ed.), *Societies, Culture and Kinship, 1580–1850* (Leicester, 1993) p. 73. See also, P. Seaver, *Wallington's World, A Puritan Artisan in Seventeenth-Century London* (Stanford, 1985) pp. 72–82.

217. See, for example, David Hey (ed.), *Richard Gough, The History of Myddle* (Harmondsworth, 1981) p. 93. See J. E. Cashin, *A Family Venture, Men and Women of the Southern Frontier* (Oxford, 1991) pp. 16–20, for an excellent discussion of how settlers on the southern frontier in America used genealogy to 'preserve kinship networks'. For other reliance on genealogy, see G. Holles Wood, *Memorials of the Holles Family, 1493–1656* (1937).

218. Rétif de la Bretonne, *Monsieur Nicolas,* 14 vols (Paris, 1883) vol. 1, pp. 122.

219. Wheaton, 'Affinity and Descent', p. 114.

220. Coke MSS, Bundle 44, 19 September 1640. This collection is now in the BL but I was unable to use the new numbering because sorting and binding were incomplete.

221. See D. Levine and K. Wrightson, *The Making of an Industrial Society, Whickham, 1560–1765,* (Oxford, 1991) pp. 329–44 for further consideration of the balance between the co-residential kin relationships and wider family relationships in the lives of villagers.

222. Stephanie Coontz, *The Social Origins of Private Life* (London, 1988) p. 120.

223. Wheaton, 'Affinity and Descent', pp. 115–16.
224. See John Addy, *Death, Money and the Vultures, passim* for examples of family involvement.
225. In cases of intestacy, the widow had an automatic right to become the executor although she could waive this right.
226. Baulant, 'The Scattered Family', pp. 106–9.
225. Baulant, 'The Scattered Family', p. 116.

Notes to Chapter 4: The Descriptive Family – 2: Co-resident Relations

1. Keith Wrightson, *English Society, 1580–1680* (London, 1982) p. 66; Vivien Brodsky [Elliott], 'Widows in Late Elizabethan London: Remarriage, Economic Opportunity and Family Orientations', in Lloyd Bonfield et al. (eds.), *The World We Have Gained, Histories of Population and Social Structure* (Oxford, 1986), p. 124; P. Laslett, 'Parental Deprivation in the Past', in P. Laslett, *Family Life and Illicit Love in Earlier Generations* (Cambridge, 1977), p. 169; Micheline Baulant, 'The Scattered Family: Another Aspect of Seventeenth-Century Demography', in Robert Forster and Orest Ranum (eds), *Family and Society, Selections from the Annales, ESC* (Baltimore and London, 1976), p. 116 *et passim*; Darrett B. and Anita H. Rutman, "Now-Wives and Sons-in-Law", Parental Death in a Seventeenth-century Virginia County', in T. W. Tate and D. L. Ammerman (eds), *The Chesapeake in the Seventeenth Century: Essays on Anglo-American Society* (Chapel Hill, 1979); and Lorena S. Walsh, '"Till Death Us Do Part", Marriage and Family in Seventeenth-century Maryland', in Tate and Ammerman (eds), *The Chesapeake*, p. 151.
2. Roger Wells (ed.), *Victorian Village. The Diaries of the Reverend John Coker Egerton of Burwash 1857–1888* (Stroud, 1992) p. 96.
3. T. H. Brookes, unpublished Memoirs, in the possession of the author.
4. See Walsh, 'Till Death Us Do Part', pp. 126–7.
5. See my forthcoming *Potter, Pycroft and Paul: The Sweet Trinity and Katharine Buildings*.
6. Lady A. E. Newdigate-Newdegate, *Gossip from a Muniment Room* (London, 1898, 2nd edition) p. 5.
7. Bagot Collection, la 197, 3 July 1606.
8. T. H. Hollingsworth, 'The Demography of the British Peerage', *Population Studies*, **18**, supplement (1964), p. 20.
9. F. J. Furnivall (ed.), *Child Marriages, Divorces and Ratifications ... in the Diocese of Chester* (Early English Text Society, 108, 1897).
10. See Jean-Louis Flandrin, *Families in Former Times: Kinship, Household and Sexuality* (Cambridge, 1979) pp. 185–6.
11. 5 Elizabeth I, c. 4, clause 19, Memorandum on the Statute of Artificers; S. Brigden, 'Youth and the English Reformation', *Past and Present*, **95** (1982) p. 46.

12. Claude Delasselle, 'Les Enfants abandonnés à Paris au XVIIIe siècle', *Annales ESC* (1975) p. 189.

13. Baulant, 'The Scattered Family', p. 105.

14. David Hey (ed.), *Richard Gough, The History of Myddle*, (Harmondsworth, 1981) p. 234.

15. Ibid., pp. 184–5.

16. Ibid., p. 182.

17. Flandrin, *Families in Former Times*, p. 13.

18. Pierre de Lancre, *Tableau de l'inconstance des mauvais anges* (1612); cited in Jean-François Soulet, *La Vie quotidienne dans les Pyrénées, sous l'ancien régime du XVIe au XVIIIe siècles* (Paris, 1974) p. 221.

19. Richard Parkinson (ed.), *The Life of Adam Martindale* (Chetham Society, Manchester, 1845) p. 88.

20. Ibid., p. 101.

21. Ibid., p. 119.

22. Hey, *History of Myddle, passim*.

23. See, for example, E. Claverie and P. Lamaison, *L'Impossible marriage, Violente et parente en Gevaudan 17e, 18e et 19e siècles* (Paris, 1982) *passim*.

24. Abel Hugo, *La France Pittoresque* (Paris, 1835) vol. I, p. 299; Flandrin *Families in Former Times*, pp. 112–16.

25. Ibid., vol. II, pp. 29–30.

26. Edward Shorter, *The Making of the Modern Family* (London, 1976) p. 57.

27. Martine Segalen, *Love and Power in the Peasant Family* (Oxford, 1983) p. 5.

28. Hugo, *La France Pittoresque*, vol. I, p. 234.

29. Segalen, *Love and Power*, p. 82.

30. This paragraph summarises the work done by Martine Segalen, *Love and Power*, pp. 78–111; see Ed. du Vieux Meunier Breton, Anna Selle, *Thumette Bigoudène* (Rennes, 1974) p. 114, cited in Segalen, *Love and Power*, p. 107; the general point is borne out by Claverie and Lamaison, *L'Impossible mariage*, pp. 78–9.

31. Parkinson (ed.), *Life of Adam Martindale*, p. 190.

32. Joyce Jeffreys' Account Book, BL. Eg. 3054.

33. See W. W. Skeat (ed.), *A. [J.] Fitzherbert, The Book of Husbandry, 1534* (English Dialect Society, 13, 1882) pp. 93–8.

34. Cited in Nancy F. Cott, 'Eighteen-Century Family and Social Life Revealed in Massachusetts Divorce Records', *Journal of Social History*, **10** (1976) p. 33.

35. Dorothy M. Meads (ed.), *The Diary of Lady Margaret Hoby, 1599–1605* (1930) *passim*; for these specific references, see extracts reprinted in David Englander, Diana Norman, Rosemary O'Day and W. R. Owens (eds), *Culture and Belief in Europe, 1450–1600* (Oxford, 1990) pp. 212–18.

36. Sarah Heller Mendelson, 'Stuart Women's Diaries and Occasional Memoirs', in Mary Prior (ed.), *Women in English Society, 1500–1800* (London, 1985) p. 190; The range of activities practised was close to those listed in, for example, William Whately, *A Bride-Bush* p. 24.

J. E. Cashin, *A Family Venture. Men and Women of the Southern Frontier* (Oxford, 1991) pp. 67–9, shows how settler women in the nineteenth-century South had to relearn hard manual labour common in the seventeenth and eighteenth centuries.

37. Wrightson, *English Society, 1580–1680*, p. 94; M. St Clare Byrne (ed.), *The Lisle Letters: An Abridgement* (Chicago, 1983) p. 17.

38. Diary of Samuel Sewell, vol. II, 24 January 1703/4.

39. Cited in E. S. Morgan, *The Puritan Family* (revised edition, New York, 1966), p. 43.

40. See R. Middleton, *Colonial America, A History 1667–1760* (Oxford, 1992) p. 237.

41. Elizabeth Fox-Genovese, *Within the Plantation Household* (Chapel Hill and London, 1988) pp. 22–4.

42. Bagot Collection, la 578, Francis Kinnersley to Walter Bagot, 4 May 1609; See below, pp. 159–60 [Adam Eyre].

43. I owe this reference to my postgraduate student, Margaret Smith.

44. Park Honan, *Jane Austen, Her Life* (New York, 1987) p. 41.

45. See Egerton MS 2645, 265, for a request that Lady Joan Barrington attend her daughter in childbirth.

46. L. Pollock, *With Faith and Physic, The Life of a Tudor Gentlewoman, Lady Grace Mildmay, 1552–1600* (London, 1993) pp. 97–143.

47. See Wendy Gibson, *Women in Seventeenth-Century France* (London, 1989) p. 87.

48. G. Davies (ed.), *The Autobiography of Thomas Raymond and the Memoirs of the Family of Guise of Elmore, Gloucs* (Camden Society XXVIII, 1917) p. 109.

49. Ibid., p. 111.

50. Anon, *Case or Petition of the Corporation of Pinmakers* (London).

51. Middleton, *Colonial America*, pp. 242–3.

52. Middleton, *Colonial America*, pp. 244–6.

53. Natalie Zemon Davis, 'City Women and Religious Change', in N. Z. Davis (ed.), *Society and Culture in Early Modern France* (Stanford, 1975) p. 94; Merry Weisner, 'Women's Defense of their Public Role', in Mary Beth Rose (ed.), *Women in the Middle Ages and the Renaissance* (Syracuse, 1986) pp. 1–28; Mary Prior, 'Women and the Urban Economy: Oxford 1500–1800', in M. Prior (ed.), *Women in English Society 1500–1800* (London, 1985) pp. 93–117.

54. James B. Collins, 'The Economic Role of Women in Seventeenth-Century France', *French Historical Studies*, **16** (1989), pp. 436–70.

55. William Chester Jordan, *Women and Credit in Pre-industrial and Developing Societies* (Philadelphia, 1993) pp. 23–82.

56. A. Bideau, 'La Mortalité des enfants dans le Chatellenie de Thoissey-en-Dombes', *Démographie Urbaine XVe–XIXe siècles* (Lyons, 1977) pp. 111–41; Fiona Newall, 'Wet Nursing and Child Care in Aldenham, Hertfordshire, 1595–1726', in Valerie Fildes (ed.), *Women as Mothers in Preindustrial England* (London, 1990) pp. 122–38.

57. Davies, *Thomas Raymond ... and the Guise Family*, p. 112.

58. Miranda Chaytor, 'Household and Kinship: Ryton in the Late Sixteenth and Early Seventeenth centuries, *History Workshop Journal*, **10** (1980) p. 25.

59. Segalen, *Love and Power*, p. 107.
60. Hughes Lapaire, *Le Berry vu par un Berrichon* (Paris, 1928) pp. 38–9, cited in Segalen, *Love and Power*, p. 16.
61. The quotation is cited in Segalen, *Love and Power*, p. 17.
62. Ibid., pp. 18–19.
63. See Chapter 2.
64. See pp. 155–8.
65. Gibson, *Women in Seventeenth-Century France*, pp. 50–2.
66. Claverie and Lamaison, *L'Impossible mariage*, pp. 93–110.
67. Pierre Bourdieu, 'Marriage Strategies as Strategies of Social Reproduction' *Annales, ESC 27* (1972) pp. 1105–25, in Robert Forster and Orest Ranum (eds), *Family and Society, Selections from the Annales, ESC* (Baltimore and London, 1976) pp. 117–44.
68. See Chapter 3 above.
69. See Ralph Houlbrooke, *The English Family, 1450–1700* (London, 1984) p. 72. Miranda Chaytor has observed that marriage formed part of family strategy among urban dwellers late in the sixteenth century.
70. See Chapter 3.
71. Bagot Collection, la 613, Jane Lane to Walter Bagot, 7 October 1611/12.
72. Bagot Collection, la 852, Jane Skipworth to Lewis Bagot, 14 April 1610; la 854, Jane Skipworth to Walter Bagot, 19 September 1610. See p. 82.
73. Bagot Collection, la 628, 25 November 1589.
74. Daniel Scott Smith, 'Parental Control and Marriage Patterns: An Analysis of Historical Trends in Higham, Massachusetts', *Journal of Marriage and the Family*, **35** (1973) pp. 423–4; Carl Degler, *At Odds: Women and the Family in America from the Revolution to the Present* (Oxford and New York, 1980) p. 10.
75. See Chapter 3.
76. V. B. Elliott, 'Single Women in the London Marriage Market: Age, Status and Nobility, 1598–1619', in R. B. Outhwaite (ed.), *Marriage and Society: Studies in the Social History of Marriage* (London, 1981) p. 90.
77. Elliott, 'Single Women', p. 89.
78. Bagot Collection, la 598, Lettice Kinnersley to Walter Bagot, 14 September 1608.
79. See Michael Mitterauer and Reinhard Sieder, *The European Family: Patriarchy to Partnership from the Middle Ages to the Present* (Oxford, 1982) pp. 64–6, where the authors appear to argue the contrary.
80. Cott, 'Eighteenth-Century Family and Social Life, pp. 25–7.
81. Alan Macfarlane (ed.), *Diary of Ralph Josselin* (London, 1976), 12.5.1645.
82. Alan Macfarlane, *The Family Life of Ralph Josselin, A Seventeenth-Century Clergyman: An Essay in Historical Anthropology* (Cambridge, 1970), p. 107.
83. I am struck by the number of references, at various social levels and in two of these societies, to the practice of women reading aloud to their menfolk. See, for example, R. Chartier, *A History of Private Life*, vol. III (Cambridge, Mass., 1989) p. 120; Thomas Turner, *The Diary*

of a Georgian Shopkeeper (Oxford, 1979) p. 2; S. Hardy, *The Diary of a Suffolk Farmer's Wife*, 1854–69 (London, 1992) p. 27.

84. Curwin Papers, III, 46; Morgan, *The Puritan Family*, pp. 55–9.

85. GLRO P92/SAV/750; cited in Jeremy Boulton, *Neighbourhood and Society* (Cambridge, 1987) p. 131.

86. R. Latham and W. Matthews (eds), *The Diary of Samuel Pepys* (London, 1970) vol. I, pp. 75, 79, 85, 165.

87. Baulant, 'The Scattered Family', p. 106.

88. Cott, 'Eighteenth-Century Family and Social Life', p. 32.

89. Mary Beth Norton, 'Gender and Defamation in Seventeenth-Century Maryland', *William and Mary Quarterly*, 3rd Series, 44 (1987) p. 23.

90. Ibid., p. 9. See Natalie Zemon Davis, *Fiction in the Archives, Pardon Tales and their Tellers in Sixteenth-Century France* (Oxford, 1987) p. 92, for the suggestion that making meals was frequently the occasion for an 'obedience struggle'.

91. Cited in Cott, 'Eighteenth-Century Family and Social Life, p. 30.

92. Cited in ibid., pp. 32–3.

93. J. A. Sharpe, *Defamation and Sexual Slander in Early Modern England* (Borthwick Institute, University of York, Paper 58, 1980) pp. 1–10, 15–17; Martin Ingram, *Church Courts, Sex and Marriage in England, 1570–1640* (Cambridge, 1987) p. 165.

94. K. V. Thomas, 'The Double-Standard', *Journal of the History of Ideas*, **20** (1959) pp. 195–216.

95. L.J.R.O. B/C/3/7; there are other cases of males performing penance for adultery and incontinence in the same year.

96. L.J.R.O. See, for example B/C/3/7, 25 and 30 January 1599/1600, and all the L. J. R. O. B/C/series.

97. L.J.R.O. B/C/3/7, 7 February 1599/1600.

98. L.J.R.O. B/C/3/7, 14 February 1599/1600.

99. Sarah Hanley, 'Engendering the State: Family Formation and State Building in Early Modern France', *French Historical Studies*, **16** (1989) pp. 16–21.

100. Natalie Zemon Davis, 'City Women and Religious Change', pp. 90–4; Jeffrey R. Watt, 'Divorce in Early Modern Neuchatel, 1547–1806', *Journal of Family History*, **14**, (1989).

101. S. H. Mendelson, 'Stuart Women's Diaries', p. 193.

102. BL, Egerton MS 2644, f. 251.

103. BL, Additional MS 69941, f. 114.

104. Parkinson (ed.), *Life of Adam Martindale*, pp. 17–19.

105. Egerton MS 2545, f. 327; printed in Arthur Searle (ed.), *Barrington Family Letters 1628–1632* (Camden Fourth Series, 28, 1983).

106. BL, Additional MS 69936 f. 128, 9 November 1696, M. Fanshaw to Sir Thomas Coke.

107. skewbald horse.

108. H.J. Morehouse (ed.), *A Dyurnall ... [Adam Eyre]*, Surtees Society, Yorkshire Diaries, LXV (1875, published 1877) pp. 10,12–13,15, 19, 67–8,116, 49, 39, 42, 49, 54, 84.

109. Wendy Gibson, *Women in Seventeenth-Century France*, p. 87; for a recent study of divorce and separation, see Lawrence Stone, *The Road to Divorce, England 1530–1987* (Oxford, 1990).

110. John Demos, *A Little Commonwealth: Family Life in Plymouth Colony* (New York, 1970) pp. 92–7.

111. Wendy Gibson, *Women in Seventeenth-Century France*, p. 62.

112. Demos, *Little Commonwealth*, p. 92; L.J.R.O. B/C/3 series, e.g. B/C/3/; Natalie Zemon Davies, *The Return of Martin Guerre*, 25; Samuel Pyeatt Menefee, *Wives for Sale* (Oxford, 1981) pp. 19–20.

113. For example, L.J.R.O. B/C/3/7, 17 April 1600. See also, R. O'Day and J. Berlatsky (eds), *The Letter Book of Thomas Bentham* ... (Camden Miscellany, XXVII (1979) p. 125, for sympathetic approach to women in marriage in 1561.

114. Menefee, *Wives for Sale*, pp. 1–7, 59, 31 *et passim*.

115. L. Pollock, *With Faith and Physic*, p. 10; see Craig R.Thompson (ed.), *The Colloquies of Erasmus* (Chicago, 1965) pp. 115–27, reprinted, with an introduction, in David Englander et al. (eds), *Culture and Belief in Europe*, pp. 58–66.

116. Cited in Segalen, *Love and Power*, p. 58; See Mitterauer & Sieder, *The European Family*, pp. 65–6.

117. Pierre Bourdieu, 'Marriage Strategies as Strategies of Social Reproduction', pp. 1105–25.

118. Linda Pollock, *Forgotten Children, Parent–Child Relations from 1500 to 1900* (Cambridge, 1983) *passim*.

119. *The Times*, 26 May 1834, p. 6 f.

120. Gibson, *Women in Seventeenth-Century France*, p. 51.

121. Cited in Cott, 'Eighteenth-Century Family and Social Life', p. 29.

122. Parkinson (ed.), *Life of Adam Martindale*, p. 206; *Life of Mrs Abigail Bailey* cited in L. Pollock, *Forgotten Children*, p. 119; Diary of John Richards, 1660–1721, cited in L. Pollock, *Forgotten Children*, p. 152.

123. L. Pollock, *Forgotten Children*, p. 92.

124. Parkinson (ed.), *Life of Adam Martindale*, pp. 108–9, 207–10, 211–18; Macfarlane (ed.), *Diary of Ralph Josselin*.

125. D. H. J. Clifford, *The Diaries of Lady Anne Clifford* (Stroud, 1990) pp. 31–2, 35, 38, 42–3, 47–51, 53, 54–5.

126. Davies, *Thomas Raymond ... and the Guise Family*, p. 112.

127. Newdigate-Newdegate, *Gossip from a Muniment Room*, p. 22.

128. L. Pollock, *With Faith and Physic*, p. 7.

129. Thomas Heywood (ed.), *The Diary of Rev. Henry Newcome* (Chetham Society, 18, 1849) pp. 15, 59 (19 February 1661/2), 60 (22 February 1661/2).

130. Parkinson (ed.), *Life of Adam Martindale*, pp. 208–9.

131. Peter Earle, *The Making of the English Middle Class: Business, Society and Family Life in London 1660–1730* (1989) pp. 232–4; see G. Davies (ed.) *The Autobiography of Thomas Raymond and Memoirs of the Family of Guise of Elmore, Gloucs* (Camden Society, XXVIII, 1917), pp. 111–123.

132. Henri Misson, *Memoirs and Observations in his Travels over England*, (translation, London, 1719) p. 33.

133. L. Pollock, *Forgotten Children*, pp. 112–14.

134. Diary of Nehemiah Wallington. Guildhall Library, London, The published extracts from this diary omit this reference. Ms, F. 435.

135. BL, Additional MS 69941, f. 67.

136. L. Pollock, *Forgotten Children*, pp. 111–17.

137. See R. O'Day, *Education and Society in Britain, 1500–1800* (London, 1982) *passim*.

138. See, for example, the hard grind to which peasant children in the backward Gévaudan were exposed. Claverie and Lamaison, *L'Impossible mariage*, p. 78.

139. E. Fox-Genovese, *Within the Plantation Household*, pp. 107–17.

140. Philip Greven Jr, *Four Generations: Population, Land and Family in Colonial Andover, Massachusetts* (Ithaca, 1970) pp. 238–40, 249–50; Richard S. Dunn, 'Servants and Slaves: the Recruitment and Employment of Labour', in Jack P. Greene and J. R. Pole (eds), *Colonial British America* (Baltimore, 1984) pp. 186–8.

141. Patricia Crawford, 'The Construction and Experience of Maternity in Seventeenth-Century England', in Fildes (ed.), *Women as Mothers*, pp. 16–17; For good examples, see Rachel, Countess of Westmorland, 'Book of Advice for the Children', Northampton Record Office, West. Misc. MS 35, especially f. 45v; Grace, Lady Mildmay, *Autobiography*.

142. P. Crawford, 'Construction and Experience of Maternity', pp. 23–7; see D. J. H. Clifford (ed.), *The Diaries of Lady Anne Clifford* (Stroud, 1990) p. 123.

143. Journal of Elizabeth Turner, 5 May 1672, Kent Archive Office; M. Holden, *The Woman's Almanack for the year … 1688* (1688) p. 9.

144. Valerie Fildes, *Breasts, Bottles and Babies* (Edinburgh, 1986) part II.

145. V. Fildes, 'Maternal Feelings re-assessed: Child Abandonment and Neglect in London and Westminster, 1550–1800', in Fildes, *Women as Mothers*, pp. 139–78, especially p. 153.

146. The girl was sixteen.

147. For Reformation Augsburg, Dr Lyndal Roper has done just this most successfully.

148. *Diaries of Lady Ann Clifford*, p. 123.

149. See Laurel Ulrich Thatcher, *Good Wives: Image and Reality in the Lives of Women in Northern New England, 1650–1750* (New York, 1982); Catherine M. Scholten, *Childbearing in American Society, 1650 to 1850* (New York, 1985); Mary Beth Norton, *Liberty's Daughters: The Revolutionary Experience of American Women, 1750–1800* (Boston, Mass., 1980).

150. BL, Egerton MS 2644, f. 269.

151. Fox-Genovese, *Within the Plantation Household*, p. 10.

152. Parkinson (ed.), *Life of Adam Martindale*, p. 120.

153. Jean-Louis Flandrin, *Families in Former Times: Kinship, Household and Sexuality* (Cambridge, 1979) p. 74; see also, Claverie and Lamaison, *L'Impossible mariage, passim*.

154. Lutz K. Berkner and John W. Shaffer, 'The Joint Family in the Nivernais', *Journal of Family History*, 3 (1978) p. 152.

155. Ibid., pp. 156–7.

156. Ibid., p. 160.

157. See also, A. Pardailhé-Galabrun, *The Birth of Intimacy: Privacy and Domestic Life in Early Modern Paris* (Oxford, 1991) p. 69.

158. Chaytor, 'Household and Kinship', pp. 36–8, 45–7.

159. G. Davies (ed.), *The Autobiography of Thomas Raymond and Memoirs of the Family of Guise of Elmore, Gloucs* (Camden Society, XXVIII, 1917) pp. 111ff.

160. James A. Henretta, 'Wealth and Social Structure', in Jack P. Greene and J. R. Pole (eds), *Colonial British America* (Baltimore and London, 1991 reprint) p. 283. See also, J. E. Cashen, *A Family Venture*, pp. 10–20.

161. David Levine, *Reproducing Families* (Cambridge, 1987) p. 160.

162. Jean Cuisenier and Martine Segalen (eds), *Le Cycle de la vie familiale, dans les sociétés européennes* (The Hague, 1977) *passim*, and Segalen, *Love and Power*, pp. 59–70.

163. Baulant, 'The Scattered Family', p. 114.

164. Bristol Census, 1689, cited in Demos, *Little Commonwealth*, p. 74.

165. Parkinson (ed.), *Life of Adam Martindale*, p. 30.

166. For example, the residential governess of Grace Sherrington (Mildmay) was Mistress Hamblyn, yet she was Grace's cousin. L. Pollock, *With Faith and Physic*, p. 6; Keith Wrightson and David Levine, *Poverty and Piety in an English Village: Terling, 1525–1700* (London, 1979) p. 85; Chaytor, 'Household and Kinship', p. 29; Ralph Houlbrooke, *The English Family*, p. 46.

167. Rector of Myddle, c. 1596–1629.

168. A jocular reference to the personal tithe.

169. Hey (ed.), *History of Myddle*, p. 41.

170. BL, Egerton MS, 3054 Account Book of Joyce Jeffrey; Ralph Josselin paid his maid servant £1 18s p. a. in 1641, see Macfarlane (ed.), *The Diary of Ralph Josselin*, p. 11.

171. David R. Ransome, 'Wives for Virginia 1621', *William and Mary Quarterly*, XLVIII (1991) pp. 14–15.

172. Hey (ed.), *History of Myddle*, pp. 246–7.

173. Cissie Fairchilds, *Domestic Enemies, Servants and their Masters in Old Regime France* (Baltimore and London, 1984) p. 61.

174. BL, Additional MS 4454, Katharine Austen's Miscellanies, f. 38v.

175. Hey (ed.), *History of Myddle*, p. 242.

176. Ibid., p. 32, p. 244; an excellent photograph of the 'house' of a day labourer or old person in Gévaudan occurs in Claverie and Lamaison, *L'Impossible mariage*, plate 6. It is no more than a hovel.

177. Cott, 'Eighteenth-Century Family and Social Life', p. 23.

178. Cited in ibid., p. 23; see also, Rhys Issac, *The Transformation of Virginia* (Chapel Hill, 1982), for the crowded living conditions of all in this period, and of the poorest until well into the nineteenth century.

179. Flandrin, *Families in Former Times*, p. 100; see also, Latham and Matthews (eds), *Diary of Samuel Pepys*, vol. I, pp. 67, 181.

180. Pardailhé-Galabrun, *The Birth of Intimacy*, pp. 73–83.

181. Flandrin, *Families in Former Times*, p. 102; see also, Claverie and Lamaison, *L'Impossible mariage*, p. 37.

182. Flandrin, *Families in Former Times*, p. 106.

183. See Fairchilds, *Domestic Enemies*, pp. 38–40.

184. Pardailhé-Galabrun, *Birth of Intimacy*, pp. 52–4.

185. Flandrin, *Families in Former Times*, p. 140; Macfarlane, *Diary of Ralph Josselin*, 5. 8. 1644; Parkinson (ed.) *Life of Adam Martindale*, p. 30; M. St Clare Byrne (ed.), *The Lisle Letters: An Abridgement* (Chicago, 1981) vol. V, pp. 448–9, 453, 730.

186. See Flandrin, *Families in Former Times*, p. 142, where he falls, hook line and sinker, for this propaganda.

187. See, for example, L.J.R.O. B/C/3/ series; D'Day and Benatsky (eds), *Letter Book of Thomas Bentham*, p. 222. Letter 221; Claverie and Lamaison, *L'Impossible mariage*, pp. 230, 233ff.; many of the cases of infanticide occurred among the servant girls of Gevaudan and the fathers of their children were often their masters.

188. Devon Record Office, Q/SB Box 59, 33; cited in P. Crawford, 'Construction and Experience of Maternity', p. 17.

189. G. Rouger (ed.), *Rétif De la Bretonne, De la vie de mon pére* (Paris, 1970) p. 130.

190. Claverie and Lamaison, *L'Impossible mariage*, pp. 187–8.

191. Parkinson (ed.), *Life of Adam Martindale*, pp. 207–10.

192. Parkinson (ed.), *Life of Adam Martindale*, p. 208; Macfarlane (ed.), *Diary of Ralph Josselin*, p. 39.

193. Demos, *A Little Commonwealth*, p. 74.

194. James Horn, 'Servant Emigration to the Chesapeake in the Seventeenth Century', in Thad W. Tate and David L. Ammerman, *The Chesapeake in the Seventeenth Century, Essays in Anglo-American Society* (Chapel Hill, 1979) p. 95; Russell Minard, 'British Migration to the Chesapeake Colonies', in Lois Green et al. (eds), *Colonial Chesapeake Society* (Chapel Hill, 1988) pp. 44–132.

195. See Ransome, 'Wives for Virginia, 1621', pp. 1–18.

196. See Middleton, *Colonial America*, p. 199; Allan Kulikoff, *Tobacco and Slaves: The Development of Southern Cultures in the Chesapeake, 1689–1800* (Chapel Hill, 1986) passim.

197. Francis G. Walett (ed.), *The Diary of Ebenezer Parkman, 1719–1755*, pp. 10–13, 33, 37, 55, 64–5; cited in Dunn, 'Servants and Slaves', p. 187.

198. Henretta, 'Wealth and Social Structure', p. 283.

199. See Kulikoff, *Tobacco and Slaves*; Philip D. Morgan and Michael L. Nicholls, 'Slaves in Piedmont Virginia, 1700–1790', *William and Mary Quarterly*, XLVI, pp. 211–51; Richard R. Beeman, *The Evolution of the Southern Backcountry: A Case Study of Luxembourg County, Virginia, 1746–1832* (Philadelphia, 1984); James A. Henretta, 'Families and Farms: Mentalités in Preindustrial America', *William and Mary Quarterly*, XXXV (1978) pp. 3–32.

200. See Allan Kulikoff, 'A Prolifick People': Black Population Growth in the Chesapeake Colonies, 1700–1790', *Southern Studies*, XVI (1977) pp. 391–428; for an excellent summary, see Middleton, *Colonial America*, pp. 275–9.

201. W. E. Burghardt DuBois, *The Negro American Family* (Atlanta, 1908) pp. 21–2; E. Franklin Frazier, *The Negro Family in the United States* (Chicago, 1939) p. 134; Kenneth M. Stampp, *The Peculiar Institution* (New York, 1956) pp. 345–6; Stanley M. Elkins, *Slavery: A Problem in American Institutional and Intellectual Life* (Chicago, 1959) p. 53.

202. John W. Blassingame, *The Slave Community* (New York, 1972) pp. 87–8; Eugene D. Genovese, *Roll Jordan, Roll: The World the Slaves Made* (New York, 1974) pp. 451–2; Herbert G. Gutman, *The Black Family in Slavery and Freedom, 1750–1925* (New York, 1976) pp. 45–184; James Trussell and Richard Steckel, 'The Age of Slaves at Menarche and Their First Birth', *Journal of Interdisciplinary History*, **8** (1978) pp. 477–505; Richard H. Steckel, 'Slave Marriage and the Family', *Journal of Family History*, **5** (1980) pp. 407–20.

203. Robert W. Fogel and Stanley L. Engermann, *Time on the Cross*, vol. I (1974) p. 83; Richard Sutch, 'The Breeding of Slaves for Sale and the Westward Expansion of Slavery, 1850–1860', in Engermann and Genovese (eds), *Race and Slavery in the Western Hemisphere* (Princeton, 1975) p. 195.

204. Fox-Genovese, *Within the Plantation Household*, pp. 24–6.

205. Ibid., pp. 100–102. See also, Cashin, *A Family Venture*, pp. 116–18.

206. See, for example, Stephanie Coontz, *The Social Origins of Private Life, A History of American Families, 1600–1900* (London and New York, 1988).

207. The most influential and sophisticated exposition of the 'strategies of family formation' and their relationship to economic conditions is to be found in David Levine, *Family Formation in an Age of Nascent Capitalism* (New York, San Francisco, London, 1977).

208. Richard S. Dunn, 'Servants and Slaves', p. 239.

209. Henretta, 'Wealth and Social Structure', in Greene and Pole (eds), *Colonial British America* (Baltimore, 1984) p. 281; Hermann Wellenreuther, 'A View of Socio-Economic Structures in England and the British Colonies on the Eve of the American Revolution', in Eric Angermann et al. (eds), *New Wine in Old Skins: A Comparative View of Socio-Political Structures and Values Affecting the American Revolution* (Stuttgart, 1976) pp. 15–21.

210. Dunn, 'Servants and Slaves'; Henretta, 'Wealth and Social Structure', p. 281.

211. See Louise A. Tilly and Joan W. Scott, *Women, Work and Family* (1987 edn) pp. 74–5, for comment on the contrast in the nineteenth century.

212. B. A. Holderness, *Pre-Industrial England* (London, 1976) p. 154; Levine, *Reproducing Families*, p. 100.

213. Henretta, 'Wealth and Social Structure', p. 284.

214. Hans Medick, 'The Proto-Industrial Family Economy: the Structural Function of Household and Family during the Transition from Peasant Society to Industrial Capitalism', *Social History*, **3** (1976) pp. 291–316; Joan Thirsk, 'Industries in the Countryside', in F. J. Fisher (ed.), *Essays in the Economic and Social History of Tudor and Stuart England* (Cambridge, 1961) pp. 70–88.

215. Levine, *Reproducing Families*, p. 104.
216. For a highly readable account, see John Rule, *The Experience of Labour in Eighteenth-Century Industry* (London, 1981).
217. Coontz, *The Social Origins of Private Life*, p. 122.
218. For example, Daniel Defoe, *A Tour Through the Whole Island of Great Britain*, 2 vols (London, 1962).
219. Levine, *Family Formation in an Age of Nascent Capitalism*.
220. An interesting but only partially successful attempt to penetrate behind the theoretically rigid distinction between the supposed 'separate spheres' of public and domestic life, to obtain an understanding of life-experience, is Leonore Davidoff and Catherine Hall, *Family Fortunes: Men and Women of the English Middle Class, 1780–1850* (London, 1987).
221. Ibid., pp. 22–3.
222. Michael Katz, Michael Doucet and Mark Stern, *The Social Organization of Industrial Capitalism* (Cambridge, Mass., 1982) pp. 14–63.
223. Peter Stearns, 'The Middle Class: Toward a Precise Definition', *Comparative Studies in Society and History*, **21** (1979). See an excellent discussion of the problem in S. Coontz, *The Social Origins of Private Life*, pp. 187–90.
224. Many of the features identified by L. Davidoff as characteristic of the eighteenth century family – the fact that the family network itself supported commercial enterprises; the training of the young in the families of relatives; the cementing of business partnerships by sibling and cousin marriage; the late age at marriage, which encouraged youthful intimacy and independence; the proximity and interchangeability of home and work; and the strengthening of family bonds through letter writing, visiting, feasts and celebrations of rites of passage – were all extensions of an earlier world. Leonore Davidoff, 'The Family in Britain', in M. Thompson (ed.), *The Cambridge Social History of Britain, 1750–1950* (Cambridge, 1990) pp. 78–80.
225. For example, L. Davidoff, in 'The Family in Britain', denied hindsight, asserts that regular mealtimes were imposed by business practice for the first time (p. 78), and apparently believes that incest first became an offence when a law was passed against it in 1908 (p. 110), although it had long been an offence heard in the Church courts.
226. Coontz, *The Social Origins of Private Life*, p. 182.
227. Nancy Cott, *Bonds of Womanhood, passim*; Coontz, *The Social Origins of Private Life* (New Haven, 1977) p. 185.
228. See p. 93, above, for the suggestion that roles were defined by place within the family rather than by gender alone; but see p. 270.
229. Turner, *The Diary of a Georgian Shopkeeper*, p. 4.
230. Ibid., p. 9.
231. Ibid.
232. Ibid., p. 12.
233. Ibid., p. 68.

234. Davidoff and Hall, *Family Fortunes*, pp. 52–9.
235. Shirley Nicholson, *A Victorian Household, Based on the Diaries of Marion Sambourne* (London, 1988) p. 39.
236. Ibid., pp. 39–47.
237. Ibid., pp. 21, 23–24.
238. Ibid., pp. 14–16, 53–8.
239. Ibid., pp. 15–16. Linley was the great, great grandfather of the present Viscount Linley.
240. Ibid., p. 47.
241. Ibid., pp. 32–5, 50–2.
242. H. G. Wells, *Experiment in Autobiography* (London, 1934) vol. I, pp. 45–6.
243. Ibid., p. 59.
244. Ibid., pp. 60–1.
245. Ibid., p. 46.
246. Sheila Hardy, *The Diary of a Suffolk Farmer's Wife*, 1854–1869 (London, 1992) p. 34.
247. Ibid., p. 32.
248. Coontz, *The Social Origins of Private Life*, pp. 41–72.
249. For further elaboration of this point, see Daniel E. Sutherland, *Americans and their Servants: Domestic Service in the United States from 1880 to 1920* (Baton Rouge, 1981) especially pp. 7–18.

Notes to Chapter 5: A Day's Work for a Day's Victuals

1. Patrick Joyce, *Work, Society and Politics*, 1980, p. 55.
2. See above, pp. 191–6, 18–19.
3. For the opposing view, see Neil J. Smelser, *Social Change in the Industrial Revolution* (1959) pp. 193–205.
4. See, for example, L. Davidoff, 'The Separation of Home and Work? Landladies and Lodgers in Nineteenth- and Twentieth-Century England', in S. Burman (ed.), *Fit Work for Women* (London, 1979) pp. 64–5.
5. Barbara Tucker, 'The Family and Industrial Discipline in Ante-Bellum New England', *Labor History*, **21** (1979–80) p. 56.
6. Patrick Joyce, *Work, Society and Politics* (London, 1980) pp. 134–55.
7. William Ashworth, *The Genesis of Modern British Town Planning* (1968) pp. 118–46.
8. See Rosemary O'Day and David Englander, *Mr Charles Booth's Inquiry: Life and Labour of the People in London Reconsidered* (London, 1993) pp. 141–2.
9. The later edition, which contained 57 case studies, is more commonly used by scholars.
10. Frédéric Le Play, *Les Ouvriers européens* (Paris, 1855) pp. 286–7.
11. Frédéric Le Play, *La Réforme sociale* (1872) pp. 363, 364, 367.

12. Le Play, *Les Ouvriers européens*, pp. 292–4.

13. AICP, *First Report of a Committee on the Sanitary Condition of the Labouring Classes in the City of New York, with Remedial Suggestions* (New York, 1853) p. 24.

14. *The Times*, quoted in R. A. Lewis, *Edwin Chadwick and the Public Health Movement*, (1952) p. 221.

15. Thomas Beames, *The Rookeries of London* (1852 edition), p. 244.

16. Gareth Stedman Jones, *Outcast London* (Oxford, 1971) p. 169.

17. See O'Day and Englander, *Mr Charles Booth's Inquiry, passim*.

18. Eugène Buret, *De la misère des classes laborieuses en Angleterre et en France, 1840* cited in A. L. Shapiro, 'Paris', in M. J. Daunton (ed.), *Housing the Workers* (Leicester, 1990) p. 33, and Louis Chevalier, *Labouring Classes and Dangerous Classes* (London, 1973) pp. 140–1.

19. *Third Annual Report of the Bureau of Statistics of Labour ... 1872, Massachusetts Senate Documents*, no. 180 (1872) p. 437.

20. O. Handlin, *Boston's Immigrants* (New York, 1970 pbk edition) p. 106.

21. Roy Lubove, *The Progressives and the Slums, Tenement House Reform in New York City, 1890–1917* (Pittsburgh, 1962) pp. 2–3.

22. Lubove, *Progressives*, p. 18; for tenement life, see Jacob A. Riis, *How the Other Half Lives: Studies Among the Tenements of New York* (New York, 1957).

23. Lubove, *Progressives*, p. 17.

24. Ibid., pp. 122–4; Irving Howe, *The Immigrant Jews of New York* (London, 1976) p. 89.

25. Select Committee of the House of Commons on Public Petitions (1865), App. 274, No. 3848.

26. *North British Daily Mail*, 22 November 1869.

27. *Report of the Committee of Internal Health*, 1849, 13; Tenement House Committee of 1894, *Report*, pp. 256–7, 266–72; Lubove, *Progressives*, pp. 7–8.

28. A. K. Chalmers, *Public Health Administration*, pp. 260–1; 267–8; 270; 274; 262–3; 502–3; 524–6; 527.

29. Lynn H. Lees, 'Patterns of Lower-Class Life: Irish Slum Communities in Nineteenth-Century London', in Stephan Thernstrom and Richard Sennett (eds), *Nineteenth-Century Cities, Essays in the New Urban History* (New Haven, 1969) pbk, p. 363.

30. F. Engels, *The Condition of the Working Class in England in 1844*, (London, 1952) p. 36; D. Wardle, *Education and Society in Nineteenth-Century Nottingham* (Cambridge, 1971) p. 20.

31. Joyce, *Work*, pp. xx–xxi, 55–8, 111–20.

32. I. C. Taylor, 'The Insanitary Housing Question and Tenement Dwellings in Nineteenth-Century Liverpool', in A. Sutcliffe (ed.), *Multi-Storey Living, The British Working-Class Experience* (London, 1974) pp. 48, 51; J. H. Treble, 'Liverpool Working-Class Housing, 1801–1851', in S. D. Chapman (ed.), *History of Working Class Housing, A Symposium* (Newton Abbott, 1971) p. 199; Privy Council, *Eighth Report of the Medical Officer of the Privy Council, 1865, App. no. 2, Report on Housing of the Poor in Towns*, p. 79.

33. *Report of the Urban Land Enquiry* (1914) pp. 35, 39–40.
34. Joyce, *Work* pp. 52–4.
35. Le Play, *Les Ouvriers européens*, pp. 229–36.
36. Charles Booth, *Life and Labour of the People in London* (Poverty Series) vol. I, pp. 159–61.
37. Roger Wells (ed.), *Victorian Village. The Diaries of the Reverend John Coker Egerton of Burwash 1857–1888* (Stroud, 1992) p. 59.
38. Ibid., pp. 31, 53.
39. Ibid., p. 46.
40. Ibid., p. 47.
41. Ibid., pp. 36–7.
42. Ibid., pp. 35–6.
43. Ibid., p. 48.
44. Ibid., p. 56.
45. Ibid., p. 60.
46. Ibid., p. 88.
47. Ibid., p. 127.
48. Ibid., p. 138.
49. Ibid., p. 179.
50. Ibid., p. 205.
51. Ibid., p. 98.
52. Ibid., p. 120.
53. Ibid., pp. 73, 91.
54. Ibid., p. 76.
55. Ibid., p. 71.
56. Ibid., p. 78.
57. Ibid., p. 85.
58. Ibid., p. 87.
59. Ibid., p. 123.
60. Ibid., p. 138.
61. Ibid., p. 139.
62. Ibid., p. 140.
63. Ibid., p. 146.
64. Ibid., p. 148.
65. Ibid., pp. 162–3.
66. Ibid., p. 90.
67. Ibid., p. 92.
68. Ibid., p. 100.
69. Ibid., p. 148.
70. Ibid., pp. 162–3, 169.
71. Lyn H. Lees, 'Patterns of Lower-Class Life'.
72. Henry Mayhew, *London Labour and the London Poor, 1861–1862* (New York, 1968), vol. 1, p. 44.
73. Stedman Jones, *Outcast London*, pp. 61–2.
74. Le Play, *Les Ouvriers européens*, vol. 6, pp. 287–301.
75. See David Garrioch, *Neighbourhood and Community in Paris, 1740–1790* (Cambridge, 1986) pp. 56–62.
76. Mayhew, *London Labour*, vol. 1, p. 39.
77. Ibid., p. 43.

78. See Park Honan, *Jane Austen, Her Life* (New York, 1987) p. 43; H. G. Wells, *Experiment in Autobiography* (London, 1934) pp. 112–15, 119, 125–31; S. Hardy, *The Diary of a Suffolk Farmer's Wife, 1854–69*, (London, 1992) pp. 11–19; 168.
79. Mayhew, *London Labour*, vol. 1, p. 40.
80. Ibid., p. 48.
81. Ibid., p. 152.
82. Cited in Garrioch, *Neighbourhood*, p. 70.
83. Mayhew, *London Labour*, p. 136.
84. Le Play, *La Réforme sociale*, pp. 352–8.
85. J. W. Scott and L. A. Tilly, 'Women's Work and the Family in Nineteenth-Century Europe', in *Comparative Studies in Society and History*, **17** (1975) pp. 36–64.
86. Leonore Davidoff, 'The Family in Britain', in F. M. L. Thompson (ed.), *The Cambridge Social History of Britain, 1750–1950* (Cambridge, 1990) p. 122.
87. Ellen Ross, 'Fierce Questions and Taunts: Married Life in Working-Class London', *Feminist Studies*, VIII (1982) pp. 575–601. This position has been slightly modified in E. Ross, *In Time of Trouble: Motherhood and Survival among the London Poor* (Oxford, forthcoming).
88. Howe, *The Immigrant Jews*, p. 259: a warning this, to the architectural historians!
89. O. Hufton, 'Women and the Family Economy in Eighteenth-Century France', *French Historical Studies*, **9** (1975) pp. 1–22.
90. Garrioch, *Neighbourhood*, pp. 80–1.
91. For an excellent discussion, see Davidoff, 'The Separation of Home and Work?' pp. 64–97.
92. Booth, *Life and Labour*, vol. I, pp. 158–9.
93. For the classic account of landlord/tenant relations, read David Englander, *Landlord and Tenant in Urban Britain* (Oxford, 1983).
94. British Library of Political and Economic Science, Coll. Misc., 43, Ledger of the Inhabitants of Katharine Buildings, 1886–90.
95. Lynn H. Lees, 'Patterns of Lower-Class Life', pp. 376–7.
96. See Stephanie Coontz, *The Social Origins of Private Life* (London, 1988) p. 325, for detailed references.
97. Michael Katz, Michael Doucet and Mark Stern, *The Social Organisation of Industrial Capitalism* (Cambridge, Mass., 1982) pp. 336, 343.
98. Oscar Handlin, *Boston's Immigrants, 1790–1880*, (New York, 1970) pp. 51–3.
99. Howe, *The Immigrant Jews*, p. 276.
100. John Buchanan, 'How to Assimilate the Foreign Element in our Population', *Forum*, XXXII (1901–2) p. 689; Robert E. Park and Herbert A. Miller, *Old World Traits Transplanted* (New York, 1921) pp. 40–1; *New York Times*, 6 March 1892, p. 4.
101. Hamilton Holt (ed.), *The Life Stories of [undistinguished] Americans as Told by Themselves* (New York and London, 1990) esp. pp. 61–92 in the stories of a French dressmaker, a German nurse girl and an Irish cook.

102. Robert Bieder, 'Kinship as a Factor in Migration', *Journal of Marriage and the Family*, **35** (1973); Lawrence Glasco, 'Migration and Adjustment in the Nineteenth-Century City', Tamara Hareven and M. Vinovskis (eds.), *Family and Population*; Virginia Yans-McLaughlin, *Family and Community: Italian Immigrants in Buffalo, 1880–1930* (Ithaca, 1977); Mayhew, *London Labour*, vol. 1, p. 109.

103. John Cumbler, *Working-Class Community in Industrial America: Work, Leisure and Struggle in Two Industrial Cities, 1880–1930* (Westport, 1979) p. 118.

104. Francis Early, 'The French-Canadian Family Economy and Standard-of-Living in Lowell, Massachusetts, 1870', *Journal of Family History*, **16** (1982) pp. 184–8.

105. Handlin, *Boston's Immigrants*, p. 61.

106. See Jerry Wilcox and Hilda Golden, 'Prolific Immigrants and Dwindling Natives?: Fertility Patterns in Western Massachusetts, 1850 and 1880', *Journal of Family History*, **16** (1982) p. 277; Michael Katz and Mark Stern, 'Fertility, Class, and Industrial Capitalism: Erie County, New York, 1855–1915,' *American Quarterly*, **33** (1981) pp. 75–6; Susan Bloomberg et al., 'A Census Probe into Nineteenth-Century Family History: Southern Michigan, 1850–1880', *Journal of Family History*, **5** (1971) pp. 26–45.

107. Coontz, *The Social Origins*, pp. 295–6.

108. Howe, *The Immigrant Jews*, p. 171.

109. See R. H. Bremner, 'The Big Flat: History of a New York Tenement House', *American Historical Review*, LXIV (1958) pp. 54–62; R. Lubove, *Progressives*, p. 9.

110. Lubove, *Progressives*, p. 35.

111. Ibid., pp. 102–3.

112. Booth, *Life and Labour*, vol. II, p. 37.

113. Octavia Hill, 'Blocks of Model Dwellings: (2) Influence on Character' in Booth, *Life and Labour*, vol. II, pp. 29–36.

114. Charles F. Wingate, 'The Moral Side of the Tenement-House Problem', *The Catholic World* (1885) p. 160.

115. E. R. L. Gould, 'The Housing Problem in Great Cities', *Quarterly Journal of Economics*, **14** (1899–1900), p. 378.

116. Elsie Clews Parsons, *The Family* (New York, 1906).

117. Beatrice Potter, The Wholesale Clothing Trade, BLPES, Passfield VII. 1.8.

118. See Rosemary O'Day, 'Katharine Buildings' in R. Finnegan and M. Drake (eds), *Studying Family and Community History: From Family Tree to Family History*, vol. I (Cambridge, 1994) pp. 129–66.

119. Shapiro, 'Paris', p. 55.

120. Edmond Demolins, 'Les Habitations ouvrières', in *La Réforme Sociale*, vol. 1 (1881) pp. 301–6.

121. R. Sennett, *Families Against the City: Middle Class Homes of Industrial Chicago, 1872–90* (Cambridge, Mass., 1970) see also, B. Laslett, 'The Family as a Public and Private Institution: an Historical Perspective', *Journal of Marriage and the Family*, **35** (1973) and C. E. Clark Jr.

'Domestic Architecture as an Index to Social History: the Romantic Revival and the Cult of Domesticity in America, 1840–1870', *Journal of Interdisciplinary History*, **9** (1976).

122. E. R. L. Gould, 'Homewood – A Model Suburban Development', *Review of Reviews*, XVI (1897) pp. 43, 47; *New York Times*, 18 February 1900, p. 23 cited in R. Lubove, Progressives, p. 110.

123. Lubove, *Progressives*, p. 132.

124. M. Daunton, 'Rows and Tenements: American Cities, 1880–1914' in Daunton (ed.), *Housing the Workers*, p. 255; R. W. DeForest and L. Veiller (eds), *The Tenement House Problem* (New York, 1903) vol. I, pp. 7–10.

125. Daunton, 'Rows and Tenements', p. 258.

126. *Report of the Tenement House Commission+* (Louisville, 1909).

127. C. E. Clark, Jr, *The American Family Home, 1800–1960* (Chapel Hill, 1986).

128. Holt, *Life Stories*, p. 91.

129. Lubove, *Progressives*, pp. 67, 103; J. A. Riis, 'What Settlements Stand For', Outlook, LXXXIX (1908) pp. 69–72; Standish Meacham, *Toynbee Hall and Social Reform, 1880–1914* (New Haven, 1987) pp. 1–23.

Notes to the Conclusion

1. Beatrice Potter, Passfield VII, 1.8. pp. 11–15; see Rosemary O'Day, 'Before the Webbs: Beatrice Potter's Early Investigations for Charles Booth's Inquiry', *History*, June 1993.

2. Robert Cleaver, *A Godly Forme of Household Government* (1598) pp. 236–7.

3. For example, Leonore Davidoff, 'The Family in Britain', in F. M. L. Thompson (ed.), *The Cambridge Social History of Britain, 1750–1950* (Cambridge, 1990) vol. 2, pp. 71–129.

4. Ferrar Papers, Magdalene College, Cambridge: see especially, letters dated 3 May 1630, Nicholas Ferrar to Arthur Woodenoth? goldsmith; July 1631, Anna Collett to John and Susanna Collett; August 1630, Margaret Woodenoth to Mary Ferrar; 19 October 1630, Margaret Woodenoth to Mary Ferrar; 22 September 1631, Anna Collett to Nicholas Ferrar; 16 December 1633, Nicholas Ferrar to Richard Ferrar; the Collett Letters, Bodleian Library, Oxford; A. L. Maycock, *Nicholas Ferrar of Little Gidding* (London, 1938) p. 147; J. E. B. Mayor (ed.), *Nicholas Ferrar: Two Lives by his Brother John and by Dr Jebb* (Cambridge, 1855) p. 232. For a full discussion of the women of Little Gidding, see the forthcoming work of Margaret Smith.

5. See Stephanie Coontz, *The Social Origins of Private Life* (London, 1988) pp. 41–72.

6.   Rosemary O'Day, *Katharine Buildings, 1886–1890: a Database, and Potter, Pycroft and Paul: The Sweet Trinity and Katharine Buildings*, forthcoming; for a preliminary study of family life in Katharine Buildings see Rosemary O'Day, 'Katherine Buildings', in R. Finnegan and M. Drake (eds), *Studying Family and Community History: From Family Tree to Family History*, vol. I (Cambridge, 1994) pp. 129–66.

Bibliography

Addy, John, *Death, Money and the Vultures: Inheritance and Avarice, 1660–1750* (London, 1992).

AICP, *First Report of a Committee on the Sanitary Condition of the Labouring Classes in the City of New York, with Remedial Suggestions* (New York, 1853).

Amussen, Susan Dwyer, *An Ordered Society: Gender and Class in Early Modern England* (Oxford: Basil Blackwell, 1988).

Anderson, Gregory, *Victorian Clerks* (Manchester: Manchester University Press, 1976).

Anderson, Michael, *Family Structure in Nineteenth-Century Lancashire* (London, 1971).

Anderson, Michael, 'What is New about the Modern Family?', in M. Drake (ed.), *Time, Family and Community* (Oxford: Blackwell, 1994).

Anon., *Case or Petition of the Corporation of Pinmakers* (London).

Anon., *A Strange and Wonderful Relation of the Burying Alive of Joan Bridges of Rochester in the County of Kent* (London, 1646).

Aries, Philippe, *Centuries of Childhood* (London: Jonathan Cape, 1962).

Ashworth, William, *The Genesis of Modern British Town Planning* (1968).

Aspinall-Oglander, C., *Nunwell Symphony* (Hogarth Press, 1945).

Auwers, Linda, 'Fathers, Sons, and Wealth in Colonial Windsor, Connecticut', *Journal of Family History*, **3** (1978).

Bailyn, Bernard, *New England Merchants in the Seventeenth Century* (New York, 1964).

Micheline Baulant, 'The Scattered Family: Another Aspect of Seventeenth-Century Demography', in Robert Forster and Orest Ranum (eds), *Family and Society, Selections from the Annales, ESC* (Baltimore & London: Johns Hopkins University Press, 1976).

Baxter, Richard, *Gildas Salvianus or The Reformed Pastor* (London, 1656).

Beames, Thomas, *The Rookeries of London* (1852 edition).

Beeman, Richard R., *The Evolution of the Southern Backcountry: A Case Study of Luxembourg County, Virginia, 1746–1832* (Philadelphia, 1984).

308

Benedicti, Jean, *La Somme des pechez* (Paris, 1601 edition of work first published in 1584).

Berkner, Lutz K. and John W. Shaffer, 'The Joint Family in the Nivernais', *Journal of Family History*, **3** (1978).

Berlanstein, Lenard, 'Illegitimacy, Concubinage, and Proletarianization in a French Town, 1760–1914', *Journal of Family History*, **5** (1980).

Bettey, J. H., 'Marriages of Convenience by Copyholders in Dorset during the Seventeenth Century', *Proceedings of the Dorset Natural History and Archaeological Society*, **98** (1976).

Bettey, J. H. (ed.), *Calendar of the Correspondence of the Smyth Family of Ashton Court, 1548–1642* (Bristol Record Society, 1982).

Betts, Lillian W., 'The Tenement-House Exhibit', *Outlook*, LXIV (1900).

Bideau, A., 'La Mortalite des Enfants dans la Chatellenie de Thoissey-en-Dombes', *Demographies Urbaine XVe–XIXe siècles* (Lyons, 1977).

Bideau, Alain, 'A Demographic and Social Analysis of Widowhood and Remarriage: the Example of the Castellany of Thoissey-en-Dombes, 1670–1840', *Journal of Family History*, **5** (1980).

Bieder, Robert, 'Kinship as a Factor in Migration', *Journal of Marriage and the Family*, **35** (1973).

Biraben, Jean-Noel, 'A Southern French Village: The Inhabitants of Montplaisant in 1644', in P. Laslett and Richard Wall (eds), *Household and Family in Past Time* (Cambridge, 1972).

Bissell, L. A., 'From One Generation to Another: Mobility in Seventeenth-Century Windsor, Connecticut', *William and Mary Quarterly*, 3rd Series, **31** (1974).

Blassingame, John W., *The Slave Community* (New York, 1972).

Blayo, Yves, 'Size and Structure of Households in a Northern French Village between 1836 and 1861', in P. Laslett and R. Wall (eds), *Household and Family in Past Time* (Cambridge University Press, 1972).

Bloomberg, Susan et al., 'A Census Probe into Nineteenth-Century Family History: Southern Michigan, 1850–1880', *Journal of Family History*, **5** (1971).

Boas, F. S. (ed.), *The Diary of Thomas Crosfield* (London: Oxford University Press, 1935).

Bonfield, Lloyd, *Marriage Settlements, 1601–1740: The Adoption of the Strict Settlement* (Cambridge University Press, 1983).

Bonfield, Lloyd, Richard Smith and Keith Wrightson (eds), *The World We Have Gained, Histories of Population and Social Structure* (Oxford: Basil Blackwell, 1986).

Bosanquet, Helen, *The Family* (London, 1915).

Bossuet, J. B., *Catéchisme du diocèse de Meaux* (Paris, 1687).

Bossy, John, 'The Counter-reformation and the People of Catholic Europe', *Past and Present*, **40** (1970).

Bossy, John, *Christianity in the West, 1400–1700* (Oxford University Press, 1985).

Boulton, Jeremy, *Neighbourhood and Society* (Cambridge University Press, 1987).

Bourdieu, Pierre, 'Marriage Strategies as Strategies of Social Reproduction', in Robert Forster and Orest Ranum (eds), *Family and*

Society. Selections from the Annales, ESC (Baltimore and London: Johns Hopkins University Press, 1976).

Bourdoise, A., *L'Idée d'un bon ecclésiastique* (Paris, 1667).

Brace, Charles Loring, *The Dangerous Classes of New York and Twenty Years' Work Among Them* (New York, 1880).

Bremner, Robert H., 'The Big Flat: History of a New York Tenement House', *American Historical Review*, LXIV (1958) pp. 54–62.

Brigden, Susan, 'Youth and the English Reformation', *Past and Present*, **95** (1982).

Briggs, Asa and Anne Macartney, *Toynbee Hall. The First Hundred Years* (London: RKP, 1984).

Briggs, Robin, *Communities of Belief* (Oxford University Press, 1989).

Brodsky, Vivien, 'Widows in Late Elizabethan London: Remarriage, Economic Opportunity and Family Orientations', in Lloyd Bonfield, Richard Smith and Keith Wrightson (eds), *The World We Have Gained, Histories of Population and Social Structure* (Oxford: Basil Blackwell, 1986).

Brown, Elizabeth A. R., 'Authority, the Family and the Dead in Late Medieval France', *French Historical Studies*, **16** (1990).

Buchanan, John T., 'How to Assimilate the Foreign Element in our Population', *Forum*, XXXII (1901–2).

Bureau of Statistics of Labour, *Third Annual Report of the Bureau of Statistics of Labour ... 1872, Massachusetts Senate Documents*, no. 180 (Massachusetts, 1872).

Burton, Orville Vernon, *In My Father's House are Many Mansions: Family and Community in Edgefield South Carolina* (Chapel Hill: University of North Carolina Press, 1985).

Bush, M. L., *The English Aristocracy, A Comparative Synthesis* (Manchester University Press, 1984).

Byrne, M. St Clare (ed.), *The Lisle Letters: An Abridgement* (Chicago, 1983).

I. M. Calder (ed.), *Letters of John Davenport, Puritan Divine* (New Haven: Yale University Press, 1937).

Carlton, Charles, *Going to the Wars: The Experience of the British Civil Wars* (London: Routledge, 1992).

Carr, Lois Green and Russell R. Menard, 'Immigration and Opportunity: the Freedman in Early Colonial Maryland', in Thad W. Tate and David L. Ammerman (eds), *The Chesapeake in the Seventeenth Century: Essays on Anglo-American Society* (Chapel Hill: University of North Carolina Press, 1979).

Carr, Lois Green and Lorena S. Walsh, 'The Planter's Wife: the Experience of White Women in Seventeenth-Century Maryland', *William and Mary Quarterly*, 3rd series, **34** (1977).

Cashin, Joan E., *A Family Venture: Men and Women of the Southern Frontier* (Oxford and New York: Oxford University Press, 1991).

Chalmers, A. K., *Public Health Administration* (London, 1905).

Chartier, Roger (ed.), *A History of Private Life*, vol. III (Cambridge, Mass.: Harvard, 1989).

Chaytor, Miranda, 'Household and Kinship: Ryton in the Late Sixteenth and Early Seventeenth Centuries', *History Workshop Journal*, **10** (1980).

Chinn, Carl, *They Worked All Their Lives* (Manchester University Press, 1988).

Chrisman, M., 'Family and Religion in Two Noble Families: French Catholic and English Puritan', *Journal of Family History*, **8** (1983).

Clark, Alice, *Working Life of Women in the Seventeenth Century* (London: George Routledge & Sons, 1919; new edition, RKP, 1982).

Clark, C. E. Jr, *The American Family Home, 1800–1960* (Chapel Hill: University of North Carolina Press, 1986).

Clark, C. E. Jr, 'Domestic Architecture as an Index to Social History: the Romantic Revival and the Cult of Domesticity in America, 1840–1870', *Journal of Interdisciplinary History*, **9** (1976).

Claverie, Elisabeth and Pierre Lamaison, *L'Impossible Marriage, Violente et parente en Gévaudan 17ᵉ, 18ᵉ et 19ᵉ siècles* (Paris: Hachette, 1982).

Robert Cleaver, *A Godlie Forme of Household Government* (London, 1598); see also John Dod, for a later edition of Cleaver's work.

Clifford, A. (ed.), *Tixall Letters* (London, 1815).

Clifford, D. J. H. (ed.), *The Diaries of Lady Anne Clifford* (Stroud: Alan Sutton, 1990).

Clinton, Catherine, *The Plantation Mistress: Woman's World in the Old South* (New York: Pantheon Books, 1982).

Cobbett, Thomas, *A Fruitfull and Usefull Discourse Touching the Honour Due from Children to Parents and the Duty of Parents Towards their Children* (London, 1656).

Collins, James B., 'The Economic Role of Women in Seventeenth-Century France', *French Historical Studies*, **16** (1989).

Collomp, A., 'Famille nucléaire et famille élargie en Provence au XVIIIᵉ siècle', *Annales, ESC* (1972).

Committee of Internal Health, *Report* (New York, 1849).

Connor, Seymour V., 'A Statistical Review of the Settlement of Peter's Colony, 1841–1848', *Southwestern Historical Quarterly*, **57** (1953–4).

Coontz, Stephanie, *The Social Origins of Private Life* (London: Verso, 1988).

Council of Hygiene and Public Health of the Citizen's Association of New York, *Report Upon the Sanitary Conditions of the City* (New York, 1865).

Corrie, G. E. (ed.), *Sermons by Hugh Latimer* (Cambridge: Parker Society, 1844).

Corrie, G. E. (ed.), *Sermons and Remains of Hugh Latimer* (Cambridge: Parker Society, 1845).

Cott, Nancy F., 'Eighteenth-Century Family and Social Life Revealed in Massachusetts Divorce Records', *Journal of Social History*, **10** (1976).

Cott, Nancy F., *Bonds of Womanhood* (New Haven: Yale University Press, 1977).

Cotton, John, *The Covenant of God's Free Grace* (London, 1645).

Crawford, Patricia, 'The Construction and Experience of Maternity in Seventeenth-Century England', in Valerie Fildes (ed.), *Women as Mothers in Preindustrial England* (London: Routledge, 1990).

Cressy, David, 'Kinship and Kin Interaction in Early Modern England', *Past and Present*, **113** (1986).

Crossick, Geoffrey and Heinz-Gerhard Haupt (eds), *Shopkeepers and Master Artisans in Nineteenth-Century Europe* (London: Methuen, 1984).

Cuisenier, Jean and Martine Segalen (eds), *Le Cycle de la vie familiale dans les sociétés européennes* (The Hague, 1977).

Cumbler, John, *Working-Class Community in Industrial America: Work, Leisure and Struggle in Two Industrial Cities, 1880–1930* (Westport, 1979).

Darrow, Margaret, 'French Noblewomen and the New Domesticity, 1750–1850', *Feminist Studies*, 5 (1979) pp. 41–65.

Daunton, Martin, 'Rows and Tenements: American Cities, 1880–1914', in M. Daunton (ed.), *Housing the Workers* (Leicester University Press, 1990).

Davidoff, Leonore, 'The Family in Britain', in F. M. L. Thompson (ed.), *The Cambridge Social History of Britain, 1750–1950* (Cambridge University Press, 1990).

Davidoff, Leonore, 'The Separation of Home and Work? Landladies and Lodgers in Nineteenth- and Twentieth-Century England', in S. Burman (ed.), *Fit Work for Women* (London: Croom Helm, 1979).

Davidoff, Leonore and Catherine Hall, *Family Fortunes, Men and Women of the English Middle Class, 1780–1850* (London: Hutchinson Educational, 1987).

Davies, K. M., 'Continuity and Change in Literary Advice on Marriage', in R. B. Outhwaite (ed.), *Marriage and Society: Studies in the Social History of Marriage* (London: Europa Publications, 1981).

Davies, Margaret Llewellyn (ed.), *Maternity Letters from Working Women* (1915; London: Virago edition, 1978).

Davis, Natalie Zemon, 'City Women and Religious Change', in N. Z. Davis (ed.), *Society and Culture in Early Modern France* (Stanford, California: Stanford University Press, 1975).

Davis, Natalie Zemon, *Fiction in the Archives, Pardon Tales and their Tellers in Sixteenth-Century France* (Oxford University Press, 1987).

Davis, Natalie Zemon, *The Return of Martin Guerre* (Harmondsworth: Penguin, 1985).

Dayuss, Kathleen, *Her People* (London: Virago, 1982).

De Mause, L., *The History of Childhood: The Evolution of Parent–Child Relationships as a Factor in History* (London: Souvenir Press, 1976).

Defoe, Daniel, *A Tour Through the Whole Island of Great Britain* (London: Everyman, 1962) 2 volumes.

DeForest, R. W. and L. Veiller (eds), *The Tenement House Problem* (New York, 1903) 2 vols.

Degler, Carl, *At Odds: Women and the Family in America: From the Revolution to the Present* (Oxford and New York, 1980).

Delamont, Sara and Lorna Duffin (eds), *The Nineteenth Century Woman. The Cultural and Physical World* (London: Croom Helm, 1978).

Delaselle, Claude, 'Les Enfants abandonnées à Paris au XVIIIe siècle', *Annales, ESC* (1975).

Demolins, Edmond, 'Les Habitations ouvrières', in *La Réforme Sociale*, vol. I (1881).

Demos, John, *A Little Commonwealth: Family Life in Plymouth Colony* (New York, 1970).

Depauw, Jacques, 'Illicit Sexual Activity and Society in Eighteenth-Century Nantes', in Robert Forster and Orest Ranum (eds), *Family and Society*.

Selections from the Annales, ESC (Baltimore and London: Johns Hopkins University Press, 1976).

Dickens, A. G. (ed.), 'The Clifford Letters', *Surtees Society*, **172** (1957).

Dod, John and Robert Cleaver, *A Godlie Forme of Household Government* (London, 1598).

DuBois, W. E. Burghardt, *The Negro American Family* (Atlanta, 1908).

Dunn, Richard S., 'Servants and Slaves: the Recruitment and Employment of Labour', in Jack P. Greene and J. R. Pole (eds), *Colonial British America* (Baltimore and London: Johns Hopkins University Press, 1991 reprint).

Dupaquier, J. et al. (eds), *Marriage and Remarriage in Populations of the Past* (London: Academic Press, 1981).

Durston, Christopher, *The Family in the English Revolution* (Oxford: Basil Blackwell, 1989).

'Dwellings and Families in 1890', Extra Census Bulletin, no. 19, *US Census* (1890).

Dyhouse, Carol, *Girls Growing Up in Victorian and Edwardian England* (London: RKP, 1981).

Earle, Peter, 'The Female Labour Market in London in the Late Seventeenth and Early Eighteenth Centuries', *Economic History Review*, 2nd series, XLII (1989).

Earle, Peter, *The Making of the English Middle Class: Business, Society and Family Life in London, 1660–1730* (London: Methuen, 1989).

Early, Francis, 'The French-Canadian Family Economy and Standard-of-Living in Lowell, Massachusetts, 1870', *Journal of Family History*, **16** (1982).

Eliot, John, *The Harmony of the Gospels* (Boston, Massachusetts, 1678).

Elkins, Stanley M., *Slavery: A Problem in American Institutional and Intellectual Life* (Chicago, 1959).

Elliott, Vivien Brodsky, 'Single Women in the London Marriage Market: Age, Status and Mobility, 1598–1619', in R. B. Outhwaite (ed.), *Marriage and Society: Studies in the Social History of Marriage* (London: Europa Publications, 1981).

Engels, F., *The Condition of the Working Class in England in 1844* (London: Allen & Unwin, 1952).

Engerman, Stanley L., 'Studying the Black Family', *Journal of Family History*, **3** (1978).

Englander, David, Diana Norman, Rosemary O'Day and W. R. Owens (eds), *Culture and Belief in Europe, 1450–1600* (Oxford: Basil Blackwell, 1990).

Englander, David, *Landlord and Tenant in Urban Britain* (Oxford University Press, 1983).

Englander, David, 'Stille Huppah (Quiet Marriage) among Jewish Immigrants in Britain', *The Jewish Journal of Sociology*, XXXIV (1992).

Erickson, Amy Louise, 'Common Law Versus Common Practice: the Use of Marriage Settlements in Early Modern England', *Economic History Review*, 2nd series, XLIII (1990).

Ernst, Robert, *Immigrant Life in New York City, 1825–1863* (New York, 1949).

Eyre, Adam, 'A Dyurnall or Catalogue of all my accons and expences', *Yorkshire Diaries and Autobiographies* (Surtees Society, **65**, 1875).

Ezell, Margaret J. M., *The Patriarch's Wife: Literary Evidence and the History of the Family* (Chapel Hill and London: University of North Carolina Press, 1987).

Fairchilds, Cissie, *Domestic Enemies. Servants and their Masters in Old Regime France* (Baltimore and London: Johns Hopkins University Press, 1984).

Fairfax, Sally, 'Diary of a Little Colonial Girl', *The Virginia Magazine of History and Biography*, **11** (1904).

Fildes, Valerie, *Women as Mothers in Preindustrial England* (London: Routledge, 1990).

Fildes, Valerie, 'Maternal Feelings Re-assessed: Child Abandonment and Neglect in London and Westminster, 1550–1800', in V. Fildes (ed.), *Women as Mothers in Preindustrial England* (London: Routledge, 1990).

Fildes, Valerie, *Breasts, Bottles and Babies* (Edinburgh, 1986).

Filmer, Robert, 'In Praise of the Vertuous Wife' (c. 1643) printed in Ezell, *The Patriarch's Wife*, above.

Flandrin, Jean-Louis, *Families in Former Times: Kinship, Household and Sexuality* (Cambridge University Press, 1979).

Flandrin, Jean-Louis, *Les Amours Paysannes* (Paris, 1975).

Fogel, Robert W. and Stanley L. Engermann, *Time on the Cross* (1974).

Forbes, Harriette (ed.), *The Diary of Rev. Ebenezer Parkman* (Massachusetts: The Westborough Historical Society, 1899).

Forster, Robert and Orest Ranum (eds), *Family and Society. Selections from the Annales, ESC* (Baltimore and London: Johns Hopkins University Press, 1976).

Fox Genovese, Elizabeth, *Within the Plantation Household* (Chapel Hill and London: University of North Carolina Press, 1988).

Frame, Donald M. (ed.), *The Complete Works of Michel de Montaigne* (Stanford, California: Stanford University Press, 1958).

Frazier, E. Franklin, *The Negro Family in the United States* (Chicago, 1939).

Furnivall, F. J. (ed.), *Philip Stubbes' Anatomy of the Abuses in England in Shakespeare's Youth, AD 1583* (New Shakespeare Society, 6th series, vols 6 and 12, 1877–82).

Furnivall, F. J. (ed.), *Child Marriages, Divorces and Ratifications … in the Diocese of Chester* (Early English Text Society, 1897).

Gampel, G., 'The Planter's Wife Revisited: Equity Law and the Chancery Court in Seventeenth-Century Maryland', in B. J. Harris and J. K. McNamara (eds), *Women and the Structure of Society* (Durham, N. C.: Duke University Press, 1984).

Gandy, Ida, *Round About the Little Steeple: The Story of a Wiltshire Parson, 1573–1623* (Stroud: Alan Sutton, 1989).

Garrioch, David, *Neighbourhood and Community in Paris, 1740–1790* (Cambridge University Press, 1986).

Gataker, T., *A Good Wife God's Gift. A Marriage Sermon on Proverbs 19.14* (London, 1620).

Gelis, J., et al. (eds), *Entrer dans la vie: Naissances et enfances dans la France Traditionelle* (Paris, 1978).

Genovese, Eugene D., *Roll Jordan, Roll: The World the Slaves Made* (New York: Pantheon Books, 1974).

George, C. H. and K., *The Protestant Mind of the English Reformation, 1570–1640* (Princeton, New Jersey: Princeton University Press, 1961).

Gibson, Wendy, *Women in Seventeenth-Century France* (London: Macmillan, 1989).

Glanz, L. M., 'The Legal Position of English Women under the Early Stuart Kings and the Interregnum, 1603–1660', unpublished Ph.D. thesis, Loyola University, 1973.

Glass, D. V., 'Two Papers on Gregory King', in D. V. Glass and D. E. C. Eversley (eds), *Population in History: Essays in Historical Demography* (London: Edward Arnold, 1965).

Glass, D. V. and D. E. C. Eversley (eds), *Population in History: Essays in Historical Demography* (London: Edward Arnold, 1965).

Goldberg, P. J. P. (ed.), *Woman is a Worthy Wight. Women in English Society c. 1200–1500* (Stroud: Alan Sutton, 1992).

Gottlieb, Beatrice, *The Family in the Western World* (New York and Oxford: Oxford University Press, 1993).

Goody, Jack, *The Development of the Family and Marriage in Europe* (Cambridge University Press, 1983).

Goody, J., J. Thirsk and E. P. Thompson (eds), *Family and Inheritance: Rural Society in Western Europe, 1200–1800* (Cambridge University Press, 1976).

Goubert, Pierre, *The French Peasantry in the Seventeenth Century* (Cambridge University Press, 1986).

Gouesse, Jean-Marie, 'Parente, famille et mariage en Normandie aux XVIIIᵉ et XVIIIᵉ siècles', *Annales, ESC*, **27** (1972).

Gouge, William, *Of Domesticall Duties* (London, 1622).

Gould, E. R. L., *The Housing of the Working People*, Eighth Special Report of the Commissioner of Labor, Washington, DC, 1895.

Gould, E. R. L., 'The Housing Problem in Great Cities', *Quarterly Journal of Economics*, **14** (1899–1900).

Gould, E. R. L., 'Homewood – A Model Suburban Settlement', *Review of Reviews*, XVI (1897).

Greene, Jack P. and J. R. Pole (eds), *Colonial British America* (Baltimore and London: Johns Hopkins University Press, 1991 reprint).

Greven, Philip, 'The Average Size of Families and Households in the Province of Massachusetts in 1764 and the United States in 1790: An Overview', in P. Laslett and R. Wall (eds), *Household and Family in Past Time* (Cambridge University Press, 1972).

Greven, Philip J. Jr, 'Family Structure in Seventeenth-Century Andover, Massachusetts', *William and Mary Quarterly*, 3rd series, **23** (1966). This is reprinted in Maris A. Vinovskis (ed.), *Studies in America – Historical Demography* (New York, 1979).

Greven, Philip J. Jr, *Four Generations: Population, Land and Family in Colonial Andover, Massachusetts* (Ithaca: Cornell University Press, 1970).

Griffin, Richard, Lord Braybrooke (ed.), *The Private Correspondence of Jane Lady Cornwallis, 1613–44 ...* (London, 1842).

Gullman, James M., 'Determinants of Age at Marriage in Colonial Perquimans County, North Carolina', *William and Mary Quarterly*, XXXIX (1982).

Gutman, Herbert G., *The Black Family in Slavery and Freedom, 1750–1925* (New York, 1976).

Hajnal, J., 'European Marriage Patterns in Perspective', in D. V. Glass and D. E. C. Eversley (eds), *Population in History: Essays in Historical Demography* (London: Edward Arnold, 1965).

Hall, Catherine, 'The Early Formation of Victorian Domestic Ideology', in S. Burman (ed.), *Fit Work for Women* (London: Croom Helm, 1979).

J. O. Halliwell (ed.), *The Autobiography and Correspondence of Sir Simonds D'Ewes* (London, 1845).

Handlin, Oscar, *Boston's Immigrants, 1790–1880* (1941; New York: Atheneum, references from 1970 revised and enlarged edition).

Hanley, Sarah, 'Engendering the State: Family Formation and State Building in Early Modern France', *French Historical Studies*, 16 (1989).

Hardwicke, Julia, 'Widowhood and Patriarchy in Seventeenth-Century France', *Journal of Social History*, 26 (1992).

Hardy, Sheila, *The Diary of a Suffolk Farmer's Wife, 1854–69* (London: Macmillan, 1992).

Hareven, Tamara, 'The Family Life Cycle in Historical Perspective: A Proposal for a Developmental Approach', in Cuisenier, J. and M. Segalen (eds), *Le Cycle de la vie familiale dans les sociétés europpéennes* (The Hague, 1977).

Hareven, T. and M. Vinovskis (eds), *Family and Population*.

Hartmann, Edward G., *The Movement to Americanize the Immigrant* (New York, 1948).

Henretta, James A., 'Wealth and Social Structure', in Jack P. Greene and J. R. Pole (eds), *Colonial British America* (Baltimore and London: Johns Hopkins University Press, 1991 reprint).

Henretta, James A., 'Families and Farms: Mentalités in Preindustrial America', *William and Mary Quarterly*, XXXV (1978).

Herlihy, David, *Medieval Households* (Cambridge, Mass.: Harvard University Press, 1985).

Hey, David G., *An English Rural Community: Myddle under the Tudors and Stuarts* (Leicester University Press, 1974).

Hey, David (ed.), *Richard Gough, The History of Myddle* (Harmondsworth: Penguin, 1981).

Heywood, Thomas (ed.), *The Diary of Rev. Henry Newcome* (Chetham Society, 18, 1849).

Hill, Octavia, *Homes of the London Poor* (London, 1875).

Holderness, B. A., *Pre-Industrial England* (London: Dent, 1976).

Holden, M., *The Woman's Almanack for the Year … 1688* (London, 1688).

Hollingsworth, Mary F. and T. H., 'Plague Mortality Rates by Age and Sex', *Population Studies*, XXV (1971).

Hollingsworth, T. H., *Historical Demography* (1969).

Hollingsworth, T. H., 'A Demographic Study of the British Ducal Families', *Population Studies*, II (1957) reprinted in D. V. Glass and D. E. C. Eversley (eds), *Population in History: Essays in Historical Demography* (London: Edward Arnold, 1965).

Hollingsworth, T. H., 'The Demography of the British Peerage', supplement to *Population Studies*, **18** (1964).

Holt, Max P., 'Patterns of Clientele and Economic Opportunity at Court During the Wars of Religion; The Household of François, Duke of Anjou', *French Historical Studies*, **13** (1984).

Holt, Hamilton (ed.), *The Life Stories of [Undistinguished] Americans as Told by Themselves* (New York and London, 1990).

Homans, G. C., *English Villagers of the Thirteenth-Century* (Cambridge, Mass, 1940).

Honan, Park, *Jane Austen, Her Life* (New York, 1987).

Horn, James, 'Servant Emigration to the Chesapeake in the Seventeenth Century', in Thad W. Tate and David L. Ammerman (eds), *The Chesapeake in the Seventeenth Century: Essays on Anglo-American Society* (Chapel Hill: University of North Carolina Press, 1979).

Houlbrooke, Ralph A., *The English Family, 1450–1700* (London: Longman, 1984).

Howe, Irving, *The Immigrant Jews of New York* (London: Littman Library of Jewish Civilization, RKP, 1976).

Howell, Cicely, *Land, Family and Inheritance in Transition: Kibworth Harcourt, 1280–1700* (Cambridge University Press, 1983).

Hufton, Olwen, 'Women and the Family Economy in Eighteenth-Century France', *French Historical Studies*, **9** (1975).

Hugo, Abel, *La France pittoresque* (Paris, 1835).

Hunt, David, *Parents and Children in History: The Psychology of Family Life in Early Modern France* (New York, 1970).

Huntington, J. O. S., 'Tenement-House Morality', *Forum*, III (1887).

Hurstfield, Joel, *The Queen's Wards, Wardship and Marriage under Elizabeth I* (London: Jonathan Cape, 1973, 2nd edition).

Ingram, Martin, *Church Courts, Sex and Marriage in England, 1570–1640* (Cambridge University Press, 1987).

Ingram, Martin, 'Spousals Litigation in the English Ecclesiastical Courts, c. 1350–c. 1640', in R. B. Outhwaite (ed.), *Marriage and Society* (London: Europa Publications, 1981).

Isaac, Rhys, *The Transformation of Virginia* (Chapel Hill, 1982).

Jackson, C. (ed.), *The Autobiography of Mrs Alice Thornton, of East Newton, Co. York* (Surtees Society, LXII, 1873).

James, Mervyn, *Family, Lineage and Civil Society* (Oxford: Clarendon Press, 1974).

Jones, Gareth Stedman, *Outcast London* (Oxford University Press, 1971).

Jordan, David W., 'Political Stability and the Emergence of a Native Elite in Maryland', in Thad W. Tate and David L. Ammerman (eds), *The Chesapeake in the Seventeenth-Century: Essays on Anglo-American Society* (Chapel Hill: University of North Carolina Press, 1979).

Jordan, William Chester, *Women and Credit in Pre-industrial and Developing Societies* (Philadelphia: University of Pennsylvania Press, 1993).

Joyce, Patrick, *Work, Society and Politics* (London: Methuen, paperback edition, 1982).

Katz, Michael, Michael Doucet and Mark Stern, *The Social Organization of Industrial Capitalism* (Cambridge, Mass.: Harvard University Press, 1982).

Katz, Michael and Mark Stern, 'Fertility, Class and Industrial Capitalism: Erie County, New York, 1855–1915', *American Quarterly*, **33** (1981).

Katzman, David M., *Seven Days a Week: Women and Domestic Service in Industrializing America* (New York, 1978).

Kay, Richard, *The Diary of Richard Kay* (Manchester: Chetham Society, 1968).

Kettering, Sharon, 'The Patronage Power of Early Modern French Noblewomen', *Historical Journal*, **32** (1989).

Kettering, Sharon, 'Friendship and Clientage in Early Modern France', *French History*, **6** (1992).

Kordi, Mohammed El, *Bayeux au XVIIe et XVIIIe siècles* (Paris, 1970).

Kulikoff, Allan, *Tobacco and Slaves: The Development of Southern Cultures in the Chesapeake, 1689–1800* (Chapel Hill: University of North Carolina Press, 1986).

Kulikoff, Allan, 'A Prolifick People: Black Population Growth in the Chesapeake Colonies, 1700–1790', *Southern Studies*, XVI (1977).

Kussmaul, A., *Servants in Husbandry in Early Modern England* (Cambridge University Press, 1981).

Ladurie, Emmanuel Le Roy, *Love Death and Money in the Pays D'Oc* (Harmondsworth: Penguin Books, 1984).

Ladurie, Emmanuel Le Roy, 'A System of Customary Law: Family Structures and Inheritance Customs in Sixteenth-Century France', in Robert Forster and Orest Ranum (eds), *Family and Society. Selections from the Annales, ESC* (Baltimore and London: Johns Hopkins University Press, 1976).

Lafon, Jacques, *Les Epoux Bordelais, 1450–1550* (Paris, 1952).

Lancre, Pierre de, *Tableau de l'inconstance des mauvais anges* (1612) cited in Soulet, Jean-François, *La Vie quotidienne dans les Pyrénées, sous l'ancien régime du XVIe au XVIIIe siècles* (Paris, 1974).

Lapaire, Hughes, *Le Berry vu par un Berrichon* (Paris, 1928).

Larminie, Vivienne (ed.), *The Undergraduate Account Book of John and Richard Newdigate, 1618–1621* (Camden Miscellany, XXX, 1990).

Laslett, B., 'The Family as a Public and Private Institution: an Historical Perspective', *Journal of Marriage and the Family*, **35** (1973).

Laslett, Peter, *The World We Have Lost* (London: Methuen, 1965, 2nd edition 1971).

Laslett, Peter, *The World We Have Lost Further Explored* (London: Methuen, 1983).

Laslett, Peter, *Family Life and Illicit Love in Earlier Generations: Essays in Historical Sociology* (Cambridge University Press, 1977).

Laslett, Peter, 'Parental Deprivation in the Past', in Peter Laslett, *Family Life and Illicit Love in Earlier Generations: Essays in Historical Sociology* (Cambridge University Press, 1977).

Laslett, Peter and Richard Wall (eds), *Household and Family in Past Time* (Cambridge University Press, 1972).

Laslett, Peter, 'Mean Household Size in England since the Sixteenth Century', in P. Laslett and R. Wall (eds), *Household and Family in Past Time* (Cambridge University Press, 1972).

Latham, R. and W. Matthews (eds), *The Diary of Samuel Pepys* (London: Bell & Hyman, 1970).

Latimer, Hugh, see G. E. Corrie, above.

Lawson, Deodat, *The Duty and Property of a Religious Householder* (Boston, Massachusetts, 1693).

Lebrun, François, *La Vie conjugale sous l'ancien régime* (Paris, 1975).

Lees, Lynn H., 'Patterns of Lower-Class Life: Irish Slum Communities in Nineteenth-Century London', in Stephan Thernstrom and Richard Sennet (eds), *Nineteenth-Century Cities: Essays in the New Urban History* (New Haven, Conn.: Yale University Press, 1969).

Lemon, James T., 'Spatial Order: Households in Local Communities and Regions', in Jack P. Greene and J. R. Pole (eds), *Colonial British America* (Baltimore and London: Johns Hopkins University Press, 1991 reprint).

Le Play, Frédéric, *La Réforme sociale* (1872).

Le Play, Frédéric, *Les Ouvriers européens* (Paris, 1855).

Levine, David, *Family Formation in an Age of Nascent Capitalism* (London: Academic Press, 1977).

Levine, David, *Reproducing Families* (Cambridge University Press, 1987).

Levy, Barry, *Quakers and the American Family: British Settlement in the Delaware Valley* (New York, 1988).

Lewis, Jane (ed.), *Labour and Love. Women's Experience of Home and Family, 1850–1940* (Oxford and New York: Basil Blackwell, 1986).

Lewis, R. A., *Edwin Chadwick and the Public Health Movement* (London: Longman, 1952).

Liberal Land Enquiry, *Report of the Liberal Land Enquiry* (1914) 2 vols.

Lockridge, Kenneth A., *A New England Town: The First Hundred Years, Dedham, Massachusetts, 1636–1736* (New York, 1970).

Lowndes, G. A., 'The History of the Barrington Family', *Transactions of the Essex Archaeological Society*, 1, New Series (1878).

Lubove, Roy, *The Progressives and the Slums: Tenement House Reform in New York City, 1890–1917* (University of Pittsburgh Press, 1962).

Macfarlane, Alan (ed.), *The Diary of Ralph Josselin* (London: Oxford University Press for The British Academy, 1976).

Macfarlane, Alan, *Marriage and Love in England, 1300–1840* (Oxford: Basil Blackwell, 1986).

Macfarlane, Alan, *The Family Life of Ralph Josselin: A Seventeenth-Century Clergyman: An Essay in Historical Anthropology* (Cambridge University Press, 1970).

Macfarlane, Alan, *The Origins of English Individualism: The Family, Property and Social Transition* (Oxford: Basil Blackwell, 1978).

Maillard, C., *Le Bon mariage* (Douai, 1643).

Marshall, J. D. (ed.), *The Autobiography of William Stout of Lancaster, 1665–1752* (Manchester: Chetham Society, 1967).

Mather, Cotton, *Diary* (Massachusetts Historical Society Collections, 7th series, 1911 and 1912).

Mather, Increase, *Diary* (Massachusetts Historical Society Proceedings, 2nd series, 1899).

Matthews, William, *American Diaries* (Berkeley and Los Angeles: University of California Press, 1945).

Matthews, William, *British Diaries* (London: Cambridge University Press, 1950).

Matthews, William, *American Diaries in Manuscript* (Athens: University of Georgia Press, 1974).

Mayhew, Henry, *London Labour and the London Poor, 1861–1862* (New York: Dover Publications, 1968) 4 vols.

Maza, Sarah C., *Servants and Masters in Eighteenth-Century France. The Uses of Loyalty* (Princeton, New Jersey: Princeton University Press, 1983).

McLaren, Angus, *Reproductive Rituals* (London and New York: Methuen, 1984).

Meacham, Standish, *Toynbee Hall and Social Reform, 1880–1914: The Search for Community* (New Haven: Yale University Press, 1987).

Meads, Dorothy M. (ed.), *The Diary of Lady Margaret Hoby, 1599–1605* (1930).

Medick, Hans, 'The Proto-Industrial Family Economy: the Structural Function of Household and Family during the Transition from Peasant Society to Industrial Capitalism', *Social History*, 3 (1976).

Mendelson, Sarah Heller, 'Stuart Women's Diaries and Occasional Memoirs', in M. Prior (ed.), *Women in English Society, 1500–1800* (London: Methuen, 1985).

Menefee, Samuel Pyeatt, *Wives for Sale* (Oxford: Basil Blackwell, 1981).

Merle, Louis, *La Métairie et l'évolution agraire de la Gâtine poitevine, de la fin du Moyen Age a la Révolution* (Paris, 1958).

Middleton, Richard, *Colonial America: A History 1607–1760* (Oxford: Basil Blackwell, 1992).

Mildmay, Grace, 'The Journal of Lady Mildmay', *Quarterly Review* (1911).

Minard, Russell, 'British Migration to the Chesapeake Colonies', in Lois Green et al. (eds), *Colonial Chesapeake Society* (Chapel Hill: University of North Carolina Press, 1988).

Misson, Henri, *Memoirs and Observations in his Travels over England*, 1719 translation from the French (London, 1719).

Mitson, Anne, 'The Significance of Kinship Networks in the Seventeenth Century: South-West Nottinghamshire', in C. Phythian Adams (ed.), *Societies, Culture and Kinship, 1580–1850* (Leicester University Press, 1993).

Mitterauer, Michael and Reinhard Seider, *The European Family: Patriarchy to Partnership from the Middle Ages to the Present* (Oxford: Basil Blackwell, 1982).

Morehouse, H. J. (ed.), *A Dyurnall ... [Adam Eyre]* (Surtees Society, Yorkshire Diaries, LXV, 1875, published 1877).

Morgan, Edmund S., *The Puritan Family* (revised edition, New York, 1966).

Morgan, Philip D. and Michael L. Nicholls, 'Slaves in Piedmont Virginia, 1700–1790', *William and Mary Quarterly*, XLVI (1900).

Mount, F., *The Subversive Family: An Alternative History of Love and Marriage* (London: Jonathan Cape, 1982).

Mowman, J. M. (ed.), *Letters of Lady Rachel Russell* ... (London: 1820).

Newall, Fiona, 'Wet Nursing and Child Care in Aldenham, Hertfordshire, 1595–1726', in Valerie Fildes (ed.), *Women as Mothers in Preindustrial England* (London: Routledge, 1993).

Lady Newdigate-Newdegate (ed.), *Gossip from a Muniment Room, being Passages in the Lives of Anne and Mary Fitton, 1574 to 1618* (2nd edition, London, 1898).

Nicholson, Shirley, *A Victorian Household, Based on the Diaries of Marion Sambourne* (London: Barrie & Jenkins, 1988).

Norton, Mary Beth, 'Gender and Defamation in Seventeenth-Century Maryland', *William and Mary Quarterly*, 3rd series, **44** (1987).

Norton, Mary Beth, *Liberty's Daughters: The Revolutionary Experience of American Women, 1750–1800* (Boston, Mass., 1980).

Norton, Susan L., 'Marital Migration in Essex County, Massachusetts, in the Colonial and Early Federal Periods', *Journal of Marriage and the Family*, **35** (1973). This is reprinted in Maris A. Vinovskis (ed.), *Studies in American Historical Demography* (New York, 1979).

O'Day, Rosemary, 'Before the Webbs: Beatrice Potter's Early Investigations for Charles Booth's Inquiry', *History*, **78** (1993).

O'Day, Rosemary, *Education and Society in Britain, 1500–1800* (London: Longman, 1982).

O'Day, Rosemary, 'Hugh Latimer: Prophet of the Kingdom', *Historical Research*, **65** (1992).

O'Day, Rosemary, 'Katharine Buildings', in R. Finnegan and M. Drake (eds), *Studying Family and Community History: From Family Tree to Family History*, vol. I (Cambridge University Press, 1994).

O'Day, Rosemary, *The English Clergy. The Emergence and Consolidation of a Profession, 1558–1642* (Leicester University Press, 1979).

O'Day, Rosemary and David Englander, *Mr Charles Booth's Inquiry: Life and Labour of the People in London Reconsidered* (London: Hambledon Press, 1993).

O'Day, R. and J. Berlatsky, *The Letter Book of Thomas Bentham* ... (Camden Miscellany, XXVII, 1979).

Outhwaite, R. B., 'Age at Marriage in England from the Late Seventeenth to the Nineteenth Century', *Transactions of the Royal Historical Society*, 5th series, **23** (1973).

Outhwaite, R. B. (ed.), *Marriage and Society: Studies in the Social History of Marriage* (London: Europa Publications, 1981).

Outhwaite, R. B., 'Marriage as Business', in N. McKendrick and R. B. Outhwaite (eds), *Business Life and Public Policy* (Cambridge University Press, 1986).

Ozment, Steven, *When Fathers Ruled: Family Life in Reformation Europe* (Cambridge, Mass.; Harvard University Press 1983).

Pardailhé-Galabrun, Annik, *The Birth of Intimacy: Privacy and Domestic Life in Early Modern Paris* (Oxford: Polity Press, 1991).

Paris, C. B., *Marriage in Seventeenth-Century Catholicism* (Paris, 1975).

Park, Robert E. and Herbert A. Miller, *Old World Traits Transplanted* (New York, 1921).

Parkinson, Richard (ed.), *The Life of Adam Martindale* (Manchester: Chetham Society, 1845).

Parkinson, Richard (ed.), *The Autobiography of Henry Newcome* (Manchester: Chetham Society, 1852).

Parsons, Elsie Clews, *The Family* (New York, 1906).

Peyronnet, J.–C., 'Famille élargie ou famille nucléaire? En Limousin au début du XIXe siècle', *Revue d'histoire moderne et contemporaine* (1975).

Phillips, Roderick, *Family Breakdown in Late Eighteenth-Century France: Divorces in Rouen, 1792–1893* (Oxford University Press, 1980).

Pillorget, R., *La Tige et le rameau: Familles Anglaises et Françaises XVIe–XVIIIe siècle* (Paris, 1991).

Pinchbeck, I. and M. Hewitt, *Children in English Society* (London: RKP, 1969) 2 vols.

Pollock, F. and F. W. Maitland, *The History of English Law before the Time of Edward I*, a reprint of the second edition of 1898 (Cambridge University Press, 1968).

Pollock, Linda, *Forgotten Children, Parent–Child Relations from 1500 to 1900* (Cambridge University Press, 1983).

Pollock, Linda, *A Lasting Relationship* (London: Fourth Estate, 1987).

Pollock, Linda, 'Embarking on a Rough Passage: the Experience of Pregnancy in Early Modern Society', in Valerie Fildes (ed.), *Women as Mothers in Preindustrial England* (London: Routledge, 1990).

Pollock, Linda, *With Faith and Physic: The Life of a Tudor Gentlewoman, Lady Grace Mildway, 1552–1600* (London, 1993).

Potter, Jim, 'Demographic Development and Family Structure', in Jack P. Greene and J. R. Pole (eds), *Colonial British America* (Baltimore and London: Johns Hopkins University Press, 1991 reprint).

Prior, Mary, 'Women and the Urban Economy: Oxford, 1500–1800', in M. Prior (ed.), *Women in English Society* (London: Methuen, 1985).

Prior, Mary, (ed.), *Women in English Society, 1500–1800* (London: Methuen, 1985).

Prior, Mary, 'Conjugal Love and the Flight from Marriage: Poetry as a Source for the History of Women and the Family', in Valerie Fildes (ed.), *Women as Mothers in Preindustrial England* (London: Routledge, 1990).

Privy Council, *Eighth Report of the Medical Officer of the Privy Council, 1865, Appendix no. 2, Report on Housing of the Poor in Towns* (1865).

Pryor, E. T., Jr, 'Rhode Island Family Structure: 1875 and 1960', in P. Laslett and R. Wall (eds), *Household and Family in Past Time* (Cambridge University Press, 1972).

Ransome, David R., 'Wives for Virginia, 1621', *William and Mary Quarterly*, XLVIII (1991).

Razi, Z., 'Family, Land and the Village Community in Later Medieval England', *Past and Present*, **93** (1981).

Razi, Z., *Life, Marriage and Death in a Mediaeval Parish: Economy, Society and Demography in Halesowen 1270–1400* (Cambridge University Press, 1980).

Rétif de la Bretonne, *La Vie de Mon Père* (Paris, 1794).

Rétif de la Bretonne, *Monsieur Nicolas* (Paris, 1883) 14 volumes.

Riis, Jacob A., *How the Other Half Lives: Studies Among the Tenements of New York* (New York: Sagamore Press, reprint, 1957).

Riis, Jacob A., *The Peril and Preservation of the Home* (Philadelphia, 1903).

Riis, Jacob A., 'What Settlements Stand For', *Outlook*, LXXXIX (1908) pp. 69–72.

Roberts, Elizabeth, *A Woman's Place. An Oral History of Working Class Women 1890–1914* (Oxford and New York, 1914).

Roper, Lindal, 'Luther: Sex, Marriage and Motherhood', *History Today*, December 1983.

Rose, Mary Beth (ed.), *Women in the Middle Ages and the Renaissance* (Syracuse, 1986).

Ross, Ellen, 'Fierce Questions and Taunts: Married Life in Working-Class London 1870–1914', *Feminist Studies*, VIII (1982).

Ross, Ellen, *In Time of Trouble: Motherhood and Survival among the London Poor* (Oxford University Press, forthcoming).

Rouger, G. (ed.), *Rétif de la Bretonne, De la vie de mon père* (Paris, 1970).

Ruggles, Steven, *Prolonged Connections: The Rise of the Extended Family in Nineteenth-Century England and America* (Maddison: University of Wisconsin Press, Social Demgraphy Series, 1987).

Rule, John, *The Experience of Labour in Eighteenth-Century Industry* (London: Croom Helm, 1981).

Rutman, Darrett B. and Anita H., ' "Now-Wives and Sons-in-Law": Parental Death in a Seventeenth-Century Virginia County', in Thad W. Tate and David L. Ammerman (eds), *The Chesapeake in the Seventeenth Century: Essays on Anglo-American Society* (Chapel Hill, 1979).

Saunders, H. W. (ed.), *The Official Papers of Sir Nathaniel Bacon ... J. P. 1580–1620* (Camden Third Series, XXVI, 1915).

Schochet, Gordon J., *Patriarchalism in Political Thought* (New York, 1975).

Schnucker, Robert V., 'Puritan Attitudes towards Childhood Discipline, 1560–1634', in Valerie Fildes (ed.), *Women as Mothers in Preindustrial England* (London: Routledge, 1990).

Scholten, Catherine M., *Childbearing in American Society, 1650 to 1850* (New York, 1985).

Scott, J. W. and L. A. Tilly, 'Women's Work and the Family in Ninteenth-Century Europe', in *Comparative Studies in Society and History*, **17** (1975).

Searle, Arthur (ed.), *Barrington Family Letters 1628–1632* (Camden Fourth Series, **28**, 1983).

Select Committee of the House of Commons on Public Petitions (1865), App. 274, no. 3848 (1865).

Seaver, P., *Wallington's World: A Puritan Artisan in Seventeenth-Century London* (Stanford, Cal., 1985).

Segalen, Martine, 'The Family Cycle and Household Structure: Five Generations in a French Village', in R. Wheaton and T. Hareven (eds), *Family and Sexuality in French History* (Philadelphia, 1980).

Segalen, Martine, *Love and Power in the Peasant Family* (Oxford: Basil Blackwell, 1983).

Sennett, Richard, *Families Against the City: Middle Class Homes of Industrial Chicago, 1872–90* (Cambridge, Mass., 1970).

Sewall, Samuel, *Diary* (Massachusetts Historical Society Collections, 1892).

Shammas, Carole, 'English-born and Creole Elites in Turn-of-the-Century Virginia', in Thad W. Tate and David L. Ammerman (eds), *The Chesapeake in the Seventeenth Century: Essays on Anglo-American Society* (Chapel Hill, 1979).

Shammas, Carole, 'The Domestic Environment in Early Modern England and America', *Journal of Social History*, **14** (1980) pp. 1–24.

Shapiro, Anne-Louise, 'Paris', in M. J. Daunton (ed.), *Housing the Workers* (Leicester University Press, 1990).

Sharpe, J. A., *Defamation and Sexual Slander in Early Modern England* (Borthwick Institute, University of York, Borthwick Paper, **58**, 1980).

Shorter, Edward, *The Making of the Modern Family* (London: Collins, 1976).

Skeat, W. W. (ed.), *A. [J.] Fitzherbert, The Book of Husbandry, 1534* (English Dialect Society, **13**, 1882).

Slater, Miriam, *Family Life in the Seventeenth Century. The Verneys of Claydon House* (London: RKP, 1984).

Smelser, Neil J., *Social Change in the Industrial Revolution* (1959).

Smith, Daniel Scott, 'Parental Control and Marriage Patterns: An Analysis of Historical Trends in Higham, Massachusetts', *Journal of Marriage and the Family*, **35** (1973).

Smith, David Blake, *Inside the Great House: Planter Family Life in Eighteenth-Century Chesapeake Society* (Ithaca: Cornell University Press, 1980).

Smith, R. M., 'Kin and Neighbors in a Thirteenth-Century Suffolk Community', *Journal of Family History*, **4** (1979).

Smith, S. R., 'Growing Old in Early Stuart England', *Albion*, **8** (1976).

Smith, S. R., 'London Apprentices as Seventeenth-Century Adolescents', *Past and Present*, **61** (1973).

Soulet, Jean-François, *La Vie quotidienne dans les Pyrénées, sous l'ancien régime du XVIe au XVIIIe siècles* (Paris, 1974).

Spufford, Margaret, *Contrasting Communities: English Villagers in the Sixteenth and Seventeenth Centuries* (Cambridge University Press, 1974).

Stampp, Kenneth M., *The Peculiar Institution* (New York, 1956).

Stearns, Peter N., 'Old Women: Historical Observations', *Journal of Family History*, **5** (1980).

Stearns, Peter N., 'The Middle Class: Towards a Precise Definition', *Comparative Studies in Society and History*, **21** (1979).

Steckel, Richard H., 'Slave Marriage and the Family', *Journal of Family History*, **5** (1980).

Stone, Lawrence, *The Family, Sex and Marriage in England 1500–1800* (London: Weidenfeld & Nicholson, 1977).

Stone, Lawrence, *The Crisis of the Aristocracy, 1558–1641* (Oxford: Clarendon Press, 1965). (An abridged paperback edition appeared under the same imprint in 1967).

Stone, Lawrence and Jeanne Fawtier Stone, *An Open Elite? England 1540–1880* (Oxford: Oxford University Press, 1984).

Stone, Lawrence, *The Road to Divorce, England 1530–1987* (Oxford University Press, 1990).

Sutch, Richard, 'The Breeding of Slaves for Sale and the Westward Expansion of Slavery, 1850–1860', in S. L. Engermann and E. Genovese (eds), *Race and Slavery in the Western Hemisphere* (Princeton, New Jersey: Princeton University Press, 1975).

Sutcliffe, Anthony (ed.), *Multi-Storey Living, The British Working-Class Experience* (London: Croom Helm, 1974).

Sutherland, Daniel E., *Americans and their Servants: Domestic Service in the United States from 1880 to 1920* (Baton Rouge: Louisiana State University Press, 1981).

Thad W. Tate and David L. Ammerman (eds), *The Chesapeake in the Seventeenth Century: Essays in Anglo-American Society* (Chapel Hill, 1979).

Taylor, I. C., 'The Insanitary Housing Question and Tenement Dwellings in Nineteenth-Century Liverpool', in A. Sutcliffe (ed.), *Multi-Storey Living, the British Working-Class Experience* (London: Croom Helm, 1974).

Tebbutt, Melanie, *Making Ends Meet, Pawnbroking and Working-Class Credit* (Leicester University Press, 1983).

Tenement House Committee, *Report* (New York, 1894).

Thatcher, Laurel Ulrich, *Good Wives: Image and Reality in the Lives of Women in Northern New England, 1650–1750* (New York, 1982).

Thirsk, Joan, 'Industries in the Countryside', in F. J. Fisher (ed.), *Essays in the Economic and Social History of Tudor and Stuart England* (Cambridge University Press, 1961).

Thirsk, J., 'Younger Sons in the Seventeenth Century', *History*, **54** (1969).

Thomas, K. V., 'Women and the Civil War Sects', in *Past and Present*, **13** (1958) p. 42.

Thomas, K. V., 'The Double-Standard', *Journal of the History of Ideas*, **20** (1959).

Thompson, Craig R. (ed.), *The Colloquies of Erasmus* (University of Chicago Press, 1965).

Thompson, R., *Women in Stuart England and America: A Comparative Study* (London: Routledge and Kegan Paul, 1974).

Tilly, Louise A. and Joan W. Scott, *Women, Work and Family* (London: Routledge, 1987).

Todd, Barbara J., 'The Remarrying Widow: a Stereotype Reconsidered', in M. Prior (ed.), *Women in English Society, 1500–1800* (London: Methuen, 1985).

Todd, Margo, 'Humanists, Puritans and the Spiritualized Household', *Church History*, **49** (1980).

Traer, James F., *Marriage and the Family in Eighteenth Century France* (Ithaca, New York: 1980).

Treble, J. H., 'Liverpool Working-Class Housing, 1801–1851', in S. D. Chapman (ed.), *History of Working-Class Housing, A Symposium* (Newton Abbott: David & Charles, 1971).

Trumbach, R., *The Rise of the Egalitarian Family: Aristocratic Kinship and Domestic Relations in Eighteenth-Century England* (London: Academic Press, 1978).

Trussell, James and Richard Steckel, 'The Age of Slaves at Menarche and Their First Birth', *Journal of Interdisciplinary History*, **8** (1978).

Tucker, Barbara, 'The Family and Industrial Discipline in Ante-Bellum New Enland', *Labor History*, **21** (1979–80).

Turner, Thomas, *The Diary of a Georgian Shopkeeper* (Oxford University Press, 1979).

Urban Land Enquiry, *Report of the Urban Land Enquiry* (1914).

Vann, Richard, 'Toward a New Lifestyle: Women in Pre-Industrial Capitalism', in R. Bridenthal and C. Coonz (eds), *Becoming Visible: Women in European History* (Boston, Mass. 1977).

Vann, Richard, 'Wills and the Family in an English Town', *Journal of Family History*, **4** (1979) pp. 346–68.

Vicinus, Martha (ed.), *A Widening Sphere* (London: Methuen, 1980).

Vicinus, Martha (ed.), *Suffer and Be Still, Women in the Victorian Age* (London: Methuen, 1980).

Vinovskis, Maris A. (ed.), *Studies in American Historical Demography* (New York, 1979).

Wadsworth, Benjamin, *The Well Ordered Family or Relative Duties* (Boston, Mass., 1712).

Walett, Francis G. (ed.), *The Diary of Ebenezer Parkman*, 1719–1755, cited in Richard S. Dunn, 'Servants and Slaves: the Recruitment and Employment of Labour', in Jack P. Greene and J. R. Pole (eds), *Colonial British America* (Baltimore: Johns Hopkins University Press, and London, 1991 reprint).

Wall, Richard, 'The Age at Leaving Home', *Journal of Family History*, **3** (1978).

Wall, Richard, 'Work, Welfare and the Family: An Illustration of the Adaptive Family Economy', in Lloyd Bonfield, Richard Smith and Keith Wrightson (eds), *The World We Have Gained, Histories of Population and Social Structure* (Oxford: Basil Blackwell, 1986).

Walsh, Lorena S., '"Till Death Us Do Part": Marriage and Family in Seventeenth-Century Maryland', in Thad W. Tate and David L. Ammerman (eds), *The Chesapeake in the Seventeenth Century: Essays in Anglo-American Society* (Chapel Hill, 1979).

Wardle, David, *Education and Society in Nineteenth-Century Nottingham* (Cambridge University Press, 1971).

Warnicke, Retha M., *Women of the English Renaissance and Reformation* (Westport, Connecticut and London: Greenwood Press, 1983).

Watt, Jeffrey R., 'Divorce in Early Modern Neuchâtel, 1547–1806', *Journal of Family History*, 14 (1989).

Weisner, Merry, 'Women's Defense of their Public Role', in Mary Beth Rose (ed.), *Women in the Middle Ages and the Renaissance* (Syracuse, 1986).

Wellenreuther, Hermann, 'A View of Socio-economic Structures in England and the British Colonies on the Eve of the American Revolution', in Eric Angermann et al. (eds), *New Wine in Old Skins: A Comparative View of Socio-political Structures and Values Affecting the American Revolution* (Stuttgart, 1976).

Wells, Robert V., 'Demographic Change and the Life Cycle of American Families', *Journal of Interdisciplinary History*, 11 (1971). This is reprinted in Maris A. Vinovskis (ed.), *Studies in American Historical Demography* (New York, 1979).

Wells, H. G., *Experiment in Autobiography* (London: Victor Gollanz and the Cresset Press, 1934).

Wells, Roger (ed.), *Victorian Village. The Diaries of the Reverend John Coker Egerton of Burwash 1857–1888* (Stroud: Alan Sutton, 1992).

Whateley, William, *A Bride-bush; or, a Direction for Married Persons* (London, 1617 and 1623 editions).

Whateley, William, *A Care-cloth: or a Treatise of the Cumbers and Troubles of Marriage* ... (London: 1624).

Wheaton, Robert, 'Affinity and Descent in Seventeenth-Century Bordeaux', in Robert Wheaton and Tamara K. Hareven (eds), *Family and Sexuality in French History* (Philadelphia, 1976).

Wheaton, Robert and Tamara K. Hareven (eds), *Family and Sexuality in French History* (Philadelphia, 1976).

Whitbread, Helena (ed.), *The Diaries of Anne Lister, 1791–1840* (1988).

White, Alfred T., 'Better Homes for Workingmen', National Confederation of Charities and Correction, *Proceedings* (1885).

White, Alfred T., *Improved Dwellings for the Laboring Classes: The Need, and the Way to meet It on Strict Commercial Principles, in New York and Other Cities* (New York, 1879).

Wilcox, Jerry and Hilda Golden, 'Prolific Immigrants and Dwindling Natives?: Fertility Patterns in Western Massachusetts, 1850 and 1880', *Journal of Family History*, 16 (1982).

Wilson, J. H., 'The Illusion of Change: Women and the American Revolution', in A. F. Young (ed.), *The American Revolution* (University of Illinois Press, 1976).

Wilson, F. P., *The Plague in Shakespeare's London* (1963).

Wingate, Charles F., 'The Moral Side of the Tenement-House Problem', *The Catholic World*, LXI (1885).

Wood, A. C. (ed.), *G. Holles, Memorials of the Holles Family, 1493–1656* (Camden Third Series, IV, 1937).

Wright, Louis and Maryon Tinling (eds), *The Secret Diary of William Byrd of Westover, 1709–1712* (Virginia: The Dietz Press, 1941).

Wrightson, Keith, *English Society, 1580–1680* (London: Hutchinson, 1982).

Wrightson, Keith, 'Household and Kinship in Sixteenth-Century England', *History Workshop Journal*, 12 (1981).

Wrightson, Keith, 'Infanticide in Earlier Seventeenth-Century England', *Local Population Studies*, 15 (1975).

Wrightson, Keith and David Levine, *Poverty and Piety in an English Village: Terling, 1525–1700* (London: Academic Press, 1979).

Wrigley, E. A., 'Mortality in Pre-Industrial England: The Example of Colyton, Devon, over Three Centuries', *Daedalus*, 97 1968).

Wrigley, E. A. and R. S. Schofield, *The Population History of England, 1541–1871. A Reconstruction* (London: Edward Arnold, 1981).

Yans-McLaughlin, Virginia, *Family and Community: Italian Immigrants in Buffalo, 1880–1930* (Ithaca, New York, 1977).

Unpublished Dissertations

Ford, Judith, 'Wills and Will-makers' in Bedfordshire, 1500–1540', Open University PhD, 1992.
Waciega, L. W., 'Widowhood and Womanhood in Early America: the Experience of Women in Philadelphia and Chester Counties, 1750–1850', unpublished Templetion University PhD thesis, 1986.

Manuscript Primary Sources

Account Book of Joyce Jeffrey, British Library, Egerton MS. 3045
Autobiography of Mary Rich, Countess of Warwick, BL, Additional MSS 27351–5, 7 and 8.
Bagot Collection, Folger Shakespeare Library, Washington, DC.
Barrington Papers, British Library, Egerton MSS 2644, 2655.
Coke Papers, British Library (formerly held at Melbourne Hall, Derbyshire and cited using HMCR references).
Katharine Austen's Miscellanies, British Library, Additional MS 4454.
Diary of James Whitehall, Rector of Checkley, Staffordshire, William Salt Library, Stafford, HM 308/40.
Ferrar Papers, Little Gidding, Magdalen College, Cambridge.
Memoirs of Rev. Thomas Henry Brookes, 1895–1980, in the author's possession.
Original Wills proved in the Diocese of Lichfield, 1560–1700, Lichfield Joint Record Office.
Potter, Beatrice, The Wholesale Clothing Trade, Passfield VII, 1.8.

Newspapers

New York Times
North British Daily Mail
The Times

Index